ARCTIC OCEAN
172–173

Europe-Asia
Boundary

ASIA
102–125

EUROPE
84–101

PACIFIC
OCEAN
166–167

AFRICA
126–143

INDIAN
OCEAN
170–171

PHYSICAL WORLD 18–19
POLITICAL WORLD 34–35
WORLD OCEANS 162–173

AUSTRALIA,
NEW ZEALAND &
OCEANIA
144–155

AUSTRALIA

ANTARCTICA
156–161

YOU ARE HERE

NATIONAL GEOGRAPHIC
KiDS

WORLD ATLAS

FIFTH EDITION

NATIONAL GEOGRAPHIC
WASHINGTON, D.C.

TABLE OF CONTENTS

FRONT OF THE BOOK

GETTING STARTED	6
How to Use This Atlas	6
UNDERSTANDING MAPS	8
Exploring Your World	8
Kinds of Maps	10
How to Read a Map	12
PLANET EARTH	14
Earth in Space	14
Earth in Motion	16
THE PHYSICAL WORLD	18
Physical Map	18
The Land	20
World Climate	22
Factors Influencing Climate	24
World Vegetation	26
Environmental Hot Spots	28
Endangered Species	30
Natural Disasters	32
THE POLITICAL WORLD	34
Political Map	34
World Population	36
Population Trends	38
World Languages & Literacy	40
World Religions	42
World Economies	44
World Trade	46
World Water	48
World Food	50
World Energy	52

NORTH AMERICA 54

PHYSICAL & POLITICAL MAPS	56
ABOUT THE CONTINENT	58
CANADA	62
UNITED STATES	64
MEXICO & CENTRAL AMERICA	66
Belize	
Costa Rica	
El Salvador	
Guatemala	
Honduras	
Mexico	
Nicaragua	
Panama	
WEST INDIES & THE BAHAMAS	68
Antigua & Barbuda	
Bahamas	
Barbados	
Cuba	
Dominica	
Dominican Republic	
Grenada	
Haiti	
Jamaica	
St. Kitts & Nevis	
St. Lucia	
St. Vincent & the Grenadines	
Trinidad & Tobago	

SOUTH AMERICA 70

PHYSICAL & POLITICAL MAPS	72
ABOUT THE CONTINENT	74
NORTHWESTERN SOUTH AMERICA	78
Bolivia	
Colombia	
Ecuador	
Peru	
Venezuela	
NORTHEASTERN SOUTH AMERICA	80
Brazil	
Guyana	
Suriname	
SOUTHERN SOUTH AMERICA	82
Argentina	
Chile	
Paraguay	
Uruguay	

EUROPE 84

PHYSICAL & POLITICAL MAPS	86
ABOUT THE CONTINENT	88
NORTHERN EUROPE	92
Denmark	
Estonia	
Finland	
Iceland	
Latvia	
Lithuania	
Norway	
Sweden	
WESTERN EUROPE	94
Andorra	
Austria	
Belgium	
France	
Germany	
Ireland	
Italy	
Liechtenstein	
Luxembourg	
Malta	
Monaco	
Netherlands	
Portugal	
San Marino	
Spain	
Switzerland	
United Kingdom	
Vatican City	
EASTERN EUROPE	96
Belarus	
Czechia	
Hungary	
Moldova	
Poland	
Slovakia	
Ukraine	
THE BALKANS & CYPRUS	98
Albania	
Bosnia & Herzegovina	
Bulgaria	
Croatia	
Cyprus	
Greece	
Kosovo	
Macedonia	
Montenegro	
Romania	
Serbia	
Slovenia	
EUROPEAN RUSSIA	100

North America: Mexican boy, page 58

South America: Llama, page 75

Europe: Colosseum, pages 90–91

Title page (left to right): spider monkey, Costa Rica; Lower Yellowstone Falls, Wyoming, U.S.A; Cuna craftswoman, Panama; Montreal skyline, Quebec, Canada; Siberian tiger; Guggenheim Museum, Bilbao, Spain; young girl, Gambia; fall foliage, U.S.A.

ASIA 102

PHYSICAL & POLITICAL MAPS	104
ABOUT THE CONTINENT	106
ASIAN RUSSIA	110
CENTRAL ASIA	112

Kazakhstan
Kyrgyzstan
Tajikistan
Turkmenistan
Uzbekistan

| EASTERN ASIA | 114 |

China
Japan
Mongolia
North Korea
South Korea

| EASTERN MEDITERRANEAN | 116 |

Armenia
Azerbaijan
Georgia
Israel
Jordan
Lebanon
Syria
Turkey

| SOUTHWESTERN ASIA | 118 |

Bahrain
Iran
Iraq
Kuwait
Oman
Qatar
Saudi Arabia
United Arab Emirates
Yemen

| SOUTHERN ASIA | 120 |

Afghanistan
Bangladesh
Bhutan
India
Maldives
Myanmar
Nepal
Pakistan
Sri Lanka

| SOUTHEASTERN ASIA | 122 |

Brunei
Cambodia
Laos
Malaysia
Philippines
Singapore
Thailand
Vietnam

| INDONESIA & TIMOR-LESTE | 124 |

AFRICA 126

PHYSICAL & POLITICAL MAPS	128
ABOUT THE CONTINENT	130
NORTHERN AFRICA	134

Algeria
Egypt
Libya
Morocco
Tunisia

| WESTERN AFRICA | 136 |

Benin
Burkina Faso
Cabo Verde
Côte d'Ivoire
Gambia
Ghana
Guinea
Guinea-Bissau
Liberia
Mali
Mauritania
Niger
Nigeria
Senegal
Sierra Leone
Togo

| EASTERN AFRICA | 138 |

Burundi
Djibouti
Eritrea
Ethiopia
Kenya
Rwanda
Somalia
Tanzania
Uganda

| CENTRAL AFRICA | 140 |

Cameroon
Central African Republic
Chad
Congo
Democratic Republic of the Congo
Equatorial Guinea
Gabon
Sao Tome & Principe
South Sudan
Sudan

| SOUTHERN AFRICA | 142 |

Angola
Botswana
Comoros
Lesotho
Madagascar
Malawi
Mauritius
Mozambique
Namibia
Seychelles
South Africa
Swaziland
Zambia
Zimbabwe

AUSTRALIA, NEW ZEALAND & OCEANIA 144

PHYSICAL & POLITICAL MAPS	146
ABOUT THE REGION	148
AUSTRALIA & NEW ZEALAND	152
OCEANIA	154

Fiji
Kiribati
Marshall Islands
Micronesia,
    Federated States of
Nauru
Palau
Papua New Guinea
Samoa
Solomon Islands
Tonga
Tuvalu
Vanuatu

ANTARCTICA 156

| ABOUT THE CONTINENT | 158 |

Antarctica: Penguins, page 158

THE OCEANS 162

Investigating the Oceans	164
Pacific Ocean	166
Atlantic Ocean	168
Indian Ocean	170
Arctic Ocean	172

BACK OF THE BOOK

FLAGS & FACTS	174
GLOSSARY	184
GEO FACTS & FIGURES	187
OUTSIDE WEBSITES & ABBREVIATIONS	190
INDEX: PLACE-NAMES	191
INDEX: OCEAN FEATURES	203
MAP DATA SOURCES & ILLUSTRATIONS CREDITS	206

Australia, New Zealand & Oceania: Maori man, page 148

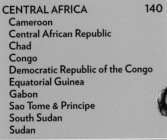

Africa: Mother and child, page 131

Asia: Panda, page 106

How to Use This Atlas

This atlas is a window for exploring the world. To learn about maps, use the first section, Understanding Maps. Basic facts about Earth as a planet are presented in the section called Planet Earth. Maps in the Physical World section focus on different aspects of nature and the environment. The Political World section contains world maps about how humans live on the planet. In the pages that follow, the maps, photographs, and essays are arranged by continent and region. You can find details about specific countries in the Flags & Facts section beginning on page 174.

"YOU ARE HERE"
Locator globes help you see where one area is in relation to others. On regional pages (as shown here), the area covered by the main map is yellow on the globe, and its continent is green. On pages with continent maps, the locator globe shows the whole continent in yellow. The surrounding land is gray.

80   NORTHEASTERN SOUTH AMERICA

THE CONTINENT:
SOUTH AMERICA

THE BASICS

STATS

Largest country
Brazil
3,287,594 sq mi
(8,514,877 sq km)
Smallest country
Suriname
63,251 sq mi (163,820 sq km)
Most populous country
Brazil 207,353,000
Least populous country
Suriname 592,000
Predominant languages
Portuguese, English, Dutch, Hindi
Predominant religions
Christianity, Hinduism, Islam
Highest GDP per capita
Brazil $15,200
Lowest GDP per capita
Guyana $7,900
Highest life expectancy
Brazil 74 years
Lowest life expectancy
Guyana 68 years

GEO WHIZ

Guyana's roughly 300 species of catfish are hunted for the international aquarium trade.

Brazil's Pantanal is the world's largest freshwater wetland.

Paramaribo, Suriname's capital, is a melting pot of Dutch, Hindu, Chinese, East Indian, and Javanese cultures. Dutch is the only official language.

Northeastern South America

GOAL! Maracanã Stadium in Rio de Janeiro is packed with enthusiastic soccer fans. Brazil has a long history of producing world-class soccer teams, winning the coveted World Cup five times as of 2017.

Brazil dominates the region as well as the continent in size and population. It is the world's fifth largest country in area, and it is home to half of South America's 419 million people. São Paulo and Rio de Janeiro are among the world's largest cities, and the country's vast agricultural lands make it a top global exporter of coffee, soybeans, beef, orange juice, and sugar. The vast Amazon rain forest, once a dense wilderness of unmatched biodiversity, is now threatened by farmers, loggers, and miners. Lands colonized by the British, Dutch, and French make up sparsely settled Guyana and Suriname as well as French Guiana, a French overseas department. Formerly known as the Guianas, these lands are populated by people of African, South Asian, and European heritage.

STATS & FACTS
At the left-hand edge of each continent opener and regional page is a bar that includes basic information about the subject. This feature is a great first stop if you're writing a report.

CHARTS & GRAPHS
Each region includes a chart or graph that shows information visually.

VAST WATERSHED

The United States and South America are shown at the same scale.

Amazon Basin

SOUTH AMERICA

The Amazon River basin includes 2.4 million square miles (6.1 million sq km). It would cover much of the contiguous, or lower 48, U.S. states.

NATIONAL RHYTHM. Samba, often called Brazil's national music, combines the music traditions of the country's populations— Amerindian, Portuguese, and African. Here a samba band practices on Rio de Janeiro's Ipanema Beach.

WHERE ARE THE PICTURES?
If you want to know where a picture in a regional section of this atlas was taken, look for the map in the photo essay. Find the label that describes the picture you're curious about, and follow the line to its location.

Maps use symbols to represent political and physical features. At right is the key to the symbols used in this atlas. If you are wondering what you're looking at on a map, check here.

INDEX AND GRID

Look through the index for the place-name you want. Next to it is a page number in bold, a letter, and another number. Go to the page. Draw imaginary lines from the letter along the side of the map and the number along the top. Your place will be close to where the lines meet.

Boulia, Australia **153** C6
Bourke, Australia **153** E7
Boyoma Falls, Dem. Rep.
   of the Congo **141** E5
Brahmaputra (river), Asia
   121 C7
Braila, Romania **99** B7
Brasília, Brazil **81** E5

COLOR BARS

Every section of this atlas has its own color. Look for the color on the Table of Contents pages and across the top of every page in the atlas. Within that color bar, you'll see the name of the section and the title for each topic or map. These color bars are a handy way to find the section you want.

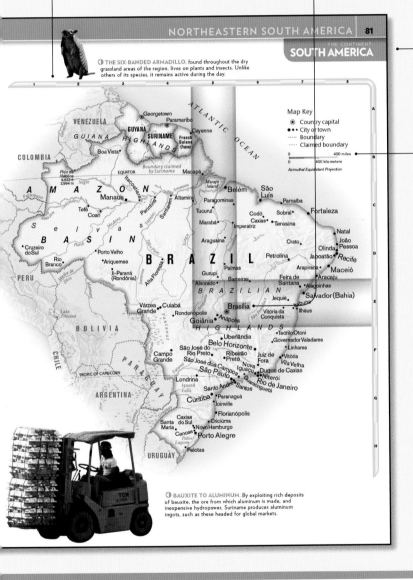

NORTHEASTERN SOUTH AMERICA | 81

SOUTH AMERICA
THE CONTINENT

North America

South America

Europe

Asia

Africa

Australia, New Zealand & Oceania

Antarctica

BAR SCALE

To find out how far on Earth's surface it is from one place on a map to another, use the scale. A bar scale appears on every map. It shows how distance on paper relates to distance in the real world.

MAP KEY

• • • City or town	791 ft. / 241 m ▲ Mountain peak with elevation above sea level	⊣╟ Waterfall	Dry salt lake
⊛ Country capital	-282 ft. / -86 m • Low point with elevation below sea level	Dam	Glacier
⊙ Other capital*		Canal	Swamp
◆ Small country	...... Defined boundary	Ice shelf	Sand
∴ Ruin	... ... Disputed or undefined boundary	Reef	Tundra
■ Point of interest		Lake	Lava
★ Pole	...... Claimed boundary	Intermittent lake	Below sea level
*This includes capitals for states, provinces, territories, dependencies, and other political entities.	River		

Exploring Your World

Earth is a big place. Even from space you can't see it all at one time. But with a map you can see the whole world or just a part of it. Thanks to the Internet, you can download programs that allow you to experience Earth from space, pick a place you want to explore, and zoom closer and closer until you are "standing" right there! These screenshots (right) take you from Chicago to space at the click of a mouse. You can even find a satellite view of your neighborhood (box below).

Compare the computer-enhanced satellite images with the maps on the opposite page. You will see how the same places can be shown in very different ways.

COMPUTER ENHANCED VIEWS OF ...

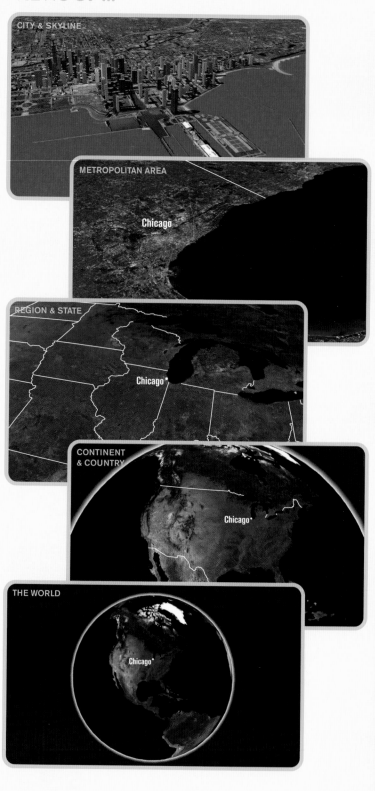

CITY & SKYLINE

METROPOLITAN AREA
Chicago

REGION & STATE
Chicago

CONTINENT & COUNTRY
Chicago

THE WORLD
Chicago

FIND YOUR HOUSE

This SkylineGlobe image shows the offices of National Geographic in Washington, D.C. To see where you live, go to showmystreet.com, one of several websites that allow you to view satellite imagery of the world.

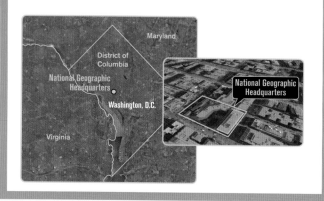

Maryland

District of Columbia

National Geographic Headquarters

Washington, D.C.

National Geographic Headquarters

Virginia

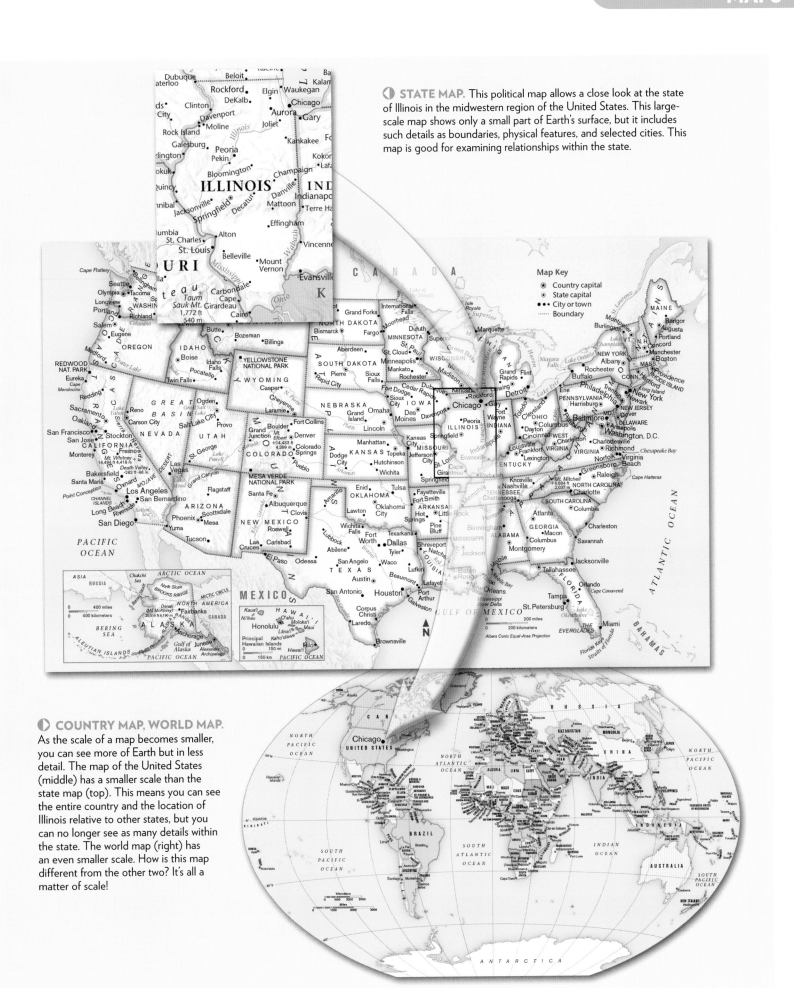

STATE MAP. This political map allows a close look at the state of Illinois in the midwestern region of the United States. This large-scale map shows only a small part of Earth's surface, but it includes such details as boundaries, physical features, and selected cities. This map is good for examining relationships within the state.

Map Key
- ⊛ Country capital
- ⊛ State capital
- ● City or town
- ⋯⋯ Boundary

COUNTRY MAP, WORLD MAP.
As the scale of a map becomes smaller, you can see more of Earth but in less detail. The map of the United States (middle) has a smaller scale than the state map (top). This means you can see the entire country and the location of Illinois relative to other states, but you can no longer see as many details within the state. The world map (right) has an even smaller scale. How is this map different from the other two? It's all a matter of scale!

Kinds of Maps

Maps are special tools that tell a story about Earth. Some maps show physical features, such as mountains or vegetation. Other maps illustrate different human features on Earth—political boundaries, urban centers, and economic systems.

Maps are not perfect. A globe is a scale model of Earth with accurate relative sizes and locations. Because maps are flat, they involve distortions of size, shape, and direction. Also, cartographers—people who create maps—make choices about what information to include. Because of this, it is important to study many different types of maps to learn the complete story of Earth.

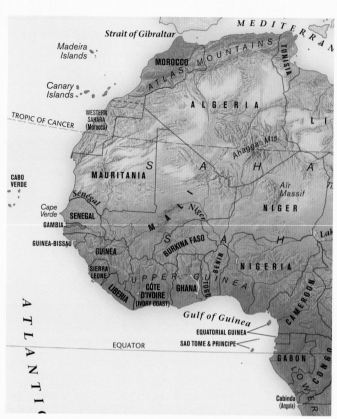

⬤ **PHYSICAL MAPS.** Earth's natural features—landforms, water bodies, and vegetation—are shown on physical maps. The map above uses color and shading to illustrate mountains, lakes, rivers, and deserts in western Africa. Country names and borders are added for reference, but they are not natural features.

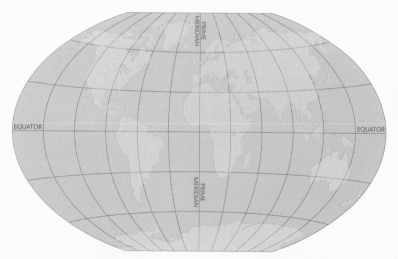

⬤ **MAP PROJECTIONS.** To create a map, cartographers transfer an image of the round Earth onto a flat surface, a process called projection. Some types of projection include cylindrical, conic, azimuthal, and interrupted. Each has certain advantages, but all have some distortions. The world maps in the thematic section of this atlas are a projection called Winkel Tripel (above), a compromise projection that moderates size and shape distortions. As you use this atlas, look for different map projections on the regional maps, identified below the scale bar.

MAKING MAPS

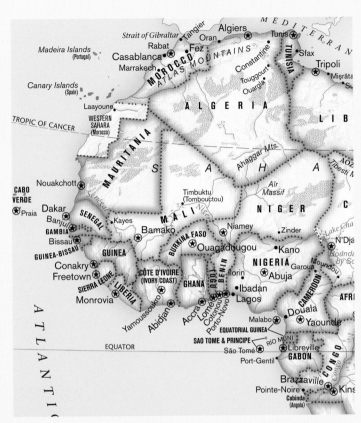

POLITICAL MAPS. These maps represent human characteristics of the landscape, such as boundaries, cities, and other place-names. Natural features are added only for reference. On the map above, capital cities are represented with a star inside a circle, while other cities are located with black dots.

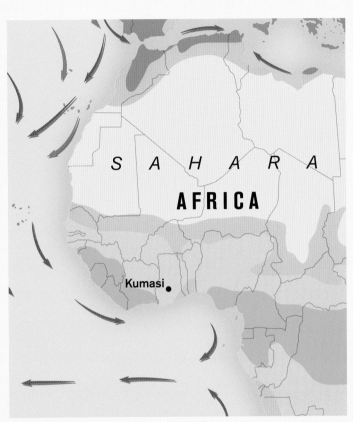

THEMATIC MAPS. Patterns related to a particular topic, or theme, such as population distribution, appear on these maps. The map above displays a region's climate zones, which range from tropical wet (bright green) to tropical wet and dry (light green) to semiarid (dark yellow) to arid (light yellow).

Long ago, cartographers worked with pen and ink, carefully handcrafting maps based on explorers' observations and diaries. Today, mapmaking is a high-tech business. Cartographers use Earth data stored in "layers" in a geographic information system (GIS) and special computer programs to create maps that can be easily updated as new information becomes available. These cartographers are making changes to a map in another National Geographic Kids atlas.

Satellites in orbit around Earth act as eyes in the sky, recording data about the planet's land and ocean areas. The data is converted to numbers that are transmitted back to computers that are specially programmed to interpret the data. They record it in a form that cartographers can use to create maps.

How to Read a Map

Every map has a story to tell, but first you have to know how to read the map.

Maps are useful for finding places because every place on Earth has a special address called its absolute location. Imaginary lines, called latitude and longitude, create a grid that makes finding places easy because every spot on Earth has a unique latitude and longitude. In addition, special tools, making use of the Global Positioning System (GPS), communicate with orbiting satellites to determine absolute location.

Maps are also useful for determining distance and direction. The map scale shows the relationship between distance on the map and actual distance on Earth. Since north is not always at the top of every map, a compass rose or arrow is used to indicate direction.

Maps represent other information by using a language of symbols. To find out what each symbol means, you must use the map key. Think of this key as your secret decoder, identifying information represented by each symbol on the map.

LATITUDE AND LONGITUDE. Lines of latitude run west to east parallel to the Equator. They measure distance in degrees from 0° latitude (Equator) to 90°N (North Pole) or to 90°S (South Pole). Lines of longitude run north to south and measure distance in degrees east or west from 0° longitude (prime meridian) to 180° longitude. The prime meridian runs through Greenwich, England.

Latitude

Longitude

ABSOLUTE LOCATION. The imaginary grid composed of lines of latitude and longitude helps us locate places on a map. Suppose you are playing a game of global scavenger hunt. The prize is hidden at absolute location 30°S, 60°W. On the map at right, look south of the Equator to find the line of latitude labeled 30°S and west of 0° longitude to find the line of longitude labeled 60°W. Trace these lines with your fingers until they meet (arrow at right). The prize must be located in central Argentina.

SYMBOLS

Points, lines, and areas are the three main types of map symbols. Points, which can be either dots or small icons, represent the location or the number of things, such as cities or landmarks. Lines are used to show boundaries, roads, or rivers and can vary in color or thickness. Area symbols use patterns or color to show regions, such as a sandy area or a neighborhood.

POINT
A point symbol, a black dot, indicates a city, such as Omdurman.

LINE
Sudan's country boundary appears as a line symbol: a dotted line with a colored edge.

AREA
Sandy places, such as parts of the Libyan Desert, are shown by a tan, speckled area.

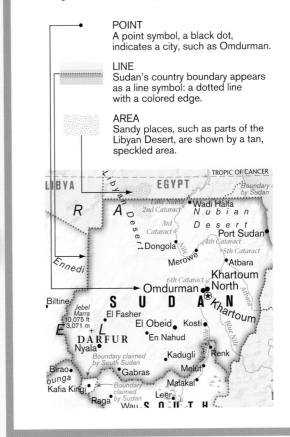

SCALE & DIRECTION

The scale on a map can be shown as a fraction, as words, or as a line or bar. It relates distance on the map to distance in the real world. Sometimes the type of map projection is named below the scale. Maps may include an arrow or compass rose to indicate north on the map. Maps in this atlas are oriented north, so they do not use a north indicator.

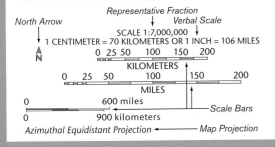

Representative Fraction

North Arrow
Verbal Scale

SCALE 1:7,000,000
1 CENTIMETER = 70 KILOMETERS OR 1 INCH = 106 MILES
0 25 50   100   150   200
KILOMETERS
0   25   50   100   150   200
MILES
0   600 miles
Scale Bars
0   900 kilometers
Azimuthal Equidistant Projection ◄——— Map Projection

◐ APPLYING WHAT YOU'VE LEARNED. Now that you know how to read a map, can you find Sapporo in the eastern Asian country of Japan? The index for this atlas says Sapporo is on page 115 B10. Go to page 115, place one finger on the B at the side of the map and another finger on the 10 at the top. Now trace straight across from the B and down from the 10. Sapporo is near where your fingers meet!

Earth in Space

Earth is part of a cosmic family called the solar system. It is one of the planets that revolves around a giant solar nuclear reactor that we call the sun.

The extreme heat and pressure on the sun cause atoms of hydrogen to combine in a process called fusion, producing new atoms of helium and releasing tremendous amounts of energy. This energy makes life on Earth possible.

Time on Earth is defined by our relationship to the sun. It takes Earth, following a path called an orbit, approximately 365 days—one year—to make one full revolution around the sun. As Earth makes its way around the sun, it also turns on its axis, an imaginary line that passes between the North and South Poles. This motion, called rotation, occurs once every 24 hours and results in day and night.

◗ TIME ZONES. Long ago, when people lived in relative isolation, they measured time by the position of the sun. That meant that noon in one place was not the same as noon in a place 100 miles (160 km) to the west. Later, with the development of long-distance railroads, people needed to coordinate time. In 1884, a system of 24 standard time zones was adopted. Each time zone reflects the fact that Earth rotates west to east 15 degrees each hour. Time is counted from the prime meridian (0° longitude).

Callisto

Titan

Triton

Charon

Haumea

Jupiter

Saturn

Uranus

Neptune

Pluto

Makemake

Eris

Note: Art shows relative sizes of the sun and planets, but distances are not to scale.

SOLAR SYSTEM. The sun and its family of planets are located near the outer edge of the Milky Way, a giant spiral galaxy. Earth is the third planet from the sun and one of the four "terrestrial" planets. These planets—Mercury, Venus, Earth, and Mars—are made up of solid rocky material. Beyond these inner planets are the four gas giants—Jupiter, Saturn, Uranus, and Neptune. Recently, astronomers—scientists who study space—have named a new category called "dwarf" planets that includes Pluto, Ceres, Eris, Haumea, and Makemake. More of these dwarf planets may soon be identified. Many planets, including Earth, have one or more moons orbiting them. The art above names a few: Io, Callisto, Titan, Triton, and Charon.

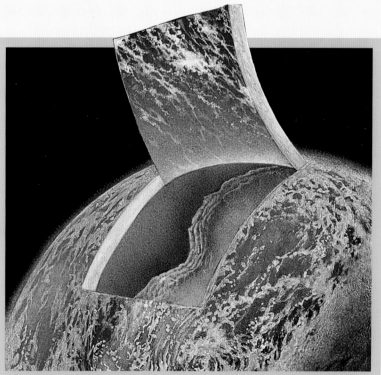

ENVELOPE OF AIR. Earth is enclosed within a thick layer of air called the atmosphere. Made up of a mixture of nitrogen, oxygen, and other gases, the atmosphere provides us with the life-giving air that we breathe. It also protects us from dangerous radiation from the sun. Weather systems move through the atmosphere, redistributing heat and moisture and creating Earth's climates.

Earth in Motion

If we could step into a time machine and travel 500 million years into the past, we probably would not recognize Earth. Back then, most of the landmasses we call continents were joined together in a single giant landmass called Pangaea (below). So how did the continents break away from Pangaea and move to their current positions? The answer lies in a process called plate tectonics. These maps and diagrams tell the story.

A LOOK WITHIN. Earth's crust is a thin shell of solid rock that covers the partially molten rock of the mantle (upper and lower). Currents of heat rising and falling within the mantle break the crust into large pieces called plates. As plates creep across Earth's surface, they reshape its features. Major plates appear on the map at right. Earthquakes and volcanoes are most frequent where plates collide or grind past each other.

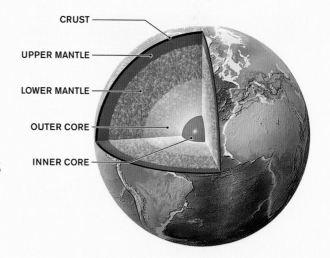

CRUST
UPPER MANTLE
LOWER MANTLE
OUTER CORE
INNER CORE

CONTINENTS ON THE MOVE

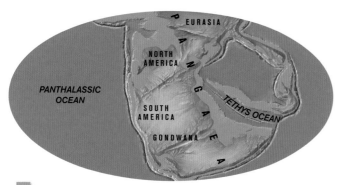

1 PANGAEA. About 240 million years ago, Earth's landmasses were joined together in one supercontinent—Pangaea—that extended from pole to pole.

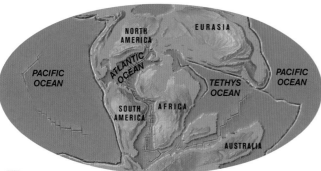

2 BREAKUP. By 94 million years ago, Pangaea had broken into what would become today's continents. Dinosaurs roamed Earth during this period of warmer climates.

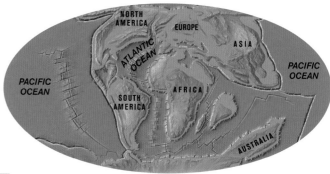

3 EXTINCTION. About 65 million years ago, an asteroid smashed into Earth (red * on map), possibly leading to the extinction of half of all species, including the dinosaurs—one of several major extinctions.

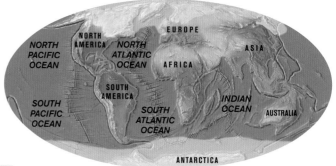

4 ICE AGE. By 18,000 years ago, the continents had drifted close to their present positions, but most far northern and far southern lands were buried beneath huge glaciers.

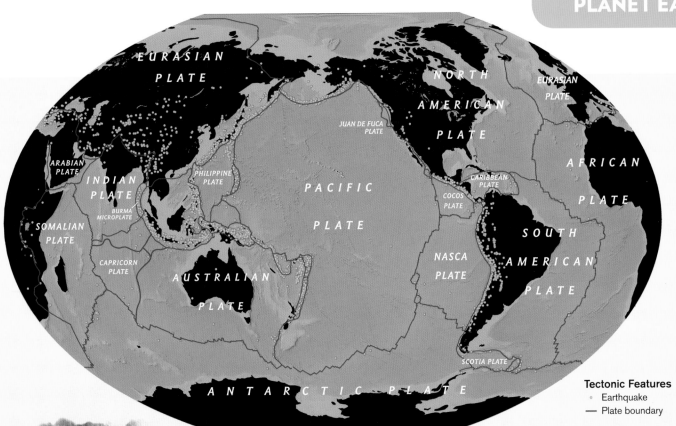

Tectonic Features
· Earthquake
— Plate boundary

Earth Shapers

Earth's features are constantly undergoing change—being built up, destroyed, or just rearranged. Plates are in constant, very slow motion. Some plates collide, others pull apart, and still others slowly grind past each other. As the plates move, mountains are uplifted, volcanoes erupt, and new land is created.

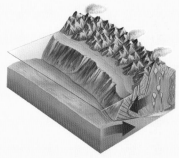

⬢ **VOLCANOES** form when molten rock, called magma, rises to Earth's surface. Some volcanoes occur as one plate pushes beneath another plate. Other volcanoes result when a plate passes over a column of magma, called a hot spot, rising from the mantle.

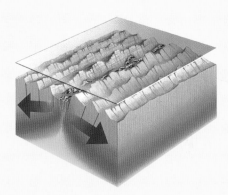

⬢ **SPREADING** results when oceanic plates move apart. The ocean floor cracks, magma rises, and new crust is created. The Mid-Atlantic Ridge spreads a few centimeters—about an inch—a year, pushing Europe and North America farther apart.

⬢ **FAULTING** happens when two plates grind past each other, creating large cracks along the edges of the plates. A famous fault is the San Andreas, in California, U.S.A., where the Pacific and North American plates meet, causing damaging earthquakes.

⬢ **SUBDUCTION** occurs when an oceanic plate dives under a continental plate. This often results in volcanoes and earthquakes, as well as mountain building.

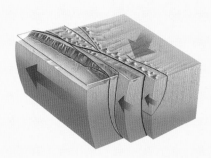

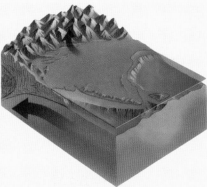

⬢ **COLLISION** of two continental plates causes plate edges to break and fold, creating mountains, Earth's highest landforms. The Himalaya are the result of the Indian plate colliding with the Eurasian plate, an ongoing process that began 50 million years ago.

The Physical World

Earth is dominated by large landmasses called continents—seven in all—and by an interconnected global ocean that is divided into four parts by the continents. More than 70 percent of Earth's surface is covered by oceans. Land areas cover the remaining 30 percent.

Different landforms give variety to the surface of the continents. The Rockies and Andes mark the western edge of North and South America, and the Himalaya tower above southern Asia. The Plateau of Tibet forms the rugged core of Asia, while the Northern European Plain extends from the North Sea to the Ural Mountains. Much of Africa is a plateau, and dry plains cover large areas of Australia. In Antarctica, mountains rise more than 16,000 feet (4,897 m) beneath massive ice sheets.

Mountains and trenches make the ocean floors as varied as the surface of any continent (see page 164). The Mid-Atlantic Ridge runs the length of the Atlantic Ocean. In the western Pacific Ocean, trenches drop to depths greater than 36,000 feet (10,984 m).

◑ LAND AND WATER. This world physical map shows Earth's seven continents—North America, South America, Europe, Africa, Asia, Australia, and Antarctica—as well as the four oceans: Pacific, Atlantic, Indian, and Arctic. Some people regard the area from Antarctica to 60°S, where the oceans merge, as a fifth ocean called the Southern Ocean.

ARCTIC OCEAN

Islands
Ellesmere I.
Oodaaq I.
Franz Josef Land
North Land
New Siberian Islands
East Siberian Sea
Baffin Bay
GREENLAND
Svalbard
Novaya Zemlya
Kara Sea
Laptev Sea
Baffin Island
Greenland Sea
Barents Sea
Central Siberian Plateau
Bering Sea
Kamchatka Peninsula
Iceland
Norwegian Sea
Scandinavia
Ob
West Siberian
Yenisey
Lena
Angara
Lena
Sea of Okhotsk
Aleutian Islands
Labrador Sea
British Isles
North Sea
Baltic Sea
Northern European Plain
Ural Mountains
Siberian Plain
Ob
Irtysh
Amur
Sakhalin
Labrador
Ireland
Great Britain
EUROPE
Volga
Ural
The Steppes
Lake Baikal
Altay Mountains
Kuril Islands
Hokkaido
Island of Newfoundland
Alps
El'brus 18,510 ft 5,642 m
Caspian Sea
ASIA
Aral Sea
Gobi
Sea of Japan (East Sea)
JAPAN
Honshu
NORTH ATLANTIC OCEAN
Corsica
Sardinia
Iberian Peninsula
Dundee
Black Sea
Caucasus Mts.
Tian Shan
North China Plain
Yellow
Korea
Yellow Sea
Nampo Islands
Kyushu
NORTH PACIFIC OCEAN
Azores
Madeira Is.
Sicily
Crete
Cyprus
Mediterranean Sea
Zagros Mountains
Taklimakan Desert
Kunlun Mountains
Plateau of Tibet
East China Sea
Kyushu
Ryukyu Is.
Atlas Mountains
Dead Sea -1,401 ft -427 m
Persian Gulf
HIMALAYA
Brahmaputra
Yangtze
Salween
Taiwan
Canary Is.
Libyan Desert
Nile
Red Sea
Arabian Peninsula
Mt. Everest 29,035 ft 8,850 m
Ganges
Hainan
Philippine Sea
Mariana Islands
SAHARA
Arabian Sea
INDIA
Deccan Plateau
Bay of Bengal
Luzon
South China Sea
MICRONESIA
Cape Verde Islands
SAHEL
Niger
Blue Nile
Ethiopian Highlands
Gulf of Aden
Somali Peninsula
Andaman Islands
Indochina Peninsula
Mekong
Andaman Sea
Caroline Islands
Marshall Islands
Upper Guinea
AFRICA
Lake Victoria
Nicobar Is.
Sri Lanka
Malay Peninsula
Gilbert Is.
Bioko
Gulf of Guinea
Congo
Lower Guinea
São Tomé
Congo Basin
Kilimanjaro 19,340 ft 5,895 m
Lake Tanganyika
Maldive Islands
Sumatra
Borneo
Greater Sunda Islands
Celebes
Moluccas
New Guinea
Bismarck Archipelago
Solomon Is.
MELANESIA
CA
Ilian Is.
San Francisco
Zambezi
Seychelles
Java
INDONESIA
Lesser Sunda Is.
Arafura Sea
Coral Sea
Vanuatu
SOUTH ATLANTIC OCEAN
Namib Desert
Kalahari Desert
Comoros Is.
Madagascar
INDIAN OCEAN
New Caledonia
Fiji Is.
Drakensberg
Mascarene Is.
Réunion
Rodrigues
Mauritius
Western Plateau
Central Lowlands
AUSTRALIA
Great Dividing Range
SOUTH PACIFIC OCEAN
Cape of Good Hope
Lake Eyre -49 ft -15 m
Murray
Darling
Great Australian Bight
Mt. Kosciuszko 7,310 ft 2,228 m
North I.
Prince Edward Islands
Crozet Islands
Kerguelen Islands
Tasmania
Tasman Sea
NEW ZEALAND
Falkland Islands
South Georgia
Scotia Sea
South Sandwich Islands
South I.
Auckland Islands
South Shetland Islands
South Orkney Islands
Antarctic Peninsula
WEDDELL SEA
South Magnetic Pole
Land
Ronne Ice Shelf
Queen Maud Land
EAST ANTARCTICA
TRANSANTARCTIC MTS.
Victoria Land
Ross Sea
Vinson Massif 16,067 ft 4,897 m
ARCTIC MOUNTAINS
ANTARCTICA
Ross Ice Shelf

90° 60° 30°W 0° 30°E 60° 90° 120° 150° 180°

The Land

A closer look at Earth's surface reveals many varied forms and features that make each place unique. This drawing of an imaginary landscape captures 41 natural and human-made features and shows how they relate to each other. For example, a large moving "river" of ice (called a glacier) descends from a high mountain range, and a harbor, built by people, creates safe anchorage for ships.

Such features can be found all over the world because the same forces are at work around the globe. Volcanoes and movement of the plates of Earth's crust are constantly creating and building up new landforms, while external forces such as wind, water, and ice continuously wear down surface features.

Earth is dynamic—constantly changing, never the same.

RIVER

As a river moves through flatlands, it twists and turns. Above, the Rio Los Amigos winds through a rain forest in Peru.

CANYON

Steep-sided valleys called canyons are created mainly by running water. Buckskin Gulch (above) is the deepest slot canyon in the American Southwest.

DESERT

Deserts are a land feature created by climate, specifically by a lack of water. Above, a camel caravan crosses the Sahara, in northern Africa.

OASIS

Occasionally, water rises from deep below a desert, creating an oasis—a fertile area that supports trees and sometimes crops—such as this one in Africa.

Mountain peak
Mountain range
Glacier
Iceberg
Basin
Divide
Valley
Canal
Lagoon
Beach
Plain
Delta
Gulf
Harbor
Breakwater
Desert
Mesa
Oasis
Plateau
Escarpment
Waterfall
Lake
Canyon
River
Fork
Hills
Tributary

A NAME FOR EVERY FEATURE.
Land has a vocabulary all its own, each name identifying a specific feature of the landscape. A cape, for example, is a broad chunk of land extending out into the sea. It is not pointed, however, because then it would be a point. Nor does it have a narrow neck. A sizable cape or point with a narrow neck is a peninsula. The narrow neck is an isthmus. Such specific identifiers have proven useful over the centuries. In the early days of exploration, even the simplest maps showed peninsulas, bays, and straits. Sailors used these landmarks to reach safe harbor or to avoid disastrous encounters.

◐ **EXPLORING THE LANDSCAPE.**
How many of these landscape features have you seen on your travels or in the area where you live?

MOUNTAIN

Mountains are Earth's tallest landforms, and Mount Everest in Asia (above) rises highest of all at 29,035 feet (8,850 m) above sea level.

GLACIER

Glaciers, such as Hubbard in Alaska, U.S.A. (above), move slowly from mountains to the sea. Climate change may be causing them to melt.

VALLEY

Valleys, cut by running water or moving ice, may be broad and flat or narrow and steep, such as the Indus River Valley in Ladakh, India (above).

WATERFALL

Waterfalls form when a river reaches an abrupt change in elevation. Above, South America's Kaieteur Falls, in Guyana, drops 800 feet (244 m).

World Climate

Weather is the condition of the atmosphere—temperature, precipitation, humidity, wind—at a given place at a given time. Climate, however, is the average weather for a particular place over a long period of time. Climate is not a random occurrence. It is a pattern that is controlled by factors such as latitude, elevation, prevailing winds, temperature of ocean currents, and location on land relative to water. Climate is generally constant, but many people are concerned that the activity of humans may be causing a change in the patterns of climate.

THE BASICS

According to the National Oceanic and Atmospheric Administration (NOAA), 2016 ranks first as the hottest year on record, and future years may be even hotter. The 2016 global annual temperature for combined land and ocean surfaces was 1.78° F (.99° C) warmer than the mid-20th-century average.

Ice cores taken from Antarctica and Greenland allow scientists to gain detailed information about the history of Earth's climate and its atmosphere—especially the presence of green-house gases—dating back thousands of years.

According to climatologists—people who study climate—Earth experienced what is called the Little Ice Age, which lasted from the 17th century to the late 19th century. During that time, temperatures were cold enough to cause glaciers to advance.

CLIMATE GRAPHS. Temperature and precipitation data provide a snapshot of the climate at a particular place. This information can be shown in a special type of graph called a climate graph (below). Average monthly temperatures (scale on the left side of the graphs) are represented by the lines at the tops of the colored areas, while average monthly precipitation totals (scale on the right side of the graphs) are reflected in the bars. For example, the graph for Belém, Brazil, shows a constant warm temperature of about 80°F (27°C) with abundant rainfall year-round. In contrast, the graph for Fairbanks, Alaska, shows a cool, variable temperature with only limited precipitation.

(Map labels: Fairbanks; Subarctic Current; North Pacific Drift; Hawaiian Islands; California Current; ROCKY MOUNTAINS; NORTH AMERICA; Des Moines; Gulf Stream; TROPIC OF CANCER; Monterrey; Gulf of Mexico; North; North Equatorial Current; PACIFIC OCEAN; Equatorial Countercurrent; EQUATOR; South Equatorial Current; Peru Current; ANDES; AMAZONIA; SO AME; TROPIC OF CAPRICORN)

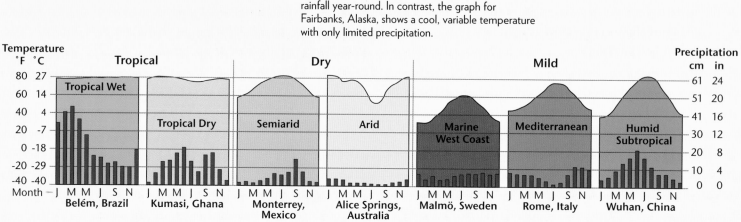

Climate graphs — Temperature °F °C scale (left): 80/27, 60/14, 40/4, 20/-7, 0/-18, -20/-29, -40/-40. Precipitation cm in scale (right): 61/24, 51/20, 41/16, 30/12, 20/8, 10/4, 0/0. Month axis: J M M J S N.

Tropical: Tropical Wet — Belém, Brazil; Tropical Dry — Kumasi, Ghana

Dry: Semiarid — Monterrey, Mexico; Arid — Alice Springs, Australia

Mild: Marine West Coast — Malmö, Sweden; Mediterranean — Rome, Italy; Humid Subtropical — Wuhan, China

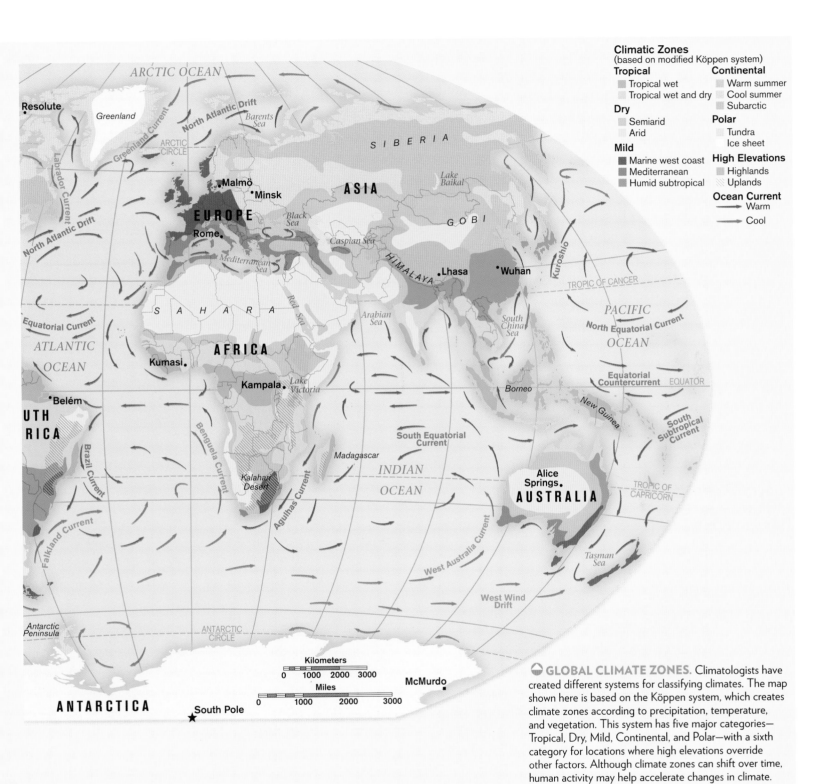

Climatic Zones
(based on modified Köppen system)

Tropical
Tropical wet
Tropical wet and dry

Dry
Semiarid
Arid

Mild
Marine west coast
Mediterranean
Humid subtropical

Continental
Warm summer
Cool summer
Subarctic

Polar
Tundra
Ice sheet

High Elevations
Highlands
Uplands

Ocean Current
→ Warm
→ Cool

ARCTIC OCEAN

Resolute

Greenland

Greenland Current

North Atlantic Drift

Barents Sea

ARCTIC CIRCLE

SIBERIA

Labrador Current

North Atlantic Drift

Malmö

Minsk

ASIA

Lake Baikal

EUROPE

Black Sea

GOBI

Rome

Caspian Sea

Mediterranean Sea

Kuroshio

HIMALAYA

Lhasa

Wuhan

TROPIC OF CANCER

Equatorial Current

SAHARA

Red Sea

Arabian Sea

PACIFIC

ATLANTIC OCEAN

AFRICA

South China Sea

North Equatorial Current

OCEAN

Kumasi

Kampala

Lake Victoria

Borneo

Equatorial Countercurrent

EQUATOR

Belém

New Guinea

UTH RICA

Brazil Current

Benguela Current

Madagascar

South Equatorial Current

INDIAN OCEAN

South Subtropical Current

Kalahari Desert

Agulhas Current

Alice Springs

TROPIC OF CAPRICORN

Falkland Current

AUSTRALIA

West Australia Current

Tasman Sea

West Wind Drift

Antarctic Peninsula

ANTARCTIC CIRCLE

McMurdo

Kilometers
0 1000 2000 3000

Miles
0 1000 2000 3000

ANTARCTICA

South Pole

⊖ **GLOBAL CLIMATE ZONES.** Climatologists have created different systems for classifying climates. The map shown here is based on the Köppen system, which creates climate zones according to precipitation, temperature, and vegetation. This system has five major categories—Tropical, Dry, Mild, Continental, and Polar—with a sixth category for locations where high elevations override other factors. Although climate zones can shift over time, human activity may help accelerate changes in climate.

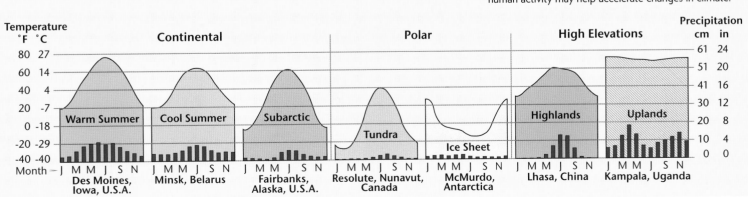

| Temperature | | Continental | | Polar | | High Elevations | Precipitation |
| °F °C | | | | | | | cm in |

Continental | **Polar** | **High Elevations**

Warm Summer — Des Moines, Iowa, U.S.A.
Cool Summer — Minsk, Belarus
Subarctic — Fairbanks, Alaska, U.S.A.
Tundra — Resolute, Nunavut, Canada
Ice Sheet — McMurdo, Antarctica
Highlands — Lhasa, China
Uplands — Kampala, Uganda

Month — J M M J S N (repeated)

Temperature scale: 80 27 / 60 14 / 40 4 / 20 -7 / 0 -18 / -20 -29 / -40 -40

Precipitation scale: 61 24 / 51 20 / 41 16 / 30 12 / 20 8 / 10 4 / 0 0

Factors Influencing Climate

Earth's climate is a bit like a big jigsaw puzzle. To understand it, you need to fit all the pieces together, because climate is influenced by a number of different, but interrelated factors. These include latitude, topography (shape of the land), elevation above sea level, wind systems, ocean currents, and distance from large bodies of water. Climate has always affected the way we live, but can humans affect climate? Pollution from industries and motor vehicles may be changing Earth's climate.

TOPOGRAPHY. Mountain ranges are natural barriers to the movement of air. In North America, prevailing westerly winds carry air full of moisture from the Pacific Ocean to the West Coast. As air rises over the Coast Ranges, light precipitation falls. Farther inland, the much taller Sierra Nevada range triggers heavy precipitation as air rises higher. On the leeward side of the Sierra Nevada, sinking air warms, water evaporates, and dry "rain shadow" conditions prevail. As winds continue across the interior plateau, the air remains dry because there is no significant source of moisture.

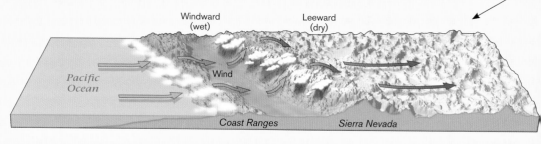

Cool → Warm → Temperature changes as air moves over mountains

ELEVATION. In general, climate conditions become cooler as elevation increases. Since cooler air holds less moisture, less precipitation falls. As temperature and moisture conditions change, vegetation also changes. In the mountain diagram (below), a dense mixed forest grows near the base of the mountain on the windward side. As elevation increases and temperatures decline, the mixed forest changes to all evergreen, followed by alpine meadows, until finally the mountain's rocky peaks are covered by snow and ice. As air moves down the leeward slope of the mountain, it warms and evaporates moisture, causing the leeward side to be drier and have less vegetation.

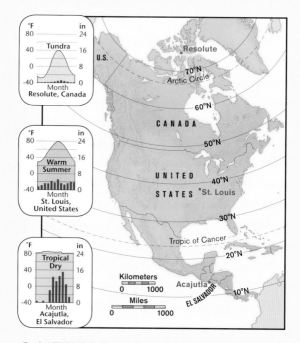

WINDWARD

LATITUDE. Energy from the sun drives global climates. Latitude—distance north or south of the Equator—affects the amount of solar energy received. Places near the Equator (Acajutla, El Salvador, above) have warm temperatures year-round. As distance from the Equator increases (St. Louis, U.S.A., and Resolute, Canada, above), average temperatures decline, and cold winters become more pronounced.

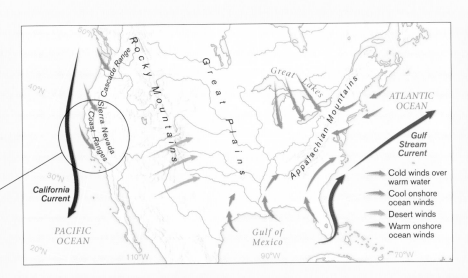

⬤ **DIGGING OUT.** Arctic winds roar across Canada, picking up moisture from the Great Lakes (purple arrows on map, left). As the moist air crosses over the frozen land, temperatures fall and heavy precipitation—called lake effect snow—occurs, burying cars and roads as shown here in Oswego, New York, U.S.A.

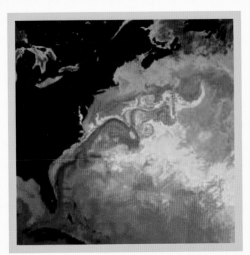

⬤ **WARM CURRENT.**
The Gulf Stream, a warm ocean current averaging 50–93 miles (80–150 km) wide, sweeps up the East Coast of North America (red arrow on map above). One branch continues across the North Atlantic Ocean and above the Arctic Circle (map, page 23). In the color-enhanced satellite image (left), the Gulf Stream looks like a dark red river moving up the coast. This "river" of warm water influences climate along its path, bringing moisture and mild temperatures to the East Coast of the United States and causing ice-free ports above the Arctic Circle in Europe.

CLIMATE CHANGE

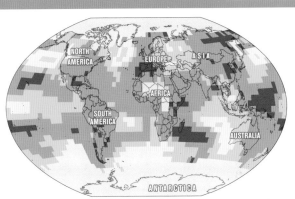

Land & Ocean Temperature Averages (January–July 2017)

No data ▪ Cooler than average ▪ Near average ▪ Warmer than average ▪ Much warmer than average ▪ Record warmest

Earth's climate history is a story of change, with warm periods followed by periods of bitter cold. The early part of the 21st century has seen some of the warmest temperatures ever recorded (map, above). Scientists are concerned that this warming trend may be related to human activity and may pose many risks to people, including rising sea levels. As average temperatures rise, glaciers melt and ocean waters expand, causing sea levels to rise and flood coastal areas, indicated by the red areas in Florida (below, right).

LEEWARD

Current

2100

World Vegetation

Natural vegetation—plants that would grow under ideal conditions at a particular place—depends on several factors. The quality and type of soil and climate are key. In fact, vegetation often reflects patterns of climate. (Compare the vegetation map at right with the world climate map on pages 22–23.) Forests thrive in places with ample precipitation; grasses are found where there is less precipitation or only seasonal rainfall; and xerophytes—plants able to survive lengthy periods with little or no water—are found in arid areas that receive very little annual precipitation.

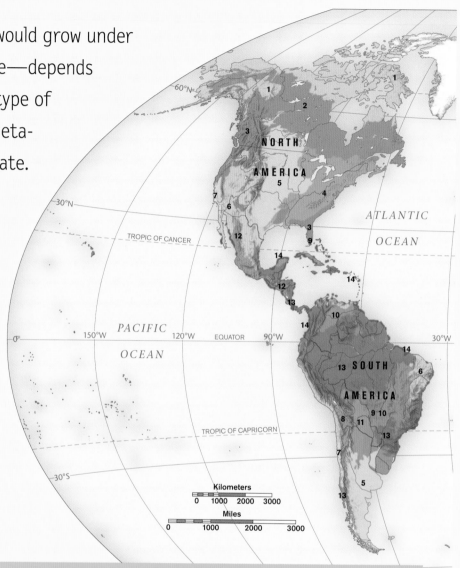

TUNDRA

With only two to three months of above-freezing temperatures, tundra plants are mostly dwarf shrubs, short grasses, mosses, and lichens (above). Much of Canada's Yukon has tundra vegetation, which turns red as winter approaches.

TEMPERATE CONIFEROUS

Needleleaf trees with cones to protect their seeds from bitter winters grow in cold climates with short summers, such as occur in British Columbia, Canada (above). These trees are important in lumber and papermaking industries.

TEMPERATE BROADLEAF

Broadleaf trees that grow in mid-latitude areas with mild temperatures, such as in Shenandoah National Park in Virginia, U.S.A. (above), are deciduous, meaning they lose their leaves in winter. Many of these forests have been cleared for cropland.

TEMPERATE GRASSLAND

Grasslands, such as this tall-grass prairie in south-western Missouri, U.S.A., are found in areas where precipitation is too low to support forests. Many temperate grasslands have been converted to cropland for grain production.

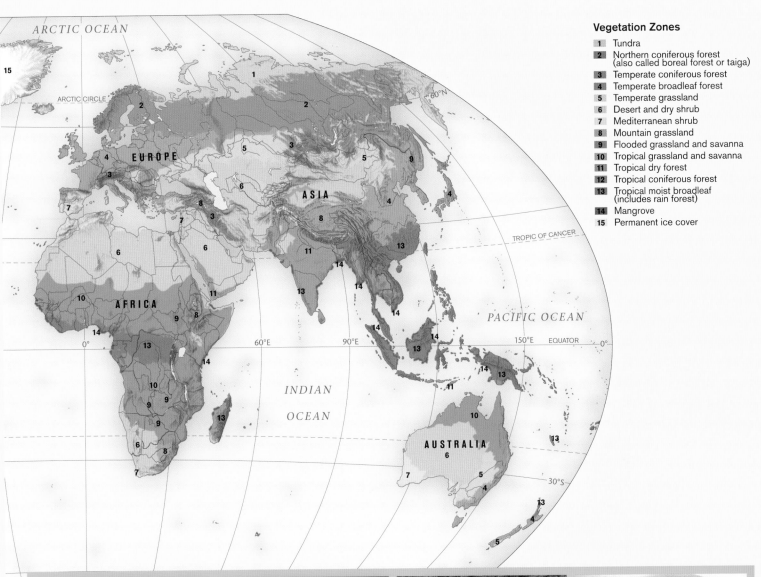

ARCTIC OCEAN

ARCTIC CIRCLE

EUROPE

ASIA

AFRICA

INDIAN

OCEAN

PACIFIC OCEAN

TROPIC OF CANCER

EQUATOR

AUSTRALIA

Vegetation Zones

1 Tundra
2 Northern coniferous forest (also called boreal forest or taiga)
3 Temperate coniferous forest
4 Temperate broadleaf forest
5 Temperate grassland
6 Desert and dry shrub
7 Mediterranean shrub
8 Mountain grassland
9 Flooded grassland and savanna
10 Tropical grassland and savanna
11 Tropical dry forest
12 Tropical coniferous forest
13 Tropical moist broadleaf (includes rain forest)
14 Mangrove
15 Permanent ice cover

6 DESERT AND DRY SHRUB

Deserts, areas that receive less than 10 inches (25 cm) of rainfall a year, have vegetation that is specially adapted to survive under dry conditions, such as these dry shrubs and cacti growing in the Sonoran Desert in Arizona, U.S.A.

10 TROPICAL GRASSLAND

Tall grasses and scattered trees that can survive a hot, dry season dominate low latitude grasslands, also called savannas. Africa's grasslands are home to game animals, such as this male lion crossing the savanna in Botswana.

13 RAIN FOREST

A waterfall tumbles over a cliff in the Costa Rican rain forest. Rain forest trees can grow to as much as 200 feet (61 m) above the forest floor. The overlapping branches of the tallest trees keep sunlight from reaching the forest floor.

CROPLAND

People remove natural vegetation in many places to create fields to grow crops to feed both people and animals. Here, a farmer in the Catskill Mountains of New York, U.S.A., cultivates land that was likely once a temperate forest.

Environmental Hot Spots

People are putting more and more pressure on the environment by dumping pollutants into the air and water and by removing natural vegetation to extract mineral resources or to create cropland for farming. In more developed countries, industries create waste and pollution; farmers use fertilizers and pesticides that run off into water supplies; and motor vehicles release exhaust fumes into the air. In less developed countries, forests are cut down for fuel or to clear land for farming; grasslands are turned into deserts as farmers and herders overuse the land; and expanding urban areas face problems of water quality and sanitation.

Environmental Stresses
- Megacity with more than 10 million people
- Deforestation
- Desertification
- Major air pollution
- Major human impact to the oceans

HUMAN FOOTPRINT. This map uses population density, land use, transportation, and energy production and use to identify environmental hot spots—areas of Earth where human impact is greatest.

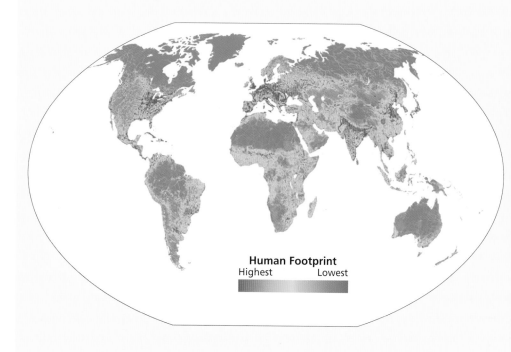

Human Footprint
Highest   Lowest

AIR POLLUTION

Poor air quality is a serious environmental problem. Industrial plants are a major source of pollution. Smoke, which contains particles that combine with moisture in the air to create acid rain, is released from a factory in Poland (above).

EUROPE
London
Paris
Moscow
Istanbul
ASIA
Beijing
Tianjin
Tokyo
Osaka
Shanghai
Chongqing
Cairo
Delhi
Dhaka
Guangzhou
Shenzhen
Karachi
Kolkata
(Calcutta)
AFRICA
Mumbai
(Bombay)
Chennai
(Madras)
Bengaluru
(Bangalore)
Manila
Lagos
Kinshasa
Jakarta
Rio de Janeiro
São Paulo
AUSTRALIA
Buenos Aires

Kilometers
0   1000   2000   3000

Miles
0   1000   2000   3000

DEFORESTATION

Loss of forest cover, such as on this hillside in Malaysia, contributes to a buildup of carbon dioxide in the atmosphere, as well as to a loss of biodiversity—variety of species— common problems in the tropics.

DESERTIFICATION

Villagers in Mauritania (above) shovel sand away from their schoolhouse. In semiarid areas, which receive limited and often unreliable rainfall, land that is overgrazed or overcultivated can become desertlike.

OCEAN POLLUTION

Plastic trash, ranging from bottles and bags to microscopic bits, is a serious threat to sea birds and other marine life. Scientists estimate eight million tons (7.3 million t) of plastic, including this trash off Dakar, Senegal, end up in the oceans every year.

Endangered Species

Earth's environment is made up of a complex system of life-forms ranging from microscopic organisms to giant blue whales. Throughout Earth's history, species such as the dinosaurs have become extinct. Scientists have concluded that in recent years many species are becoming endangered at an increasing rate as humans spread into natural areas for agricultural and urban use and contribute to climate change by using fossil fuels. Loss of species could mean less food, fewer medical discoveries to fight disease, and loss of plants and animals that enrich our lives each day.

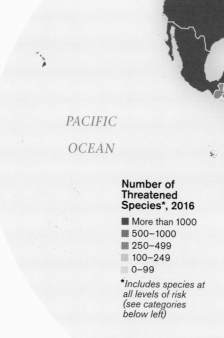

NORTH AMERICA

PACIFIC OCEAN

Number of Threatened Species*, 2016

- More than 1000
- 500–1000
- 250–499
- 100–249
- 0–99

*Includes species at all levels of risk (see categories below left)

SPECIES AT RISK

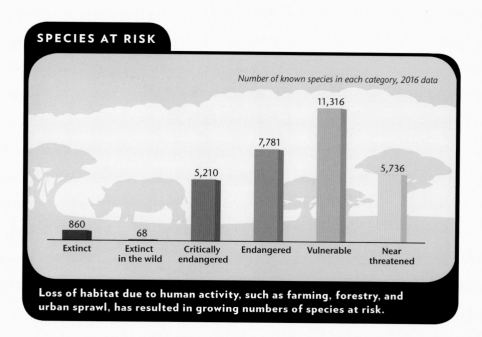

Number of known species in each category, 2016 data

Category	Number
Extinct	860
Extinct in the wild	68
Critically endangered	5,210
Endangered	7,781
Vulnerable	11,316
Near threatened	5,736

Loss of habitat due to human activity, such as farming, forestry, and urban sprawl, has resulted in growing numbers of species at risk.

Extinct*	Extinct in the wild	Critically endangered	Endangered	Vulnerable	Near threatened
no reasonable doubt that the last example of the species has died	best available evidence indicates the species is extinct in its natural habitat, surviving only in captivity	best available evidence indicates the species faces extremely high risk of extinction in the wild	best available evidence indicates the species faces very high risk of extinction in the wild	best available evidence indicates the species faces high risk of becoming endangered in the wild	best available evidence indicates the species is not yet vulnerable, but is likely to be without ongoing conservation action

*Categories and definitions are based on IUCN Red List.

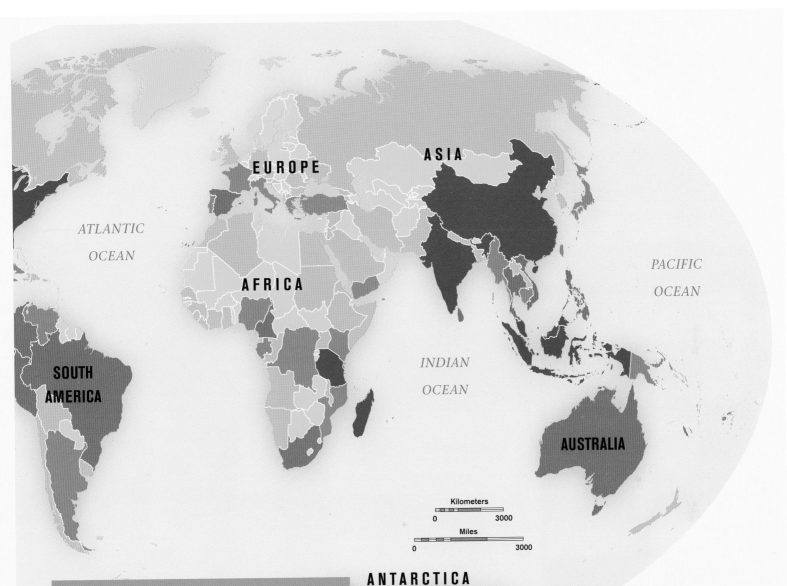

EUROPE

ASIA

ATLANTIC
OCEAN

PACIFIC
OCEAN

AFRICA

INDIAN
OCEAN

SOUTH
AMERICA

AUSTRALIA

Kilometers

0   3000

Miles

0   3000

ANTARCTICA

CRITICALLY ENDANGERED

Human activity poses the greatest threat to Earth's rich variety of species. Climate change and loss of habitat put many species at great risk. Experts estimate that species are facing extinction at a greater rate than at any other time in human history. The species shown here were declared critically endangered as of 2016.

Diademed Sifaka

Eastern Gorilla

Chinese Pangolin

Swift Parrot

Canterbury Knobbled Weevil

Geometric Tortoise

Torrey Pine

Gentiana kurroo

Natural Disasters

Every world region has its share of natural disasters. The Ring of Fire—grinding tectonic plate boundaries that follow the coasts of the Pacific Ocean—shakes with volcanic eruptions and earthquakes (page 17). Coastal areas can be swept away by quake-caused tsunamis. The U.S. heartland endures blizzards in winter and dangerous tornadoes that can strike in spring, summer, or fall. Tropical cyclones batter many coastal areas with ripping winds, torrents of rain, and huge storm surges along their deadly paths.

NORTH AMERICA

ROCKY MOUNTAINS

Tri-State Tornado (1925)

Hurricane Sandy (2012)

Mid-Atlantic

Galveston Hurricane (1900)

Hurricane Katrina (2005)

Hurricane Harvey (2017)

Hurricane Irma (2017)

Hawaiian Islands

Middle America Trench

Haiti (2010)

Hurricane Maria (2017)

Hurricane Mitch (1998)

Galapagos Is.

SOUTH AMERICA

ANDES

Peru-Chile Trench

East Pacific Rise

Valdivia (1960)

Chile Rise

ANDES

Natural Disasters
(1900–2017)

← Typical storm track of hurricane, typhoon, or cyclone

▢ "Tornado Alley" (highest concentration of tornadoes worldwide)

· Earthquake greater than 6.5 magnitude

· Tsunami quake epicenter

● Notable tornado

● Notable hurricane, typhoon, or cyclone

▲ Notable volcanic eruption

⬤ **TORNADO.** A funnel cloud roars across open country near Campo, Colorado, U.S.A. More of these storms occur in "Tornado Alley" (see map) than anywhere else on Earth.

◐ **RAGING HURRICANE.** In early September 2017, Hurricane Irma roared through the Caribbean and southeastern United States. With peak sustained winds of 185 miles an hour (298 km/h), the storm destroyed almost every structure on the small island of Barbuda (right) in the Lesser Antilles.

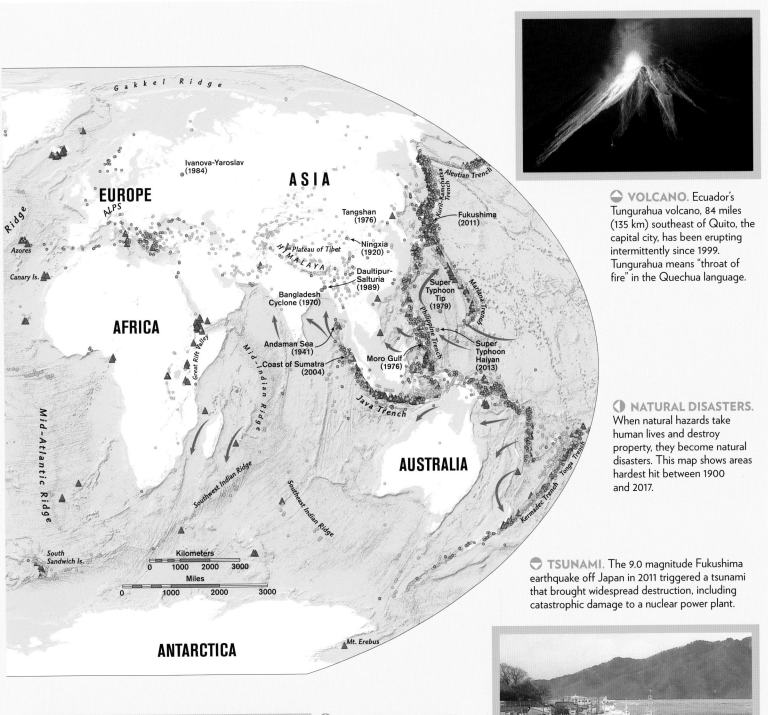

Gakkel Ridge

Ivanova-Yaroslav
(1984)

ASIA

EUROPE
ALPS

Ridge

Kuril-Kamchatka Trench

Aleutian Trench

Azores

Tangshan
(1976)

Fukushima
(2011)

Canary Is.

Plateau of Tibet

HIMALAYA

Ningxia
(1920)

Daultipur-
Salturia
(1989)

Super
Typhoon
Tip
(1979)

Mariana Trench

Bangladesh
Cyclone (1970)

AFRICA

Great Rift Valley

Mid-Indian Ridge

Andaman Sea
(1941)

Coast of Sumatra
(2004)

Moro Gulf
(1976)

Philippine Trench

Super
Typhoon
Haiyan
(2013)

Java Trench

Mid-Atlantic Ridge

Southwest Indian Ridge

Southeast Indian Ridge

AUSTRALIA

Kermadec Trench

Tonga Trench

South
Sandwich Is.

Kilometers
0   1000   2000   3000
Miles
0   1000   2000   3000

Mt. Erebus

ANTARCTICA

VOLCANO. Ecuador's Tungurahua volcano, 84 miles (135 km) southeast of Quito, the capital city, has been erupting intermittently since 1999. Tungurahua means "throat of fire" in the Quechua language.

NATURAL DISASTERS. When natural hazards take human lives and destroy property, they become natural disasters. This map shows areas hardest hit between 1900 and 2017.

TSUNAMI. The 9.0 magnitude Fukushima earthquake off Japan in 2011 triggered a tsunami that brought widespread destruction, including catastrophic damage to a nuclear power plant.

MEASURING QUAKES. Scientists, like this one, use an instrument called a seismograph to measure and record the strength of tremors caused by shifts in Earth's crust.

The Political World

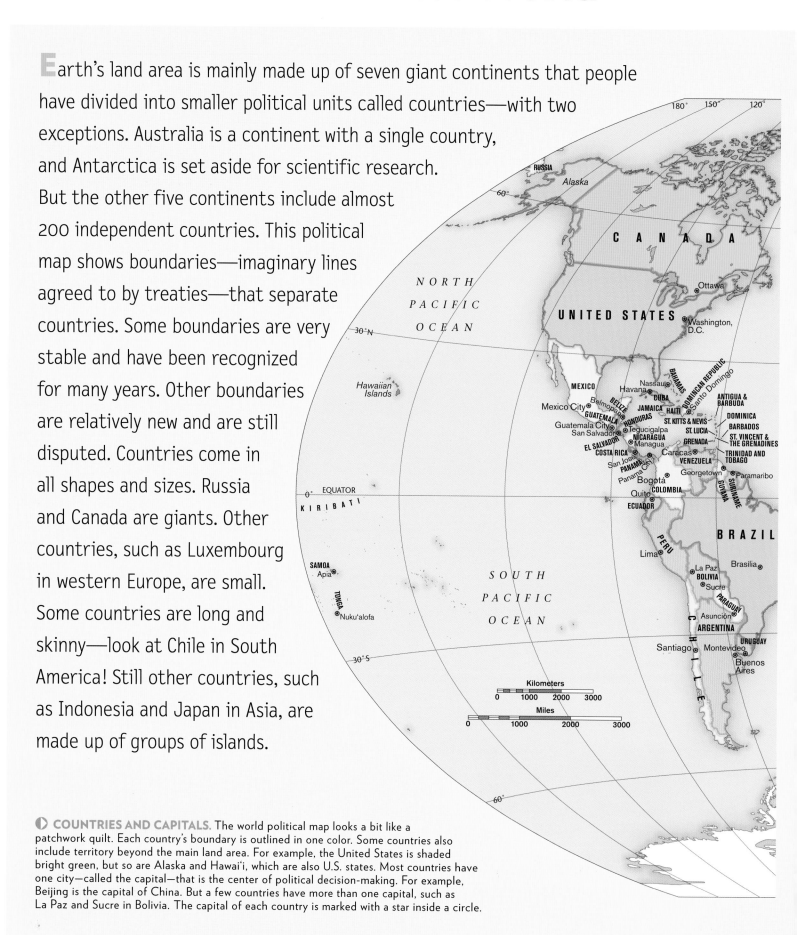

Earth's land area is mainly made up of seven giant continents that people have divided into smaller political units called countries—with two exceptions. Australia is a continent with a single country, and Antarctica is set aside for scientific research. But the other five continents include almost 200 independent countries. This political map shows boundaries—imaginary lines agreed to by treaties—that separate countries. Some boundaries are very stable and have been recognized for many years. Other boundaries are relatively new and are still disputed. Countries come in all shapes and sizes. Russia and Canada are giants. Other countries, such as Luxembourg in western Europe, are small. Some countries are long and skinny—look at Chile in South America! Still other countries, such as Indonesia and Japan in Asia, are made up of groups of islands.

COUNTRIES AND CAPITALS. The world political map looks a bit like a patchwork quilt. Each country's boundary is outlined in one color. Some countries also include territory beyond the main land area. For example, the United States is shaded bright green, but so are Alaska and Hawai'i, which are also U.S. states. Most countries have one city—called the capital—that is the center of political decision-making. For example, Beijing is the capital of China. But a few countries have more than one capital, such as La Paz and Sucre in Bolivia. The capital of each country is marked with a star inside a circle.

ARCTIC OCEAN

Greenland
Svalbard

Reykjavik ⊛ ICELAND

RUSSIA

NORWAY
SWEDEN
FINLAND

Oslo ⊛ Helsinki
Copenhagen ⊛ Stockholm
DENMARK   ESTONIA
UNITED   LATVIA
KINGDOM   LITHUANIA   Moscow
Dublin   Minsk
IRELAND   NETH. POLAND BELARUS
London ⊛ BELG. Berlin Warsaw ⊛ Kiev
Paris ⊛ LUX. GERMANY CZECHIA
       AUSTRIA SLOVAKIA UKRAINE
       SWITZ. SLOVENIA HUNGARY MOLDOVA
FRANCE CROATIA ROMANIA
       BOSN.& HERZE. SERBIA BULGARIA
PORTUGAL Madrid ITALY MONT. KOSOVO
SPAIN Rome MACEDONIA GEORGIA
Lisbon   Athens ⊛ Ankara ARMENIA AZERBAIJAN
Rabat Algiers Tunis ⊛ GREECE TURKEY
MOROCCO TUNISIA MALTA CYPRUS SYRIA
       ⊛ Tripoli LEBANON IRAQ Baghdad
WESTERN   ISRAEL Cairo JORDAN
SAHARA ALGERIA LIBYA EGYPT

Astana

KAZAKHSTAN

Tashkent
Bishkek
UZBEKISTAN KYRGYZSTAN
TURKMENISTAN Dushanbe
Ashgabat TAJIKISTAN
AFGHANISTAN Kabul
Tehran IRAN Islamabad
PAKISTAN

Ulaanbaatar ⊛

MONGOLIA

Beijing ⊛

CHINA

NORTH
KOREA
Pyongyang
⊛ Seoul
SOUTH
KOREA

JAPAN
Tokyo

NORTH
PACIFIC
OCEAN

NORTH
ATLANTIC
OCEAN

(Morocco)

Nouakchott
CABO   SENEGAL
VERDE   Dakar MAURITANIA MALI NIGER
GAMBIA Bamako BURKINA Niamey CHAD
GUINEA-BISSAU FASO Ouagadougou N'Djamena SUDAN Khartoum Asmara
Bissau GUINEA BENIN NIGERIA
Conakry CÔTE GHANA Abuja
Freetown D'IVOIRE TOGO CENTRAL SOUTH
SIERRA LEONE Accra Lomé CAMEROON AFRICAN SUDAN Juba
Monrovia LIBERIA EQUATORIAL Yaoundé REPUBLIC ETHIOPIA Addis Ababa
Yamoussoukro Abidjan GUINEA Bangui
SAO TOME & PRINCIPE GABON CONGO DEM. REP. OF Kampala UGANDA
Libreville Brazzaville THE CONGO RWANDA Kigali KENYA
      Kinshasa BURUNDI Nairobi
Luanda ⊛ Bujumbura Dodoma
ANGOLA TANZANIA Dar es Salaam
      Lilongwe COMOROS SEYCHELLES
SOUTH   ZAMBIA MALAWI Moroni
ATLANTIC Lusaka MOZAMBIQUE MADAGASCAR
OCEAN   Harare Antananarivo
NAMIBIA ZIMBABWE MAURITIUS
Windhoek BOTSWANA Port Louis
Gaborone   Maputo
(Tshwane) Pretoria SWAZILAND
Bloemfontein LESOTHO
SOUTH
Cape Town AFRICA

Riyadh
SAUDI
ARABIA
BAHRAIN KUWAIT
QATAR
U.A.E.
YEMEN Muscat OMAN
Sanaa DJIBOUTI
ERITREA
SOMALIA
Mogadishu

MALDIVES

New Delhi
Kathmandu Thimphu
NEPAL BHUTAN
INDIA Dhaka BANGLADESH
Nay Pyi Taw
MYANMAR (BURMA) Hanoi
Yangon (Rangoon) LAOS Vientiane VIETNAM
Bangkok THAILAND
Phnom Penh CAMBODIA
SRI LANKA
Colombo Sri Jayewardenepura Kotte
Male
Kuala Lumpur MALAYSIA
SINGAPORE
BRUNEI Bandar Seri Begawan

Male

INDIAN OCEAN

Victoria

TAIWAN

Manila ⊛ PHILIPPINES

Ngerulmud
PALAU
FEDERATED STATES
OF MICRONESIA

MARSHALL
ISLANDS
Palikir
Majuro

Tarawa KIRIBATI

NAURU

INDONESIA
Jakarta

Dili
TIMOR-LESTE
(EAST TIMOR)

PAPUA
NEW GUINEA
Honiara
Port Moresby

SOLOMON
ISLANDS
Funafuti

TUVALU

VANUATU
Port-Vila FIJI
Suva

SOUTH
ATLANTIC
OCEAN

AUSTRALIA

SOUTH
PACIFIC
OCEAN

Canberra ⊛

NEW ZEALAND
Wellington ⊛

ANTARCTICA

World Population

How big is a billion? It's hard to imagine. But Earth's population is 7.4 billion and rising, with more than a billion living in both China and India. And more than 60 million people are added to the world each year. Most population growth occurs in the less developed countries of Asia, Africa, and Latin America, while some countries in Europe are hardly increasing at all. Population changes can create challenges for countries. Fast-growing countries with young populations need food, housing, and schools. Countries with low growth rates and older populations need workers to sustain their economies.

MOST POPULOUS COUNTRIES

	(2017 estimates)	
1.	China	1,379,303,000
2.	India	1,281,936,000
3.	United States	326,626,000
4.	Indonesia	260,581,000
5.	Brazil	207,353,000

MOST CROWDED COUNTRIES

	Population Density (People per sq mi/sq km; 2017 estimates)	
1.	Monaco	30,645.0 / 15,322.5
2.	Singapore	21,891.9 / 8,449.0
3.	Bahrain	4,815.5 / 1,856.5
4.	Maldives	3,414.9 / 1,317.8
5.	Malta	3,412.6 / 1,317.5

◗ **DENSITY.** Demographers, people who study population, use density to measure how concentrated population is, but density is just an average. For example, the population density of Egypt is more than 250 people per square mile (97 people per sq km). This incorrectly assumes that the population is evenly spread throughout the country. Actually, most people live along the Nile River. Likewise, Earth's population is not evenly spread across the land. Some places are almost empty, others are very crowded.

◗ **CITY DWELLERS.**
More than half the world's people have shifted from rural areas to urban centers, with some countries adding more than 100 million to their urban populations between 1950 and 2015 (map, right). In more developed countries, about 75 percent of the population is urban, compared with just 46 percent in less developed countries. But the fastest growing urban areas are in less developed countries, where thousands flock to cities, such as Dhaka, Bangladesh (photo, far right), in search of a better life. In 2016, there were 31 cities with populations of 10 million or more.

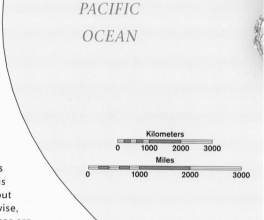

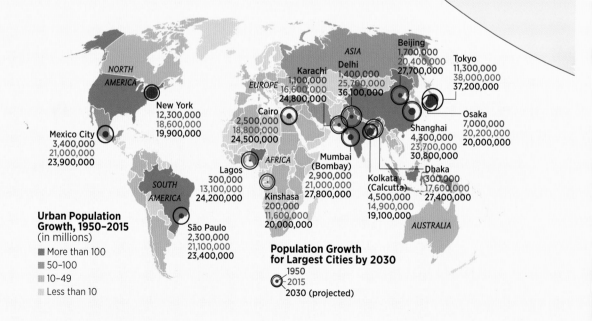

Urban Population Growth, 1950–2015
(in millions)
- ■ More than 100
- ■ 50–100
- ■ 10–49
- ■ Less than 10

Population Growth for Largest Cities by 2030
- 1950
- ⊙ 2015
- 2030 (projected)

NORTH AMERICA
Los Angeles
Mexico City
PACIFIC OCEAN

Kilometers
0   1000   2000   3000
Miles
0   1000   2000   3000

NORTH AMERICA
New York
12,300,000
18,600,000
19,900,000

Mexico City
3,400,000
21,000,000
23,900,000

EUROPE

Cairo
2,500,000
18,800,000
24,500,000

AFRICA
Lagos
300,000
13,100,000
24,200,000

Kinshasa
200,000
11,600,000
20,000,000

SOUTH AMERICA
São Paulo
2,300,000
21,100,000
23,400,000

ASIA
Karachi
1,100,000
16,600,000
24,800,000

Delhi
1,400,000
25,700,000
36,100,000

Beijing
1,700,000
20,400,000
27,700,000

Tokyo
11,300,000
38,000,000
37,200,000

Osaka
7,000,000
20,200,000
20,000,000

Shanghai
4,300,000
23,700,000
30,800,000

Mumbai (Bombay)
2,900,000
21,000,000
27,800,000

Kolkata (Calcutta)
4,500,000
14,900,000
19,100,000

Dhaka
300,000
17,600,000
27,400,000

AUSTRALIA

C.E. 1 50 100 150 200 250 300 350 400 450 500 550 600 650 700 750 800 850
Year

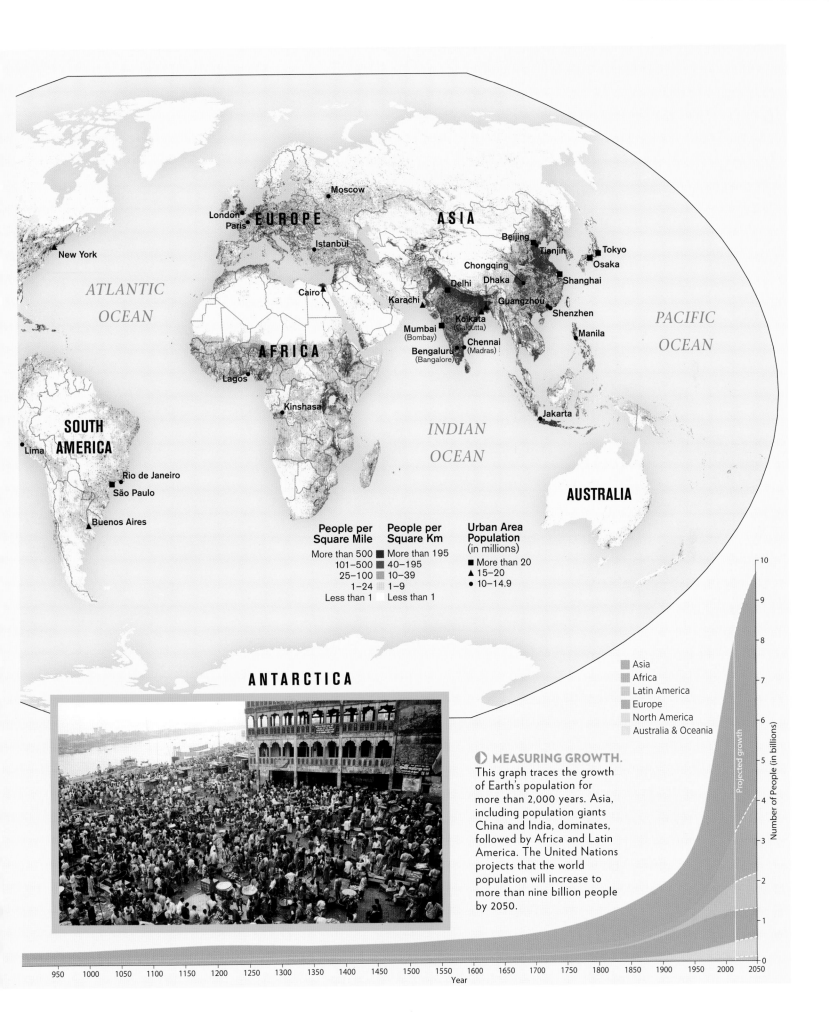

People per Square Mile
- More than 500
- 101–500
- 25–100
- 1–24
- Less than 1

People per Square Km
- More than 195
- 40–195
- 10–39
- 1–9
- Less than 1

Urban Area Population (in millions)
- ■ More than 20
- ▲ 15–20
- ● 10–14.9

- Asia
- Africa
- Latin America
- Europe
- North America
- Australia & Oceania

◗ **MEASURING GROWTH.**
This graph traces the growth of Earth's population for more than 2,000 years. Asia, including population giants China and India, dominates, followed by Africa and Latin America. The United Nations projects that the world population will increase to more than nine billion people by 2050.

Number of People (in billions)

Projected growth

Year

POLITICAL WORLD

Population Trends

Population growth rates are slowing, total fertility rates are declining, and populations are aging. Nevertheless, world population will continue to increase for many years to come because the base population is so large. More than 60 million people are added, on average, to the world's population each year, 90 percent of whom are born in less developed countries where poverty is greatest.

In more affluent countries, life expectancy is higher and populations are aging. By 2050, almost one-quarter of the world's population will be 60 years of age or older.

POPULATION GROWTH RATE (%)	
Lowest (2017 estimates)	
1. Lebanon	-1.1
2. Latvia	-1.08
3. Lithuania	-1.08
4. Moldova	-1.05
5. Bulgaria	-0.61

POPULATION GROWTH RATE (%)	
Highest (2017 estimates)	
1. South Sudan	3.83
2. Angola	3.52
3. Malawi	3.31
4. Burundi	3.25
5. Uganda	3.2

◗ **POPULATION GROWTH.**
This map shows projected population change (%) from 2015 to 2050. Russia, China, Japan, and much of Europe face a decline in population due to low birth rates and women waiting longer to have children. Countries in Africa can expect to see an opposite trend as fertility rates remain high.

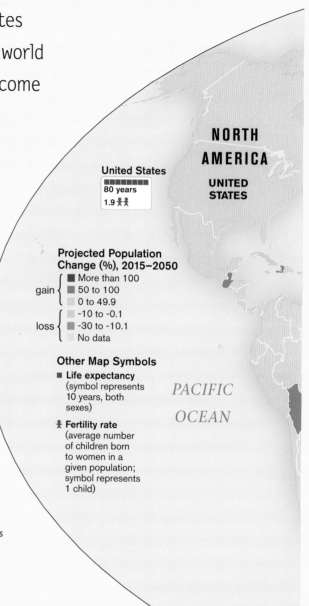

United States
80 years
1.9

NORTH AMERICA

UNITED STATES

Projected Population Change (%), 2015–2050

gain
- More than 100
- 50 to 100
- 0 to 49.9

loss
- -10 to -0.1
- -30 to -10.1
- No data

Other Map Symbols
- **Life expectancy** (symbol represents 10 years, both sexes)
- **Fertility rate** (average number of children born to women in a given population; symbol represents 1 child)

PACIFIC OCEAN

POPULATION PYRAMIDS

A population pyramid compares population by age and sex and can be used to predict future trends. Countries, such as Nigeria, with high birth rates and high percentages of young people have a pyramid-shaped graph, which suggests continued growth. Countries with low birth rates, such as Italy, have narrow bases with bulges in the higher age brackets, indicating an aging population.

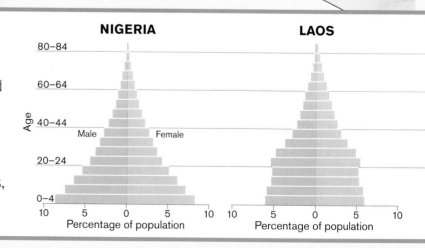

NIGERIA

LAOS

Age

Male   Female

Percentage of population

Percentage of population

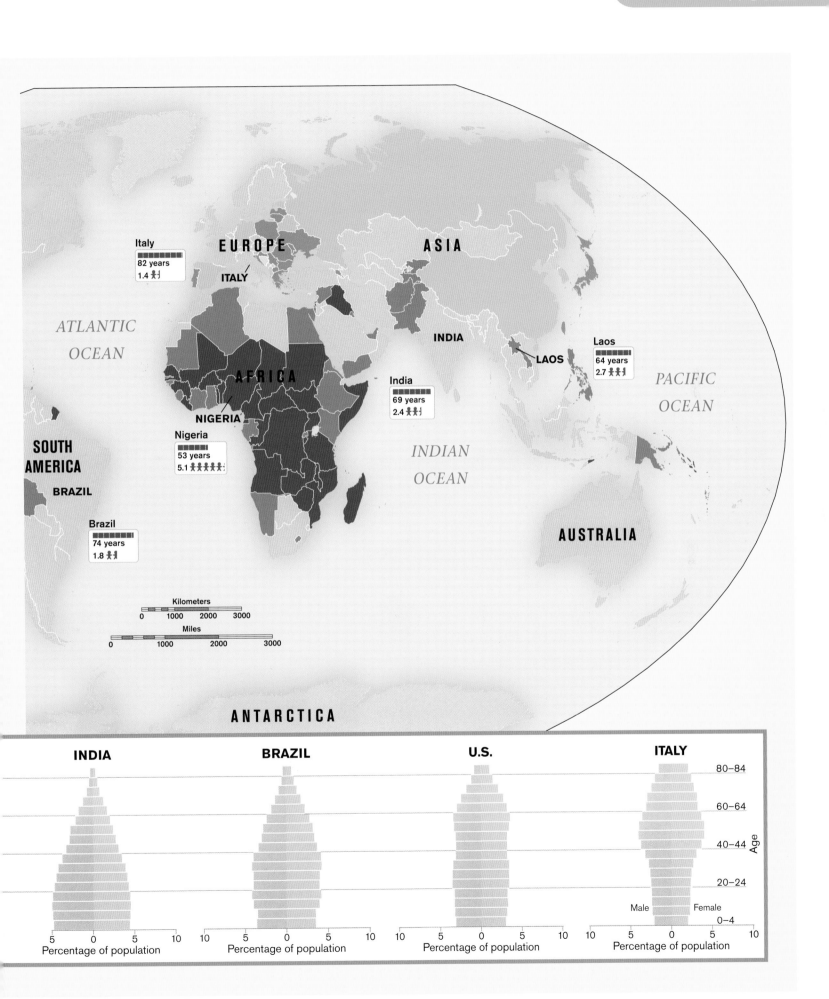

Italy
82 years
1.4

Brazil
74 years
1.8

Nigeria
53 years
5.1

India
69 years
2.4

Laos
64 years
2.7

EUROPE

ASIA

ATLANTIC OCEAN

ITALY

INDIA

LAOS

PACIFIC OCEAN

AFRICA

NIGERIA

INDIAN OCEAN

SOUTH AMERICA

BRAZIL

AUSTRALIA

Kilometers
0   1000   2000   3000

Miles
0   1000   2000   3000

ANTARCTICA

INDIA

BRAZIL

U.S.

ITALY

80–84

60–64

40–44

Age

20–24

Male   Female

0–4

5   0   5   10
Percentage of population

10   5   0   5   10
Percentage of population

10   5   0   5   10
Percentage of population

10   5   0   5   10
Percentage of population

World Languages & Literacy

Earth's 7.4 billion people live in 195 independent countries, but they speak more than 5,000 languages. Experts believe that humans may once have spoken as many as 10,000 languages. Some countries, such as Germany, have one official language. Other countries, such as Zimbabwe, have many official languages.

Literacy is the ability to read and write in one's native language. High literacy rates are associated with more developed countries. But literacy is also a gender issue, since women in less developed countries often lack access to education.

NORTH AMERICA

SOUTH AMERICA

PACIFIC OCEAN

LEADING LANGUAGES

2016 data

Population of first language speakers (in millions)

897 — Chinese (Mandarin)
436 — Spanish
371 — English
329 — Hindi/Urdu
290 — Arabic
242 — Bengali
218 — Portuguese
153 — Russian
148 — Punjabi
128 — Japanese

Languages*

Some languages have only a few hundred speakers, but 26 languages stand out with more than 50 million speakers each. Earth's population giant, China, has almost 900 million speakers of Mandarin as their first language, almost double the next largest group of language speakers. Colonial expansion, trade, and migration account for the spread of the other most widely spoken languages. With growing use of the Internet, English is becoming the language of the technology age.

Colors of bars correspond to language families shown on the map.

⬤ **EDUCATION AND LITERACY.** These Nenet boys in Siberia spend hours learning the national language—Russian—but this may result in the loss of their native language. Literacy can lead to good jobs in the future for these boys and improved economic success for their country.

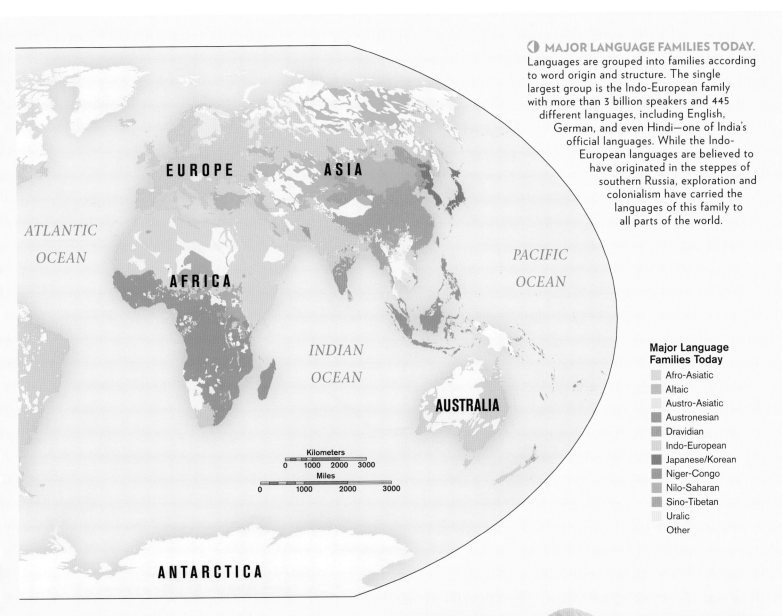

EUROPE

ASIA

ATLANTIC OCEAN

AFRICA

PACIFIC OCEAN

INDIAN OCEAN

AUSTRALIA

Kilometers
0   1000   2000   3000

Miles
0   1000   2000   3000

ANTARCTICA

◖ MAJOR LANGUAGE FAMILIES TODAY. Languages are grouped into families according to word origin and structure. The single largest group is the Indo-European family with more than 3 billion speakers and 445 different languages, including English, German, and even Hindi—one of India's official languages. While the Indo-European languages are believed to have originated in the steppes of southern Russia, exploration and colonialism have carried the languages of this family to all parts of the world.

Major Language Families Today

- Afro-Asiatic
- Altaic
- Austro-Asiatic
- Austronesian
- Dravidian
- Indo-European
- Japanese/Korean
- Niger-Congo
- Nilo-Saharan
- Sino-Tibetan
- Uralic
- Other

◖ ONE LANGUAGE, TWO FORMS. Some languages, including Chinese, use characters instead of letters. The Golden Arches provide a clue to the meaning of the characters on the restaurant sign. Many signs, such as the one in the foreground, also show words in pinyin, a spelling system that uses the Western alphabet.

◖ UNIVERSAL LANGUAGE. The widespread use of technology—for example, the electronic games that hold the attention of these children in France—has crossed the language barrier. Computers, the Internet, and electronic communication devices use a universal language that knows no national borders.

World Religions

Rooted in people's attempts to explain the unknown, religion takes many forms. Some belief systems, such as Christianity, Islam, and Judaism, are monotheistic, meaning that followers believe in just one supreme being. Others, like Hinduism, Shintoism, and most indigenous belief systems, are polytheistic, meaning that followers believe in many gods.

All of the major religions have their origins in Asia, but they have spread around the world. Christianity, with the largest number of followers, has three main divisions—Roman Catholic, Eastern Orthodox, and Protestant. Islam, with almost one-fourth of all believers, has two main divisions—Sunni and Shia. Together, Hinduism and Buddhism account for more than another one-fifth of believers. Judaism, dating back some 4,000 years, is the oldest of all the major monotheistic religions.

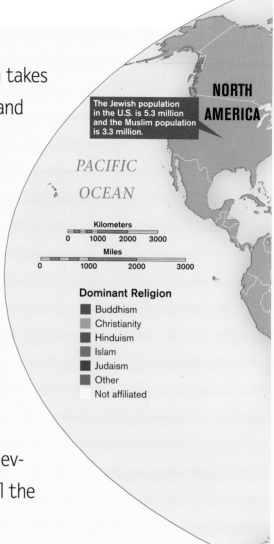

The Jewish population in the U.S. is 5.3 million and the Muslim population is 3.3 million.

NORTH AMERICA

PACIFIC OCEAN

Kilometers
0   1000   2000   3000

Miles
0   1000   2000   3000

Dominant Religion
- Buddhism
- Christianity
- Hinduism
- Islam
- Judaism
- Other
- Not affiliated

BUDDHISM

Founded about 2,500 years ago in northern India by a Hindu prince named Gautama Buddha, Buddhism spread throughout eastern and southeastern Asia. Buddhist temples house statues, such as the Mihintale Buddha (above) in Sri Lanka.

CHRISTIANITY

Based on the teachings of Jesus Christ, born some 2,000 years ago in the area of modern-day Israel, Christianity has spread worldwide and actively seeks converts. Followers in Switzerland (above) participate in a procession with lanterns and crosses.

HINDUISM

Dating back more than 4,000 years, Hinduism is practiced mainly in India. Hindus follow sacred texts known as the Vedas and believe in reincarnation. During the festival of Diwali, Hindus light candles (above) to symbolize the victory of good over evil.

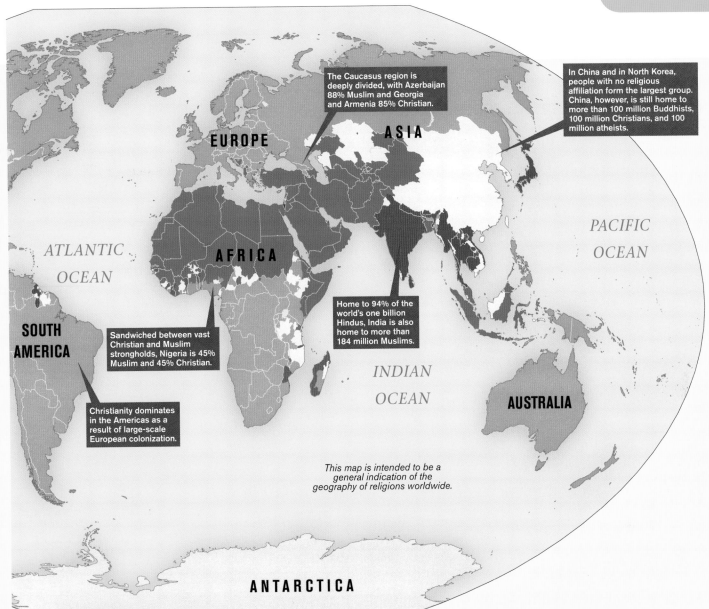

The Caucasus region is deeply divided, with Azerbaijan 88% Muslim and Georgia and Armenia 85% Christian.

In China and in North Korea, people with no religious affiliation form the largest group. China, however, is still home to more than 100 million Buddhists, 100 million Christians, and 100 million atheists.

EUROPE

ASIA

ATLANTIC OCEAN

PACIFIC OCEAN

AFRICA

Home to 94% of the world's one billion Hindus, India is also home to more than 184 million Muslims.

SOUTH AMERICA

Sandwiched between vast Christian and Muslim strongholds, Nigeria is 45% Muslim and 45% Christian.

INDIAN OCEAN

AUSTRALIA

Christianity dominates in the Americas as a result of large-scale European colonization.

This map is intended to be a general indication of the geography of religions worldwide.

ANTARCTICA

ISLAM

Muslims believe that the Koran, Islam's sacred book, records the words of Allah (God) as revealed to the Prophet Muhammad around 610 C.E. Believers (above) circle the Kabah in the Haram Mosque in Mecca, Saudi Arabia, the spiritual center of the faith.

JUDAISM

The traditions, laws, and beliefs of Judaism date back some 4,000 years to Abraham, its founder, and to the Torah, the first five books of the Old Testament. Followers pray before the Western Wall (above), which stands below Islam's Dome of the Rock in Jerusalem, Israel.

RELIGIOUS FOLLOWERS

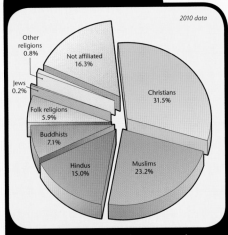

2010 data

Other religions 0.8%

Not affiliated 16.3%

Jews 0.2%

Folk religions 5.9%

Christians 31.5%

Buddhists 7.1%

Hindus 15.0%

Muslims 23.2%

Most people identify with a major religion. Some are nonreligious.

World Economies

A country's economy can be divided into three parts, or sectors—primary, which includes agriculture, forestry, fishing, and mining; secondary, which includes industry and manufacturing; and tertiary, which includes services ranging from retail sales to mail delivery, to teaching or jobs in medicine. Sometimes a fourth sector, called quaternary, is added. This includes information technology, research, and knowledge creation. The map shows that the economies of the United States, western Europe, and Japan are dominated by service sector jobs. These countries rely heavily on the use of technology and enjoy a high gross domestic product (GDP) per capita—the value of goods and services produced each year, averaged per person in each country. The overall quality of life in these countries is good. In contrast, many people in Africa and Asia still depend on the primary sector, which generates a low GDP per capita.

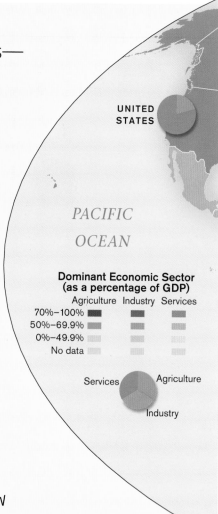

UNITED
STATES

PACIFIC
OCEAN

**Dominant Economic Sector
(as a percentage of GDP)**

	Agriculture	Industry	Services
70%–100%			
50%–69.9%			
0%–49.9%			
No data			

Services Agriculture

Industry

⬤ **INFORMATION.** Computers and other technologies have opened employment opportunities dealing with information and knowledge creation. These college students in the United Kingdom learn skills in an information technology lab that will prepare them for 21st-century jobs.

⬤ **INDUSTRY.** A man assembles a hybrid Prius car on an automated assembly line in a Toyota factory in Japan. The manufacture of cars is an important industrial activity and a key part of the global economy.

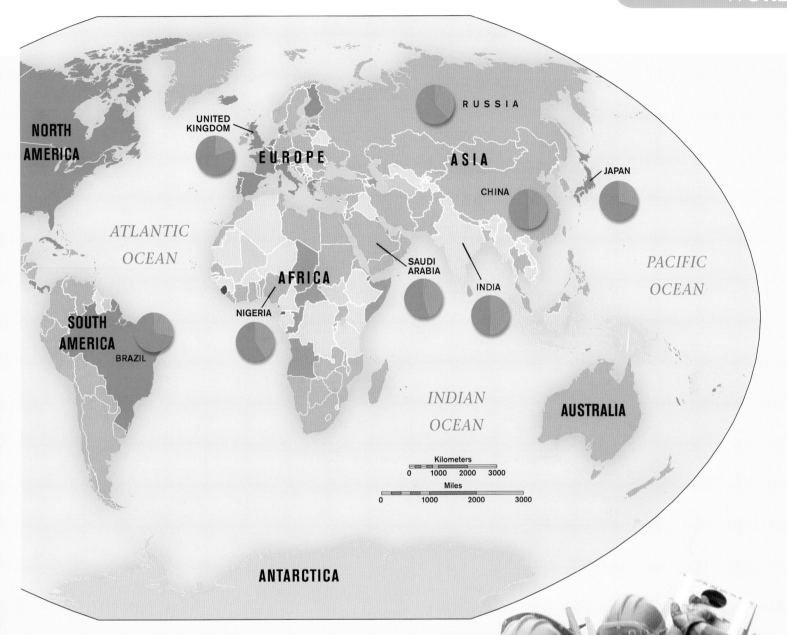

⬤ **AGRICULTURE.** People in less developed countries, such as these women in Mozambique, often grow a variety of crops just to support their families. This practice is called subsistence agriculture. In more developed countries, farmers use machines to produce large quantities of commercial crops.

⬤ **SERVICES.** People employed in the service sector, such as these national forest firefighters in Washington State, U.S.A., use their skills and training to provide services rather than products. Teachers, lawyers, and store clerks, among others, are also part of the service sector.

World Trade

World trade has expanded rapidly since the end of World War II in 1945. In fact, trade has grown faster than world production. Some countries, such as the United States, China, and Germany, have complex economies that involve trading many different products as well as commercial services, such as financial and information management. But many less developed countries rely on only a few products—sometimes even just one product—to generate trade income (map, right).

Wealthy countries often protect their economies by negotiating agreements and imposing taxes that limit trade in products from other countries. The World Trade Organization works to reduce such trade barriers so that all countries can compete in the global economy.

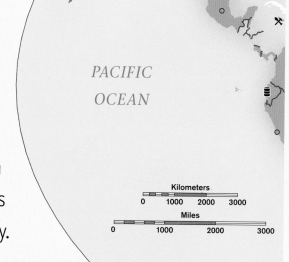

NORTH AMERICA

PACIFIC OCEAN

Kilometers
0   1000   2000   3000

Miles
0   1000   2000   3000

◗ **TRADE.** The map (right) shows the richest and poorest economies around the world. The wealth of economies can be measured in terms of gross national income (GNI) per person—income derived from all economic activity.

TOP MERCHANDISE EXPORTERS

(2015 data, billion U.S. dollars)	
1. China	$2,275
2. United States	$1,505
3. Germany	$1,329
4. Japan	$625
5. Netherlands	$567

TOP MERCHANDISE IMPORTERS

(2015 data, billion U.S. dollars)	
1. United States	$2,308
2. China	$1,682
3. Germany	$1,050
4. Japan	$648
5. United Kingdom	$626

TOP COMMERCIAL SERVICE EXPORTERS

(2015 data, billion U.S. dollars)	
1. United States	$690
2. United Kingdom	$345
3. China	$285
4. Germany	$247
5. France	$240

TOP COMMERCIAL SERVICE IMPORTERS

(2015 data, billion U.S. dollars)	
1. United States	$469
2. China	$466
3. Germany	$289
4. France	$228
5. United Kingdom	$208

◗ **GLOBAL EXCHANGE.** The world economy depends on container ports where ships deliver goods for sale or redistribution. Some ports, called transshipment ports, move containers from one form of transportation (such as a ship) to another (such as a truck) so that goods can be delivered to a final destination.

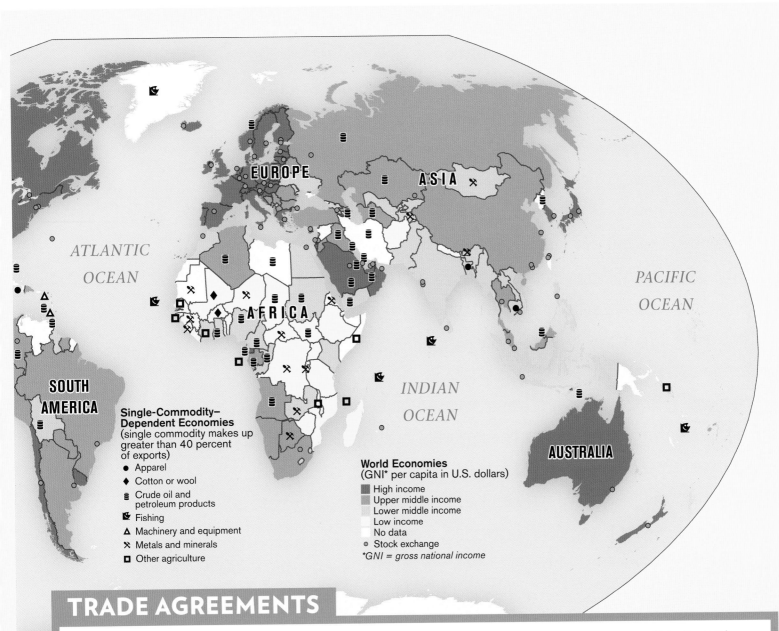

**Single-Commodity–
Dependent Economies**
(single commodity makes up
greater than 40 percent
of exports)

- ● Apparel
- ◆ Cotton or wool
- ▤ Crude oil and
  petroleum products
- ◪ Fishing
- △ Machinery and equipment
- ✕ Metals and minerals
- ▢ Other agriculture

World Economies
(GNI* per capita in U.S. dollars)

- High income
- Upper middle income
- Lower middle income
- Low income
- No data
- ○ Stock exchange

GNI = gross national income

TRADE AGREEMENTS

Trade within regions is
increasing. Neighboring
countries agree to offer
each other trade benefits
that can improve the
economy of the whole
region. Such agreements
allow products, workers,
and money to move more
easily among the partners.
But these agreements may
also prevent trade with
other countries that may
be able to provide products
at a lower cost.

**Major Regional
Trade Agreements**

- **APEC:** Asia-Pacific
  Economic Cooperation
- **ASEAN:** Association of
  Southeast Asian Nations
- **APEC & ASEAN**
- **COMESA:** Common
  Market for Eastern and
  Southern Africa
- **ECOWAS:** Economic
  Community of West
  African States
- **EU:** European Union
- **MERCOSUR:** Southern
  Common Market
- **NAFTA:** North America
  Free Trade Agreement
  & APEC
- **SAFTA:** South Asian
  Free Trade Area

World Water

Water is Earth's most precious resource. Although more than two-thirds of the planet is covered by water, freshwater, which is needed by plants and animals—including humans—is only about 2.5 percent of all the water on Earth. Much of this is trapped deep underground or frozen in ice sheets and glaciers. Of the small amount of water that is fresh, less than one percent is available for human use.

The map at right shows each country's access to renewable freshwater supplies. Watersheds are large areas that drain into a particular river or lake. Unfortunately, human activity often puts great stress on watersheds. For example, in Brazil, plans are being made to build large dams on the Amazon. This will alter the natural flow of water in this giant watershed. In the United States, heavy use of chemical fertilizers and pesticides has created toxic runoff that threatens the health of the Mississippi watershed.

Access to clean freshwater is critical for human health. But in many places, safe water is scarce due to population pressure and pollution.

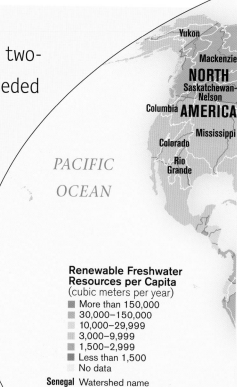

Yukon
Mackenzie
NORTH
Saskatchewan-Nelson
Columbia **AMERICA**
Mississippi
Colorado
Rio Grande

PACIFIC OCEAN

Renewable Freshwater Resources per Capita
(cubic meters per year)
■ More than 150,000
■ 30,000–150,000
■ 10,000–29,999
■ 3,000–9,999
■ 1,500–2,999
■ Less than 1,500
□ No data
Senegal Watershed name
――― Watershed boundary

WATER FACTS

Rivers that have been dammed to generate electricity are the source of almost 90 percent of Earth's renewable energy resources.

North America's Great Lakes hold about 20 percent of Earth's available freshwater.

If all the glaciers and ice sheets on Earth's surface melted, they would raise the level of Earth's oceans by about 216 feet (66 m).

If all the world's water could be placed in a gallon jug, the freshwater available for humans to use would equal only about one tablespoon.

⊘ **BIG SPLASH!** Water sports are a favorite recreational activity, especially in hot places such as Albuquerque, New Mexico, U.S.A., where these young people cool down in a giant wave pool.

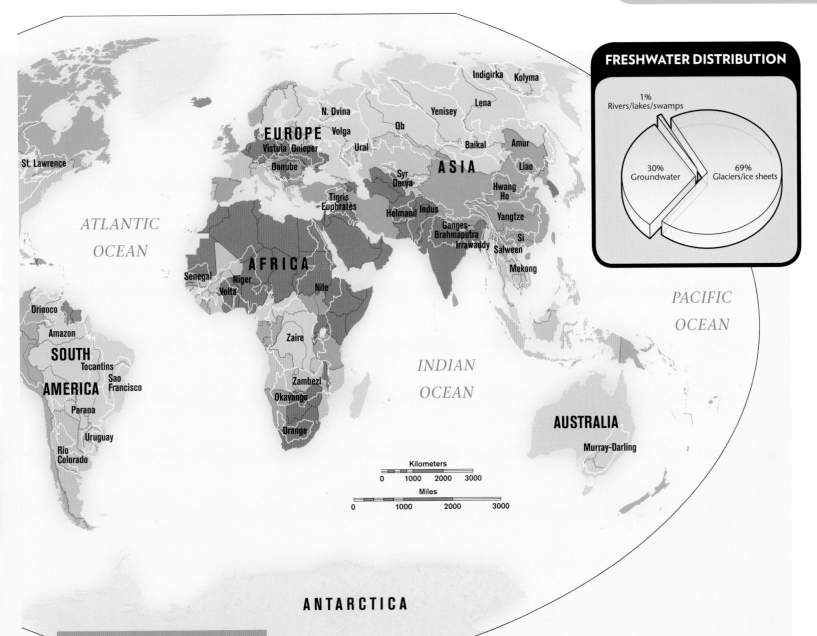

FRESHWATER DISTRIBUTION

1%
Rivers/lakes/swamps

30%
Groundwater

69%
Glaciers/ice sheets

ATLANTIC
OCEAN

St. Lawrence

EUROPE
Vistula Dnieper
Danube

N. Dvina
Volga
Ural

Ob
Yenisey

Indigirka Kolyma
Lena

ASIA
Baikal
Amur
Liao

Tigris
Euphrates
Syr
Darya
Helmand Indus
Ganges-
Brahmaputra
Irrawaddy
Hwang
Ho
Yangtze
Si
Salween
Mekong

AFRICA
Senegal
Niger
Volta
Nile

Orinoco
Amazon
SOUTH
Tocantins
Sao
Francisco
AMERICA
Parana
Uruguay
Rio
Colorado

Zaire
Zambezi
Okavango
Orange

INDIAN
OCEAN

PACIFIC
OCEAN

AUSTRALIA
Murray-Darling

ANTARCTICA

Kilometers
0 1000 2000 3000

Miles
0 1000 2000 3000

WATER CYCLE

The amount of water on Earth has remained more or less constant over the past two billion years—only the form changes. As the sun warms Earth's surface, liquid water is changed to water vapor in a process called evaporation. Plants lose water from their leaves in a process called transpiration. As water vapor rises into the air, it cools and changes again, becoming clouds in a process called condensation. Droplets fall from clouds as precipitation, which travels as groundwater or runoff back to the lakes, rivers, and oceans, where the cycle starts again.

Water vapor becomes clouds

Precipitation falls and
runs off into the ground

Lake

River

Water evaporates

Groundwater

Ocean

World Food

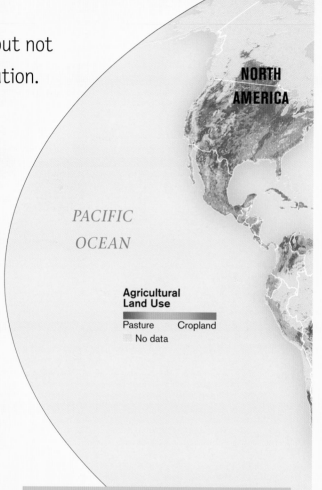

Earth produces enough food for all its inhabitants, but not everyone gets enough to eat. It's a matter of distribution. Agricultural regions (map, right) are unevenly spread around the world, and it is sometimes difficult to move food supplies from areas of surplus to areas of great need. Africa, in particular, has regions where hunger and malnourishment rob people of healthy, productive lives.

In recent decades, food production has increased, especially production of meat and cereals, such as corn, wheat, and rice, and the harvesting of fish. Grains dominate the calorie supply of people, especially in Africa and Asia. But increased yields of grain require intensive use of fertilizers and irrigation, which are not only expensive but also possibly a threat to the environment.

NORTH
AMERICA

PACIFIC
OCEAN

**Agricultural
Land Use**

Pasture   Cropland
No data

TOP CATCH

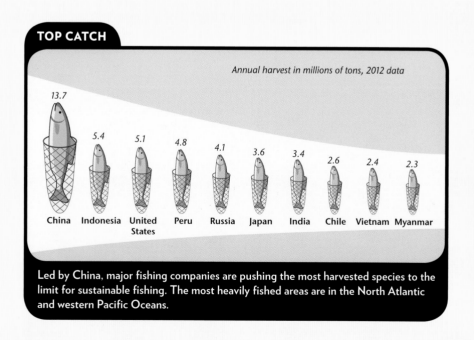

Annual harvest in millions of tons, 2012 data

China	Indonesia	United States	Peru	Russia	Japan	India	Chile	Vietnam	Myanmar
13.7	5.4	5.1	4.8	4.1	3.6	3.4	2.6	2.4	2.3

Led by China, major fishing companies are pushing the most harvested species to the limit for sustainable fishing. The most heavily fished areas are in the North Atlantic and western Pacific Oceans.

⊖ **HEADED TO MARKET.** A commercial fisherman uses a motorized winch to raise a net heavy with fish.

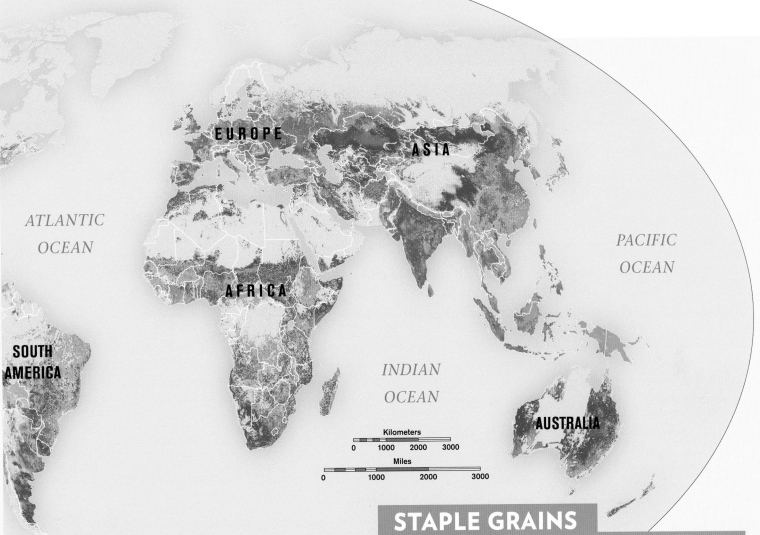

ATLANTIC
OCEAN

EUROPE

ASIA

PACIFIC
OCEAN

AFRICA

SOUTH
AMERICA

INDIAN
OCEAN

AUSTRALIA

Kilometers
0   1000   2000   3000

Miles
0   1000   2000   3000

STAPLE GRAINS

CORN. A staple in prehistoric Mexico and Peru, corn (or maize) is native to the New World. By the time Columbus's crew first tasted it, corn was already a hardy crop in much of North and South America.

WHEAT. One of the two oldest grains (barley is the other), wheat was important in ancient Mediterranean civilizations. Today, it is the most widely cultivated grain. Wheat grows best in temperate climates.

RICE. Originating in Asia many millennia ago, rice is the staple grain for about half the world's people. It is a labor-intensive crop that grows primarily in paddies (flooded fields) and thrives in the hot, humid tropics.

CASTING NETS. Fishermen in Orissa, India, cast their nets on the Birupa River. Fish is an important source of protein in their diets. Any surplus catch can be sold in the local market.

World Energy

Almost everything people do requires energy. But energy comes in different forms. Traditional energy sources, such as burning wood and dried animal dung, are still used by many people in the developing world. Industrialized countries and urban centers around the world rely on coal, oil, and natural gas—called fossil fuels because they formed long ago from ancient deposits of decayed plant and animal material. As the map shows, these deposits are unevenly distributed on Earth, and many countries frequently cannot afford them.

Carbon dioxide from the burning of fossil fuels along with other emissions may be contributing to climate change. Concerned scientists are looking at new ways to harness sources of renewable energy, such as water, wind, sun, and biofuels (wood, plant materials, and garbage).

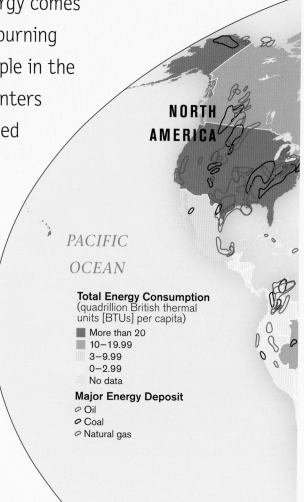

NORTH
AMERICA

PACIFIC

OCEAN

Total Energy Consumption
(quadrillion British thermal
units [BTUs] per capita)
- More than 20
- 10–19.99
- 3–9.99
- 0–2.99
- No data

Major Energy Deposit
- Oil
- Coal
- Natural gas

OIL, GAS, AND COAL

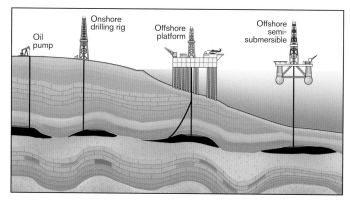

Oil
pump

Onshore
drilling rig

Offshore
platform

Offshore
semi-
submersible

⬤ **DRILLING FOR OIL AND GAS.** The type of equipment used depends on whether the oil or natural gas is in the ground or under the ocean. This illustration shows some of the different kinds of onshore and offshore drilling equipment.

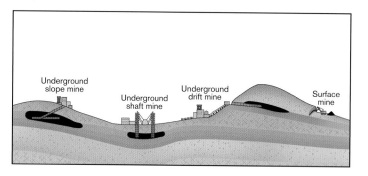

Underground
slope mine

Underground
shaft mine

Underground
drift mine

Surface
mine

⬤ **COAL MINING.** The mining of coal made possible the industrial revolution, which began in the mid-1700s in England, and coal still remains a major energy source. Work that was once done by people using picks and shovels now relies heavily on mechanized equipment. This diagram shows some of the various kinds of mines currently in use.

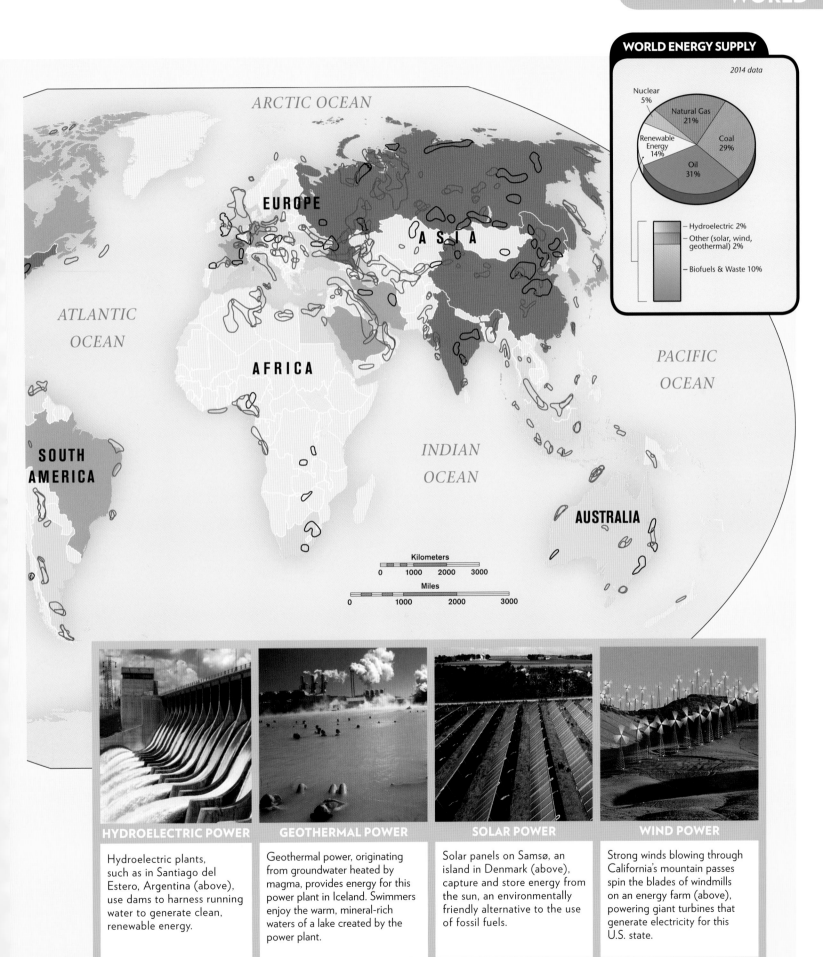

ARCTIC OCEAN

EUROPE

ASIA

ATLANTIC OCEAN

PACIFIC OCEAN

AFRICA

INDIAN OCEAN

SOUTH AMERICA

AUSTRALIA

WORLD ENERGY SUPPLY

2014 data

- Nuclear 5%
- Natural Gas 21%
- Renewable Energy 14%
- Coal 29%
- Oil 31%

- Hydroelectric 2%
- Other (solar, wind, geothermal) 2%
- Biofuels & Waste 10%

Kilometers
0 1000 2000 3000

Miles
0 1000 2000 3000

HYDROELECTRIC POWER

Hydroelectric plants, such as in Santiago del Estero, Argentina (above), use dams to harness running water to generate clean, renewable energy.

GEOTHERMAL POWER

Geothermal power, originating from groundwater heated by magma, provides energy for this power plant in Iceland. Swimmers enjoy the warm, mineral-rich waters of a lake created by the power plant.

SOLAR POWER

Solar panels on Samsø, an island in Denmark (above), capture and store energy from the sun, an environmentally friendly alternative to the use of fossil fuels.

WIND POWER

Strong winds blowing through California's mountain passes spin the blades of windmills on an energy farm (above), powering giant turbines that generate electricity for this U.S. state.

PHYSICAL

TOTAL AREA 9,449,000 sq mi (24,474,000 sq km)	**LOWEST POINT** Death Valley, California, U.S.A. -282 ft (-86 m)	**LARGEST LAKE** Lake Superior, U.S.-Canada 31,700 sq mi (82,100 sq km)
HIGHEST POINT Denali (Mount McKinley), Alaska, U.S.A. 20,320 ft (6,194 m)	**LONGEST RIVER** Mississippi-Missouri, United States 3,780 mi (6,083 km)	

POLITICAL

POPULATION 639,613,000	**LARGEST COUNTRY** Canada 3,855,081 sq mi (9,984,670 sq km)
LARGEST METROPOLITAN AREA Mexico City, Mexico Pop. 21,157,000	**MOST DENSELY POPULATED COUNTRY** Barbados 1,761.1 people per sq mi (679.9 per sq km)

NORTH AMERICA

North America

For the Aleutian Islands and continuation of the Bering Sea, see inset map page 64.

Map Key
— Country boundary

0   600 miles
0   600 kilometers

Azimuthal Equidistant Projection

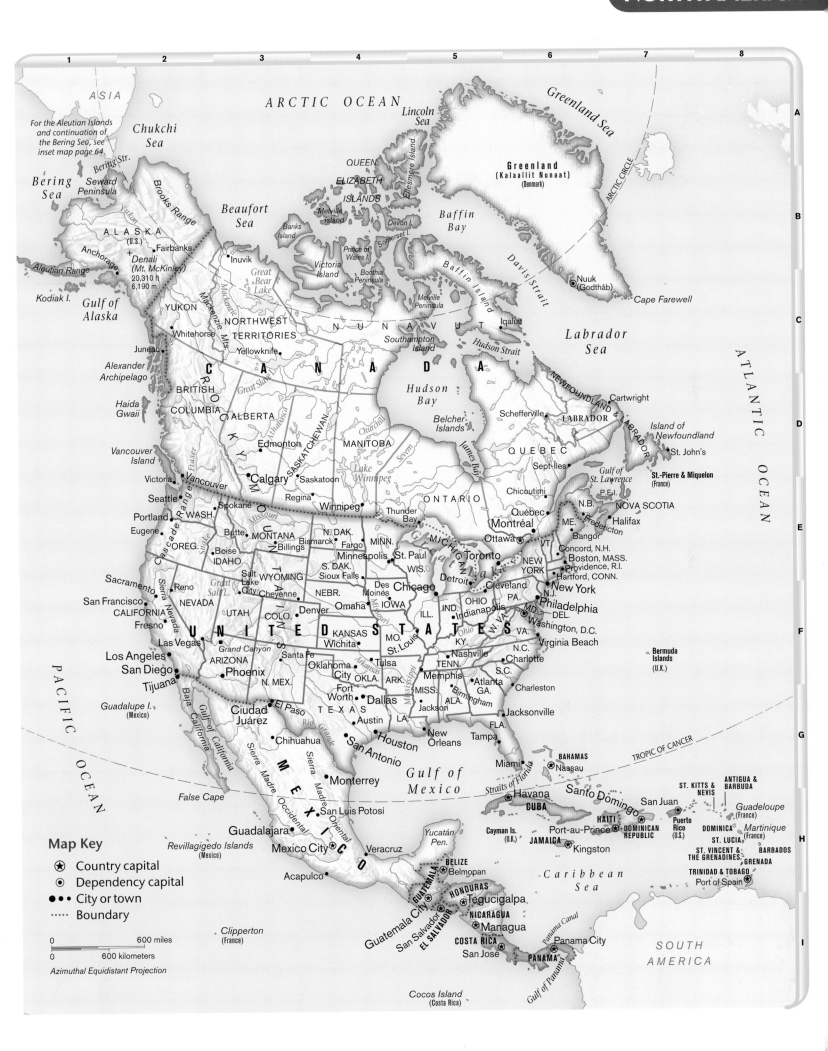

ASIA

ARCTIC OCEAN

Chukchi
Sea

*For the Aleutian Islands
and continuation of
the Bering Sea, see
inset map page 64.*

Bering Str.

Bering
Sea

Seward
Peninsula

Lincoln
Sea

Greenland
Sea

Greenland
(Kalaallit Nunaat)
(Denmark)

Beaufort
Sea

QUEEN
ELIZABETH
ISLANDS

Ellesmere Island

Melville
Island

Banks
Island

Devon I.

Baffin
Bay

Brooks Range

ALASKA
(U.S.)

Anchorage

Fairbanks

+Denali
(Mt. McKinley)
20,310 ft
6,190 m

Inuvik

Great
Bear
Lake

Prince of
Wales I.

Somerset I.

Victoria
Island

Boothia
Peninsula

Baffin Island

ARCTIC CIRCLE

Nuuk
(Godthåb)

Cape Farewell

Kodiak I.

Gulf of
Alaska

Aleutian Range

Whitehorse

YUKON

Yellowknife

NORTHWEST
TERRITORIES

Mackenzie Mts.

Great Slave
Lake

N U N A V U T

Southampton
Island

Iqaluit

Hudson Strait

Labrador
Sea

Juneau

Alexander
Archipelago

Haida
Gwaii

BRITISH
COLUMBIA

C A N A D A

Great Slave

Athabasca

R
O
C
K
Y

ALBERTA

Edmonton

SASKATCHEWAN

MANITOBA

Churchill

Lake
Winnipeg

Severn

Hudson
Bay

James Bay

Belcher
Islands

ONTARIO

QUEBEC

Schefferville

NEWFOUNDLAND & LABRADOR

Cartwright

LABRADOR

Island of
Newfoundland

Sept-Îles

St. John's

Vancouver
Island

Victoria

Vancouver

Fraser

Calgary

Saskatoon

Regina

Winnipeg

Thunder
Bay

Chicoutimi

Québec

Gulf of
St. Lawrence

St.-Pierre & Miquelon
(France)

P.E.I.

N.B.

NOVA SCOTIA

Seattle

Portland

Eugene

WASH.

OREG.

Spokane

Cascade Range

Snake

Missouri

Butte

Boise

MONTANA

IDAHO

Billings

Bismarck

Fargo

N. DAK.

S. DAK.

MINN.

WIS.

Minneapolis

St. Paul

Sioux Falls

MICHIGAN

L. Superior

Montréal

Ottawa

Toronto

Detroit

Cleveland

ME.

Fredericton

Bangor

Concord, N.H.

Boston, MASS.

Providence, R.I.

Hartford, CONN.

NEW
YORK

VT

Halifax

New York

N.J.

Philadelphia

PA.

DEL.

MD.

Washington, D.C.

Sacramento

Reno

NEVADA

Sierra Nevada

Great
Salt L.

Salt
Lake
City

WYOMING

UTAH

Cheyenne

NEBR.

Denver

COLO.

Omaha

Des
Moines

IOWA

Chicago

ILL.

IND.

OHIO

Indianapolis

Ohio

W. VA.

VA.

KY.

San Francisco

Fresno

CALIFORNIA

Las Vegas

Los Angeles

San Diego

Tijuana

ARIZONA

Grand Canyon

Phoenix

N. MEX.

Santa Fe

KANSAS

Wichita

MO.

St. Louis

Arkansas

Oklahoma
City

OKLA.

Tulsa

ARK.

Memphis

TENN.

Nashville

N.C.

Charlotte

S.C.

Virginia Beach

Bermuda
Islands
(U.K.)

Guadalupe I.
(Mexico)

Baja California

Gulf of California

El Paso

Ciudad
Juárez

Chihuahua

TEXAS

Fort
Worth

Dallas

Austin

Rio Grande

Mississippi

LA.

MISS.

Jackson

ALA.

Birmingham

Atlanta

GA.

Charleston

Jacksonville

FLA.

New
Orleans

Tampa

PACIFIC OCEAN

M E X I C O

Sierra Madre Occidental

Sierra Madre Oriental

False Cape

San Antonio

Houston

Monterrey

San Luis Potosí

Gulf of
Mexico

Miami

Straits of Florida

Havana

CUBA

BAHAMAS

Nassau

TROPIC OF CANCER

Santo Domingo

San Juan

Puerto
Rico
(U.S.)

ST. KITTS &
NEVIS

ANTIGUA &
BARBUDA

Guadeloupe
(France)

DOMINICA

Martinique
(France)

Guadalajara

Revillagigedo Islands
(Mexico)

Mexico City

Veracruz

Yucatán
Pen.

Cayman Is.
(U.K.)

Port-au-Prince

HAITI

DOMINICAN
REPUBLIC

JAMAICA

Kingston

ST. LUCIA

ST. VINCENT &
THE GRENADINES

BARBADOS

GRENADA

TRINIDAD & TOBAGO

Port of Spain

Acapulco

BELIZE

Belmopan

Caribbean
Sea

GUATEMALA

Guatemala City

San Salvador

EL SALVADOR

HONDURAS

Tegucigalpa

NICARAGUA

Managua

COSTA RICA

San José

PANAMA

Panama City

Panama Canal

Gulf of Panama

SOUTH
AMERICA

Clipperton
(France)

Cocos Island
(Costa Rica)

ATLANTIC
OCEAN

Davis Strait

PACIFIC
OCEAN

Map Key

- ⊛ Country capital
- ⊚ Dependency capital
- ••• City or town
- ..... Boundary

0   600 miles
0   600 kilometers

Azimuthal Equidistant Projection

THE CONTINENT:
NORTH AMERICA

North America

LAND OF CONTRASTS

CLASSIC CARS. American cars from the 1950s line a street in Havana, Cuba. Cuban mechanics keep old cars running by creative use of nonstandard parts.

From the windswept tundra of Alaska, U.S.A., to the rain forest of Panama, the third largest continent stretches 5,500 miles (8,850 km), spanning natural environments that support wildlife from polar bears to jaguars. Over thousands of years, Native American groups spread across these varied landscapes. But this rich mosaic of cultures largely disappeared with the arrival of European fortune hunters and land seekers. While abundant resources and fast-changing technology have brought prosperity to Canada and the United States, other countries wrestle with the most basic needs. Promise and problems abound across this contrasting realm of 23 countries and 640 million people.

DRESSED TO CELEBRATE. This boy in Mexico's southern state of Chiapas wears traditional clothing, including a brightly colored string tie and a broad-brimmed sombrero with elaborate stitching around the edge.

⬥ **HOLD TIGHT.** These daring rafters run the roaring rapids of the Kicking Horse River in British Columbia, Canada's westernmost province. Rivers tumbling down the steep slopes of the Rocky Mountains provide many recreational opportunities.

◐ **STREET MUSIC.**
People from around the world visit New Orleans, Louisiana, U.S.A., to hear jazz musicians fill the air with their music.

◑ **NIGHT SONG.**
This coyote sends his mournful howl into the dark Montana night. Members of the dog family, coyotes originated in the southwestern United States but are now found throughout North America—even in urban areas.

more about
North America

⬒ **DWELLINGS FROM THE PAST.** Between 1000 and 1300 C.E., native people known as Ancestral Puebloans built cliff dwellings called pueblos, such as this one in Mesa Verde, Colorado, U.S.A.

⬒ **HIGH FLIER.** A young Kutchin boy sails off a snowbank on snowshoes in Canada's Yukon. The Kutchin, an Athabascan tribe, live in the forested lands of eastern Alaska and western Canada. The name Kutchin means "people."

⬒ **MAYA TREASURE.** The Pyramid of the Magician marks the ruins of Uxmal on the Yucatan Peninsula. At least five million people of Maya descent still live in southern Mexico and Central America.

◑ **FROZEN SUMMER.** Because Greenland lies so far north, even summers there are cold. Here, local people navigate their boat among icebergs in waters off the village of Augpilagtoq.

SWIMMING FREE. A variety of fish swim among colorful corals in the clear blue waters of the Caribbean Sea. Tropical waters are the habitat for many species of fish.

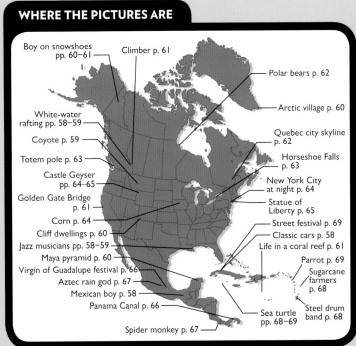

WHERE THE PICTURES ARE

Boy on snowshoes pp. 60–61
Climber p. 61
Polar bears p. 62
Arctic village p. 60
White-water rafting pp. 58–59
Quebec city skyline p. 62
Coyote p. 59
Horseshoe Falls p. 63
Totem pole p. 63
New York City at night p. 64
Castle Geyser pp. 64–65
Statue of Liberty p. 65
Golden Gate Bridge p. 61
Street festival p. 69
Corn p. 64
Classic cars p. 58
Cliff dwellings p. 60
Life in a coral reef p. 61
Jazz musicians pp. 58–59
Parrot p. 69
Maya pyramid p. 60
Sugarcane farmers p. 68
Virgin of Guadalupe festival p. 66
Aztec rain god p. 67
Mexican boy p. 58
Steel drum band p. 68
Panama Canal p. 66
Sea turtle pp. 68–69
Spider monkey p. 67

DON'T LOOK DOWN. Clinging to a sheer rock face, a young woman demonstrates great skill as she scales a steep cliff in Banff National Park in Alberta, Canada. Covering more than 2,500 square miles (6,475 sq km) in the Canadian Rockies, Banff is a major tourist attraction.

WESTERN GATEWAY. The Golden Gate Bridge marks the entrance to San Francisco Bay, U.S.A. Beyond the bridge, captured above in the warm glow of twilight, is the California port city that shares a name with the bay.

THE BASICS
STATS

Area
3,855,081 sq mi
(9,984,670 sq km)

Population
35,624,000

Predominant languages
English, French (both official)

Predominant religion
Christianity

GDP per capita
$46,400

Life expectancy
82 years

GEO WHIZ

Nunavut, Canada's newest territory, has issued license plates shaped like a polar bear for cars, motorcycles, and snowmobiles.

Canada's government is a constitutional monarchy. Britain's Queen Elizabeth II is its head of state.

Canada's Bay of Fundy, located between the eastern provinces of New Brunswick and Nova Scotia, has the highest tides in the world, with a tidal range reaching up to 53 feet (16 m).

Geologists believe the impact of a meteorite may have created Quebec's Réservoir Manicouagan more than 200 million years ago.

Canada

Topped only by Russia in area, Canada has just 36 million people. That's less than the population of the U.S. state of California. Ancient rocks yield abundant minerals. Lakes and rivers in Quebec are tapped for hydropower, and wheat farming and cattle ranching thrive across the western Prairie Provinces. Vast forests attract loggers, and mountain slopes provide a playground for nature lovers. Enormous deposits of oil sands lie waiting for technology to find a cheap way to convert them to hundreds of billions of barrels of oil. Most Canadians live within a hundred miles (161 km) of the U.S. border. Here, too, are its leading cities: Asia-focused Vancouver, ethnically diverse Toronto, national capital Ottawa, and French-speaking Montreal.

SILENT WATCHERS. Polar bears, North America's largest land carnivores, are adapted to the extreme Arctic environment around Cape Churchill in northern Manitoba. An estimated 15,000 to 20,000 polar bears live in Canada.

LONGEST COASTLINE

Country	Coastline
Canada	151,023 miles (243,042 km)
Indonesia	33,998 miles (54,716 km)
Russia	23,397 miles (37,653 km)
Philippines	22,549 miles (36,289 km)
Japan	18,486 miles (29,751 km)
Australia	16,006 miles (25,760 km)
Norway	15,626 miles (25,148 km)
United States	12,380 miles (19,924 km)
New Zealand	9,404 miles (15,134 km)
China	9,010 miles (14,500 km)

Canada has the longest coastline in the world, and at more than 150,000 miles (243,000 km) it far surpasses the length of coastline of any other country.

FRENCH ENCLAVE. Château Frontenac sparkles in Quebec City's nighttime skyline. Settled by the French in the early 1600s, the province of Quebec has maintained close ties to Europe and to its French heritage.

KNOWING WHO WE ARE. Native people of the Pacific Northwest preserve family stories and legends in massive carved poles called totems.

Map Key

- ⚝ Country capital
- ⊙ Provincial capital
- ●●● City or town
- ⋯⋯ Boundary

0 _____ 500 miles
0 _____ 500 kilometers
Azimuthal Equidistant Projection

ARCTIC OCEAN

QUEEN ELIZABETH
ISLANDS
SVERDRUP ISLANDS
Prince Patrick
Island
Ellesmere Island
Greenland
(Kalaallit Nunaat)
(Denmark)

BEAUFORT
SEA
Banks
Island
Melville I.
Bathurst
Island
Devon Island
Resolute
PARRY ISLANDS
BAFFIN
BAY

Amundsen
Gulf
Victoria
Island
Parry Channel
Prince
of Wales
Island
Somerset
Island
Pond Inlet

NORTHWEST
Cambridge
Bay
King
William I.
Gulf of Boothia
Boothia Peninsula
Igloolik
Prince
Charles
Island
BAFFIN ISLAND
DAVIS STRAIT

ARCTIC CIRCLE
Kugluktuk
Great Bear
Lake
NUNAVUT
Melville Peninsula
FOXE
BASIN

TERRITORIES
Iqaluit
Cape Dorset
ATLANTIC OCEAN

Mackenzie
Great Slave
Lake
Yellowknife
Southampton
Island
Hudson Strait

Hay River
Whale
Cove
Chesterfield
Inlet
Ivujivik
Coats
Island
Mansel
Island
Ungava
Bay
LABRADOR
SEA

C A N A D A
Fort Smith
Arviat
Ungava
Peninsula
Kuujjuaq
NEWFOUNDLAND & LABRADOR

Uranium
City
Lake
Athabasca
HUDSON
BAY
Belcher
Islands
LABRADOR
L'Anse aux
Meadows

Fort
McMurray
Reindeer
Lake
Churchill
Scheffervile
Happy Valley-
Goose Bay

ALBERTA
Churchill
Thompson
Nelson
Fort
Severn
James
Bay
Akimiski
Island
Labrador
City
Réservoir
Manicouagan
St.
John's

Edmonton
SASKATCHEWAN
Prince
Albert
MANITOBA
The Pas
Severn
Chisasibi
Sept-Îles
ISLAND OF
NEWFOUNDLAND
Cape
Race

Red Deer
North Saskatchewan
Saskatoon
Lake
Winnipeg
Fort Albany
QUEBEC
Anticosti
Island
St-Pierre &
Miquelon
(France)

Calgary
South Saskatchewan
Lake
Manitoba
ONTARIO
Rimouski
Gaspé
Peninsula
Gulf of
St. Lawrence
Cabot Strait
Cape Breton Island

Moose
Jaw
Regina
Brandon
Lake
Winnipeg
Lake
Nipigon
Saguenay
Québec
PRINCE
EDWARD
ISLAND
Charlottetown

Lethbridge
Medicine Hat
Thunder
Bay
Timmins
St. Lawrence
NEW
BRUNSWICK
NOVA
SCOTIA
Sable
Island

UNITED STATES
Lake Superior
North Bay
Sudbury
Sault
Ste. Marie
Ottawa
Kingston
Fredericton
Halifax
Bay of Fundy
Cape
Sable

Lake Huron
Lake Michigan
Oshawa
Toronto
Hamilton
London
Windsor
Lake Erie
Montréal
Niagara
Falls
Lake Ontario

ICE-AGE REMNANT. The Niagara River, which formed as glaciers of the last ice age began to melt, cascades over Canada's Horseshoe Falls. The falls, which stretch across the border between Canada and the United States, are a major tourist attraction.

THE BASICS

STATS

Area
3,794,079 sq mi
(9,826,675 sq km)

Population
326,626,000

Predominant languages
English, Spanish

Predominant religion
Christianity

GDP per capita
$57,400

Life expectancy
80 years

GEO WHIZ

Florida is known as the lightning capital of the United States. Breezes from the Gulf of Mexico and Atlantic Ocean collide over the warm Florida peninsula to create thunderstorms and the lightning associated with them.

Hawai'i is politically part of the United States but geographically part of Polynesia, a cultural region of Oceania (pages 154–155).

Lake Michigan is the only one of the Great Lakes located entirely within the United States. Each of the other four lakes spans the U.S.-Canada border.

United States

From "sea to shining sea" the United States is blessed with a rich bounty of natural resources. Mineral treasures abound—oil, coal, iron, and gold—and its croplands are among the most productive in the world. Americans have used—and too often overused— this storehouse of raw materials to build an economic base unmatched by any other country. An array of high-tech businesses populate the Sunbelt of the South and West. By combining its natural riches and the creative ideas of its ethnically diverse population, this land of opportunity has become a leading global power.

STAPLE CROP. Approximately 94 million acres (38 million ha) are planted in corn in the U.S. Most of the crop is used as livestock feed.

WORLD CITY. The lights of Manhattan glitter around New York City's Chrysler Building. The city's influence as a financial and cultural center extends across the United States and around the world.

LETTING OFF STEAM. Castle Geyser is just one of many active geological features in Yellowstone National Park in Wyoming. The park is part of a region that sits on top of a major tectonic hot spot.

LADY LIBERTY. The Statue of Liberty, in New York City's harbor, has become a symbol of hope for millions of immigrants coming to the United States.

0   200 miles
0   200 kilometers
Albers Conic Equal-Area Projection

Map Key
★ Country capital
◉ State capital
••• City or town
•••••• Boundary

CANADA

Lake of the Woods

Isle Royale

Lake Superior

St. Lawrence

Great Falls
Helena
Butte
Bozeman
Billings
Missouri
MONTANA
IDAHO
Idaho Falls
WYOMING
YELLOWSTONE NATIONAL PARK
Casper
Cheyenne
Ogden
Salt Lake City
Provo
Laramie
Fort Collins
Boulder
Denver
Grand Junction
COLORADO
Colorado Springs
Pueblo
Dodge City
MESA VERDE NATIONAL PARK
Santa Fe
Albuquerque
Clovis
NEW MEXICO
Roswell
Las Cruces
Carlsbad
El Paso

Minot
Grand Forks
Bismarck
Fargo
NORTH DAKOTA
Aberdeen
SOUTH DAKOTA
Pierre
Rapid City
NEBRASKA
Grand Island
Omaha
Lincoln
Kansas City
Manhattan
Topeka
KANSAS
Jefferson City
Wichita
Enid
Tulsa
OKLAHOMA
Oklahoma City
Lawton
Wichita Falls
Amarillo
Lubbock
Abilene
Odessa
San Angelo
TEXAS
Fort Worth
Dallas
Waco
Austin
San Antonio
Houston
Corpus Christi
Laredo
Brownsville

International Falls
Moorhead
Duluth
MINNESOTA
St. Cloud
St. Paul
Minneapolis
Mankato
Rochester
WISCONSIN
Superior
Green Bay
Madison
Milwaukee
Kenosha
Sioux Falls
Sioux City
Cedar Rapids
Fort Dodge
Dubuque
IOWA
Des Moines
Davenport
Rockford
Aurora
Chicago
ILLINOIS
Springfield
MISSOURI
St. Louis
Cape Girardeau
Springfield
ARKANSAS
Fort Smith
Fayetteville
Hot Springs
Little Rock
Pine Bluff
Texarkana
Shreveport
Natchez
LOUISIANA
Lafayette
Baton Rouge
New Orleans
Beaumont
Port Arthur
Galveston
Tyler
Lufkin

Marquette
MICHIGAN
Lake Michigan
Grand Rapids
Flint
Lansing
Peoria
Gary
Fort Wayne
INDIANA
Indianapolis
Cincinnati
Evansville
Paducah
KENTUCKY
Louisville
Lexington
Frankfort
Nashville
TENNESSEE
Memphis
Chattanooga
Knoxville
Huntsville
Birmingham
ALABAMA
Montgomery
Mobile
MISSISSIPPI
Jackson
Biloxi
Mobile Bay
Mississippi River Delta

Lake Huron
Niagara Falls
Lake Ontario
Lake Erie
Detroit
Toledo
Cleveland
OHIO
Columbus
Pittsburgh
WEST VIRGINIA
Charleston
Erie
Buffalo
Rochester

St. Lawrence
Montpelier
Burlington
Lake Champlain
VT.
N.H.
MAINE
Bangor
Augusta
Portland
Concord
Manchester
Boston
MASS.
Albany
NEW YORK
RHODE ISLAND
Providence
Hartford
CONN.
Long Island
New York
Newark
Trenton
Philadelphia
PENNSYLVANIA
Harrisburg
NEW JERSEY
Baltimore
Dover
DELAWARE
MD.
Annapolis
Washington, D.C.
Richmond
Chesapeake Bay
VIRGINIA
Norfolk
Virginia Beach
Greensboro
Raleigh
Cape Hatteras
NORTH CAROLINA
Charlotte
SOUTH CAROLINA
Columbia
Charleston
GEORGIA
Atlanta
Macon
Columbus
Savannah
Jacksonville
Tallahassee
FLORIDA
Orlando
Cape Canaveral
Tampa
St. Petersburg
Lake Okeechobee
Miami
THE EVERGLADES
Florida Keys
Straits of Florida

ATLANTIC OCEAN

MEXICO
Rio Grande

GULF OF MEXICO

BAHAMAS

Kaua'i
Ni'ihau
O'ahu
Honolulu
Moloka'i
Lāna'i
Kaho'olawe
Maui
Hawai'i
Hilo
HAWAI'I
Principal Hawaiian Islands
0   150 mi
0   150 km
PACIFIC OCEAN
For location of Alaska and Hawai'i, see map page 34.

NATION OF IMMIGRANTS

Number of immigrants obtaining legal permanent resident status in 2015

Mexico
157,227

China
70,977

India
61,380

Philippines
54,307

Cuba
54,178

Dominican Republic
50,382

From its founding, the United States has attracted people from other lands. Today, most immigrants come from **Latin America** and **Asia**.

THE BASICS

STATS

Largest country
Mexico
758,445 sq mi
(1,964,375 sq km)

Smallest country
El Salvador
8,124 sq mi (21,041 sq km)

Most populous country
Mexico
124,575,000

Least populous country
Belize
360,000

Predominant languages
English, Spanish, Mayan,
indigenous languages

Predominant religion
Christianity

Highest GDP per capita
Panama
$23,000

Lowest GDP per capita
Honduras
$5,300

Highest life expectancy
Costa Rica, Panama
79 years

Lowest life expectancy
Belize
69 years

GEO WHIZ

Mexico takes its name from the word *Mexica*, another name for the Aztec, an indigenous people who ruled the land before it fell to the Spanish in 1521.

Coral colonies growing along much of the coast of Belize form the longest barrier reef in the Western Hemisphere.

Thumb-size vampire bats live throughout Central America.

CELEBRATION.
Traditional costumes and musical instruments combine with Christian beliefs during the annual Virgin of Guadalupe festival, observed throughout Mexico. The festival marks the appearance of the Virgin Mary to a peasant in 1531.

Mexico & Central America

VITAL LINK. More than 17,000 oil tankers, cruise ships, and cargo vessels pass through the Panama Canal yearly, avoiding a long trip around South America.

Mexico and most Central American countries share a backbone of mountains, a legacy of powerful Native American empires, and a largely Spanish colonial history. Deforestation has robbed the region of much of its rain forest. Mexico dwarfs its seven Central American neighbors in area, population, and natural resources. Its economy boasts a rich diversity of agricultural crops, highly productive oil fields, a growing manufacturing base, as well as strong trade with the United States and Canada. Overall, Central American countries rely on agricultural products such as bananas and coffee, though tourism is increasing. Modern-day Mexico and Central America struggle to fulfill the hopes of their people, some of whom search for better lives by migrating north to the United States.

◗ **MYTHS AND LEGENDS.** The powerful Aztec Empire dominated much of Mexico and Central America from 1427 to 1521.

2   3   4   5   6   7   8   9

◗ **TREETOP LIVING.** This spider monkey hangs by its tail in a rain forest on the Osa Peninsula, in Costa Rica. Found in undisturbed forests from southern Mexico to Brazil, spider monkeys spend nearly all their time in trees.

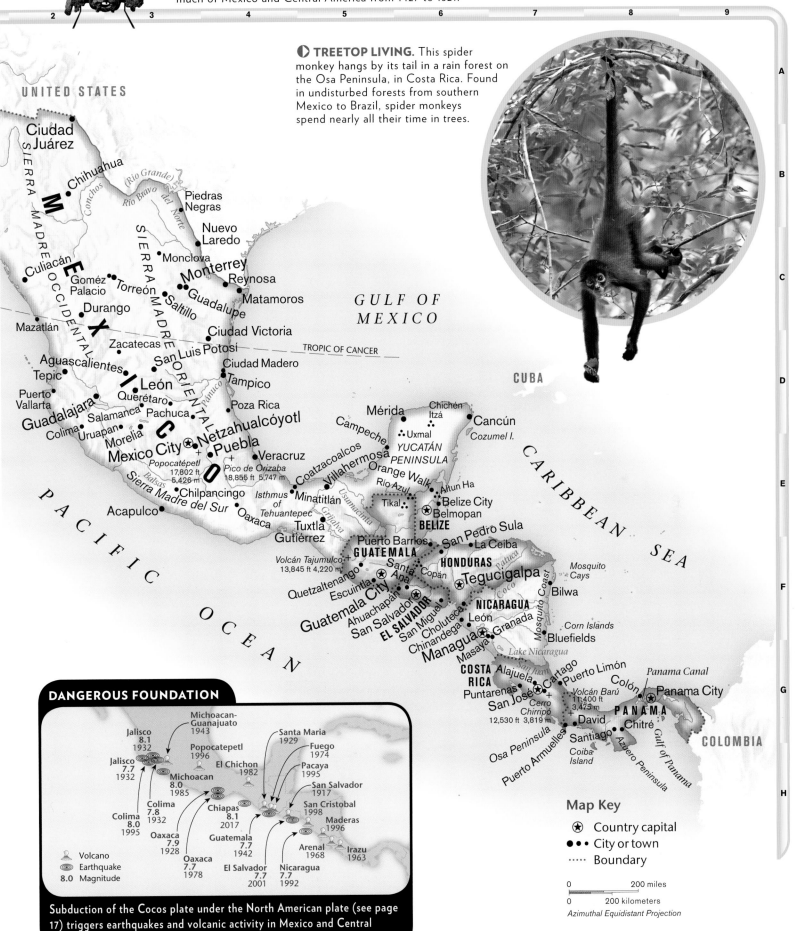

UNITED STATES

A

Ciudad Juárez

Chihuahua

SIERRA MADRE OCCIDENTAL

Conchos

Río Grande
(Río Bravo del Norte)

Piedras Negras

Nuevo Laredo

Monclova

Culiacán

Gomez Palacio

Torreón

Saltillo

Monterrey

Reynosa

Guadalupe

Matamoros

Durango

SIERRA MADRE ORIENTAL

B

C

Mazatlán

Zacatecas

San Luis Potosí

Ciudad Victoria

Ciudad Madero

TROPIC OF CANCER

GULF OF MEXICO

D

Aguascalientes

Tepic

León

Querétaro

Pánuco

Tampico

CUBA

Puerto Vallarta

Guadalajara

Salamanca

Pachuca

Poza Rica

Mérida

Chichén Itzá

Cancún

Colima

Uruapan

Morelia

Netzahualcóyotl

Puebla

Campeche

Uxmal

YUCATÁN PENINSULA

Cozumel I.

M E X I C O

Mexico City

Popocatépetl 17,802 ft 5,426 m

Veracruz

Coatzacoalcos

Villahermosa

Orange Walk

Río Azul

Altun Ha

CARIBBEAN SEA

Balsas

Chilpancingo

Pico de Orizaba 18,855 ft 5,747 m

Minatitlán

Tikal

Belize City

Belmopan

E

Sierra Madre del Sur

Acapulco

Oaxaca

Isthmus of Tehuantepec

Grijalva

Usumacinta

BELIZE

Puerto Barrios

San Pedro Sula

La Ceiba

Tuxtla Gutiérrez

Volcán Tajumulco 13,845 ft 4,220 m

GUATEMALA

Santa Ana

Copán

HONDURAS

Patuca

Mosquito Cays

F

PACIFIC OCEAN

Quetzaltenango

Escuintla

Guatemala City

Ahuachapán

Tegucigalpa

Coco

Bilwa

Mosquito Coast

San Miguel

San Salvador

EL SALVADOR

Choluteca

NICARAGUA

León

Corn Islands

Chinandega

Masaya

Granada

Bluefields

Managua

Lake Nicaragua

San Juan

Panama Canal

G

COSTA RICA

Alajuela

Cartago

Puerto Limón

Colón

Panama City

Puntarenas

San José

Volcán Barú 11,400 ft 3,475 m

Cerro Chirripó 12,530 ft 3,819 m

David

PANAMA

Chitré

Gulf of Panama

COLOMBIA

Osa Peninsula

Puerto Armuelles

Santiago

Coiba Island

Azuero Peninsula

H

DANGEROUS FOUNDATION

Michoacan-Guanajuato 1943

Santa Maria 1929

Jalisco 8.1 1932

Popocatepetl 1996

Fuego 1974

Jalisco 7.7 1932

El Chichon 1982

Pacaya 1995

Michoacan 8.0 1985

San Salvador 1917

Colima 7.8 1932

Chiapas 8.1 2017

San Cristobal 1998

Colima 8.0 1995

Oaxaca 7.9 1928

Guatemala 7.7 1942

Maderas 1996

Oaxaca 7.7 1978

El Salvador 7.7 2001

Nicaragua 7.7 1992

Arenal 1968

Irazu 1963

⛰ Volcano

◉ Earthquake

8.0 Magnitude

Map Key

⊛ Country capital

●●● City or town

····· Boundary

0   200 miles
0   200 kilometers
Azimuthal Equidistant Projection

Subduction of the Cocos plate under the North American plate (see page 17) triggers earthquakes and volcanic activity in Mexico and Central America. Major events in the last 100 years are shown here.

West Indies & the Bahamas

THE BASICS
STATS

Largest country
Cuba
42,803 sq mi (110,860 sq km)

Smallest country
St. Kitts & Nevis
101 sq mi (261 sq km)

Most populous country
Cuba
11,147,000

Least populous country
St. Kitts & Nevis
53,000

Predominant languages
Spanish, English, French, Creole

Predominant religion
Christianity

Highest GDP per capita
Trinidad & Tobago
$31,900

Lowest GDP per capita
Haiti
$1,800

Highest life expectancy
Cuba
79 years

Lowest life expectancy
Haiti
64 years

GEO WHIZ

Pico Duarte (10,417 ft/3,175 m), on Hispaniola, is the highest peak in the Caribbean.

Voodoo, which combines West African spiritualism and the worship of Roman Catholic saints, is common in Haiti. Related folk religions are found in other countries in this region.

RHYTHM OF THE TROPICS. When traditional drums were banned in Trinidad in 1884, plantation workers looked for new instruments, including 55-gallon (208-L) oil drums, which were the origin of today's steel drums or "pans."

This region of tropical islands stretches from the Bahamas, off the eastern coast of Florida, to Trinidad and Tobago, off the northern coast of South America. The Greater Antilles—Cuba, Jamaica, Hispaniola, and U.S. territory Puerto Rico—account for nearly 90 percent of the region's land area and most of its 42 million people. A necklace of smaller islands called the Lesser Antilles plus the Bahamas make up most of the rest of this region. Lush vegetation, warm waters, and scenic beaches attract tourists from across the globe. While these visitors bring much needed income, most people in this region remain poor.

WHITE GOLD. Sugarcane is an important economic resource throughout the Caribbean. This woman carries freshly cut cane on her head in a field in Barbados.

FUN IN THE SUN

International tourist arrivals, 2014 data

Country	Arrivals
Dominican Republic	5,141,377
Cuba	3,001,958
Jamaica	2,080,181
Bahamas	1,421,860
Aruba	1,072,082
U.S. Virgin Islands	730,367
Barbados	519,598
St. Maarten	499,920
Martinique	489,561
Haiti	465,174

These island countries are the region's most popular destinations for tourists seeking sandy beaches, blue waters, and warm breezes.

◐ **RARE BIRD.** The red-necked Amazon, or Jaco, parrot is found only on the island of Dominica, where it lives on flowers, seeds, and fruits.

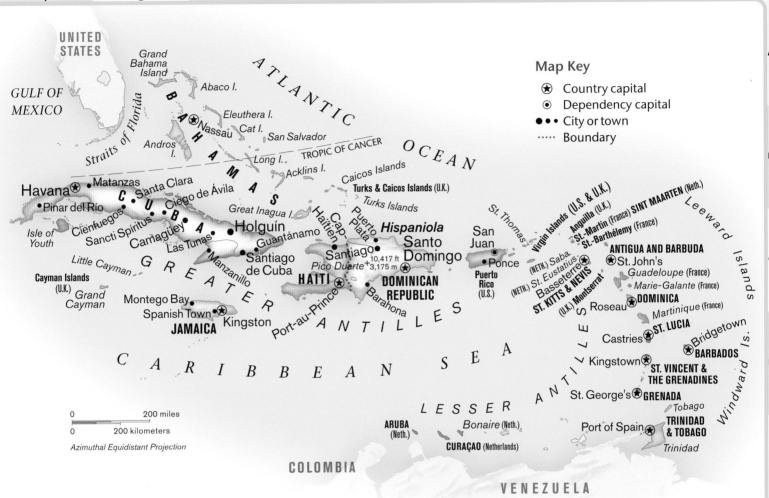

UNITED STATES

GULF OF MEXICO

Grand Bahama Island

Abaco I.

ATLANTIC

Eleuthera I.
Cat I.
San Salvador

Nassau

Straits of Florida

Andros I.

Long I.
TROPIC OF CANCER

Acklins I.

OCEAN

Havana ⊛ • Matanzas
Pinar del Río
Santa Clara
Ciego de Ávila
Cienfuegos
Sancti Spíritus
Camagüey
Las Tunas
Holguín
Manzanillo
Santiago de Cuba
Guantánamo

Isle of Youth

C U B A

G R E A T E R

Cayman Islands (U.K.)
Little Cayman
Grand Cayman

Montego Bay
Spanish Town ⊛ Kingston
JAMAICA

Caicos Islands
Turks & Caicos Islands (U.K.)
Turks Islands

Great Inagua I.

Cap-Haïtien
Puerto Plata

Santiago
Pico Duarte 10,417 ft +3,175 m ★

HAITI

Port-au-Prince

Barahona

A N T I L L E S

Hispaniola
Santo Domingo

DOMINICAN REPUBLIC

St. Thomas

San Juan
• Ponce
Puerto Rico (U.S.)

Virgin Islands (U.S. & U.K.)
(NETH.) Saba
(NETH.) St. Eustatius
Basseterre
ST. KITTS & NEVIS
(U.K.) Montserrat

Anguilla (U.K.)
St-Martin (France) **SINT MAARTEN** (Neth.)
St-Barthélemy (France)

ANTIGUA AND BARBUDA
⊛ St. John's
Guadeloupe (France)
• Marie-Galante (France)

Roseau ⊛ **DOMINICA**
Martinique (France)

Leeward Islands

Castries ⊛ **ST. LUCIA**

Kingstown ⊛
ST. VINCENT & THE GRENADINES

St. George's ⊛ **GRENADA**

⊛ Bridgetown
★ **BARBADOS**

Windward Is.

L E S S E R

A N T I L L E S

ARUBA
(Neth.)

Bonaire (Neth.)

CURAÇAO (Netherlands)

Tobago

Port of Spain ⊛ **TRINIDAD & TOBAGO**

Trinidad

C A R I B B E A N   S E A

COLOMBIA

VENEZUELA

Map Key
⊛ Country capital
⊙ Dependency capital
●●● City or town
····· Boundary

0 ——— 200 miles
0 ——— 200 kilometers
Azimuthal Equidistant Projection

◕ **WATER WORLD.** The clear waters of the Caribbean allow face-to-face interaction with sea life, such as this green sea turtle. Adult sea turtles can remain underwater for two hours without breathing.

◒ **CELEBRATION.** Stilt walkers in brightly colored costumes tower above this street in Old Havana, Cuba, during the annual celebration of Carnival. Introduced by Catholic colonizers from Spain, this festival occurs prior to the beginning of the religious season of Lent.

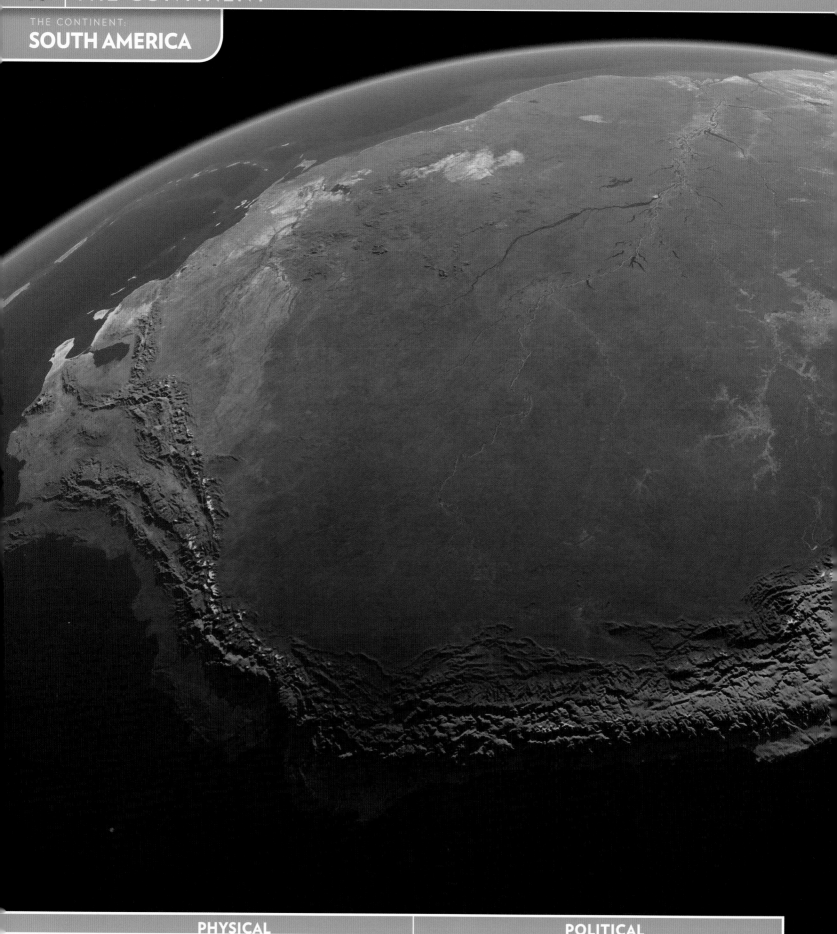

PHYSICAL			POLITICAL	
TOTAL AREA 6,880,000 sq mi (17,819,000 sq km)	**LOWEST POINT** Laguna del Carbón, Argentina -344 ft (-105 m)	**LARGEST LAKE** Lake Titicaca, Bolivia-Peru 3,200 sq mi (8,290 sq km)	**POPULATION** 418,538,000	**LARGEST COUNTRY** Brazil 3,287,594 sq mi (8,514,877 sq km)
HIGHEST POINT Cerro Aconcagua, Argentina 22,831 ft (6,959 m)	**LONGEST RIVER** Amazon 4,150 mi (6,679 km)		**LARGEST METROPOLITAN AREA** São Paulo, Brazil Pop. 21,297,000	**MOST DENSELY POPULATED COUNTRY** Ecuador 148.8 people per sq mi (57.5 per sq km)

SOUTH AMERICA

South America

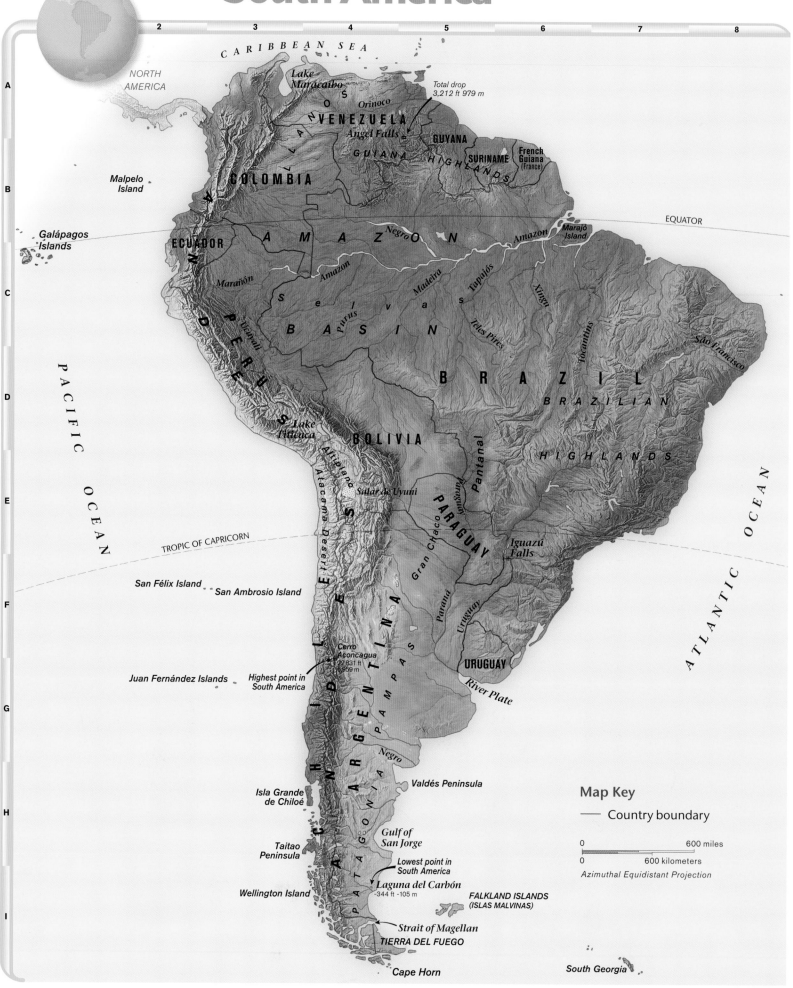

2 3 4 5 6 7 8

NORTH
AMERICA

CARIBBEAN SEA

Lake
Maracaibo

Orinoco

VENEZUELA

Angel Falls

Total drop
3,212 ft 979 m

GUYANA

GUIANA
HIGHLANDS

SURINAME

French
Guiana
(France)

COLOMBIA

Malpelo
Island

ECUADOR

Galápagos
Islands

EQUATOR

Negro

Amazon

Marajó
Island

A M A Z O N

Amazon

Marañón

Madeira

Tapajós

Xingu

São Francisco

S   e   l   v   a   s

Purus

Tocantins

Teles Pires

Ucayali

PACIFIC

B A S I N

BRAZIL

BRAZILIAN

Lake
Titicaca

BOLIVIA

Pantanal

HIGHLANDS

Altiplano

Salar de Uyuni

PACIFIC OCEAN

Atacama Desert

TROPIC OF CAPRICORN

PARAGUAY

Paraguay

Iguazú
Falls

ATLANTIC OCEAN

San Félix Island   San Ambrosio Island

Gran Chaco

Paraná

Uruguay

Cerro
Aconcagua
22,831 ft
6,959 m

A   N   D   E   S

Juan Fernández Islands

Highest point in
South America

C H I L E

A R G E N T I N A

P A M P A S

URUGUAY

River Plate

Negro

Valdés Peninsula

Isla Grande
de Chiloé

P A T A G O N I A

Gulf of
San Jorge

Taitao
Peninsula

Lowest point in
South America

Wellington Island

Laguna del Carbón
-344 ft -105 m

FALKLAND ISLANDS
(ISLAS MALVINAS)

Strait of Magellan
TIERRA DEL FUEGO

Cape Horn

South Georgia

Map Key

— Country boundary

0 ————— 600 miles

0 ————— 600 kilometers

Azimuthal Equidistant Projection

CARIBBEAN SEA

NORTH AMERICA

VENEZUELA

Santa Marta
Barranquilla
Cartagena
Maracaibo
Lake Maracaibo
Barquisimeto
Caracas
Valencia
Maracay
Cúcuta
San Cristóbal
Bucaramanga
Medellín
Manizales
Bogotá
Ibagué
Cali
Pasto
COLOMBIA

Ciudad Guayana
Orinoco
Angel Falls
Georgetown
GUYANA
Paramaribo
SURINAME
Cayenne
French Guiana (France)
GUIANA HIGHLANDS
Boundary claimed by Suriname
Boa Vista
Amapá

Malpelo Island (Colombia)

EQUATOR

Esmeraldas
Quito
ECUADOR
Guayaquil
Cuenca

Galápagos Islands (Ecuador)

A M A Z O N
Negro
Amazon
Marajó Island
Belém
Manaus
Santarém
São Luís
Parnaíba

Iquitos
Marañón
Amazon (Solimões)
Madeira
Tapajós
Fortaleza
Teresina
Marabá

PACIFIC OCEAN

Piura
Chiclayo
Trujillo
Chimbote
S e l v a s
B A S I N
Purus
Xingu
Teles Pires
Natal
João Pessoa
Campina Grande
Recife

Ucayali
Rio Branco
Porto Velho
Tocantins
PERU
Callao
Lima
Machu Picchu
Cusco
Ayacucho
Trinidad
L. Titicaca
La Paz
BOLIVIA
Santa Cruz
B R A Z I L
B R A Z I L I A N
Aracaju
Maceió
Salvador (Bahia)
Ilhéus

Arequipa
Cochabamba
Oruro
Sucre
Altiplano
Salar de Uyuni
Goiânia
Brasília
H I G H L A N D S
São Francisco
Uberlândia
Uberaba
Governador Valadares

Arica
Iquique
Tarija
Pantanal
Paraguay
Campo Grande
São José do Rio Preto
Ribeirão Preto
Belo Horizonte

TROPIC OF CAPRICORN
Antofagasta
Salta
Gran Chaco
PARAGUAY
Asunción
Londrina
Campinas
São Paulo
Santos
Rio de Janeiro
Nova Iguaçu
Iguazú Falls
Curitiba

San Félix Island (Chile)
San Ambrosio Island
San Miguel de Tucumán
Resistencia
Corrientes
Paraná
Passo Fundo
Florianópolis

La Serena
Cerro Aconcagua 22,831 ft 6,959 m
Córdoba
Santa Fe
Uruguay
Uruguaiana
Santa Maria
Porto Alegre

Valparaíso
Santiago
Mendoza
Rosario
URUGUAY
Buenos Aires
Montevideo
La Plata
River Plate

Juan Fernández Islands (Chile)

Talca
A R G E N T I N A
Pampa
Mar del Plata

Concepción
Temuco
Negro
Bahía Blanca

Puerto Montt
Isla Grande de Chiloé
Viedma
Valdés Peninsula

C O R D I L L E R A
A N D E S

ATLANTIC OCEAN

Comodoro Rivadavia
Gulf of San Jorge

Taitao Peninsula
P A T A G O N I A

Wellington I.
Laguna del Carbón -344 ft -105 m
Stanley
Falkland Islands (Islas Malvinas) (United Kingdom)

Río Gallegos
Strait of Magellan
TIERRA DEL FUEGO
Punta Arenas
Ushuaia
Cape Horn

South Georgia (U.K.)

Map Key
⊛ Country capital
⊙ Dependency capital
••• City or town
····· Boundary
····· Claimed boundary

0 — 600 miles
0 — 600 kilometers
Azimuthal Equidistant Projection

South America

A MIX OF OLD AND NEW

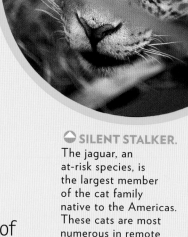

South America stretches from the warm waters of the Caribbean to the frigid ocean near Antarctica. Draining a third of the continent, the mighty Amazon carries more water than the world's next 10 biggest rivers combined. Its basin contains the planet's largest rain forest. The Andes tower along the continent's western edge from Colombia to southern Chile. The indigenous people who lived in the Andes were no match for the gold-seeking Spanish who arrived in 1532. The Spanish, along with the Portuguese, ruled most of the continent for almost 300 years. Centuries of ethnic blending have woven indigenous, European, African, and Asian heritage into South America's rich cultural fabric.

⬤ SILENT STALKER. The jaguar, an at-risk species, is the largest member of the cat family native to the Americas. These cats are most numerous in remote areas of Central and South America.

◗ ROYAL CITY. Built by an Inca ruler between 1460 and 1470, Machu Picchu reveals the Inca's skill as stone masons. Massive blocks of granite were carved so carefully that all seams fit tightly without the use of mortar.

SOUTHERN METROPOLIS. A 1,300-foot (396-m)-high block of granite called Sugar Loaf dominates the harbor of Brazil's second largest city, Rio de Janeiro. Rio was Brazil's capital until 1960 and remains the country's most popular tourist destination.

NATURAL HERITAGE.
Extending 2.5 miles (4 km) along the border between Brazil and Argentina, Iguazú Falls, which means "great water" in the local Guaraní language, is clouded in mist as the water drops 296 feet (90 m) into the Iguazú River.

MOUNTAIN BUDDIES.
An Aymara woman, with her llama, follows a traditional mountain lifestyle in the Andes of Peru.

more about
South America

⬤ **GLEAMING SANDS.** The white sands of Rio de Janeiro's 2.5-mile (4-km)-long Copacabana and Leme Beaches are among the most famous in the world, attracting tourists year-round. The beaches, which are now lined with upscale hotels that overlook Guanabara Bay, were once the site of thriving fishing villages.

⬤ **ICY COLD.** Rising to an elevation of almost 11,000 feet (3,353 m), Mount Fitz Roy in southern Argentina's Patagonia region presents major challenges to adventurous climbers who must contend with strong winds and bitter cold.

⬤ **QUIET VIGIL.** A young Panare Indian sits beside a rushing stream in Venezuela, ready to catch a fish with his spear. Many groups of native people live in relative isolation from the modern world.

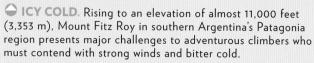

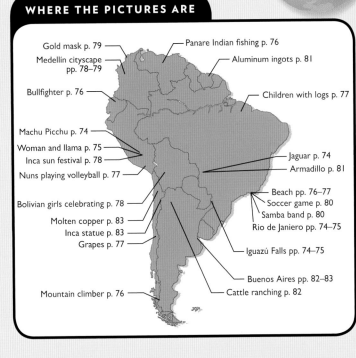

WHERE THE PICTURES ARE

Gold mask p. 79
Medellín cityscape pp. 78–79
Bullfighter p. 76
Machu Picchu p. 74
Woman and llama p. 75
Inca sun festival p. 78
Nuns playing volleyball p. 77
Bolivian girls celebrating p. 78
Molten copper p. 83
Inca statue p. 83
Grapes p. 77
Mountain climber p. 76

Panare Indian fishing p. 76
Aluminum ingots p. 81
Children with logs p. 77
Jaguar p. 74
Armadillo p. 81
Beach pp. 76–77
Soccer game p. 80
Samba band p. 80
Rio de Janiero pp. 74–75
Iguazú Falls pp. 74–75
Buenos Aires pp. 82–83
Cattle ranching p. 82

◐ **JUICY HARVEST.** Grapes hang in heavy clusters ready for harvest near Santiago, Chile. A leading exporter of table grapes, Chile is the major supplier of these grapes for the United States and European Union during winter months.

◐ **BREAK TIME.** Colonization of South America by Spain and Portugal in the 16th century brought a new religion—Roman Catholicism—to the region. Here, Catholic nuns in Arequipa, Peru, take a break from prayers to engage in a game of volleyball.

◐ **ENVIRONMENTAL TRAGEDY.** These giants of the rain forest dwarf two children in the Amazon village of Paragominas in Brazil. Harvesting such trees provides income for villagers but poses a serious long-term threat to the environment.

◑ **EL TORRO!** Introduced to South America during Spanish colonization, bullfighting is a popular sport and the focus of many festivals. Here, in Cayambe, Ecuador, a matador flashes his red cape before the bull.

Northwestern South America

⊕ **HAIL THE SUN.** The ancient Inca celebrated the new year in June with the festival of Inti Raymi. The tradition continues today in Cusco, Peru, with the Festival of the Sun, when the celestial body is honored through music and dance.

THE BASICS

STATS

Largest country
Peru 496,222 sq mi
(1,285,216 sq km)

Smallest country
Ecuador
109,483 sq mi (283,561 sq km)

Most populous country
Colombia 47,699,000

Least populous country
Bolivia 11,138,000

Predominant languages
Spanish, indigenous languages, English

Predominant religion
Christianity

Highest GDP per capita
Colombia $14,100

Lowest GDP per capita
Bolivia $7,200

Highest life expectancy
Ecuador 77 years

Lowest life expectancy
Bolivia 69 years

GEO WHIZ

On the llanos of Venezuela, capybaras, the world's largest rodents, are hunted by anacondas. These snakes can weigh as much as 550 pounds (250 kg).

Colombia is the source of some of the world's finest emeralds, a gemstone sacred to the Inca. Mines once operated by the Inca still yield quality stones.

Marine iguanas live only on Ecuador's Galapagos Islands.

Like a huge letter "C," five countries crest the continent's northwest— Venezuela, Colombia, Ecuador, Peru, and Bolivia. Each has a seacoast, except for landlocked Bolivia. Dominated by the volcano-studded Andes range, the region contains huge rain forests in the upper Amazon and Orinoco River basins. Colombia and Venezuela share an extensive tropical grassland called Los Llanos. Though the Spanish defeated the Inca in the 16th century, Quechua, their language, is still spoken in the altiplanos—high plateaus of the Andes. Despite rich oil reserves around Lake Maracaibo, many people remain poor. Venezuela has been plagued by demonstrations and civil unrest due to high prices and shortages of basic goods.

◑ **FOLKLORE CENTER.** Founded as a mining town, Oruro, Bolivia, is a UNESCO World Heritage site. Each November traditional Andean culture is celebrated with ancient dances, music, and rituals.

INDIGENOUS PEOPLE

Estimated populations, 2009–2010

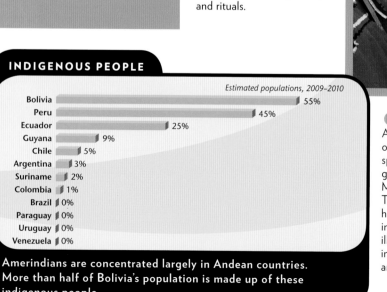

Country	Percentage
Bolivia	55%
Peru	45%
Ecuador	25%
Guyana	9%
Chile	5%
Argentina	3%
Suriname	2%
Colombia	1%
Brazil	0%
Paraguay	0%
Uruguay	0%
Venezuela	0%

Amerindians are concentrated largely in Andean countries. More than half of Bolivia's population is made up of these indigenous people.

◑ **OLD MEETS NEW.** Against a backdrop of skyscrapers, a train speeds past the old government palace in Medellín, Colombia. The city is working hard to change its image as a center of illegal drug traffic by introducing economic and social changes.

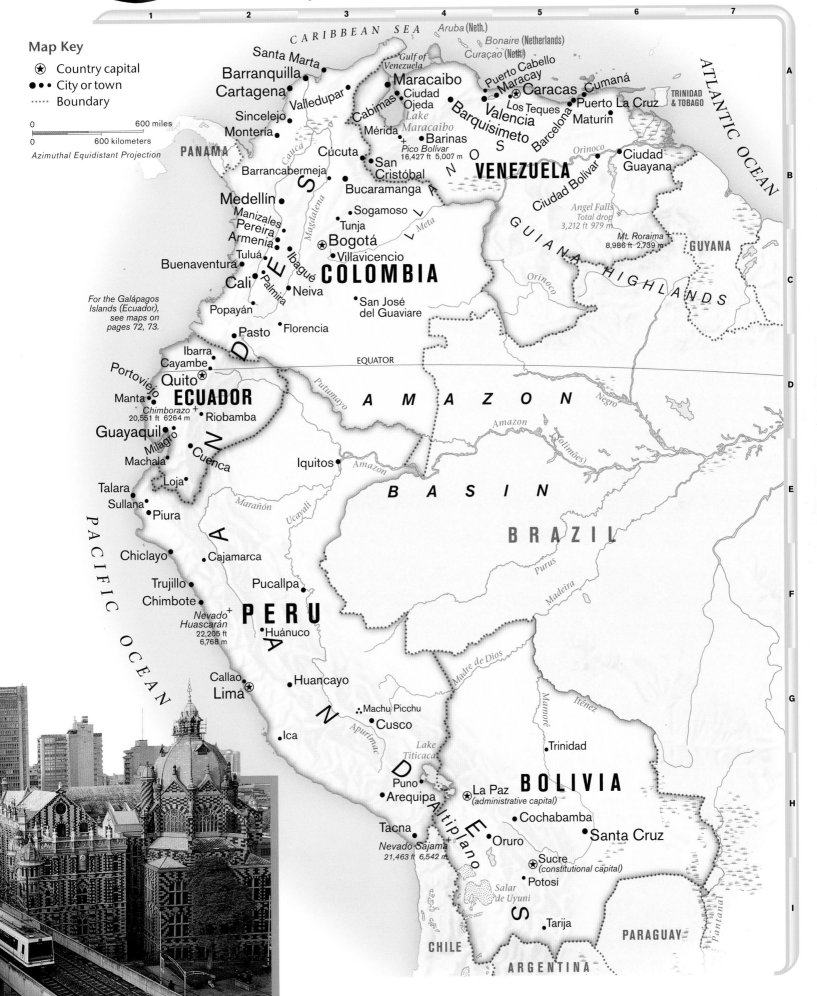

ANCIENT ARTISANS. Early cultures of Colombia left no great stone monuments, but distinguished themselves with fine gold work, such as this mask.

Map Key

⊛ Country capital

●●● City or town

⋯⋯ Boundary

0   600 miles

0   600 kilometers

Azimuthal Equidistant Projection

For the Galápagos Islands (Ecuador), see maps on pages 72, 73.

CARIBBEAN SEA

Aruba (Neth.)

Bonaire (Netherlands)

Curaçao (Neth.)

Santa Marta

Barranquilla

Cartagena

Valledupar

Gulf of Venezuela

Maracaibo

Ciudad Ojeda

Cabimas

Lake Maracaibo

Mérida

Pico Bolívar 16,427 ft 5,007 m

Puerto Cabello

Maracay

Caracas

Los Teques

Valencia

Barquisimeto

Barcelona

Cumaná

Puerto La Cruz

Maturín

TRINIDAD & TOBAGO

ATLANTIC OCEAN

Sincelejo

Montería

PANAMA

Cauca

Barrancabermeja

Cúcuta

San Cristóbal

Bucaramanga

Barinas

VENEZUELA

Ciudad Guayana

Medellín

Manizales

Pereira

Armenia

Tuluá

Ibagué

Buenaventura

Cali

Palmira

Neiva

Popayán

Magdalena

Sogamoso

Tunja

Bogotá

Villavicencio

COLOMBIA

Meta

San José del Guaviare

Ciudad Bolívar

Orinoco

Angel Falls Total drop 3,212 ft 979 m

GUIANA HIGHLANDS

Mt. Roraima 8,986 ft 2,739 m

GUYANA

Pasto

Florencia

EQUATOR

Orinoco

Ibarra

Cayambe

Portoviejo

Quito

Manta

ECUADOR

Chimborazo 20,551 ft 6264 m

Riobamba

Putumayo

AMAZON

Negro

Guayaquil

Milagro

Machala

Cuenca

Loja

Iquitos

Amazon

BASIN

Amazon (Solimões)

Talara

Sullana

Piura

Marañón

Ucayali

BRAZIL

Chiclayo

Cajamarca

Trujillo

Pucallpa

Chimbote

Nevado Huascarán 22,205 ft 6,768 m

PERU

Purus

Madeira

Callao

Lima

Huánuco

Huancayo

Apurímac

Machu Picchu

Cusco

Madre de Dios

Ica

Lake Titicaca

Trinidad

Mamoré

Iténez

Puno

Arequipa

La Paz (administrative capital)

BOLIVIA

Tacna

Nevado Sajama 21,463 ft 6,542 m

Altiplano

Cochabamba

Oruro

Santa Cruz

Sucre (constitutional capital)

Potosí

Salar de Uyuni

Tarija

Pantanal

CHILE

PARAGUAY

ARGENTINA

PACIFIC OCEAN

ANDES

THE BASICS

STATS

Largest country
Brazil
3,287,594 sq mi
(8,514,877 sq km)

Smallest country
Suriname
63,251 sq mi (163,820 sq km)

Most populous country
Brazil 207,353,000

Least populous country
Suriname 592,000

Predominant languages
Portuguese, English, Dutch, Hindi

Predominant religions
Christianity, Hinduism, Islam

Highest GDP per capita
Brazil $15,200

Lowest GDP per capita
Guyana $7,900

Highest life expectancy
Brazil 74 years

Lowest life expectancy
Guyana 68 years

GEO WHIZ

Guyana's roughly 300 species of catfish are hunted for the international aquarium trade.

Brazil's Pantanal is the world's largest freshwater wetland.

Paramaribo, Suriname's capital, is a melting pot of Dutch, Hindu, Chinese, East Indian, and Javanese cultures. Dutch is the only official language.

Northeastern South America

GOAL! Maracanã Stadium in Rio de Janeiro is packed with enthusiastic soccer fans. Brazil has a long history of producing world-class soccer teams, winning the coveted World Cup five times as of 2017.

Brazil dominates the region as well as the continent in size and population. It is the world's fifth largest country in area, and it is home to half of South America's 419 million people. São Paulo and Rio de Janeiro are among the world's largest cities, and the country's vast agricultural lands make it a top global exporter of coffee, soybeans, beef, orange juice, and sugar. The vast Amazon rain forest, once a dense wilderness of unmatched biodiversity, is now threatened by farmers, loggers, and miners. Lands colonized by the British, Dutch, and French make up sparsely settled Guyana and Suriname as well as French Guiana, a French overseas department. Formerly known as the Guianas, these lands are populated by people of African, South Asian, and European heritage.

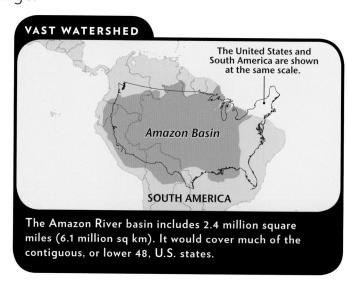

VAST WATERSHED

The United States and South America are shown at the same scale.

Amazon Basin

SOUTH AMERICA

The Amazon River basin includes 2.4 million square miles (6.1 million sq km). It would cover much of the contiguous, or lower 48, U.S. states.

NATIONAL RHYTHM. Samba, often called Brazil's national music, combines the music traditions of the country's populations—Amerindian, Portuguese, and African. Here a samba band practices on Rio de Janeiro's Ipanema Beach.

◀ **THE SIX-BANDED ARMADILLO,** found throughout the dry grassland areas of the region, lives on plants and insects. Unlike others of its species, it remains active during the day.

Map Key
★ Country capital
●●● City or town
······ Boundary
······ Claimed boundary

0   400 miles
0   400 kilometers
Azimuthal Equidistant Projection

ATLANTIC OCEAN

VENEZUELA
Georgetown
Paramaribo
GUYANA
SURINAME
Cayenne
French Guiana (France)
GUIANA HIGHLANDS
Boa Vista
COLOMBIA
Boundary claimed by Suriname
Orinoco
EQUATOR
Macapá
Pico da Neblina 9,823 ft 2,994 m
Negro
Itacoatiara
Amazon
Marajó Island
Belém
São Luís
Parnaíba
Fortaleza
A M A Z O N
Manaus
Altamira
Paragominas
Codó
Sobral
Putumayo
(Solimões)
Tucuruí
Caxias
Teresina
Tefé
Coari
Parintins
Santarém
Tapajós
Marabá
Imperatriz
Natal
Amazon
Araguaína
Crato
João Pessoa
S e l v a s
B A S I N
Madeira
Olinda
Jaboatão
Recife
Cruzeiro do Sul
Porto Velho
B R A Z I L
Petrolina
Purus
Rio Branco
Ariquemes
Palmas
Arapiraca
Maceió
PERU
Ji-Paraná (Rondônia)
Alta Floresta
Gurupi
Barreiras
Feira de Santana
Aracaju
Madre de Dios
Guaporé
Juruena
Teles Pires
Xingu
Tocantins
Alvorado
B R A Z I L I A N
Alagoinhas
Mamoré
Araguaia
Jequié
Salvador (Bahia)
Lake Titicaca
Várzea Grande
Cuiabá
Brasília
Vitória da Conquista
Itabuna
Ilhéus
BOLIVIA
Rondonópolis
Anápolis
São Francisco
H I G H L A N D S
Goiânia
Pantanal
Teófilo Otoni
Uberlândia
Governador Valadares
Paraguai
Belo Horizonte
Linhares
Campo Grande
São José do Rio Preto
Ribeirão Preto
Juiz de Fora
Vitória
Vila Velha
CHILE
P A R A G U A Y
São José dos Campos
Nova Iguaçu
Duque de Caxias
TROPIC OF CAPRICORN
Paraná
São Paulo
Guaratinguetá
Niterói
Rio de Janeiro
Londrina
Santo André
Santos
Iguazú Falls
ARGENTINA
Curitiba
Paranaguá
Joinville
Uruguay
Florianópolis
Caxias do Sul
Criciúma
Santa Maria
Novo Hamburgo
Canoas
Porto Alegre
Paraná
Patos Lagoon
Pelotas
URUGUAY

◀ **BAUXITE TO ALUMINUM.** By exploiting rich deposits of bauxite, the ore from which aluminum is made, and inexpensive hydropower, Suriname produces aluminum ingots, such as these headed for global markets.

Southern South America

Four countries make up this region, which is sometimes called the Southern Cone because of its shape. Long north-south distances in Chile and Argentina result in varied environments. Chile's Atacama Desert in the north contrasts with much cooler, moister lands in the country's south, where there are fjords and glaciers. Almost half of Chileans live in and around the country's booming capital, Santiago. Similarly, most neighboring Argentinians live in the central Pampas region, where wheat and cattle flourish on the fertile plains. Farther south lie the arid, windswept plateaus of Patagonia. Landlocked Paraguay is small in comparison, less urbanized, and one of South America's poorest countries. Uruguay is smaller still, but it possesses a strong agricultural economy, including cattle- and sheep-raising.

◗ **COWBOYS OF THE PAMPAS.** Cattle are herded by gauchos, the Argentine term for cowboys. The country's pampas, extensive grass-covered plains, support grain and cattle production on ranches called estancias.

◗ **GATEWAY CITY.** Skyscrapers in the modern skyline rise above Buenos Aires, capital of Argentina and second largest metropolitan area in South America. Situated on the Rio de la Plata, the city was established in 1536 by Spanish explorers. Its port is one of the busiest in South America.

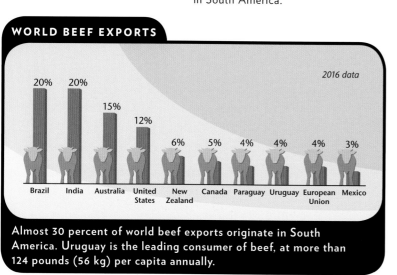

WORLD BEEF EXPORTS

2016 data

Brazil	India	Australia	United States	New Zealand	Canada	Paraguay	Uruguay	European Union	Mexico
20%	20%	15%	12%	6%	5%	4%	4%	4%	3%

Almost 30 percent of world beef exports originate in South America. Uruguay is the leading consumer of beef, at more than 124 pounds (56 kg) per capita annually.

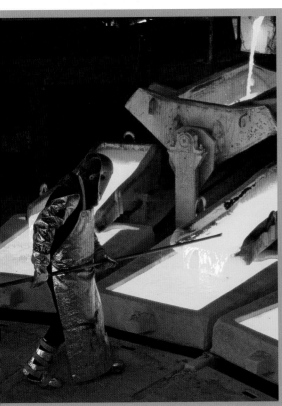

INCA TREASURE. Near the frozen summit of Argentina's Cerro Llullaillaco, archaeologists uncovered well-preserved Inca mummies and 20 clothed statues, such as this one.

DESERT RICHES. Molten copper is poured into molds at a refinery near Chuquicamata, a mine that has operated since 1910 in Chile's Atacama Desert. Chile produces 28 percent of the world's copper.

PERU

BOLIVIA

BRAZIL

Arica

Iquique

Chuquicamata
Calama

Antofagasta

Cerro Llullaillaco
22,057 ft
6,723 m

Copiapó

La Serena
Coquimbo

Viña del Mar
Valparaíso
Santiago
Rancagua
Curicó
Talca
Chillán
Concepción
Los Ángeles
Temuco
Valdivia
Osorno
Puerto Montt

Isla Grande
de Chiloé

Wellington
Island

Punta Arenas

TIERRA DEL
FUEGO

Cape Horn

Ushuaia

Río Gallegos

Laguna
del Carbón
-344 ft -105 m

Comodoro Rivadavia
Gulf of San Jorge

PACIFIC OCEAN

ANDES

CHILE

PATAGONIA

San Salvador
de Jujuy
Salta
San Miguel
de Tucumán

Catamarca
Santiago
del Estero

La Rioja

San
Juan

Cerro Aconcagua
22,831 ft 6,959 m

Córdoba

Río Cuarto

Mendoza
Godoy Cruz
San Luis

Neuquén

Colorado

Negro

ARGENTINA

PAMPAS

La Esmeralda

Gran Chaco

Paraguay

Puerto
Bahía Negra

Concepción

PARAGUAY

Asunción

Ciudad
del Este
Itaipú Dam

Formosa

Resistencia
Villarrica

Corrientes
Posadas

Paraná

Uruguay

Iguazú
Falls

Paraná

Santa Fe
Concordia
Salto
Paraná

Rivera

Patos
Lagoon

Rosario
San Nicolás

Buenos Aires

San Justo
La Plata

River Plate

URUGUAY

Montevideo

Bahía
Blanca

Mar del Plata

TROPIC OF CAPRICORN

San Matías Gulf

Valdés
Peninsula

ATLANTIC OCEAN

Strait of Magellan

Map Key

★ Country capital
◉ Dependency capital
•• City or town
···· Boundary

0   200 miles
0   200 kilometers
Azimuthal Equidistant Projection

Falkland Islands
(Islas Malvinas)
(United Kingdom)

Stanley

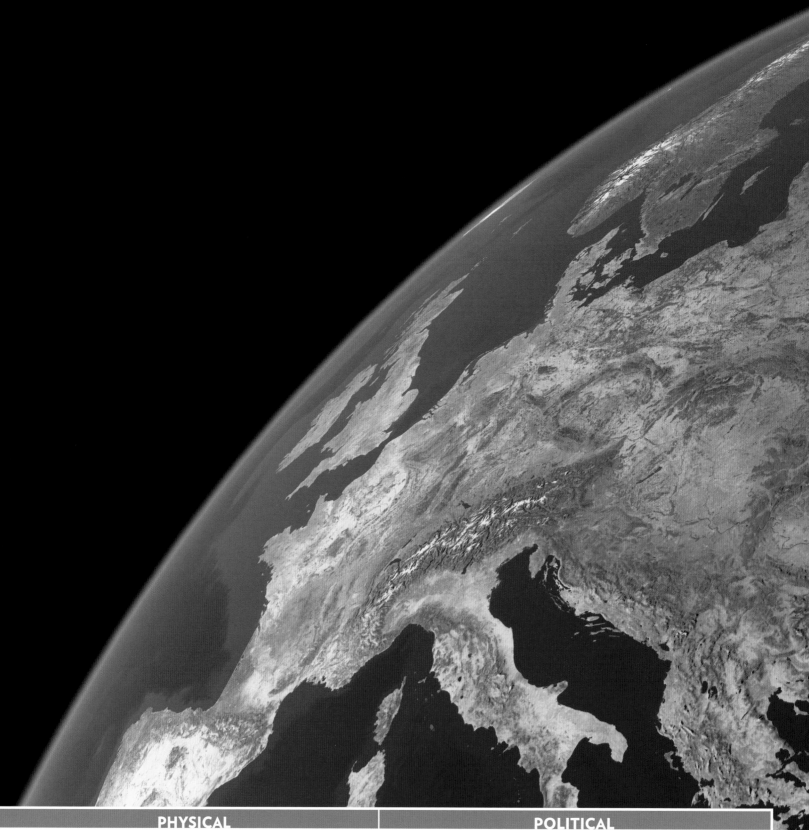

THE CONTINENT:
EUROPE

PHYSICAL

TOTAL AREA	LOWEST POINT	LARGEST LAKE ENTIRELY IN EUROPE
3,841,000 sq mi (9,947,000 sq km)	Caspian Sea	
	-92 ft (-28 m)	Ladoga, Russia
HIGHEST POINT		6,835 sq mi (17,703 sq km)
El'brus, Russia	**LONGEST RIVER**	
18,510 ft (5,642 m)	Volga, Russia	
	2,290 mi (3,685 km)	

POLITICAL

POPULATION	LARGEST COUNTRY ENTIRELY IN EUROPE
683,816,000	Ukraine
	233,031 sq mi (603,550 sq km)
LARGEST METROPOLITAN AREA	
Moscow, Russia	**MOST DENSELY POPULATED COUNTRY**
Pop. 12,260,000	Monaco
	30,645.0 people per sq mi (15,322.5 per sq km)

EUROPE

Europe

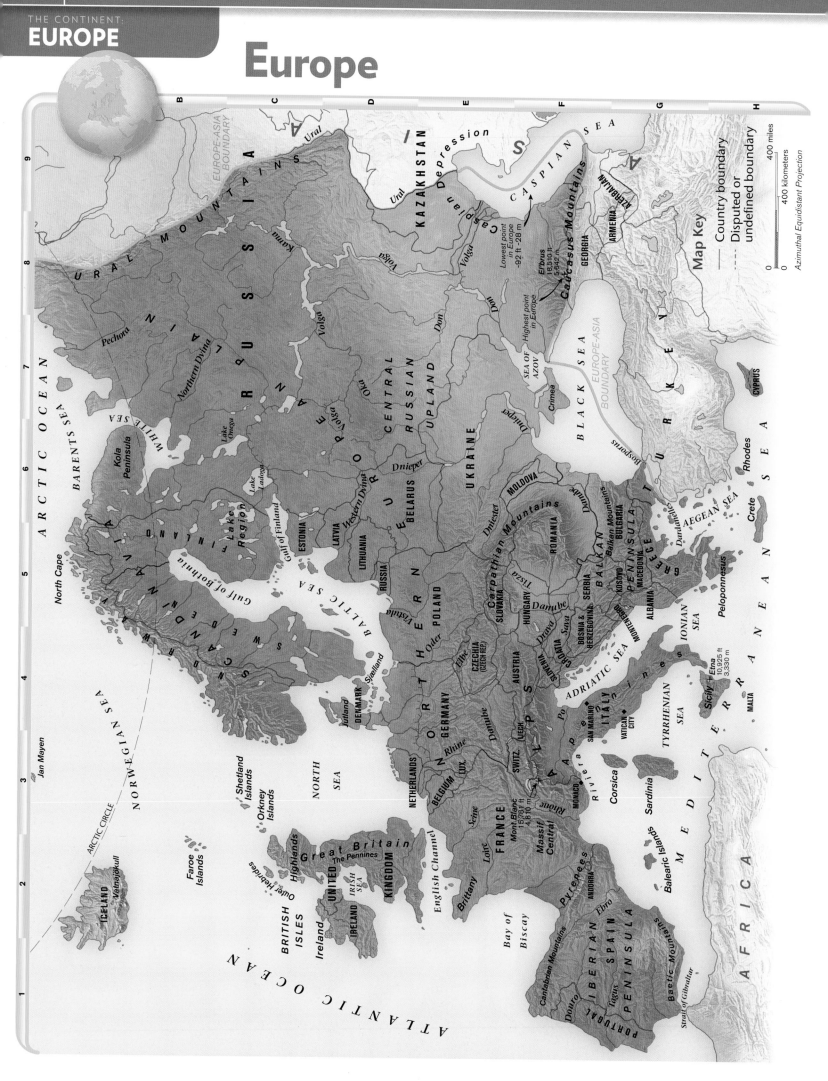

Map Key

—— Country boundary

- - - Disputed or undefined boundary

400 miles

400 kilometers

Azimuthal Equidistant Projection

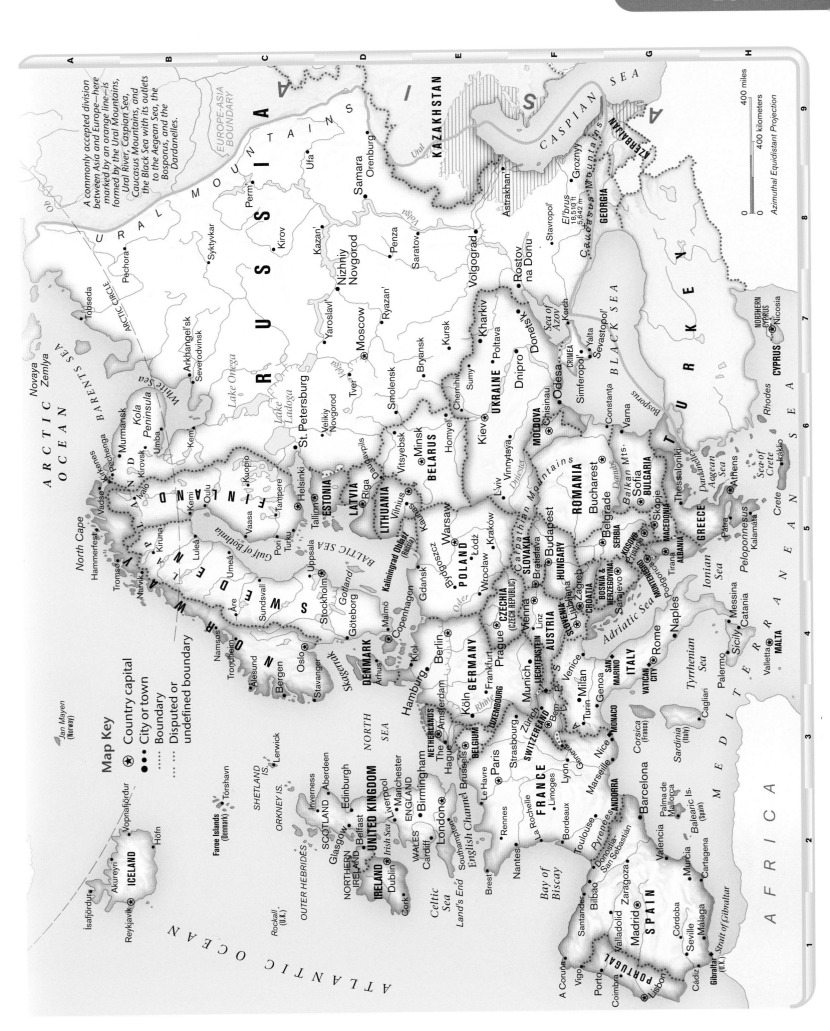

Europe

SMALL SPACES, DIVERSE PLACES

WIND POWER. A traditional windmill stands silent in Spain, calling to mind scenes from the classic Spanish novel *Don Quixote*. Modern windmills are used to generate electricity and to pump water.

A cluster of islands and peninsulas jutting west from Asia, Europe is bordered by two oceans and more than a dozen seas, which are linked to inland areas by canals and navigable rivers such as the Rhine and Danube. The fertile Northern European Plain sweeps west from the Urals. Rugged uplands form part of Europe's western coast, while the Alps shield Mediterranean lands from frigid northern winds. Here, first Greek and then Roman civilizations laid Europe's cultural foundation. Its colonial powers built wealth from vast empires, while its inventors and thinkers revolutionized world industry, economy, and politics. Today, the European Union seeks to achieve political and economic cooperation among member countries.

CHEERY GREETINGS. Laughing children clown for the camera in Klaipėda, Lithuania. The city is the northernmost ice-free port on the eastern coast of the Baltic Sea.

⬇ **WATCHFUL GUARDIAN.** A gargoyle stares out across the Paris skyline from a ledge of Notre Dame Cathedral. Gargoyles were first used in Gothic architecture as waterspouts but later were decorative additions meant to ward off evil spirits.

⬇ **ROCKY SENTINEL.** Towering 14,692 feet (4,478 m) in elevation, the Matterhorn, on the border between Switzerland and Italy, is one of Europe's most famous mountains. Frequent avalanches on its steep slopes pose challenges for mountain climbers.

⬇ **WINDOW ON THE PAST.** The brightly painted houses of Nyhavn (New Harbor), once the homes and warehouses of wealthy Copenhagen merchants, are now shops and restaurants and one of the most popular tourist attractions in Denmark's capital city.

more about
Europe

⬤ **AGELESS TIME.** This famous astronomical clock, built in 1410 in Prague, Czechia, has an astronomical dial on top of a calendar dial. Together, they keep track of time as well as the movement of the sun, moon, and stars.

◑ **CLIFF DWELLERS.** The town of Positano clings to the rocky hillside along Italy's Amalfi coast. In the mid-19th century, more than half the town's population emigrated, mainly to the United States. The economy today is based on tourism.

⬤ **SEABIRDS OF THE NORTH.** Colorful Atlantic puffins perch on a grass-covered cliff in Iceland, Europe's westernmost country. These unusual birds are skilled fishers but have difficulty becoming airborne and often crash as they attempt to land.

⬤ **CITY AT NIGHT.** A winged victory statue atop the Metropolis Building, a classic example of early 20th-century architecture, appears to watch the evening traffic on the Gran Via in Madrid, Spain.

⬤ **GLIMPSE OF THE PAST.** Rome's Colosseum is a silent reminder of a once powerful empire that stretched from the British Isles to Persia (now Iran). The concrete, stone, and brick structure could seat as many as 50,000 people.

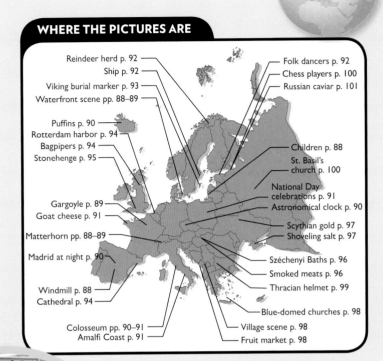

WHERE THE PICTURES ARE

Reindeer herd p. 92
Ship p. 92
Viking burial marker p. 93
Waterfront scene pp. 88–89
Puffins p. 90
Rotterdam harbor p. 94
Bagpipers p. 94
Stonehenge p. 95
Gargoyle p. 89
Goat cheese p. 91
Matterhorn pp. 88–89
Madrid at night p. 90
Windmill p. 88
Cathedral p. 94
Colosseum pp. 90–91
Amalfi Coast p. 91

Folk dancers p. 92
Chess players p. 100
Russian caviar p. 101
Children p. 88
St. Basil's church p. 100
National Day celebrations p. 91
Astronomical clock p. 90
Scythian gold p. 97
Shoveling salt p. 97
Széchenyi Baths p. 96
Smoked meats p. 96
Thracian helmet p. 99
Blue-domed churches p. 98
Village scene p. 98
Fruit market p. 98

◑ **LUNCHTIME!** Varieties of creamy, fresh goat cheese are displayed in a market in the Brittany region of northern France.

⬤ **NATIONAL PRIDE.** Young women carry banners in a parade marking Poland's National Day. Celebrated each year on May 3, it is the anniversary of the 1997 proclamation of the Polish Constitution.

THE BASICS

STATS

Largest country
Sweden
173,859 sq mi (450,295 sq km)

Smallest country
Denmark
16,639 sq mi (43,094 sq km)

Most populous country
Sweden 9,960,000

Least populous country
Iceland 340,000

Predominant languages
Swedish, Danish, Finnish,
Norwegian, Lithuanian, Latvian,
Estonian, Russian, Icelandic

Predominant religion
Christianity

Highest GDP per capita
Norway $69,200

Lowest GDP per capita
Latvia $25,700

Highest life expectancy
Iceland 83 years

Lowest life expectancy
Latvia, Lithuania 75 years

GEO WHIZ

Vatnajökull, in Iceland, is the largest glacier in Europe.

The national symbol of Denmark is a statue of Hans Christian Andersen's Little Mermaid, in Copenhagen's harbor.

During Iceland's Thorrablot winter festival, locals eat *hákarl,* a Viking dish made of rotten shark meat.

Northern Europe

This region lies in latitudes similar to Canada's Hudson Bay, but the warm North Atlantic Drift current moderates temperatures from volcanically active Iceland to Denmark and Norway. Sparsely populated but mostly urban, northern Europe is home to slightly more than 33 million people. The region's better farmlands lie in southern Sweden and Denmark's lowlands. Forested Finland shares a border with Russia. Estonia, Latvia, and Lithuania—the so-called Baltic States—are former republics of the Soviet Union.

NORDIC HERDERS. The Sami, indigenous people of northern Europe, herd their reindeer across the borders of Norway, Sweden, Finland, and Russia. Some use snowmobiles instead of horses.

MIGHTY WARSHIP. In 1628 the Swedish warship *Vasa* sank in the cold waters of Stockholm Harbor on its maiden voyage. After 333 years it was raised and reconstructed.

COLORFUL TRADITION. Costumed folk dancers perform traditional dances at an open-air museum in Tallinn, Estonia's capital city.

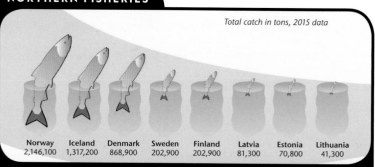

NORTHERN FISHERIES

Total catch in tons, 2015 data

Norway	Iceland	Denmark	Sweden	Finland	Latvia	Estonia	Lithuania
2,146,100	1,317,200	868,900	202,900	202,900	81,300	70,800	41,300

Large schools of fish thrive in the cold waters off northern Europe. Norway harvests the most, bringing in more than two million tons of fish annually.

⬤ MARKER FROM THE PAST. This stone memorial in Sweden marks the burial site of Viking warriors. Although known for their fierce raids, Vikings were mainly farmers and traders.

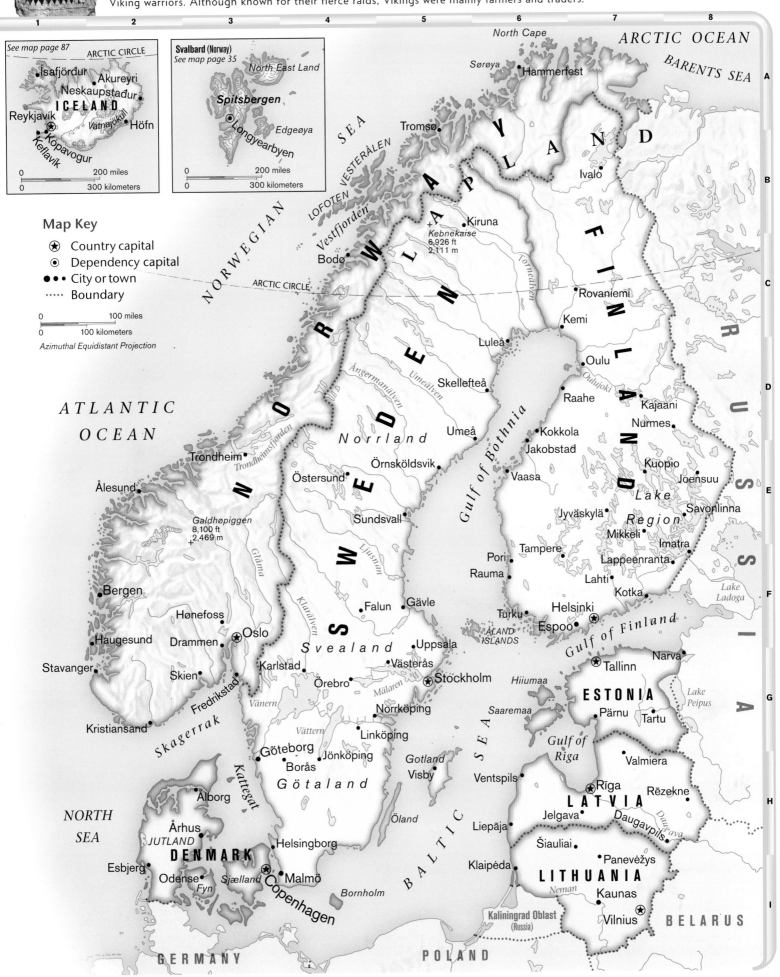

See map page 87
ARCTIC CIRCLE
Ísafjörður
Akureyri
Neskaupstadur
ICELAND
Reykjavík
Kópavogur
Vatnajökull
Höfn
Keflavík

0   200 miles
0   300 kilometers

Svalbard (Norway)
See map page 35
North East Land
Spitsbergen
Longyearbyen
Edgeøya

0   200 miles
0   300 kilometers

Map Key
⊛ Country capital
⊙ Dependency capital
●●● City or town
····· Boundary

0   100 miles
0   100 kilometers
Azimuthal Equidistant Projection

NORTH CAPE
ARCTIC OCEAN
BARENTS SEA
Sørøya
Hammerfest

L   A   P   L   A   N   D

Tromsø
Ivalo

NORWEGIAN
SEA

LOFOTEN
VESTERÅLEN
Vestfjorden
Bodø

ARCTIC CIRCLE

Kebnekaise
6,926 ft
2,111 m
Kiruna

Torneälven

F   I   N   L   A   N   D

Rovaniemi
Kemi

R   U   S   S   I   A

ATLANTIC
OCEAN

N   O   R   W   A   Y

Ångermanälven
Umeälven
Skellefteå
Luleå
Oulujoki
Oulu
Raahe
Kajaani
Nurmes

Norrland
Örnsköldsvik
Umeå

Trondheim
Trondheimsfjorden
Ålesund

Gulf of Bothnia

Kokkola
Jakobstad
Vaasa
Kuopio
Joensuu

S   W   E   D   E   N

Östersund

Galdhøpiggen
8,100 ft
2,469 m

Sundsvall

Jyväskylä
Lake
Region
Savonlinna
Mikkeli
Imatra

Ljustan

Glåma

Pori
Rauma
Tampere
Lappeenranta
Lahti

Lake
Ladoga

Bergen
Hønefoss
Drammen
Oslo
Falun
Gävle
Turku
Helsinki
Espoo
Kotka

Haugesund
Stavanger
Skien
Karlstad
Örebro
Uppsala
Västerås
Klarälven
Svealand
Stockholm
Mälaren
ÅLAND
ISLANDS
Gulf of Finland
Narva
Tallinn

Fredrikstad
Vänern
Norrköping
Hiiumaa

ESTONIA
Lake
Peipus
Pärnu
Tartu

Kristiansand
Skagerrak
Linköping
Saaremaa
Gulf of
Riga
Valmiera

Göteborg
Jönköping
Vättern
Gotland
Visby
Ventspils
Rīga
Rēzekne

Borås
Götaland
Öland
LATVIA
Jelgava
Daugavpils
Daugava

Kattegat
BALTIC
SEA
Liepāja
Šiauliai

NORTH
SEA
Ålborg
Helsingborg
Klaipėda
Panevėžys
LITHUANIA

Århus
JUTLAND
DENMARK
Kaunas

Esbjerg
Odense
Fyn
Sjælland
Malmö
Copenhagen
Bornholm
Neman
Vilnius

Kaliningrad Oblast
(Russia)
BELARUS

GERMANY
POLAND

THE BASICS

STATS

Largest country
France
248,572 sq mi (643,801 sq km)

Smallest country
Vatican City
0.2 sq mi (0.4 sq km)

Most populous country
Germany 80,594,000

Least populous country
Vatican City 1,000

Predominant languages
German, French, English, Italian,
Spanish, Dutch, Portuguese

Predominant religion
Christianity

Highest GDP per capita
Liechtenstein $139,100

Lowest GDP per capita
Portugal $28,900

Highest life expectancy
Monaco 90 years

Lowest life expectancy
Portugal 79 years

GEO WHIZ

Turiasaurus riodevensis is the largest dinosaur ever found in Europe. The fossil was discovered in northern Spain in 2006.

Mount Etna, on Sicily, is known as the home of Zeus, ruler of all Greek gods. It is also Europe's highest active volcano.

Antwerp, Belgium, is the center of the world's diamond industry.

Western Europe

Eighteen countries crowd this diverse region, which has enjoyed a central role in world affairs for centuries. The past half-century has seen bitter rivals become allies, with today's European Union growing out of the need to rebuild economic and political stability after World War II. Fertile soil in the many river valleys across the Northern European Plain and on Mediterranean hillsides gives rise to abundant harvests of a wide variety of crops. France leads in agricultural production and area, while Germany is the most populous country.

MONUMENT TO FAITH. The towering spires of La Sagrada Familia (The Holy Family) rise above Barcelona, Spain. This massive Roman Catholic church has been under construction for more than a century.

HIGHLAND TUNE. Bagpipers in formal dress parade through the streets of Edinburgh, Scotland, in the United Kingdom. Bagpipes may have arrived centuries ago with Roman invaders, but today they are most associated with the Scottish Highlands.

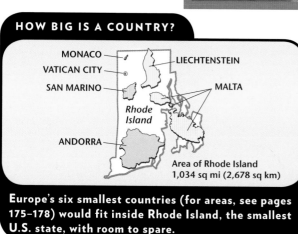

HOW BIG IS A COUNTRY?

MONACO
VATICAN CITY
SAN MARINO
Rhode Island
ANDORRA
LIECHTENSTEIN
MALTA
Area of Rhode Island
1,034 sq mi (2,678 sq km)

Europe's six smallest countries (for areas, see pages 175–178) would fit inside Rhode Island, the smallest U.S. state, with room to spare.

MODERN SPAN. Tall red arches support the Willem Bridge across the Maas River in Rotterdam, Netherlands. The Maas, which flows into the North Sea, is a major trade and transport artery, linking the Netherlands to the rest of Europe.

CELTIC POWER. These rock pillars, part of Stonehenge in southern England, United Kingdom, were erected more than 5,000 years ago and may be associated with sun worship.

Map Key

- ⊛ Country capital
- ⊙ Capital of a political division of the United Kingdom
- ••• City or town
- •••• Boundary

0 ___ 200 miles
0 ___ 200 kilometers
Azimuthal Equidistant Projection

THE BASICS

STATS

Largest country
Ukraine
233,031 sq mi (603,550 sq km)

Smallest country
Moldova
13,070 sq mi (33,851 sq km)

Most populous country
Ukraine 44,034,000

Least populous country
Moldova 3,474,000

Predominant languages
Ukrainian, Russian, Polish,
Hungarian, Czech, Belarusian,
Slovak, Moldovan

Predominant religions
Christianity, Judaism, Islam

Highest GDP per capita
Czechia $33,200

Lowest GDP per capita
Moldova $5,300

Highest life expectancy
Czechia 79 years

Lowest life expectancy
Moldova 71 years

GEO WHIZ

The Wieliczka salt mine is known as the underground salt cathedral of Poland. It features historical, religious, and mythical figures, chambers, a chapel, and an exhibit about how salt is mined—all carved in salt!

Budapest became a united city in 1873 after Count István Széchenyi built a bridge connecting Buda on the west bank of the Danube River and Pest on the east bank.

The Pinsk Marshes, one of Europe's largest wetlands, are still contaminated by radioactive waste from a 1986 nuclear reactor explosion in Chernobyl, Ukraine.

Eastern Europe

TIME TO EAT. Smoked sausages and bacon, ready for purchase in the market, are an important part of the diet in the countries of eastern Europe.

Eastern Europe stretches from the Baltic Sea southeast to the Black Sea. Before 1991, Ukraine, Belarus, and Moldova were part of the Soviet Union, with the region's other countries largely under its control. Kaliningrad, a small region of Russia separated from the main country, lies just north of Poland. Much of the region has a continental climate similar to that of the U.S. Midwest. Nearly the size of Texas, Ukraine is the region's largest country in both population and area. Like Poland, it holds rich agricultural and industrial resources. Warsaw is the region's largest city, while historic Prague and Budapest are popular tourist stops. With the exceptions of Hungarians and Moldovans, most people in these lands are linked by branches of Slavic language and ethnicity.

HEALING WATERS.
Budapest's Széchenyi Baths, built between 1909 and 1913, are famous for their medicinal thermal waters, discovered in 1879. A total of 15 baths, as well as saunas and steam rooms, are housed in buildings decorated with sculptures and mosaics by Hungary's leading artists.

◑ **ANCIENT GOLD.** Scythians, who occupied the area from what is now Ukraine into Russia from the third century B.C.E. to the second century C.E., crafted this gold collar.

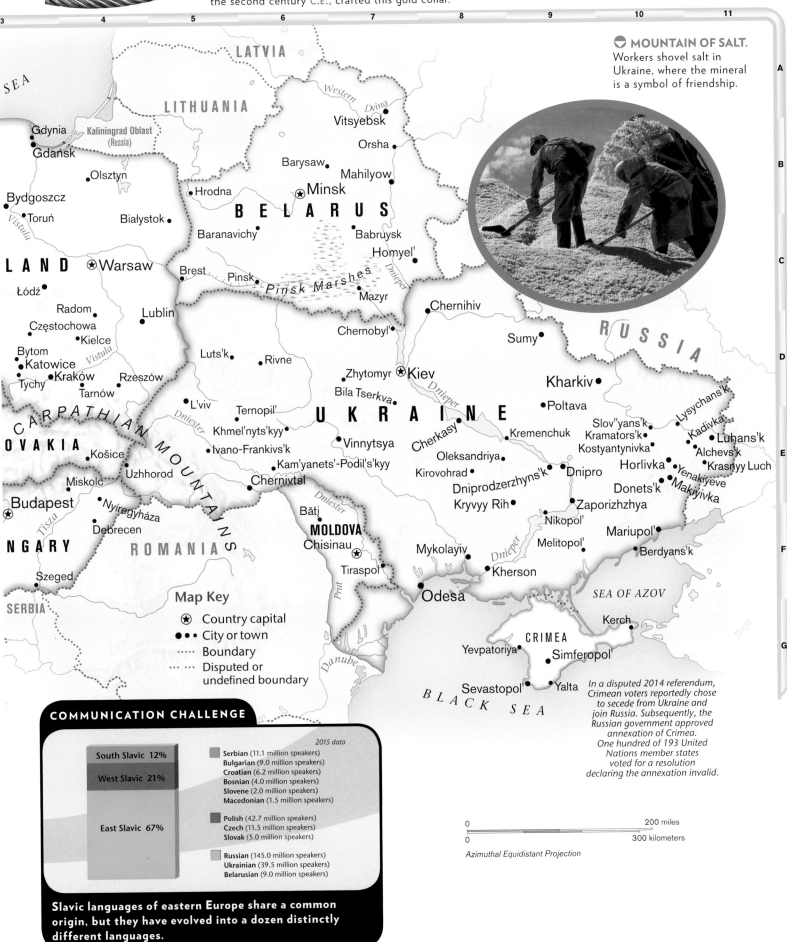

⊙ **MOUNTAIN OF SALT.** Workers shovel salt in Ukraine, where the mineral is a symbol of friendship.

Map Key

⊛ Country capital
••• City or town
····· Boundary
····· Disputed or undefined boundary

In a disputed 2014 referendum, Crimean voters reportedly chose to secede from Ukraine and join Russia. Subsequently, the Russian government approved annexation of Crimea. One hundred of 193 United Nations member states voted for a resolution declaring the annexation invalid.

0 ————— 200 miles
0 ————— 300 kilometers

Azimuthal Equidistant Projection

COMMUNICATION CHALLENGE

2015 data

South Slavic 12%

Serbian (11.1 million speakers)
Bulgarian (9.0 million speakers)
Croatian (6.2 million speakers)
Bosnian (4.0 million speakers)
Slovene (2.0 million speakers)
Macedonian (1.5 million speakers)

West Slavic 21%

Polish (42.7 million speakers)
Czech (11.5 million speakers)
Slovak (5.0 million speakers)

East Slavic 67%

Russian (145.0 million speakers)
Ukrainian (39.5 million speakers)
Belarusian (9.0 million speakers)

Slavic languages of eastern Europe share a common origin, but they have evolved into a dozen distinctly different languages.

The Balkans & Cyprus

THE BASICS

STATS

Largest country
Romania
92,043 sq mi (238,391 sq km)

Smallest country
Cyprus
3,572 sq mi (9,251 sq km)

Most populous country
Romania 21,530,000

Least populous country
Montenegro 643,000

Predominant languages
Romanian, Greek, Serbian,
Croatian, Bulgarian, Albanian,
Turkish, English

Predominant religions
Christianity, Islam

Highest GDP per capita
Cyprus $35,000

Lowest GDP per capita
Kosovo $9,600

Highest life expectancy
Greece 81 years

Lowest life expectancy
Bulgaria, Romania
75 years

GEO WHIZ

The Dalmatian, a popular breed of dog, is named for the region where it originated: Dalmatia, along the Adriatic coast of the Balkan Peninsula.

Dracula tours are popular in Romania, home of Vlad Dracula (Vlad the Impaler), who ruled the region between the Danube and the Transylvanian Alps in the 15th century.

The Balkans—named for a Bulgarian mountain range—make up a rugged land with a rough history. Ethnic and religious conflicts have long troubled the area. After 1991, seven new countries stretching from Slovenia to Macedonia emerged as a result of the breakup of Yugoslavia. Kosovo is the most recent. The Danube River winds east across the Balkans, separating Bulgaria from Romania, the region's largest country. Rimmed by four seas—the Black, Aegean, Ionian, and Adriatic—the Balkans, particularly Greece, have a long maritime history. In 2004, Cyprus, which has been uneasily divided for three decades into Turkish and Greek sections, joined the European Union along with Greece.

🔺 **TRADITIONAL LIFE.** Villagers walk down a cobbled street in Gusinje, a rural town in northeastern Montenegro. A place of rugged mountains, Montenegro is one of the countries that emerged from the former Yugoslavia.

🔻 **VIOLENT PAST.** Blue domes of Greek Orthodox churches on the island of Thira (Santorini) cling to cliffs above the remains of a volcano that erupted more than 3,000 years ago.

🔺 **COLORFUL BOUNTY.** An open-air fruit market overflows with grapes, plums, apples, and other produce that thrive in the moderate climate of the Mediterranean region. Warm, dry summers and cool, rainy winters provide ideal growing conditions for a variety of fruits, many of which had their origins in the region.

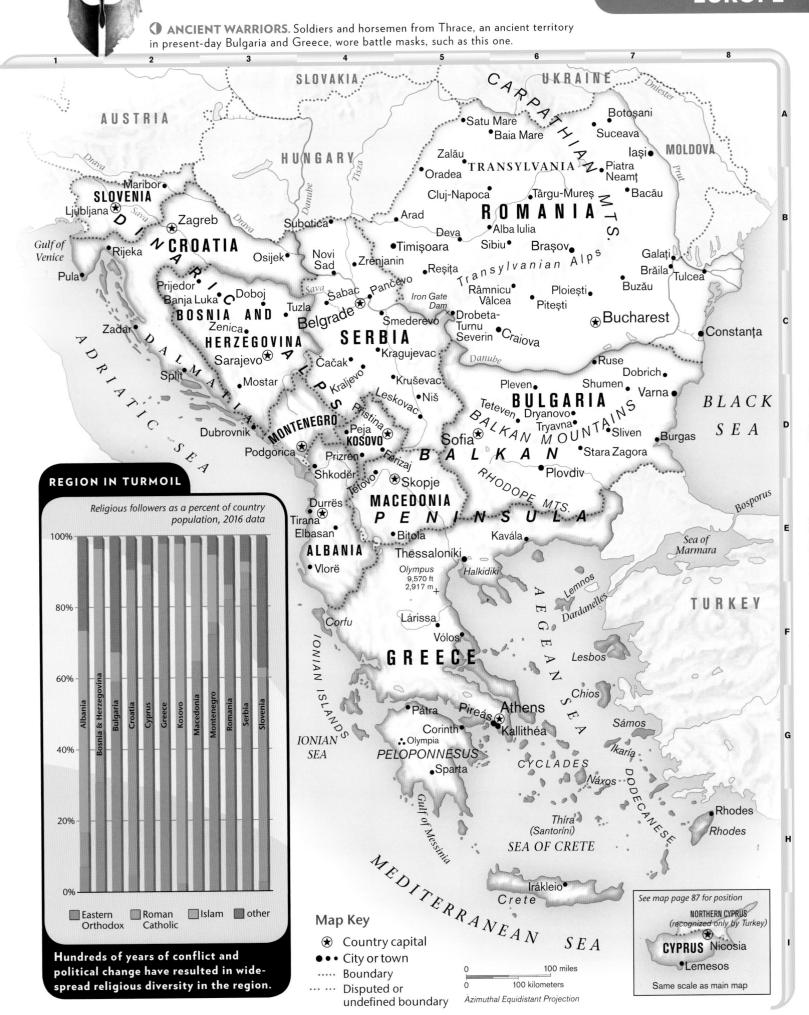

ANCIENT WARRIORS. Soldiers and horsemen from Thrace, an ancient territory in present-day Bulgaria and Greece, wore battle masks, such as this one.

REGION IN TURMOIL

Religious followers as a percent of country population, 2016 data

Albania
Bosnia & Herzegovina
Bulgaria
Croatia
Cyprus
Greece
Kosovo
Macedonia
Montenegro
Romania
Serbia
Slovenia

100%
80%
60%
40%
20%
0%

Eastern Orthodox
Roman Catholic
Islam
other

Hundreds of years of conflict and political change have resulted in widespread religious diversity in the region.

Map Key

⊛ Country capital
••• City or town
..... Boundary
·-·-· Disputed or undefined boundary

0   100 miles
0   100 kilometers
Azimuthal Equidistant Projection

See map page 87 for position
NORTHERN CYPRUS
(recognized only by Turkey)
CYPRUS ⊛ Nicosia
• Lemesos
Same scale as main map

SLOVAKIA
UKRAINE
Dniester
AUSTRIA
CARPATHIAN MTS.
HUNGARY
• Botoșani
• Satu Mare
• Suceava
• Baia Mare
Zalău
• Iași
MOLDOVA
Drava
TRANSYLVANIA
• Oradea
Piatra Neamț
Maribor •
SLOVENIA
• Cluj-Napoca
• Târgu-Mureș
• Bacău
Prut
Ljubljana ⊛
Sava
Zagreb
Subotica •
• Arad
ROMANIA
Drava
• Deva
• Alba Iulia
DINARIC
CROATIA
• Timișoara
• Sibiu
• Brașov
Galați •
Gulf of Venice
• Rijeka
Osijek •
Novi Sad
Zrenjanin •
• Reșița
Transylvanian Alps
Brăila •
Tulcea •
• Pula
Prijedor •
Doboj •
Danube
• Râmnicu Vâlcea
• Ploiești
Buzău •
Banja Luka •
Tuzla •
Pančevo •
Iron Gate Dam
Zadar •
BOSNIA AND
• Belgrade
Šabac •
Smederevo •
Drobeta-Turnu Severin
• Pitești
• Bucharest ⊛
HERZEGOVINA
Zenica •
SERBIA
• Craiova
Constanța •
Sarajevo •
Čačak •
• Kragujevac
Danube
• Ruse
Split •
DALMATIA
Mostar •
Kraljevo •
• Kruševac
Pleven •
Shumen •
Dobrich •
ADRIATIC
Leskovac •
• Niš
BULGARIA
Varna •
Teteven •
Dryanovo •
BLACK SEA
Dubrovnik •
Pristina •
BALKAN MOUNTAINS
Tryavna •
MONTENEGRO
Peja •
Sofia ⊛
• Sliven
Podgorica ⊛
KOSOVO
Prizren •
Ferizaj •
BALKAN
Stara Zagora •
Burgas •
SEA
Shkodër •
Tetovo •
Plovdiv •
Bosporus
DINARIC ALPS
Durrës •
Skopje •
MACEDONIA
RHODOPE MTS.
Tirana •
PENINSULA
Sea of Marmara
Elbasan •
• Bitola
Kavála •
ALBANIA
Vlorë •
Thessaloníki •
Olympus 9,570 ft 2,917 m
Halkidikí •
TURKEY
Corfu
Lemnos
Lárissa •
Dardanelles
IONIAN ISLANDS
GREECE
Vólos •
Lesbos
AEGEAN SEA
Chios
IONIAN SEA
Pátra •
Pireás •
Athens ⊛
Sámos
Corinth •
Kallithéa •
Ikaría
Olympia
PELOPONNESUS
CYCLADES
Náxos
DODECANESE
Gulf of Messinía
• Sparta
Rhodes •
Thíra (Santoríni)
Rhodes
SEA OF CRETE
Irákleio •
Crete
MEDITERRANEAN SEA

European Russia

THE BASICS

STATS*

Area
**6,601,631 sq mi
(17,098,242 sq km)**

Population
142,258,000

Predominant language
Russian (official)

Predominant religions
Christianity, Islam

GDP per capita
$26,500

Life expectancy
71 years

*Note: These figures are for all of Russia. For Asian Russia, see pages 110–111.

GEO WHIZ

St. Petersburg's many canals and hundreds of bridges have earned the city the nickname Venice of the North.

The fertile Northern European Plain, west of the Urals, is home to most of Russia's population and industry, whereas most of its mineral resources lie east of the Urals in the Asian portion of the country.

Arkhangel'sk, founded in 1584, is Russia's oldest Arctic port. The timber resources that are its chief export have been nicknamed "green gold."

The Kremlin is a walled fortress in Moscow, Russia's capital city, that houses the official residence of the country's president.

⊙ **CHECKMATE!** Bystanders watch intently as one player prepares to make his move in this chess game in a park in St. Petersburg. In Russia, chess is a national pastime, popular with people from all walks of life.

Home to four-fifths of Russia's 142 million people, European Russia contains most of the country's agriculture and industry. Here also is Moscow, its capital and Europe's largest city. Far to the north, Murmansk provides a year-round seaport—a gift of the warming currents of the North Atlantic Drift. This funnel-shaped portion of Russia, spanning 1,600 miles (2,575 km) from the Arctic to the Caucasus Mountains, is home to the Volga, Europe's longest river, and Mount El'brus, its highest peak. The Caucasus and Urals form a natural boundary between Europe and Asia. Although parts of Azerbaijan, Georgia, and Kazakhstan span the continental boundary, only Russia is counted as part of Europe.

EUROPE'S GREAT RIVERS

Volga	2,290 mi (3,685 km)
Danube	1,795 mi (2,888 km)
Dnieper	1,423 mi (2,290 km)
Rhine	820 mi (1,320 km)
Elbe	678 mi (1,091 km)
Vistula	651 mi (1,047 km)
Tagus	645 mi (1,038 km)
Loire	629 mi (1,012 km)
Rhône	497 mi (800 km)
Po	405 mi (652 km)

Europe's rivers, many linked by canals, form a transportation network that connects the continent's people and places to each other and the world beyond.

◗ **CATHEDRAL ON THE SQUARE.** The onion-shaped domes atop the towers of St. Basil's are a key landmark on Red Square in Moscow. Built between 1555 and 1561 to commemorate military campaigns led by Ivan the Terrible, the building is rich in Christian symbolism.

RUSSIAN DELICACY. Caviar is the eggs (called roe) of sturgeon fish caught in the Caspian Sea. The eggs are aged in a salty brine, then packaged in cans (left) for export.

1 2 3 4 5 6 7 8

ARCTIC OCEAN
NOVAYA ZEMLYA
KARA SEA
Yamal Peninsula
Gulf of Ob

NORWAY

BARENTS SEA

Kolguyev I.

LAPLAND

• Murmansk

Vorkuta •

ARCTIC CIRCLE

Kola Peninsula

Kanin Peninsula

SWEDEN

Usinsk •

FINLAND

WHITE SEA

Pechora •

Gulf of Bothnia

Pechora

U R A L

See pages 110–111 for Asian part of Russia

• Arkhangel'sk

Severodvinsk •

Ukhta •

Sosnogorsk •

S I B E R I A

Petrozavodsk •

Zheleznodorozhnyy •

Northern Dvina

Syktyvkar •

Lake Ladoga

Lake Onega

Kotlas •

S

Gulf of Finland

Berezniki •

St. Petersburg

Sukhona

EUROPE-ASIA BOUNDARY

ESTONIA

Lake Peipus

Cherepovets •

• Vologda

Kirov •

Perm' •

Pskov •

Velikiy Novgorod

Rybinsk Reservoir

M

BALTIC SEA

LATVIA

Velikiye Luki •

Rybinsk •

Kostroma •

Izhevsk •

Kama

Yaroslavl' •

O

Kaliningrad Oblast (Russia)

LITHUANIA

Tver' •

Ivanovo •

Nizhniy Novgorod •

Kazan' •

Naberezhnyye Chelny •

U

Ufa •

Vladimir •

Ul'yanovsk •

Magnitogorsk •

POLAND

Moscow ✪

Cheboksary •

Volga

N

Smolensk •

R

Sterlitamak •

T

BELARUS

Kaluga •

Ryazan' •

Oka

Syzran' •

Tol'yatti •

Ural

Tula •

Saransk •

A

CENTRAL

Bryansk •

Penza •

Samara

Belaya

Dnieper

Orel •

Lipetsk •

Novotroitsk •

I

RUSSIAN

Oka

Tambov •

Orenburg •

Orsk •

Kursk •

Voronezh •

Balakovo •

N

UPLAND

Belgorod •

Saratov •

KAZAKHSTAN

Engels •

S

UKRAINE

Kamyshin •

Don

MOLDOVA

Donets

Volgograd •

Volzhskiy •

Map Key

✪ Country capital

Shakhty •

••• City or town

Don

······ Boundary

Dnieper

Rostov na Donu •

Volga

DEPRESSION

Taganrog •

CASPIAN

0   200 miles

SEA OF AZOV

0   200 kilometers

Krasnodar •

Stavropol' •

Azimuthal Equidistant Projection

Novorossiysk •

Astrakhan' •

Maykop •

Pyatigorsk •

CASPIAN

BLACK SEA

El'brus 18,510 ft 5,642 m

CHECHNYA

SEA

Sochi •

Groznyy •

Makhachkala •

CAUCASUS MOUNTAINS

Vladikavkaz •

GEORGIA

TURKEY

ARMENIA   AZERBAIJAN

THE CONTINENT:
ASIA

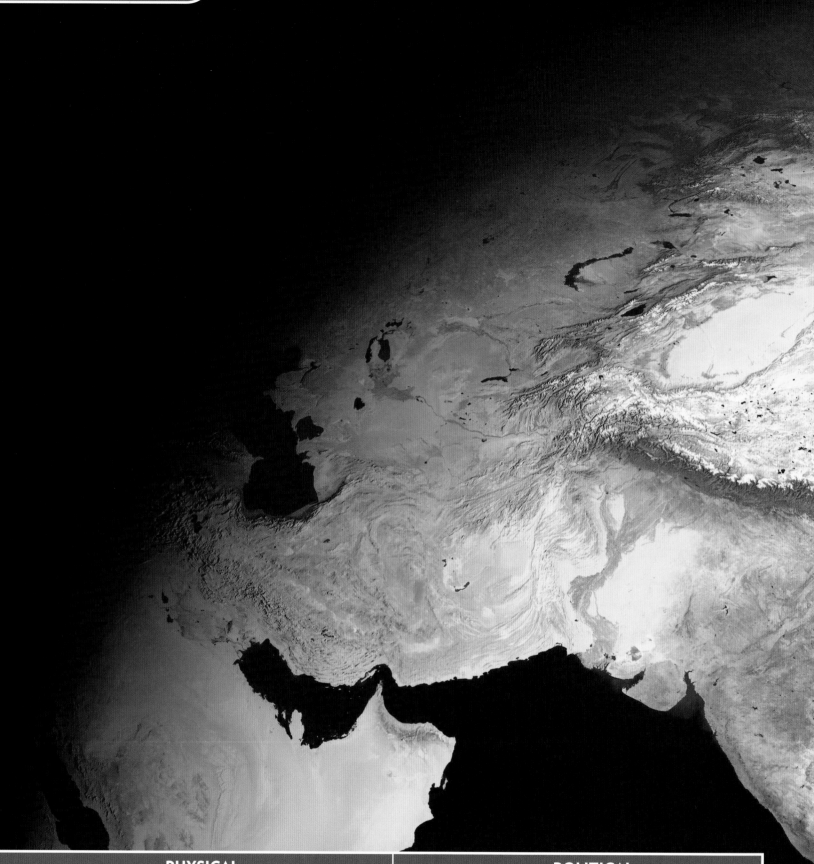

PHYSICAL

TOTAL AREA 17,208,000 sq mi (44,570,000 sq km)	**LOWEST POINT** Dead Sea, Israel-Jordan -1,388 ft (-423 m)	**LARGEST LAKE** **ENTIRELY IN ASIA** Lake Baikal 12,200 sq mi (31,500 sq km)
HIGHEST POINT Mount Everest, China-Nepal 29,035 ft (8,850 m)	**LONGEST RIVER** Yangtze (Chang), China 3,880 mi (6,244 km)	

POLITICAL

POPULATION 4,405,052,000	**LARGEST COUNTRY ENTIRELY IN ASIA** China 3,705,386 sq mi (9,596,960 sq km)
LARGEST METROPOLITAN AREA Tokyo, Japan Pop. 38,140,000	**MOST DENSELY POPULATED COUNTRY** Singapore 21,891.9 people per sq mi (8,449.0 per sq km)

ASIA

Asia

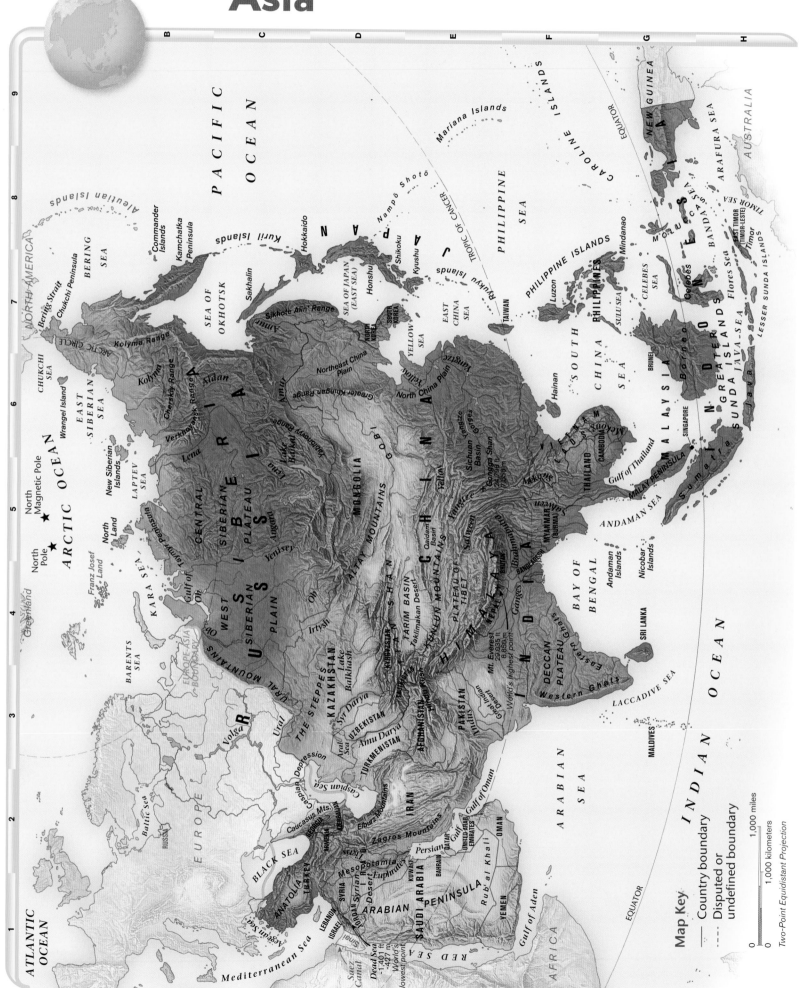

Map Key
—— Country boundary
---- Disputed or undefined boundary

0   1,000 miles
0   1,000 kilometers

Two-Point Equidistant Projection

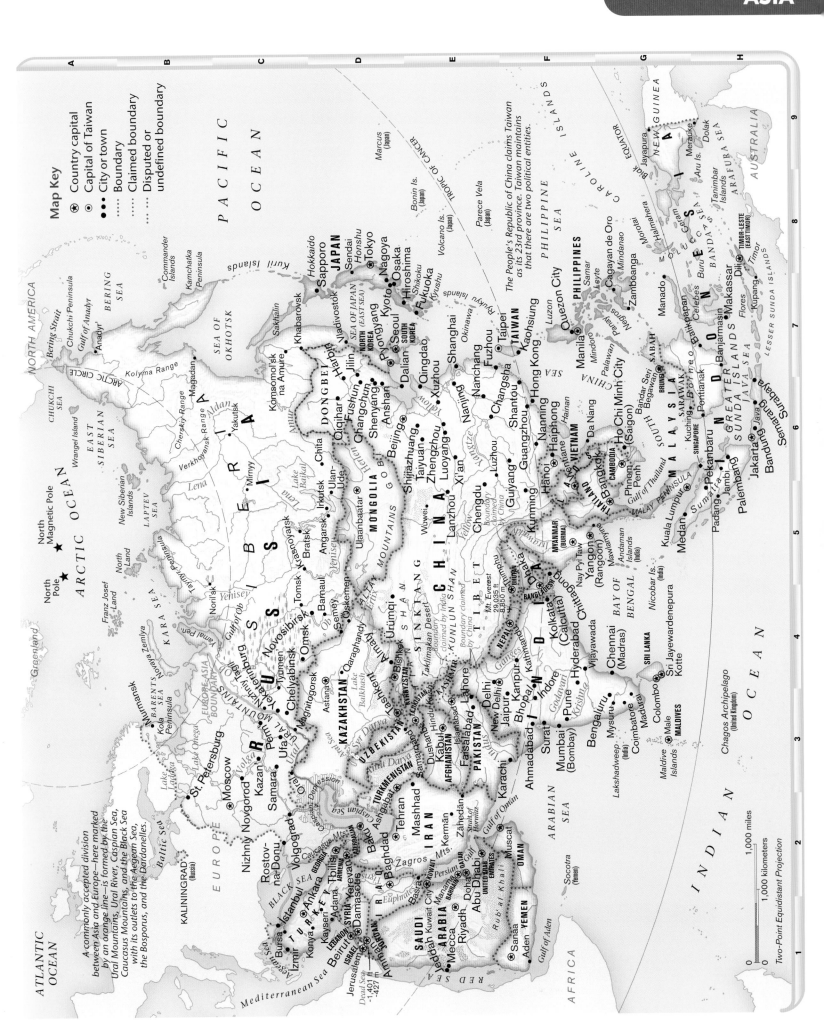

Map Key
- ⊛ Country capital
- ⊙ Capital of Taiwan
- • City or town
- ●●● Boundary
- ⋯⋯ Claimed boundary
- ⋯⋯ Disputed or undefined boundary

A commonly accepted division between Asia and Europe—here marked by an orange line—is formed by the Ural Mountains, Ural River, Caspian Sea, Caucasus Mountains, and the Black Sea with its outlets to the Aegean Sea, the Bosporus, and the Dardanelles.

The People's Republic of China claims Taiwan as its 23rd province. Taiwan maintains that there are two political entities.

ATLANTIC OCEAN

ARCTIC OCEAN

NORTH AMERICA

North Pole
North Magnetic Pole

PACIFIC OCEAN

Two-Point Equidistant Projection

0   1,000 miles
0   1,000 kilometers

INDIAN OCEAN

AUSTRALIA

AFRICA

Asia

WORLD CHAMPION

From Turkey to the eastern tip of Russia, Asia sprawls across nearly 180 degrees of longitude—almost half the globe! It boasts the highest (the Himalaya) and lowest (the Dead Sea) places on Earth's surface. Then there are Asia's people—more than four billion of them. That's more people than live on all the other continents put together. Asia has both the most farmers and the most million-plus cities. The world's first civilization arose in Sumer, in what is now southern Iraq. Rich cultures also emerged along rivers in present-day India and China, strongly influencing the world ever since.

⬤ **NEW VS. OLD.** An Afghan woman, completely covered by a traditional burka, sits among young girls dressed in Western clothes in Kabul.

◐ LUNAR NEW YEAR.
Young men carry a writhing paper dragon on poles in this Chinese New Year's parade in Singapore.

◑ WINGED HUNTER.
A Kazakh falconer sits astride his pony as he releases his golden eagle to pursue prey on the dry Asian steppe.

◑ NEON AVENUE.
Bright lights and neon signs highlight bustling Nanjing Lu, Shanghai's main shopping street. With a population of more than 24 million, Shanghai is China's largest city.

more about
Asia

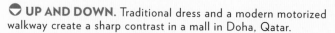

⬤ **EASTERN BELIEF.** From its origins in the foothills of the Himalaya, Buddhism has spread across much of eastern Asia. Statues of the Buddha, such as this one in Bangkok, Thailand, are an important part of the region's cultural landscape.

⬤ **UP AND DOWN.** Traditional dress and a modern motorized walkway create a sharp contrast in a mall in Doha, Qatar.

⬤ **FINAL TOUCH.** A silk kimono and perfectly applied makeup identify a *maiko,* or apprentice geisha, in Kyoto, Japan.

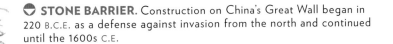

STONE BARRIER. Construction on China's Great Wall began in 220 B.C.E. as a defense against invasion from the north and continued until the 1600s C.E.

WHERE THE PICTURES ARE

Kyrgyz goat herder p. 112
Samarkand market p. 113
Baikonur Cosmodrome p. 112
Saiga antelope p. 113
Girls talking p. 118
Stone head p. 117
Galata Bridge p. 116
Swimmers p. 117
Petra p. 116
Ring p. 119
Horse and car p. 118
Mall scene p. 108
Drummer p. 118
Afghan girls p. 106
Taj Mahal p. 120
Hindu god Shiva p. 121
Elephant at work p. 122
Tigers p. 109
Mountain climbers p. 121

Natural gas well p. 111
Ger and yak p. 115
Falconer p. 107
Golden Buddha p. 108
Petronas Twin Towers p. 123
Lunar New Year pp. 106–107
Man and his cow p. 120

Nenet woman and child p. 110
Lenin's head p. 111
Brown bears p. 110
Great Wall of China pp. 108–109
Woman in lab p. 114
Tokyo city street pp. 114–115
Geisha p. 108
Shanghai city lights pp. 106–107
Terra-cotta soldiers p. 115
Panda p. 106
Jeepney p. 123
Buddhist monk p. 122
Container terminal p. 122
Rain forest p. 125
Boy with flag p. 124
Orangutan p. 125
Terraced rice fields p. 109
Ceremonial mask p. 125
Jakarta at night p. 124

MOUNTAIN STAIRWAY. Terraces cut into a steep mountainside create fields for rice on the island of Bali, in Indonesia. Rice is a staple grain crop in much of eastern Asia. In the foreground, a man nimbly climbs a palm tree to harvest coconuts.

MOTHER KNOWS BEST.
A Bengal tiger gently moves her cub to a safe hiding place before stalking her prey in India's Bandhavgarh National Park. Tigers are an endangered species.

THE BASICS

STATS*

Area
6,601,631 sq mi
(17,098,242 sq km)

Population
142,258,000

Predominant language
Russian (official)

Predominant religions
Christianity, Islam

GDP per capita
$26,500

Life expectancy
71 years

*These figures are for all of Russia. For European Russia, see pages 100–101.

GEO WHIZ

The name Siberia comes from the Turkic language and means "Sleeping Land."

It takes at least six days to travel 6,000 miles (9,656 km) on the Trans-Siberian Railway from Moscow to the Pacific port of Vladivostok. The trip crosses eight time zones.

Lake Baikal, nicknamed Siberia's "blue eye," is home to 1,500 unique species of plants and animals, including the nerpa, the world's only freshwater seal.

The Chukchi, the largest group of native people in Siberia, take their name from a word meaning "rich in reindeer." They share their name with their homeland, a peninsula bordered by the Arctic and Pacific Oceans.

A region of northern coniferous forest called taiga stretches across northern Russia as far as Norway.

Asian Russia

◔ **NOMADIC HERDERS.**
A Nenet woman and her grandson prepare to follow the family reindeer herd to northern Siberia for spring and summer grazing.

Forming more than half of Russia, this region stretches from the Ural Mountains east to the Pacific, and from the Arctic Ocean south to mountains and deserts along borders with central Asia, Mongolia, China, and North Korea. Siberia, as this region is commonly known, has limited croplands but bountiful forests (the taiga) and rich mineral resources such as oil, natural gas, and gold. The Trans-Siberian Railway, built between 1891 and 1905, opened up the region for settlement, but not too much. Fewer than 39 million people—27 percent of Russia's population—live in sprawling Siberia.

See page 101 for European part of Russia

◑ **FISHING FOR A MEAL.**
A brown bear and her cubs hunt for fish in a river below the slopes of a volcano on Russia's Kamchatka Peninsula. Part of the Pacific Ring of Fire, this peninsula has 29 active volcanoes.

◑ REVOLUTIONARY LEADER. Vladimir Ilyich Lenin, a founder of the Soviet Union, was honored with many statues. This one in Siberia is the largest still standing in Russia.

Map Key

⊛ Country capital
●●● City or town
⋯⋯ Boundary

0 _____ 500 miles
0 _____ 500 kilometers
Two-Point Equidistant Projection

DEEPEST LAKES

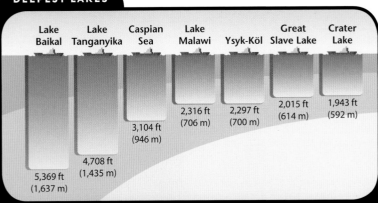

Lake Baikal	Lake Tanganyika	Caspian Sea	Lake Malawi	Ysyk-Köl	Great Slave Lake	Crater Lake
5,369 ft (1,637 m)	4,708 ft (1,435 m)	3,104 ft (946 m)	2,316 ft (706 m)	2,297 ft (700 m)	2,015 ft (614 m)	1,943 ft (592 m)

Most of Earth's surface water is stored in lakes. The deepest of all is Lake Baikal, which contains about 20 percent of Earth's total surface freshwater.

◑ COLD POWER. A liquefied natural gas well in the Yamal Peninsula in northwestern Siberia taps into Russia's largest gas reserves. Bitterly cold Arctic winters are a major challenge to this project.

THE BASICS

STATS

Largest country
Kazakhstan 1,052,084 sq mi
(2,724,900 sq km)

Smallest country
Tajikistan 55,251 sq mi
(143,100 sq km)

Most populous country
Uzbekistan 29,749,000

Least populous country
Turkmenistan 5,351,000

Predominant languages
Russian, Kazakh, Uzbek, Kyrgyz,
Tajik, Turkmen

Predominant religions
Islam, Christianity

Highest GDP per capita
Kazakhstan $25,100

Lowest GDP per capita
Tajikistan $3,000

Highest life expectancy
Uzbekistan 74 years

Lowest life expectancy
Tajikistan 68 years

GEO WHIZ

The main musical instrument of
the steppes in Kazakhstan is the
dombra, a long-necked lute with
two strings.

Uzbekistan, one of the world's
top gold-producing countries,
has the world's largest open-pit
gold mine. Muruntau Mine is said
to hold more gold reserves than
any other mine in the world.

Mountains, including the Pamir
and Tian Shan, cover more than
90 percent of Tajikistan.

Central Asia

Located along the historic Silk Road, central Asia is made up of five former Soviet republics, often referred to as the stans, or "homelands." This region has a largely Muslim population that includes Kazakhs, Turkmen, Uzbeks, Tajiks, and Kyrgyz, but Russians are also still present. Kazakhstan's short-grass steppes give way to deserts, arid plateaus, and rugged mountains to the south. The Amu Darya and the Syr Darya provide water for irrigating wheat, rice, cotton, and fruit crops. Although this landlocked region lies far from any ocean, it includes several large bodies of water, including the Caspian Sea, which is actually a saltwater lake.

⊙ **BEST FRIENDS.** A boy carries his goat in mountainous Kyrgyzstan, where almost half the land is used for pasture and hay to support herds of goats and sheep.

◑ **INTO SPACE.** Russia's Baikonur Cosmodrome, located east of the Aral Sea in Kazakhstan's desert, has been the launch site for Russian space missions since Sputnik 1 in 1957. U.S. astronauts have flown from here to the International Space Station.

◑ CRITICALLY ENDANGERED. Loss of habitat, illegal hunting, and disease have put the saiga antelope, found mainly in Kazakhstan, at risk.

Map Key
* ⊛ Country capital
* ••• City or town
* ⋯⋯ Boundary

500 miles
500 kilometers
Two-Point Equidistant Projection

◑ WHERE BARGAINING IS AN ART.
Two men haggle over the price of cherries in a bazaar in Samarqand, Uzbekistan. Located on the fabled Silk Road, the country relies on agriculture, especially cotton production, to support its economy.

VANISHING SEA

KAZAKHSTAN

Extent of Aral
Sea in 1965
Dry/Salt Lake

ARAL
SEA

Syr Darya

Amu Darya

UZBEKISTAN

The Aral Sea has lost more than 90 percent of its area due to water from feeder rivers being used to irrigate millions of acres of cotton and rice.

THE CONTINENT:
ASIA

THE BASICS
STATS

Largest country
China 3,705,386 sq mi
(9,596,960 sq km)

Smallest country
South Korea
38,502 sq mi (99,720 sq km)

Most populous country
China 1,379,303,000

Least populous country
Mongolia 3,068,000

Predominant languages
Standard Chinese (Mandarin),
Japanese, Korean, Mongol

Predominant religions
Daoism, Buddhism, Shintoism,
Christianity, Confucianism

Highest GDP per capita
Japan $41,300

Lowest GDP per capita
North Korea $1,700

Highest life expectancy
Japan 85 years

Lowest life expectancy
Mongolia, North Korea 70 years

GEO WHIZ

The only surviving breed of
wild horse, the Przewalski, is
named for the count who
"discovered" it in Mongolia in
the 1880s. Careful breeding has
saved it from extinction. About
1,500 remain.

Each year on October 9, people
in South Korea celebrate their
alphabet, which was created in
1446 to increase literacy.

Eastern Asia

China, Mongolia, the Koreas, and Japan make up eastern Asia. Rich river valleys have supported Chinese civilization for more than four millennia. The Tibetan Plateau, dry basins, and the towering Himalaya border China to the west. Mongolia, the land of Genghis Khan, lies to China's north. Despite rugged uplands that limit living space, Japan and South Korea have used technology and manufacturing to become economic powerhouses, while North Korea remains poor and isolated. China's gradual shift toward capitalism has made it a leader in global markets.

HIGH TECH. This young South Korean woman works in a laboratory that makes microcircuits in a semiconductor plant in Seoul.

NIGHTLIGHTS.
Tokyo's Shinjuku is both a shopping center and a theater district as well as the city's busiest train station. It averages more than 3.6 million passengers daily.

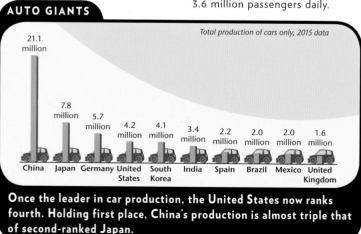

AUTO GIANTS

Total production of cars only, 2015 data

Country	Production
China	21.1 million
Japan	7.8 million
Germany	5.7 million
United States	4.2 million
South Korea	4.1 million
India	3.4 million
Spain	2.2 million
Brazil	2.0 million
Mexico	2.0 million
United Kingdom	1.6 million

Once the leader in car production, the United States now ranks fourth. Holding first place, China's production is almost triple that of second-ranked Japan.

◗ HOME ON THE STEPPE. A *ger* is the traditional Mongolian dwelling. The cowlike yak works as a pack animal and is a source of milk.

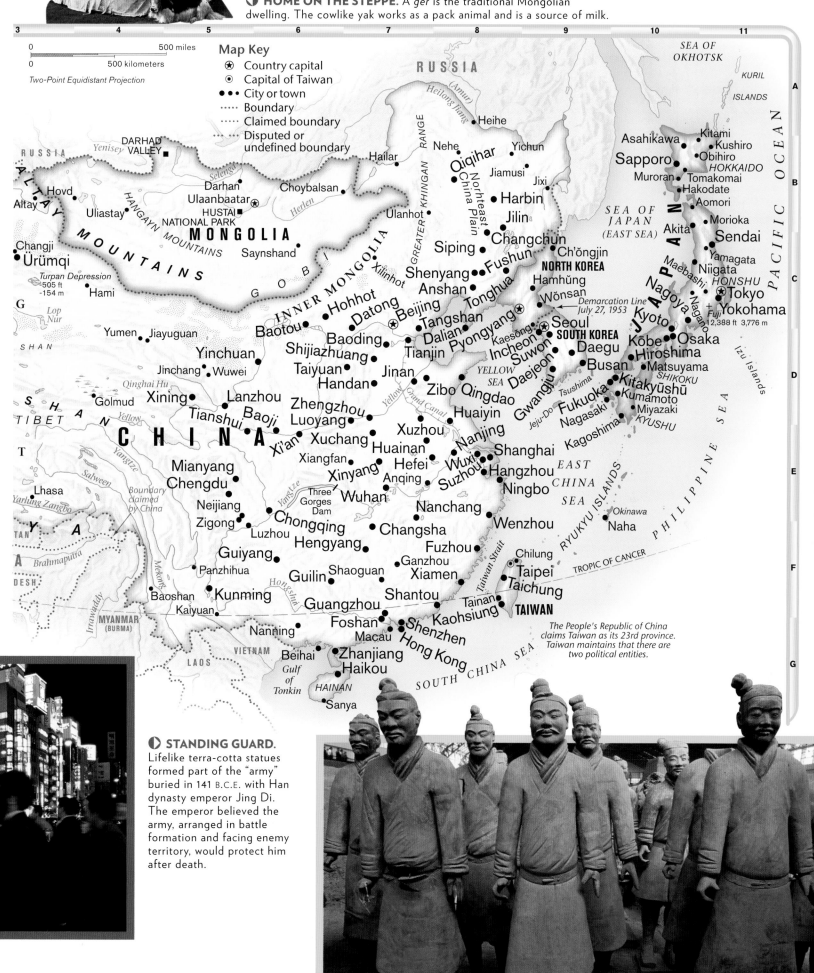

Map Key
- ★ Country capital
- ⊙ Capital of Taiwan
- ●●● City or town
- ····· Boundary
- ····· Claimed boundary
- ····· Disputed or undefined boundary

Two-Point Equidistant Projection

0   500 miles
0   500 kilometers

RUSSIA

SEA OF OKHOTSK

KURIL ISLANDS

RUSSIA
Yenisey
Heilong Jiang (Amur)
DARHAD VALLEY
Hovd
Altay
ALTAY MOUNTAINS
Uliastay
Darhan
Ulaanbaatar
Choybalsan
HUSTAI NATIONAL PARK
Selenga
Herlen
HANGAYN MOUNTAINS
MONGOLIA
Saynshand
Hailar
GREATER KHINGAN RANGE
Nehe
Heihe
Yichun
Qiqihar
Jiamusi
Jixi
Northeast China Plain
Harbin
Jilin
Changchun
Siping
Ulanhot
Shenyang
Fushun
Ch'ŏngjin
NORTH KOREA
Hamhŭng
Wŏnsan
Demarcation Line July 27, 1953
Asahikawa
Kitami
Kushiro
Sapporo
Obihiro
HOKKAIDO
Muroran
Tomakomai
Hakodate
Aomori
SEA OF JAPAN (EAST SEA)
Morioka
Akita
Sendai
Yamagata
HONSHU
Niigata
Maebashi
Nagano
Nagoya
Tokyo
Yokohama
PACIFIC OCEAN

Changji
Ürümqi
Turpan Depression -505 ft -154 m
Hami
Yumen
Jiayuguan
SHAN
G
Lop Nur
GOBI
INNER MONGOLIA
Xilinhot
Hohhot
Datong
Beijing
Tangshan
Tianjin
Baotou
Baoding
Shijiazhuang
Anshan
Tonghua
Pyongyang
Kaesŏng
Seoul
SOUTH KOREA
Incheon
Suwon
Daejeon
YELLOW SEA
Gwangju
Busan
Daegu
Jeju-Do
Tsushima
Fukuoka
Kitakyūshū
Kumamoto
Nagasaki
Miyazaki
KYUSHU
Kagoshima
Kōbe
Osaka
Hiroshima
Matsuyama
SHIKOKU
Kyoto
Fuji 12,388 ft 3,776 m
Izu Islands

Yinchuan
Jinchang
Wuwei
Taiyuan
Handan
Jinan
Zibo
Qingdao
Huaiyin
Dalian

Qinghai Hu
Golmud
Xining
Lanzhou
Zhengzhou
Luoyang
Baoji
Tianshui
Xi'an
Xuchang
Xuzhou
Nanjing
Shanghai
Huainan
Hefei
Wuxi
Suzhou
Hangzhou
Ningbo
EAST CHINA SEA
RYUKYU ISLANDS
Okinawa
Naha
PHILIPPINE SEA

TIBET
T
SHAN
Yangtze
Yellow
CHINA
Xiangfan
Xinyang
Anqing
Nanchang
Wenzhou

Lhasa
Salween
Boundary claimed by China
Yarlung Zangbo
Mianyang
Chengdu
Neijiang
Zigong
Three Gorges Dam
Wuhan
Changsha
Fuzhou
TAN
Brahmaputra
Chongqing
Luzhou
Hengyang
Ganzhou
Xiamen
Chilung
Taipei
TROPIC OF CANCER
A
YA
Guiyang
Panzhihua
Guilin
Shaoguan
Taichung
Taiwan Strait
DESH
Baoshan
Kaiyuan
Kunming
Guangzhou
Shantou
Tainan
Kaohsiung
TAIWAN
Irrawaddy
MYANMAR (BURMA)
Mekong
Hongshui
Nanning
Foshan
Macau
Shenzhen
Hong Kong
LAOS
VIETNAM
Beihai
Zhanjiang
Haikou
Gulf of Tonkin
HAINAN
Sanya
SOUTH CHINA SEA

The People's Republic of China claims Taiwan as its 23rd province. Taiwan maintains that there are two political entities.

◗ STANDING GUARD.
Lifelike terra-cotta statues formed part of the "army" buried in 141 B.C.E. with Han dynasty emperor Jing Di. The emperor believed the army, arranged in battle formation and facing enemy territory, would protect him after death.

Eastern Mediterranean

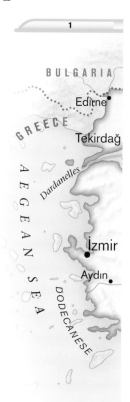

BULGARIA

Edirne

GREECE

Tekirdağ

AEGEAN SEA

Dardanelles

İzmir

Aydın

DODECANESE

THE BASICS

STATS

Largest country
Turkey
302,533 sq mi (783,562 sq km)

Smallest country
Lebanon
4,015 sq mi (10,400 sq km)

Most populous country
Turkey 80,845,000

Least populous country
Armenia 3,045,000

Predominant languages
Turkish, Arabic, Azerbaijani,
Hebrew, Georgian, Armenian,
English, French, Kurdish

Predominant religions
Islam, Judaism, Christianity

Highest GDP per capita
Israel $35,200

Lowest GDP per capita
Syria $2,900

Highest life expectancy
Israel 82 years

Lowest life expectancy
Azerbaijan 73 years

GEO WHIZ

Mount Ararat, near Turkey's
border with Iran and Armenia,
is believed by some to be the
resting place for the ark that—
according to the Bible—Noah
built to survive the great flood.

Israelis capture runoff from seasonal rains to support crops in
the Negev, a desert region that
extends across more than half
their country.

⊖ **ANCIENT MYSTERY.**
A camel walks past Al-Khazneh
in Petra, a World Heritage site
in Jordan. Carved out of the
mountainside more than 2,500
years ago, Petra was the capital
of the Nabateans.

This region forms a bridge between Europe and Asia, from the Caucasus Mountains to the desert lands of Jordan. Turkey, framed by the Black, Aegean, and Mediterranean Seas, leads the region in population and area. The historic and life-giving Tigris and Euphrates Rivers begin in Turkey and flow southeast through arid Syria and Iraq. Israel, Lebanon, Syria, and Turkey share the Mediterranean shore. While Islam claims the majority of followers across these lands, Judaism, Christianity, and other faiths are present. The holiest places to Christians and Jews occupy Israeli soil in Jerusalem, adjacent to the third holiest site for Muslims, which continues to cause tension and conflict.

BELOW SEA LEVEL

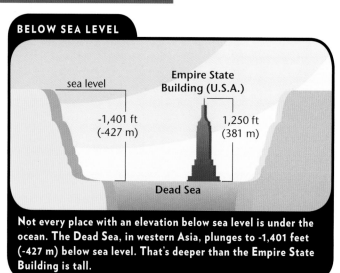

sea level

Empire State
Building (U.S.A.)

-1,401 ft
(-427 m)

1,250 ft
(381 m)

Dead Sea

Not every place with an elevation below sea level is under the
ocean. The Dead Sea, in western Asia, plunges to -1,401 feet
(-427 m) below sea level. That's deeper than the Empire State
Building is tall.

◖ **WATCHERS FROM THE PAST.** Giant stone heads, representing Greek gods, guard the first-century B.C.E. burial site of King Antiochus I in southeastern Turkey.

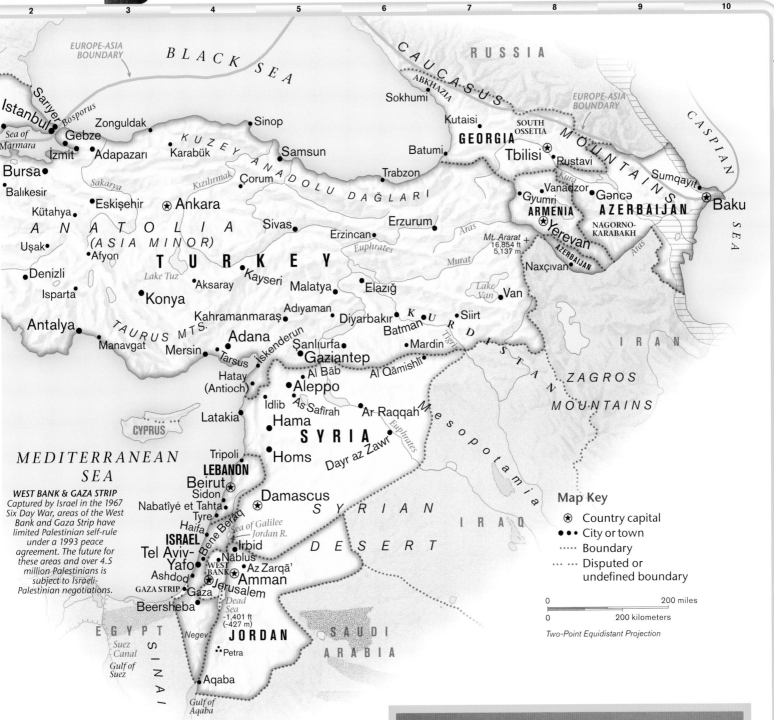

EUROPE-ASIA BOUNDARY

BLACK SEA

CAUCASUS

RUSSIA

Sarıyer
Istanbul
Sea of Marmara
Gebze
İzmit
Bursa
Adapazarı
Zonguldak
Karabük
Sinop
Samsun
Balıkesir
Sakarya
Kızılırmak
Çorum
Trabzon
Sokhumi
ABKHAZIA
Kutaisi
Batumi
SOUTH OSSETIA
GEORGIA
Tbilisi
Rustavi
Kura
Sumqayıt
CASPIAN SEA
Baku

Kütahya
Eskişehir
Ankara
Sivas
Erzurum
Aras
Gyumri
Vanadzor
Gəncə
ARMENIA
Yerevan
NAGORNO-KARABAKH
AZERBAIJAN

Uşak
ANATOLIA
(ASIA MINOR)
TURKEY
Erzincan
Murat
Mt. Ararat
16,854 ft
5,137 m
AZERBAIJAN
Aras

Afyon
Lake Tuz
Kayseri
Malatya
Elazığ
Lake Van
Van
Naxçıvan

Denizli
Isparta
Konya
Aksaray
Adıyaman
K U R D I S T A N
IRAN

Antalya
TAURUS MTS.
Kahramanmaraş
Diyarbakır
Batman
Siirt
ZAGROS MOUNTAINS

Manavgat
Adana
İskenderun
Şanlıurfa
Gaziantep
Mardin
Tigris

Mersin
Tarsus
Al Bāb
Al Qāmishlī
M e s o p o t a m i a

Hatay
(Antioch)
Aleppo
Idlib
As Safirah
Ar Raqqah
Euphrates

Latakia
CYPRUS
Hama
SYRIA
Dayr az Zawr

MEDITERRANEAN SEA
Tripoli
Homs

WEST BANK & GAZA STRIP
Captured by Israel in the 1967 Six Day War, areas of the West Bank and Gaza Strip have limited Palestinian self-rule under a 1993 peace agreement. The future for these areas and over 4.5 million Palestinians is subject to Israeli-Palestinian negotiations.

LEBANON
Beirut
Sidon
Nabatîyé et Tahta
Tyre
Bene Beraq
Damascus
S Y R I A N
D E S E R T
IRAQ

Haifa
Sea of Galilee
Jordan R.
ISRAEL
Tel Aviv-Yafo
Irbid
Nablus
WEST BANK
Az Zarqā'
Ashdod
Jerusalem
Amman
GAZA STRIP
Gaza
Dead Sea
-1,401 ft
(-427 m)
Beersheba

EGYPT
Negev
JORDAN
SAUDI ARABIA
S I N A I
Suez Canal
Gulf of Suez
Petra
Aqaba
Gulf of Aqaba

Map Key
⊛ Country capital
••• City or town
····· Boundary
·—·—· Disputed or undefined boundary

0 ——— 200 miles
0 ——— 200 kilometers
Two-Point Equidistant Projection

◖ **BETWEEN TWO WORLDS.** The Galata Bridge crosses the Golden Horn, connecting the Asian part of Istanbul, Turkey (foreground), to the Galata area in the city's European part.

◖ **SALTY EXTREME.** The land between Israel and Jordan plunges down to the surface of the Dead Sea. The water of the sea is almost six times saltier than the ocean.

Southwestern Asia

THE BASICS

STATS

Largest country
Saudi Arabia 829,995 sq mi
(2,149,690 sq km)

Smallest country
Bahrain 293 sq mi (760 sq km)

Most populous country
Iran 82,022,000

Least populous country
Bahrain 1,411,000

Predominant languages
Arabic, Persian (Farsi), Kurdish

Predominant religion
Islam

Highest GDP per capita
Qatar $127,700

Lowest GDP per capita
Yemen $2,400

Highest life expectancy
Bahrain, Qatar 79 years

Lowest life expectancy
Yemen 66 years

GEO WHIZ

The Rub' al Khali, or Empty Quarter, is the world's largest sand desert. It covers an area larger than France.

More than 4,000 years ago, the Sumerians built the world's first cities on the plain between the Tigris and Euphrates Rivers in what is now Iraq.

The ancient Romans called Yemen "Arabia Felix," meaning "Happy Arabia."

⬤ **GIRL TALK**. Young Iranian girls get together at a film festival in Tehran. The scarves they are wearing are part of the Islamic dress code, hijab, which says that women and girls must cover their heads and dress modestly.

This region, made up largely of deserts and mountains, includes the countries of the Arabian Peninsula and those that border the Persian Gulf. Islam is the dominant religion, and the two holiest places for Muslims—Mecca and Medina—are here. Arabic is the principal language everywhere but Iran, where most people speak Farsi. While water has been the most important natural resource here for millennia, global attention has focused in recent decades on the region's extensive oil reserves. Ongoing conflict and political tensions also have kept this region in headlines around the world.

⬤ **HE'S GOT THE BEAT.** This Omani drummer plays at a dance in the Arabian Sea port of Qurayyāt. Oman works hard to preserve its traditional culture.

⬤ **DIFFERENT WORLDS**. This roadside meeting in Qatar displays a contrast between horse and horsepower and between traditional Arab and Western clothing styles. Qatar has a rich history of Arabian horse breeding.

WORLD OIL RESERVES

Top world oil reserves by country, in billion barrels, 2015 data
(1 barrel = 42 gallons/159 liters)

- 298 Venezuela
- 268 Saudi Arabia
- 172 Canada
- 158 Iran
- 144 Iraq
- 104 Kuwait
- 98 United Arab Emirates
- 80 Russia
- 48 Libya

Saudi Arabia, second in oil reserves, and four other southwestern Asia countries account for almost 25 percent of all oil production.

LOST AND FOUND. Ancient treasures were destroyed, lost, or stolen during the 2003 invasion of Iraq. This ring is among the few items recovered.

BLACK SEA

GEORGIA

TURKEY

ARMENIA

AZERBAIJAN

CASPIAN
SEA

TURKMENISTAN

Tigris

KURDISTAN

L. Urmia

Orūmīyeh

Marand

Tabrīz

Ardabīl

Bojnūrd

Zākho

Dihok

Mīāndoāb

Rasht

Gorgān

Gondad-e
Kāvūs

Tall 'Afar

Nineveh

Zanjān

Sārī

Sabzevār

Mashhad

Mosul

Erbil

As
Sulaymānīyah

Qazvīn

Semnān

KHORĀSĀN

MEDITERRANEAN
SEA

Kirkuk

Kermānshāh

Sanandaj

Tehran

Kuh-e
Damāvand
18,605 ft
5,671 m

Dasht-e Kavir
(Kavir Desert)

Gonābad

SYRIA

Euphrates

Tikrīt

Hamadān

MESOPOTAMIA

ZAGROS

IRAN

Birjand

LEBANON

Sāmarrā

Arāk

Qom

ISRAEL

IRAQ

Baghdad

Isfahan

Dasht-e Lūt

Zābol

JORDAN

Turaybīl

Ar Ramādī

Al Fallūjah

Nippur

Dezfūl

Qomsheh

Yazd

Nosratābād

Karbalā

An Najaf

Al Hillah

Al 'Amārah

MOUNTAINS

Ahvāz

Kermān

Zāhedān

EGYPT

Al Quraiyāt

'Ar'ar

Ur

An Nāşirīyah

Al Başrah

Ābādān

Shīrāz

Persepolis

Marv
Dasht

Sa'īdābād

Bam

Gulf of
Aqaba

Tabūk

Al Jawf

Sakākā

Az Zubayr

KUWAIT

Būshehr

FĀRS

Jahrom

Fasā

Ţārom

Īrānshahr

An Nafūd

Kuwait
City

PERSIAN

BALUCHISTAN

Angohrān

PAKISTAN

Hā'il

Ad Dahnā

Al Jubayl

Bandar-e 'Abbās

Strait of
Hormuz

Qeshm

Chāh Bāhar

Buraydah

Ad Dammām

BAHRAIN

Ra's al-Khaimah

OMAN

AL HIJAZ

SAUDI

Manama

Al Mubarraz

GULF

Sharjah

GULF OF OMAN

Medina

Riyadh

Nafūd

Doha

Dubai

Suḩār

Al Hufūf

QATAR

Muscat

RED

Al Hillah

ARABIA

Abu Dhabi

Al Ain

UNITED ARAB
EMIRATES

TROPIC OF CANCER

'Ibrī

Qurayyāt

Nizwā

Sūr

Jeddah

ARABIAN

Al Ḩadīdah
×(meteorite craters)

OMAN

Mecca

Aţ Ţā'if

PENINSULA

Khalūf

SUDAN

SEA

Yanbu' al Bahr

Qal'at Bīshah

Jabal Tuwayq

Rub' al Khali
(Empty Quarter)

Duqm

Masira

Al Qunfudhah

ZUFĀR

ARABIAN

Abā as Sa'ūd

SEA

Jīzān

YEMEN

Mirbāţ

ERITREA

Al Hudaydah

Dhamār

Sanaa

Ridā

Ḩadramawt

Hawf

Nishtūn

Şalālah

Ta'izz

Ibb

Ash Shihr

Lahij

Al Mukallā

ETHIOPIA

Aden

Socotra
(Yemen)

DJIBOUTI

GULF OF ADEN

SOMALIA

Map Key

⊛ Country capital
••• City or town
····· Boundary

0 ——— 300 miles
0 ——— 300 kilometers

Two-Point Equidistant Projection

Southern Asia

THE BASICS

STATS

Largest country
India 1,269,212 sq mi
(3,287,263 sq km)

Smallest country
Maldives 115 sq mi (298 sq km)

Most populous country
India 1,281,936,000

Least populous country
Maldives 393,000

Predominant languages
Hindi, English, Punjabi, Bangla,
Dari, Burmese, Pashto, Urdu,
Sinhala, Nepali, Dzongkha

Predominant religions
Hinduism, Islam, Buddhism

Highest GDP per capita
Maldives $15,500

Lowest GDP per capita
Afghanistan $1,900

Highest life expectancy
Sri Lanka 77 years

Lowest life expectancy
Afghanistan 51 years

GEO WHIZ

India's rail system transports
8.4 billion passengers each
year across nearly 40,660 miles
(65,436 km) of track.

Bhutan, a Himalayan country
known as Land of the Thunder
Dragon, is the world's only
Buddhist kingdom.

⬤ **TAJ MAHAL.** In 1631 in Agra, India,
the Mughal emperor Shah Jehan began
construction of this magnificent marble
memorial to his deceased wife.

This region is home to the world's highest peaks. Three of the world's storied rivers—the Indus, Ganges, and Brahmaputra—support the hundreds of millions of people who live here. India is at the center, greater in area than the other countries combined and more than double their population. Hinduism and Buddhism originated in India where Hinduism continues to be the main religion. There are large numbers of Buddhists in Bhutan, Nepal, Sri Lanka, and Myanmar, and Muslims form the majority in Afghanistan, Pakistan, and Bangladesh. Poverty and prosperity live side by side across the region, with streams of migrants flowing from rural areas to mushrooming cities.

◑ **GOLDEN GRAIN.**
A man leads his
cow past a rice field
south of Rangpur,
Bangladesh. Rice is
the staple food for 158
million Bangladeshis
and provides employ-
ment for almost half
the rural population.

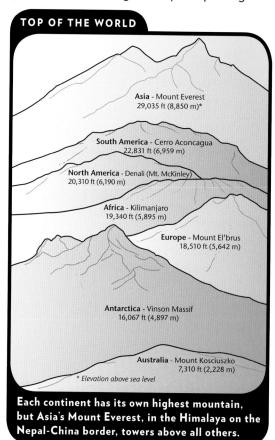

TOP OF THE WORLD

Asia - Mount Everest
29,035 ft (8,850 m)*

South America - Cerro Aconcagua
22,831 ft (6,959 m)

North America - Denali (Mt. McKinley)
20,310 ft (6,190 m)

Africa - Kilimanjaro
19,340 ft (5,895 m)

Europe - Mount El'brus
18,510 ft (5,642 m)

Antarctica - Vinson Massif
16,067 ft (4,897 m)

Australia - Mount Kosciuszko
7,310 ft (2,228 m)

* Elevation above sea level

**Each continent has its own highest mountain,
but Asia's Mount Everest, in the Himalaya on the
Nepal-China border, towers above all others.**

EASTERN BELIEF. The god Shiva (left) is part of the Hindu trinity, which also includes the gods Brahma and Vishnu. Hinduism is the world's third largest religion (after Christianity and Buddhism), with more than a billion followers.

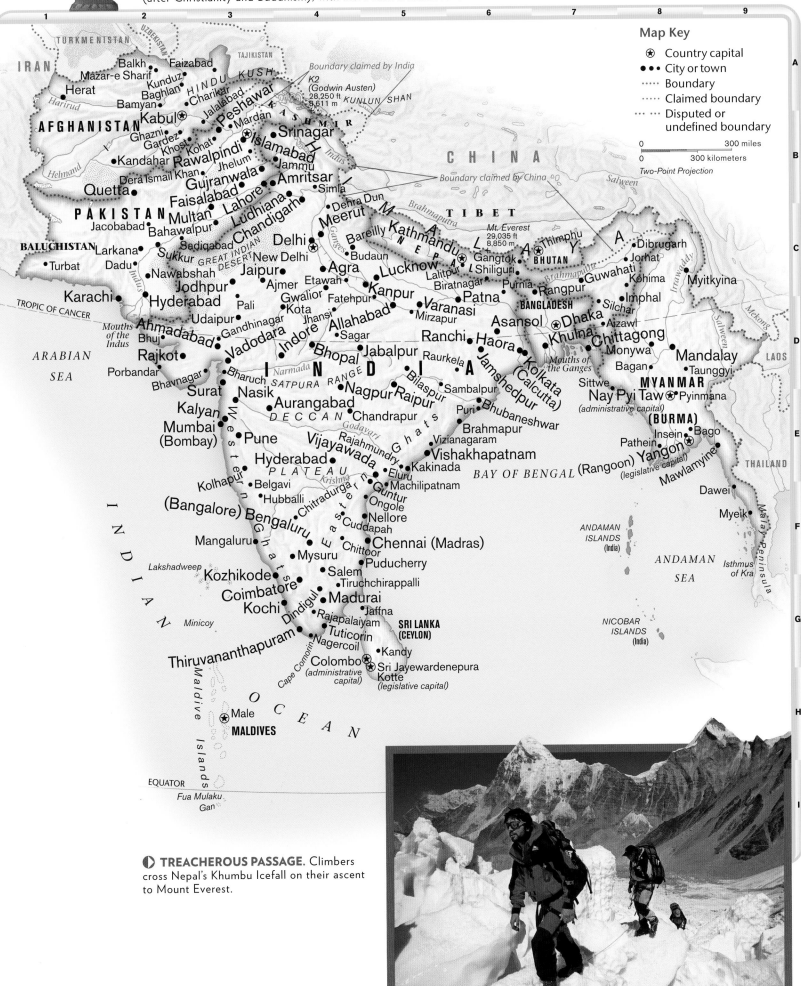

Map Key
★ Country capital
••• City or town
····· Boundary
····· Claimed boundary
····· Disputed or undefined boundary

0   300 miles
0   300 kilometers
Two-Point Projection

IRAN
TURKMENISTAN
UZBEKISTAN
TAJIKISTAN
Balkh
Faizabad
Mazar-e Sharif
Herat
Kunduz
Baghlan
Bamyan
HINDU KUSH
Charikar
Jalalabad
Boundary claimed by India
K2
(Godwin Austen)
28,250 ft
8,611 m
KUNLUN SHAN
Harirud
Kabul
AFGHANISTAN
Ghazni
Gardez
Khost
Kohat
Peshawar
Mardan
Srinagar
KASHMIR
CHINA
Helmand
Kandahar
Islamabad
Rawalpindi
Jhelum
Jammu
Simla
Boundary claimed by China
Salween
Dera Ismail Khan
Gujranwala
Amritsar
Quetta
Faisalabad
Lahore
Ludhiana
Dehra Dun
TIBET
Mt. Everest
29,035 ft
8,850 m
Thimphu
Dibrugarh
PAKISTAN
Multan
Chandigarh
Meerut
Bareilly
Kathmandu
BHUTAN
Jorhat
Jacobabad
Bahawalpur
Delhi
Budaun
Lucknow
Gangtok
Guwahati
Kohima
Myitkyina
BALUCHISTAN
Larkana
Sadiqabad
GREAT INDIAN
New Delhi
Lalitpur
Shiliguri
Brahmaputra
Turbat
Dadu
Sukkur
DESERT
Jaipur
Agra
Biratnagar
Purnia
Rangpur
Imphal
Nawabshah
Jodhpur
Ajmer
Etawah
Kanpur
Varanasi
Patna
Silchar
Karachi
Hyderabad
Pali
Gwalior
Fatehpur
Mirzapur
BANGLADESH
Dhaka
Aizawl
TROPIC OF CANCER
Udaipur
Kota
Jhansi
Allahabad
Sagar
Ranchi
Haora
Khulna
Chittagong
Mouths of the Indus
Gandhinagar
INDIA
Asansol
Monywa
ARABIAN
Ahmadabad
Bhuj
Vadodara
Indore
Bhopal
Jabalpur
Raurkela
Kolkata
(Calcutta)
Mouths of the Ganges
Bagan
Mandalay
LAOS
SEA
Rajkot
Narmada
SATPURA RANGE
Jamshedpur
Sittwe
Taunggyi
Porbandar
Bharuch
Nagpur
Bilaspur
Sambalpur
Puri
Bhubaneshwar
MYANMAR
Bhavnagar
Surat
Nasik
Aurangabad
Raipur
Brahmapur
Nay Pyi Taw
Pyinmana
Kalyan
DECCAN
Chandrapur
Godavari
Rajahmundry
Vizianagaram
(administrative capital)
Mumbai
(Bombay)
Pune
Vijayawada
Ghats
Vishakhapatnam
(BURMA)
Hyderabad
Eluru
Kakinada
Insein
Bago
PLATEAU
Krishna
Machilipatnam
BAY OF BENGAL
Pathein
Yangon
Kolhapur
Belgavi
Guntur
(Rangoon)
Mawlamyine
Hubballi
Chitradurga
Ongole
(legislative capital)
Mangaluru
Nellore
THAILAND
(Bangalore) Bengaluru
Cuddapah
Dawei
Eastern
Chittoor
Chennai (Madras)
ANDAMAN
ISLANDS
(India)
Myeik
Ghats
Mysuru
Puducherry
Lakshadweep
Kozhikode
Salem
Tiruchirappalli
ANDAMAN
SEA
Isthmus
of Kra
Coimbatore
Dindigul
Madurai
Kochi
Rajapalaiyam
Jaffna
INDIAN
Minicoy
Nagercoil
SRI LANKA
(CEYLON)
NICOBAR
ISLANDS
(India)
Thiruvananthapuram
Tuticorin
Cape Comorin
Colombo
(administrative capital)
Kandy
Sri Jayewardenepura Kotte
(legislative capital)
OCEAN
Maldive Islands
EQUATOR
Fua Mulaku
Gan
Male
MALDIVES
Malay Peninsula
Mekong
Irrawaddy

TREACHEROUS PASSAGE. Climbers cross Nepal's Khumbu Icefall on their ascent to Mount Everest.

THE CONTINENT:
ASIA

THE BASICS

STATS

Largest country
Thailand 198,116 sq mi
(513,120 sq km)

Smallest country
Singapore 269 sq mi
(697 sq km)

Most populous country
Philippines 104,256,000

Least populous country
Brunei 444,000

Predominant languages
Filipino (based on Tagalog),
English, Vietnamese, Thai,
Khmer, Lao, French, Malay,
Bahasa Melayu, Mandarin

Predominant religions
Christianity, Buddhism, Islam

Highest GDP per capita
Singapore $87,900

Lowest GDP per capita
Cambodia $3,700

Highest life expectancy
Singapore 85 years

Lowest life expectancy
Laos 64 years

GEO WHIZ

The Philippines has one of the
world's highest rates of deforestation. Studies estimate that,
based on current removal rates,
the country's virgin forests are in
danger of disappearing as soon
as 2025.

Thailand means "Land of the
Free." It is the only country in
southeastern Asia never ruled by
a colonial power.

The Plain of Jars, in northern Laos, takes its name from
hundreds of huge stone urns
spread across the ground.
Archaeologists believe Bronze
Age people made the jars and
used then to hold the cremated
remains of their dead.

Southeastern Asia

The countries of southeastern Asia have long been influenced by neighboring giants India and China. The result is a dazzling mix of cultures, rich histories, terrible conflicts, and future promise. Cambodia's spectacular 12th-century Angkor Wat provides a glimpse of former greatness. Colonial rule brought division and change, and struggles for independence took a heavy toll, as in Vietnam. Mainland countries are largely Buddhist, whereas peninsular Malaysia is mostly Muslim, and Christians dominate the Philippines. All but Laos have ocean access, with fisheries providing jobs and food for millions. Rivers like the Chao Phraya and the mighty Mekong provide transport and water-rich croplands dominated by rice growing. Tiny Singapore has gained global importance with its bustling port operations and high-tech focus.

SMILING BUDDHA.
A Buddhist monk admires a
sculpture in Cambodia's Angkor
temple complex. Built by the
Khmer between 800 and 1200
C.E., the complex includes
Buddhist and Hindu temples.

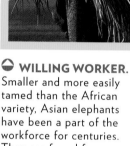

WILLING WORKER.
Smaller and more easily
tamed than the African
variety, Asian elephants
have been a part of the
workforce for centuries.
They are found from
India to Indonesia.

SHIPPING HUB.
Huge container terminals, such
as this one at Tanjong Pagar,
make Singapore the world's
busiest transshipment center,
connected to 600 ports in 123
countries around the world.

FLASHY RIDE. Colorful Philippine taxis, called jeepneys because of their origin as rebuilt World War II jeeps, are a common sight on the streets of Manila.

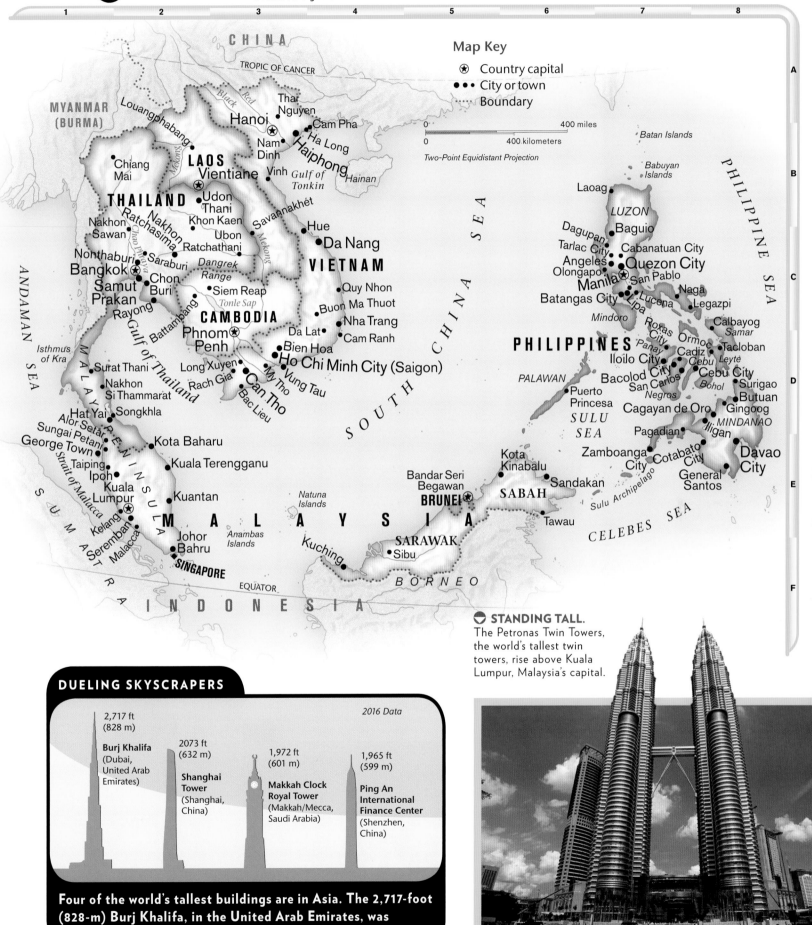

Map Key
✷ Country capital
••• City or town
•••• Boundary

CHINA
TROPIC OF CANCER

MYANMAR
(BURMA)

Louangphabang

Hanoi
Thai Nguyen
Cam Pha
Ha Long
Nam Dinh
Haiphong
Vinh Gulf of Tonkin
Hainan

LAOS
Vientiane
Chiang Mai

THAILAND
Udon Thani
Khon Kaen
Ubon Ratchathani
Savannakhet

Nakhon Sawan
Ratchasima
Nakhon Ratchasima
Nonthaburi
Saraburi
Bangkok
Samut Prakan
Chon Buri
Rayong

Hue
Da Nang

VIETNAM

Dangrek Range
Siem Reap
Tonle Sap
CAMBODIA
Phnom Penh
Battambang

Quy Nhon
Buon Ma Thuot
Nha Trang
Da Lat
Cam Ranh
Bien Hoa
Ho Chi Minh City (Saigon)
Vung Tau

Long Xuyen
Rach Gia
Can Tho
My Tho
Bac Lieu

Isthmus of Kra

Surat Thani
Nakhon Si Thammarat
Hat Yai
Songkhla

Alor Setar
Sungai Petani
George Town
Taiping
Ipoh
Kuala Lumpur
Kelang
Seremban
Malacca
Johor Bahru

Kota Baharu
Kuala Terengganu
Kuantan

MALAYSIA

Natuna Islands
Anambas Islands
Kuching
SARAWAK
Sibu

Gulf of Thailand

MALAY PENINSULA

Strait of Malacca

SINGAPORE
EQUATOR

ANDAMAN SEA

SUMATRA
INDONESIA

SOUTH CHINA SEA

Batan Islands
Babuyan Islands

Laoag
LUZON
Dagupan
Baguio
Tarlac City
Cabanatuan City
Angeles
Quezon City
Olongapo
Manila
San Pablo
Batangas City
Lipa
Lucena
Naga
Legazpi
Mindoro
Roxas City
Panay
Calbayog
Samar
Ormoc
Cadiz
Tacloban
PHILIPPINES
Iloilo City
Cebu
Leyte
Bacolod City
Cebu City
San Carlos
Bohol
Surigao
Negros
Butuan
PALAWAN
Cagayan de Oro
Gingoog
Puerto Princesa
Iligan
SULU SEA
MINDANAO
Pagadian
Zamboanga City
Cotabato City
Davao City
General Santos
Kota Kinabalu
Sandakan
Sulu Archipelago
SABAH
Tawau
CELEBES SEA

Bandar Seri Begawan
BRUNEI

BORNEO

PHILIPPINE SEA

Two-Point Equidistant Projection
0   400 miles
0   400 kilometers

STANDING TALL.
The Petronas Twin Towers, the world's tallest twin towers, rise above Kuala Lumpur, Malaysia's capital.

DUELING SKYSCRAPERS

2016 Data

2,717 ft (828 m)
Burj Khalifa (Dubai, United Arab Emirates)

2073 ft (632 m)
Shanghai Tower (Shanghai, China)

1,972 ft (601 m)
Makkah Clock Royal Tower (Makkah/Mecca, Saudi Arabia)

1,965 ft (599 m)
Ping An International Finance Center (Shenzhen, China)

Four of the world's tallest buildings are in Asia. The 2,717-foot (828-m) Burj Khalifa, in the United Arab Emirates, was completed in 2010.

THE CONTINENT:
ASIA

THE BASICS

STATS

Largest country
Indonesia 735,354 sq mi
(1,904,569 sq km)

Smallest country
Timor-Leste 5,743 sq mi
(14,874 sq km)

Most populous country
Indonesia 260,581,000

Least populous country
Timor-Leste 1,291,000

Predominant languages
Indonesian, English, Dutch,
Javanese, Tetum, Portuguese

Predominant religions
Islam, Christianity

Highest GDP per capita
Indonesia $11,700

Lowest GDP per capita
Timor-Leste $4,200

Highest life expectancy
Indonesia 73 years

Lowest life expectancy
Timor-Leste 68 years

GEO WHIZ

In 2006, two species of sharks
that use their fins to "walk"
on coral reefs were discovered
off the northwestern coast of
Indonesia's Papua province.

When seen from the air, Timor
Island resembles a crocodile.
According to local legend, a crocodile turned itself into the island
as a way of saying thank you to a
boy who saved its life.

Komodo dragons, the world's
heaviest lizard, live only on
Indonesia's Lesser Sunda Islands.
They eat all types of prey—even
people sometimes!

◗ **CITY ON THE MOVE.**
Skyscrapers and a busy freeway
are just one face of Jakarta,
Indonesia's national capital and
center of trade and industry. In
this city of more than 10 million
people, the modern and traditional, the rich and poor, live side
by side. Like the country, the city
has a very diverse population.

Indonesia & Timor-Leste

Stretching more than 2,200 miles (3,520 km) from Sumatra to New Guinea, Indonesia is the world's larg- est island nation and the fourth most populous country. Most of its 261 million people live on the volcani- cally active island of Java. Indonesia shares rain-forested Borneo with Malaysia and Brunei. Most Indonesians are of Malay ethnicity, though there are large numbers of Melanesians (see page 154), Chinese, and East Indians. Arab traders brought Islam to the islands in the 13th century, and today six of seven Indonesians are Muslim. Timor- Leste gained independence from Indonesia in 2002. It and the Philippines are Asia's only mainly Catholic countries.

◗ **PROUD CITIZEN.**
A young boy smiles broadly
as he waves the flag of Timor-
Leste (also known as East
Timor) in Díli, the capital city.

◐ SPIRIT WORLD. Masks, such as this one from Bali, Indonesia, were probably originally created for traditional dance and storytelling rituals.

◐ GIANT APE. This adult male Borneo orangutan is a critically endangered species found in the wild only on Sumatra and Borneo. This species is the world's largest tree-living mammal.

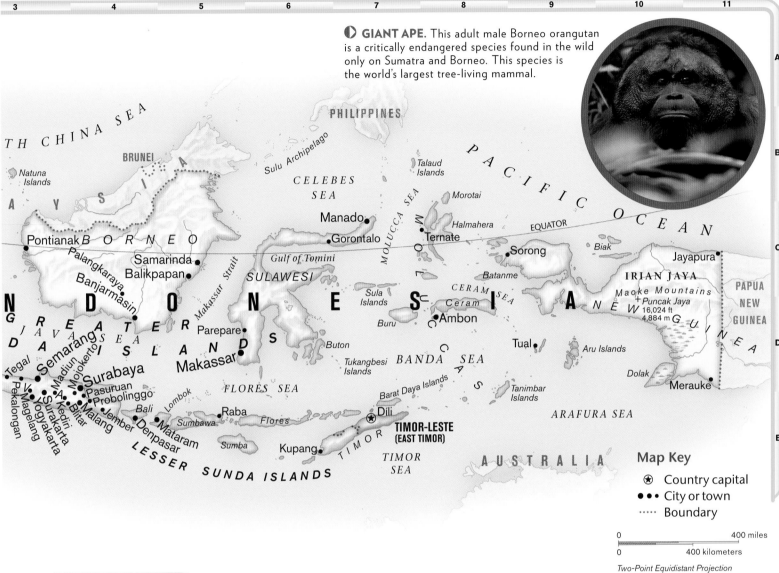

Map Key
* ⊛ Country capital
* ••• City or town
* ······ Boundary

0   400 miles
0   400 kilometers

Two-Point Equidistant Projection

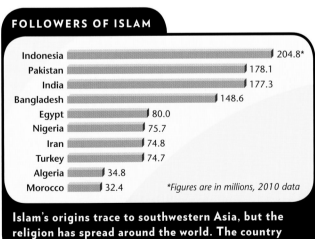

FOLLOWERS OF ISLAM

Country	Millions
Indonesia	204.8*
Pakistan	178.1
India	177.3
Bangladesh	148.6
Egypt	80.0
Nigeria	75.7
Iran	74.8
Turkey	74.7
Algeria	34.8
Morocco	32.4

*Figures are in millions, 2010 data

Islam's origins trace to southwestern Asia, but the religion has spread around the world. The country with the largest Muslim population is Indonesia.

◐ GENETIC STOREHOUSE. Only about 33 percent of Indonesia's Kalimantan Province in eastern Borneo remains covered in rain forest, which is home to many rare species. Forest loss is a result of activities such as logging and road building that are a consequence of the spread of plantation agriculture, especially oil palm cultivation.

PHYSICAL

POLITICAL

TOTAL AREA	**LOWEST POINT**	**LARGEST LAKE**	**POPULATION**	**LARGEST COUNTRY**
11,608,000 sq mi	Lake Assal, Djibouti	Victoria	1,215,763,000	Algeria
(30,065,000 sq km)	-509 ft (-155 m)	26,800 sq mi (69,500 sq km)		919,590 sq mi (2,381,741 sq km)
			LARGEST METROPOLITAN AREA	
			Lagos, Nigeria	
HIGHEST POINT	**LONGEST RIVER**		Pop. 13,661,000	**MOST DENSELY POPULATED COUNTRY**
Kilimanjaro, Tanzania	Nile			Mauritius
19,340 ft (5,895 m)	4,400 mi (7,081 km)			1721.3 people per sq mi (664.9 per sq km)

AFRICA

Africa

2 3 4 5 6 7 8

A

EUROPE

Azores

B

M E D I T E R R A N E A N   S E A

Strait of Gibraltar

Madeira Islands

MOROCCO

A T L A S   M O U N T A I N S

TUNISIA

Suez Canal

A S I A

Canary Islands

C

TROPIC OF CANCER

WESTERN SAHARA
(Morocco)

A L G E R I A

L I B Y A

EGYPT

Sinai

R E D   S E A

Lake Nasser

Ahaggar Mts.

Libyan Desert

CABO VERDE

D

MAURITANIA

S   A   H   A   R   A

Aïr Massif

Tibesti Mts.

NIGER

CHAD

Lake Chad

SUDAN

Nile

Blue Nile

White Nile

ERITREA

Danakil

DJIBOUTI

Gulf of Aden

Lowest point in Africa

Lake Assal
-509 ft
-155 m

Lake Tana

Cape Verde

SENEGAL

GAMBIA

Senegal

M A L I

Niger

GUINEA-BISSAU

BURKINA FASO

S   A   H   E   L

GUINEA

SIERRA LEONE

LIBERIA

CÔTE D'IVOIRE
(IVORY COAST)

U P P E R   G U I N E A

GHANA

TOGO

BENIN

NIGERIA

CENTRAL AFRICAN REPUBLIC

SOUTH SUDAN

ETHIOPIA

SOMALIA

E

Gulf of Guinea

EQUATORIAL GUINEA

SAO TOME & PRINCIPE

CAMEROON

Congo

C O N G O

UGANDA

Lake Turkana
(Lake Rudolf)

KENYA

EQUATOR

A T L A N T I C

GABON

*Cabinda
(Angola)*

L O W E R   G U I N E A

C O N G O

B A S I N

DEMOCRATIC REPUBLIC
OF THE CONGO

Virunga Mts.
14,787 ft
4,507 m

RWANDA

BURUNDI

Lake Victoria

Kilimanjaro
19,340 ft
5,895 m

Highest point in Africa

F

Ascension

TANZANIA

Lake Tanganyika

G R E A T   R I F T   V A L L E Y

SEYCHELLES

O C E A N

KATANGA PLATEAU

Lake Nyasa
(Lake Malawi)

COMOROS

G

St. Helena

ANGOLA

L O W E R   G U I N E A

ZAMBIA

MALAWI

MOZAMBIQUE

Mozambique Channel

MADAGASCAR

I N D I A N

Zambezi

ZIMBABWE

Victoria Falls

MAURITIUS

Réunion

TROPIC OF CAPRICORN

NAMIBIA

Namib Desert

BOTSWANA

KALAHARI DESERT

O C E A N

H

Map Key

——— Country boundary

- - - Disputed or undefined boundary

SOUTH AFRICA

SWAZILAND

Orange

LESOTHO

Drakensberg

0   600 miles

0   600 kilometers

Cape of Good Hope

Cape Agulhas

I

Azimuthal Equidistant Projection

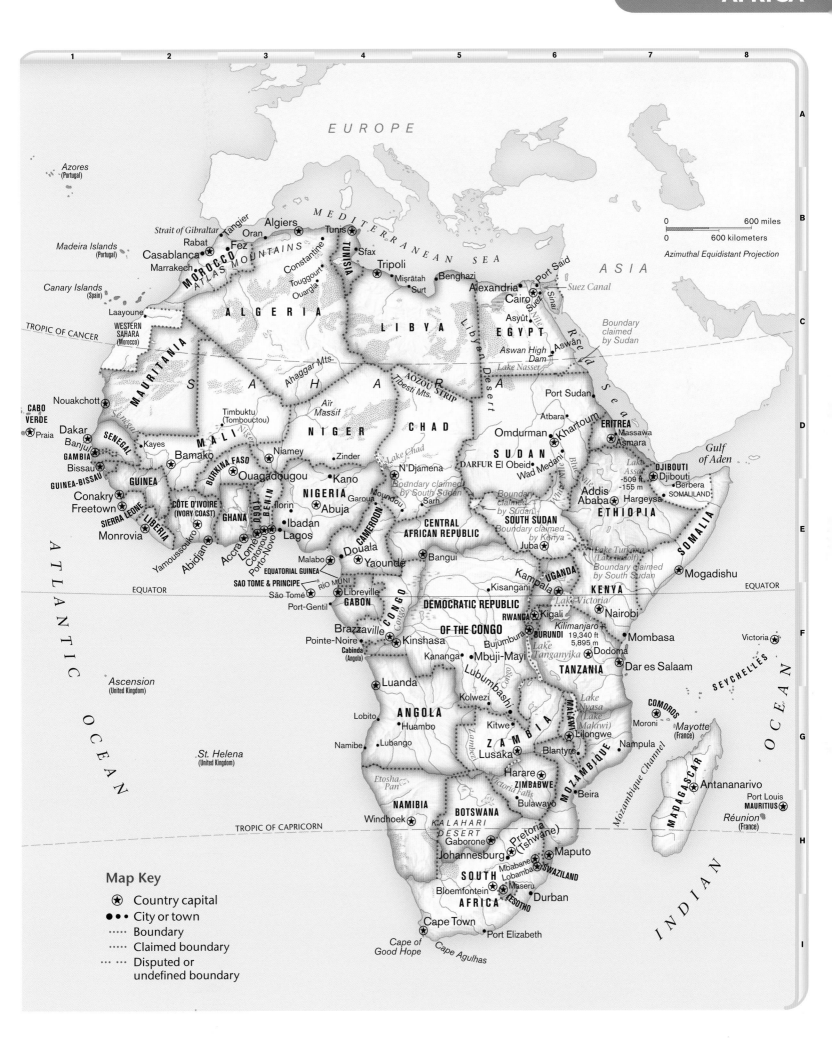

EUROPE

Azores
(Portugal)

Madeira Islands
(Portugal)

Canary Islands
(Spain)

Strait of Gibraltar Tangier
Rabat   Oran   Algiers
Casablanca   Fez
Marrakech

Tunis
Sfax
Tripoli
Mişrātah   Surt   Benghazi

MEDITERRANEAN SEA

Port Said
Alexandria
Cairo
Suez Canal

ASIA

TROPIC OF CANCER

WESTERN
SAHARA
(Morocco)
Laayoune

MOROCCO   ATLAS MOUNTAINS   Constantine
Touggourt
Ouargla

TUNISIA

ALGERIA

LIBYA

Libyan Desert

EGYPT

Asyût

Aswan High
Dam   Aswân
Lake Nasser

Red Sea

Boundary
claimed
by Sudan

Ahaggar Mts.
AOZOU
STRIP   Tibesti Mts.

Aïr
Massif

CABO
VERDE

Nouakchott

MAURITANIA

Praia

Dakar
Banjul
GAMBIA
Bissau
GUINEA-BISSAU

SENEGAL
Kayes

Timbuktu
(Tombouctou)

MALI
Bamako

NIGER
Niamey

Zinder

CHAD
N'Djamena

Lake Chad

Port Sudan

Atbara

Omdurman   Khartoum
SUDAN
DARFUR   El Obeid
Wad Medani

ERITREA
Massawa
Asmara

DJIBOUTI
Djibouti   Berbera
SOMALILAND

Gulf
of Aden

Lake
Assal
-509 ft
-155 m

Conakry
Freetown
GUINEA

SIERRA LEONE

Monrovia

LIBERIA

BURKINA FASO
Ouagadougou

CÔTE D'IVOIRE
(IVORY COAST)
Yamoussoukro
Abidjan

GHANA
Accra
Lomé
Cotonou
Porto-Novo

TOGO
BENIN

Ilorin
Ibadan
Lagos

NIGERIA
Kano

Abuja

Garoua

Moundou
Sarh

Boundary claimed
by South Sudan

CENTRAL
AFRICAN REPUBLIC

Boundary
claimed
by Sudan

SOUTH SUDAN
Juba

Boundary claimed
by Kenya

Addis
Ababa   Hargeysa

ETHIOPIA

SOMALIA

Mogadishu

EQUATOR

Malabo
EQUATORIAL GUINEA

SAO TOME & PRINCIPE
São Tomé

RIO MUNI

Douala
Yaoundé
CAMEROON

Bangui

Kampala
UGANDA
Kisangani

Lake Turkana
(Lake Rudolf)

Boundary claimed
by South Sudan

KENYA
Nairobi

EQUATOR

Libreville
Port-Gentil
GABON

CONGO
Brazzaville

DEMOCRATIC REPUBLIC

OF THE CONGO

RWANDA   Kigali
BURUNDI
Bujumbura

Lake Victoria

Kilimanjaro
19,340 ft
5,895 m

Mombasa

Victoria

SEYCHELLES

ATLANTIC OCEAN

Ascension
(United Kingdom)

Pointe-Noire
Cabinda
(Angola)
Kinshasa
Kananga   Mbuji-Mayi

Lake
Tanganyika

Dodoma
TANZANIA
Dar es Salaam

Luanda

Kolwezi

Lubumbashi

ANGOLA

Lobito

Namibe   Lubango

Huambo

Kitwe

ZAMBIA
Lusaka

Lake
Nyasa
(Lake
Malawi)

MALAWI
Lilongwe

Blantyre

Moroni

COMOROS

Mayotte
(France)

Nampula

MADAGASCAR

Antananarivo

Port Louis
MAURITIUS

St. Helena
(United Kingdom)

Etosha
Pan

Zambezi

Victoria Falls
Harare
ZIMBABWE
Bulawayo

Beira

MOZAMBIQUE

Mozambique Channel

Réunion
(France)

TROPIC OF CAPRICORN

NAMIBIA

Windhoek

KALAHARI
DESERT

BOTSWANA
Gaborone

Pretoria
(Tshwane)
Johannesburg
Maputo

Mbabane
Lobamba   SWAZILAND
Maseru
LESOTHO

INDIAN OCEAN

Bloemfontein

SOUTH
AFRICA

Durban

Cape Town
Port Elizabeth
Cape of
Good Hope   Cape Agulhas

Map Key

⭐ Country capital
●●● City or town
····· Boundary
····· Claimed boundary
····· Disputed or
undefined boundary

Africa

A COMPLEX GIANT

FASHION STATEMENT. Maasai women in Kenya adorn themselves with distinctive, colorful bead jewelry.

Africa spans nearly as far west to east as it does north to south. The Sahara—the world's largest hot desert—covers Africa's northern third, while to the south lie bands of grassland, tropical rain forest, and more desert. The East African Rift system marks where shifting tectonic plates are splitting off the continent's edge. Africa has a wealth of cultures, speaking some 1,600 languages—more than on any other continent. Though the continent is still largely rural, Africans increasingly migrate to booming cities like Lagos, Cairo, and Johannesburg. Despite rich natural resources, ranging from oil and coal to gemstones and precious metals, Africa is the poorest continent, long plagued by outside interference, corruption, and disease.

CHARGE! Sensing danger, an African elephant charges. The world's largest land mammal, African elephants are at risk due to poaching and loss of habitat.

COLORFUL NEIGHBORHOOD. South Africa's Bo-Kaap once was known as the Malay Quarter because of its early settlers. Dating to the 18th century, this multicultural suburb overlooks Cape Town's city center.

AFRICAN SAVANNA. Zebras graze on the tall grasses of the Serengeti Plain, in eastern Africa. Each year more than 200,000 zebras migrate through the Serengeti, following the seasonal rains.

CRYSTAL WATERS. A snorkeler swims in the clear blue waters off the Seychelles, one of Africa's island countries. Made up of 116 granite and coral islands, it lies about 1,000 miles (1,600 km) east of Kenya.

FREE RIDE.
A woman in Kumasi, Ghana, goes about her daily chores with her infant wrapped snugly on her back in a colorful cloth.

more about
Africa

◗ **WORSHIPPERS IN THE DESERT.** Muslim faithful gather before the Great Mosque in Mopti, Mali. An earthen structure typical of Muslim architecture in Africa's Sahel, the mosque was built between 1936 and 1943.

◗ **WINDOW ON THE PAST.** Traditional Egyptian sailing vessels called feluccas skim along the Nile River below the ruins at Qubbat al-Hawa. Tombs from ancient Egypt's 6th dynasty are carved into the hillside.

◗ **MODERN SKYLINE.** Established in 1899 as a railway supply depot, Nairobi, Kenya, is now one of Africa's most modern cities. In Maasai, an indigenous language, the name means "place of cold water."

◐ **TALL LOAD.** A woman carries a stack of brightly dyed cotton cloth, called wax prints, through a market in Lomé, Togo.

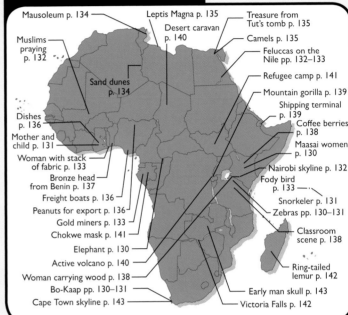

WHERE THE PICTURES ARE

Mausoleum p. 134
Leptis Magna p. 135
Treasure from Tut's tomb p. 135
Desert caravan p. 140
Muslims praying p. 132
Camels p. 135
Feluccas on the Nile pp. 132–133
Sand dunes p. 134
Refugee camp p. 141
Mountain gorilla p. 139
Shipping terminal p. 139
Coffee berries p. 138
Dishes p. 136
Maasai women p. 130
Mother and child p. 131
Nairobi skyline p. 132
Woman with stack of fabric p. 133
Fody bird p. 133
Bronze head from Benin p. 137
Snorkeler p. 131
Freight boats p. 136
Zebras pp. 130–131
Peanuts for export p. 136
Gold miners p. 133
Classroom scene p. 138
Chokwe mask p. 141
Elephant p. 130
Active volcano p. 140
Ring-tailed lemur p. 142
Woman carrying wood p. 138
Bo-Kaap pp. 130–131
Early man skull p. 143
Cape Town skyline p. 143
Victoria Falls p. 142

◒ **DIGGING FOR GOLD.** Miners dig a pit mine near the edge of the rain forest in Gabon. Oil and mineral extraction is an important part of the country's economy. While searching for traces of gold, however, they expose the fragile soil to erosion.

◒ **TROPICAL JEWEL.** A ruby red fody perches on a forest branch on Mahé Island in the Seychelles. Native to neighboring Madagascar, the fody eats seeds and insects.

THE BASICS

STATS

Largest country
Algeria 919,590 sq mi
(2,381,741 sq km)

Smallest country
Tunisia 63,170 sq mi
(163,610 sq km)

Most populous country
Egypt 97,041,000

Least populous country
Libya 6,653,000

Predominant languages
Arabic, French,
indigenous languages

Predominant religions
Islam, indigenous beliefs

Highest GDP per capita
Algeria $15,000

Lowest GDP capita
Morocco $8,300

Highest life expectancy
Algeria, Libya, Morocco 77 years

Lowest life expectancy
Egypt 73 years

GEO WHIZ

Ibn Battuta, who was born in
Tangier, Morocco, in 1304, set off
on a pilgrimage to Mecca that
turned into a 29-year, 75,000-
mile (120,675-km) journey that
took him from the Middle East
to India, China, the East Indies,
and back home.

Egypt's Aswan High Dam, which
forms Lake Nasser, produces up
to 10 billion kilowatt hours of
electricity every year and provides
water for farms along the Nile in
years of drought.

Kairouan, Tunisia, is considered
to be Islam's fourth holiest
city after Mecca, Medina, and
Jerusalem.

Northern Africa

This region, which is made up of five countries, stretches from the Atlantic Ocean in the west to the Red Sea in the east. To the north the region is bounded by the Mediterranean Sea, while to the south lies the vast dry expanse of the Sahara. The world's longest river—the Nile—winds northward through Egypt, but most of the region is arid—meaning there is too little moisture to support trees or extensive vegetation. Most of the region's population lives in coastal areas or in the fertile valley of the Nile River. In recent years, the region has experienced widespread instability as a result of tensions between conservative Islamic groups and more liberal groups seeking modernization and democratic rule.

SEA OF SAND. Towering dunes as well as barren, rocky expanses define Earth's largest hot desert—the Sahara, which separates northern Africa from the rest of the continent.

LEADER REMEMBERED. Arab influence in northern Africa is reflected in the dramatic mausoleum of Tunisia's first president, Habib Bourguiba, in the coastal town of Monastir. Bourguiba led Tunisia's fight for independence from French colonial rule. Independence was won in 1956.

SPIRIT OF THE PAST. This gold hawk pendant, found in the tomb of King Tut, may represent Horus, one of the oldest Egyptian gods.

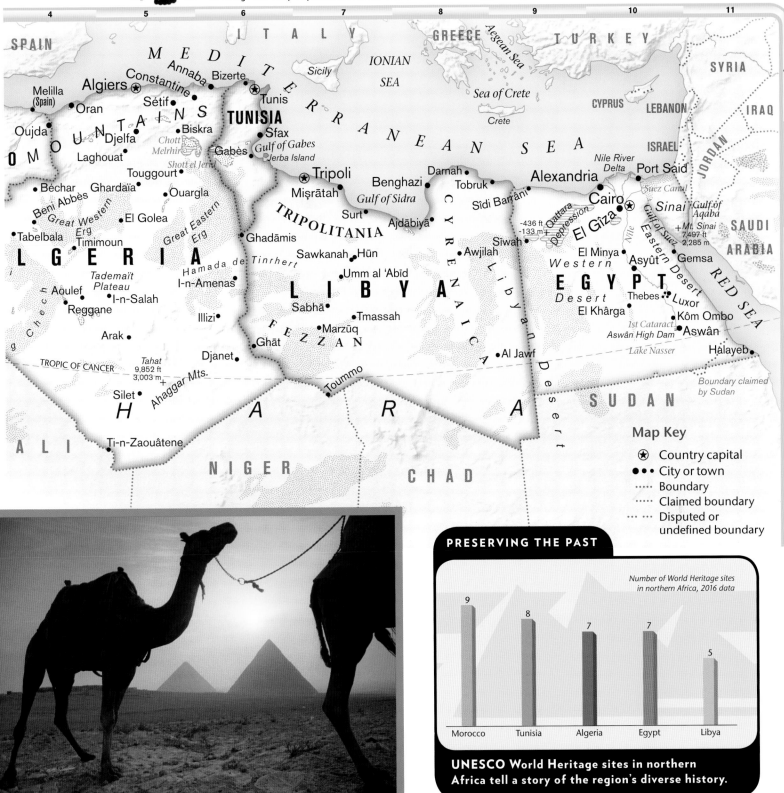

Map Key
- ★ Country capital
- ••• City or town
- ⋯⋯ Boundary
- ⋯⋯ Claimed boundary
- — — Disputed or undefined boundary

SYMBOLS OF ANCIENT EGYPT.
Camels plod through the desert as the sun sets behind the ancient pyramids of Giza. Built 4,500 years ago, the pyramids were monumental tombs of pharaohs, rulers of ancient Egypt.

PRESERVING THE PAST

Number of World Heritage sites in northern Africa, 2016 data

Morocco	Tunisia	Algeria	Egypt	Libya
9	8	7	7	5

UNESCO World Heritage sites in northern Africa tell a story of the region's diverse history.

COMPLEX CULTURE.
Leptis Magna, a World Heritage site in Libya, was founded in the seventh century B.C.E. and became a major trade center. Following Roman and later Arab conquests, it fell into ruin.

AFRICA

THE BASICS

STATS

Largest country
Niger 489,189 sq miles
(1,267,000 sq km)

Smallest country
Cabo Verde 1,557 sq miles
(4,033 sq km)

Most populous country
Nigeria 190,632,000

Least populous country
Cabo Verde 561,000

Predominant languages
French, English, Portuguese, Arabic, Spanish, indigenous languages

Predominant religions
Islam, Christianity, indigenous beliefs

Highest GDP per capita
Cabo Verde $6,700

Lowest GDP per capita
Liberia $900

Highest life expectancy
Cabo Verde 72 years

Lowest life expectancy
Guinea-Bissau 51 years

GEO WHIZ

For more than 300 years, the Slave House on Senegal's Gorée Island served as a holding pen for slaves before they were sent to the Americas and elsewhere. Today, it is a museum and a memorial.

Nigeria is a major producer and exporter of oil. Port Harcourt, in the Niger River delta, is the center of the country's oil industry.

Western Africa

Stretching from Cabo Verde in the west (inset, opposite), Mauritania in the northwest, and the barren Sahara in the north, to Nigeria in the southeast, 16 countries make up western Africa. Three countries —

RIVER TRANSPORT. Traditional river boats are an important link in the movement of cargo and people along the Niger River.

Burkina Faso, Mali, and Niger—are landlocked. The remaining 13 have coastlines along the Atlantic Ocean or the Gulf of Guinea. Early kingdoms thrived in Mali, Ghana, and Benin, but European colonization disrupted traditional societies and economies, and left a legacy of political turmoil. Today, the countries are independent, but widespread use of French and English reflects the region's colonial past. Reliance on agriculture plus falling global oil prices have left the region with a struggling economy.

WAITING FOR SHIPMENT. Sacks of peanuts create an artificial mountain in Kano, Nigeria, where they wait for transport to Lagos and then export to world markets. Nigeria produces more than half of the region's peanut crop.

FULL OF COLOR. Artistic ceramic plates brighten an outdoor marketplace in Kumasi, Ghana. This country has a long and rich cultural tradition of creating pottery for cooking and for serving food and water.

◑ **MASTER ARTISANS.** The ancient African kingdom of Benin produced outstanding bronze work. Each piece was created to honor the king.

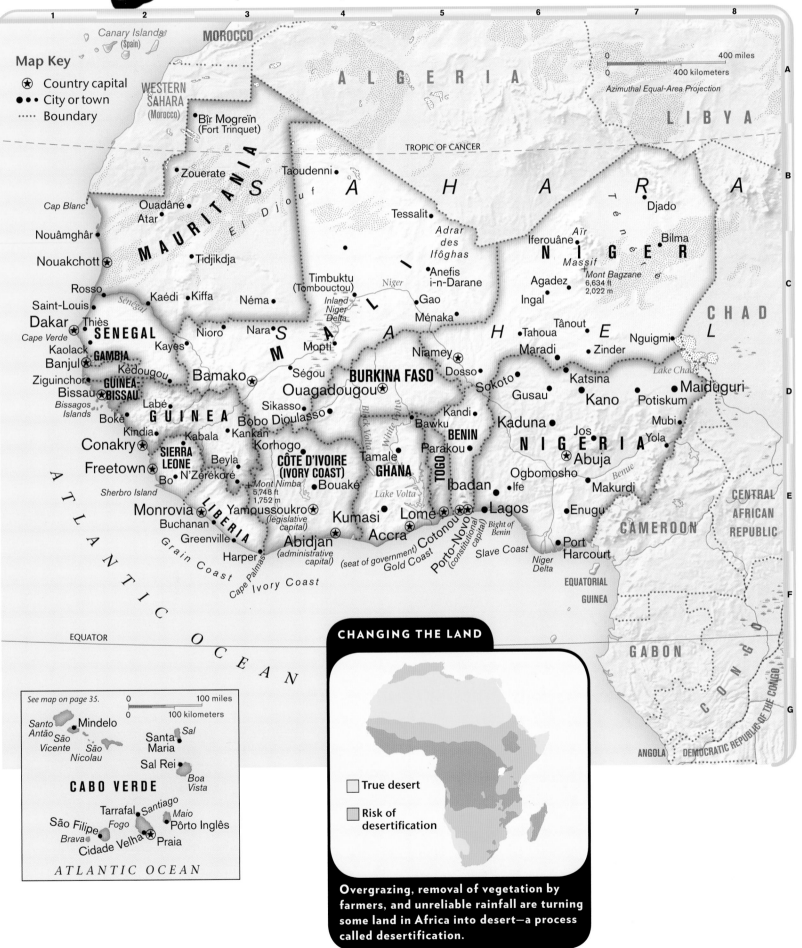

Map Key

⊛ Country capital
•• City or town
···· Boundary

0 ————— 400 miles
0 ————— 400 kilometers
Azimuthal Equal-Area Projection

MOROCCO

Canary Islands
(Spain)

WESTERN
SAHARA
(Morocco)

ALGERIA

LIBYA

TROPIC OF CANCER

Bîr Mogreïn
(Fort Trinquet)

Zouerate

Taoudenni

S   A   H   A   R   A

Djado

Cap Blanc

Ouadâne
Atar

Tessalit

Iferouâne
Aïr
Massif

Bilma

Ténéré

Nouâmghâr

MAURITANIA

Tidjikdja

Adrar
des
Ifôghas

NIGER

Agadez
Ingal

Mont Bagzane
6,634 ft
2,022 m

Nouakchott ⊛

El Djouf

Anefis
i-n-Darane

Niger

CHAD

Rosso

Kaédi Kiffa

Néma

Timbuktu
(Tombouctou)

Gao

Ménaka

Tânout

Nguigmi

Saint-Louis

Sénégal

Kayes

Nioro

Nara

Inland
Niger
Delta

M   A   L   I

Tahoua

Maradi

Zinder

Lake Chad

Dakar

Thiès

SENEGAL

Kaolack

GAMBIA

Banjul

Ziguinchor

GUINEA-
BISSAU

Bissau ⊛

Bissagos
Islands

Boké

Kédougou

Kayes

Labé

Bamako ⊛

Ségou

Mopti

Niamey ⊛

Dosso

Sokoto

Gusau

Katsina

Kano

Maiduguri

Potiskum

Mubi

BURKINA FASO

Ouagadougou ⊛

Sikasso

Bobo Dioulasso

Kandi

Bawku

Kaduna

Jos

Yola

GUINEA

Kindia

Kabala

Kankan

Korhogo

Black Volta

White Volta

BENIN

Parakou

NIGERIA

Abuja ⊛

Conakry ⊛

SIERRA
LEONE

Beyla

Bo N'Zérékoré

CÔTE D'IVOIRE
(IVORY COAST)

Tamale

GHANA

TOGO

Ibadan

Ogbomosho

Ife

Makurdi

Freetown

Sherbro Island

Mont Nimba
5,748 ft
1,752 m

Bouaké

Lake Volta

Enugu

Benue

CENTRAL
AFRICAN
REPUBLIC

Monrovia

Buchanan

LIBERIA

Yamoussoukro ⊛
(legislative
capital)

Kumasi

Lomé

Cotonou
(seat of government)

Lagos

Port
Harcourt

CAMEROON

Greenville

Grain Coast

Abidjan
(administrative
capital)

Accra

Gold Coast

Porto-Novo ⊛
(constitutional
capital)

Bight of
Benin

Slave Coast

Niger
Delta

EQUATORIAL
GUINEA

Harper

Cape Palmas

Ivory Coast

EQUATOR

A   T   L   A   N   T   I   C   O   C   E   A   N

GABON

C
O
N
G
O

ANGOLA

DEMOCRATIC REPUBLIC OF THE CONGO

See map on page 35.

0 ————— 100 miles
0 ————— 100 kilometers

Santo
Antão

Mindelo

São
Vicente

São
Nicolau

Sal

Santa
Maria

Sal Rei

Boa
Vista

CABO VERDE

Tarrafal

São Filipe

Fogo

Brava

Santiago

Cidade Velha

Maio

Pôrto Inglês

Praia

ATLANTIC OCEAN

CHANGING THE LAND

☐ True desert

☐ Risk of
desertification

Overgrazing, removal of vegetation by farmers, and unreliable rainfall are turning some land in Africa into desert—a process called desertification.

THE BASICS

STATS

Largest country
Tanzania 365,753 sq miles
(947,300 sq km)

Smallest country
Djibouti 8,958 sq miles
(23,200 sq km)

Most populous country
Ethiopia 105,350,000

Least populous country
Djibouti 865,000

Predominant languages
French, Arabic, English, Kiswahili,
indigenous languages

Predominant religions
Christianity, Islam,
indigenous beliefs

Highest GDP per capita
Djibouti, Kenya $3,400

Lowest GDP per capita
Somalia $400

Highest life expectancy
Djibouti 63 years

Lowest life expectancy
Somalia 52 years

GEO WHIZ

As part of a coming-of-age ritual, each Maasai boy must kill a lion. The Maasai are a semi-nomadic people in Kenya and Tanzania.

In 2006, the 3.3-million-year-old fossilized remains of a child were found in northern Ethiopia.

Eastern Africa

Eastern Africa's southern countries attract tourists to see big game—lions, elephants, giraffes, cape buffalos, zebras, wildebeests—that live on tropical grasslands called savannas. Some also come to the region to climb its towering volcanic mountains, such as Kilimanjaro and Mount Kenya. Along the western border lie Africa's Great Lakes, a part of the Rift Valley where tectonic forces are gradually separating eastern Africa from the rest of the continent. Religious and ethnic conflicts have plagued the region's northern countries for many years, leading to the political separation of Eritrea from Ethiopia. Civil unrest combined with drought has led to widespread famine, especially in Somalia.

EAGER LEARNERS. Tanzania, a poor country with a literacy rate of only 78 percent, lags in education. Students in this crowded village school compete for the teacher's attention.

FROM FIELD TO CUP. A worker on a coffee estate in Kenya holds freshly harvested coffee berries, which will soon be on their way to world markets. Coffee production was introduced to Kenya in 1900. Today, it directly or indirectly employs more than five million workers.

WOMAN'S WORK. This woman in Kibera, Kenya, carries a heavy load of wood gathered in a nearby forest. Villagers throughout Africa depend on wood as their main source of fuel to cook and heat their homes. This contributes to widespread deforestation.

SOURCE OF THE NILE

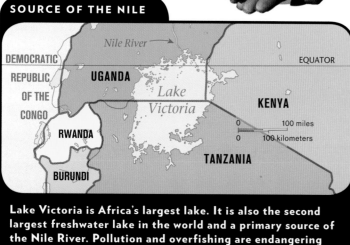

Nile River

DEMOCRATIC
REPUBLIC
OF THE
CONGO

UGANDA

Lake
Victoria

KENYA

EQUATOR

RWANDA

0   100 miles
0   100 kilometers

BURUNDI

TANZANIA

Lake Victoria is Africa's largest lake. It is also the second largest freshwater lake in the world and a primary source of the Nile River. Pollution and overfishing are endangering the lake's environment.

◑ **CRITICALLY ENDANGERED.** About half of Earth's roughly 900 wild mountain gorillas live in forests on the slopes of the Virunga Mountains. Poaching, habitat loss, and civil conflict threaten their survival.

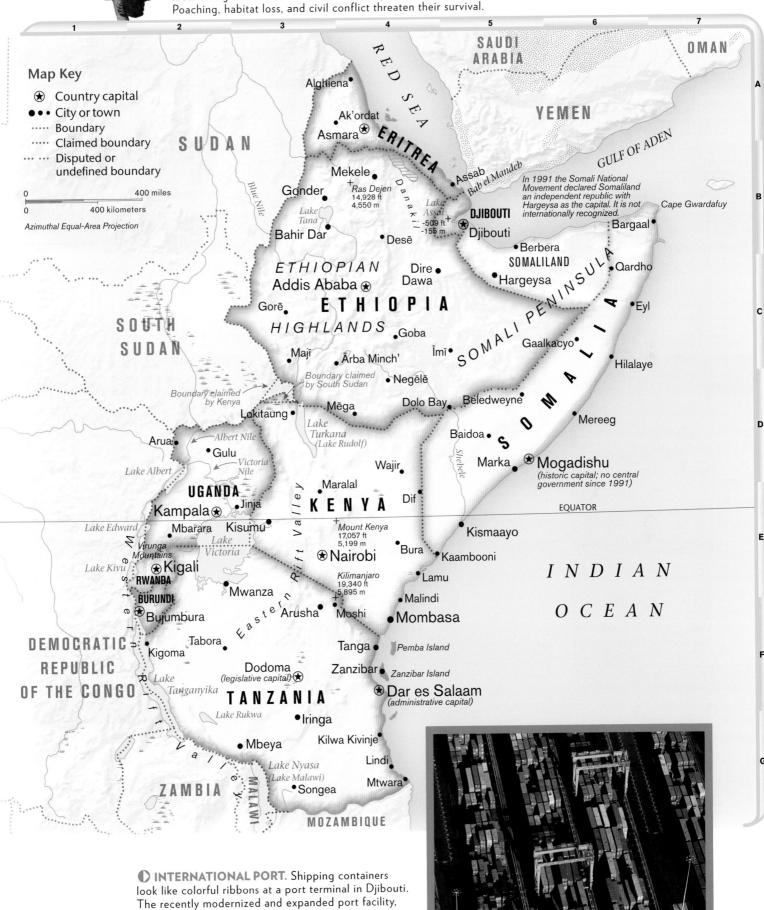

Map Key

⊛ Country capital
●●● City or town
...... Boundary
------ Claimed boundary
------ Disputed or undefined boundary

0 ————— 400 miles
0 ————— 400 kilometers

Azimuthal Equal-Area Projection

SUDAN

SOUTH SUDAN

RED SEA

SAUDI ARABIA

OMAN

YEMEN

GULF OF ADEN

Alghiena
Ak'ordat
Asmara ⊛ ERITREA
Mekele
Ras Dejen 14,928 ft 4,550 m
Gonder
Lake Tana
Bahir Dar
Desē
Assab
Bab el Mandeb
Danakil
Lake Assal -509 ft -155 m
DJIBOUTI ⊛
Djibouti

Cape Gwardafuy

In 1991 the Somali National Movement declared Somaliland an independent republic with Hargeysa as the capital. It is not internationally recognized.

Bargaal

Berbera
SOMALILAND
Hargeysa
Qardho

ETHIOPIAN
Dire Dawa
Addis Ababa ⊛
Gorē
ETHIOPIA
HIGHLANDS
Goba
Eyl

SOMALI PENINSULA

Gaalkacyo

Maji
Ārba Minch'
Īmī
Hilalaye

Negēlē
Boundary claimed by South Sudan

Boundary claimed by Kenya

Lokitaung
Mēga
Dolo Bay
Beledweyne

SOMALIA

Mereeg

Arua
Albert Nile
Gulu
Lake Turkana (Lake Rudolf)
Baidoa
Marka
Mogadishu ⊛
(historic capital; no central government since 1991)

Lake Albert
Victoria Nile

Wajir
Dif

Maralal

UGANDA
Kampala ⊛
Jinja

KENYA

EQUATOR

Lake Edward
Mbarara
Kisumu
Lake Victoria
Mount Kenya 17,057 ft 5,199 m
Nairobi ⊛
Bura
Kismaayo
Kaambooni

Virunga Mountains
Lake Kivu
Kigali ⊛
RWANDA
BURUNDI
Bujumbura ⊛
Mwanza
Kilimanjaro 19,340 ft 5,895 m
Arusha
Moshi
Malindi
Lamu
Mombasa

INDIAN OCEAN

DEMOCRATIC REPUBLIC OF THE CONGO

Kigoma
Tabora
Dodoma (legislative capital) ⊛
Tanga
Zanzibar
Pemba Island
Zanzibar Island

Lake Tanganyika
Lake Rukwa
TANZANIA
Iringa
Dar es Salaam ⊛ (administrative capital)

Eastern Rift Valley

Western Rift Valley

Mbeya
Kilwa Kivinje
Lindi

ZAMBIA
Lake Nyasa (Lake Malawi)
Songea
Mtwara

MALAWI

MOZAMBIQUE

Blue Nile

Shebele

◑ **INTERNATIONAL PORT.** Shipping containers look like colorful ribbons at a port terminal in Djibouti. The recently modernized and expanded port facility, with its deep natural harbor, is the economic mainstay of this small country in eastern Africa.

THE BASICS

STATS

Largest country
Democratic Republic of the Congo (DRC)
905,350 sq mi (2,344,858 sq km)

Smallest country
Sao Tome and Principe
372 sq mi (964 sq m)

Most populous country
Democratic Republic of the Congo
83,301,000

Least populous country
Sao Tome and Principe 201,000

Predominant languages
English, French, Arabic, Portuguese, indigenous languages

Predominant religions
Christianity, Islam, indigenous beliefs

Highest GDP per capita
Equatorial Guinea $38,600

Lowest GDP per capita
Central African Republic $700

Highest life expectancy
Sao Tome and Principe 65 years

Lowest life expectancy
Chad 50 years

GEO WHIZ

The Mbuti Pygmies, of the DRC, yodel as they beat the bush to drive cat-size antelope into nets. The hunting technique is more than a thousand years old.

The two main tributaries of the Nile join at Khartoum, in Sudan. Farmers rely on the world's longest river to water their crops.

Central Africa

The Congo, a major commercial waterway of central Africa, flows through rain forests being cut for timber and palm oil plantations. This places a large area of Earth's biodiversity at risk. To the north, Lake Chad, a large, but shallow lake, fluctuates greatly in size due to high rates of evaporation, unreliable rainfall, and overuse by the 20 million people who live near its shores. Diamonds, copper, and chromium are mined in the Democratic Republic of the Congo (DRC) and the Central African Republic. Coffee is grown in the eastern highlands of the region, and livestock and cotton contribute to the economy of Chad. Religious and ethnic conflicts led to the separation of South Sudan from Sudan in 2011. Ongoing civil unrest and drought have led to widespread famine in South Sudan.

⬤ **ACTIVE VOLCANO.** Mount Nyiragongo, in the Virunga Mountains of the DRC, contains one of the world's largest lava lakes.

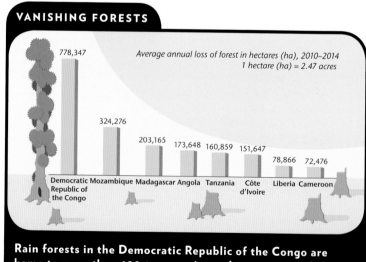

VANISHING FORESTS

Average annual loss of forest in hectares (ha), 2010–2014
1 hectare (ha) = 2.47 acres

Country	Loss (ha)
Democratic Republic of the Congo	778,347
Mozambique	324,276
Madagascar	203,165
Angola	173,648
Tanzania	160,859
Côte d'Ivoire	151,647
Liberia	78,866
Cameroon	72,476

Rain forests in the Democratic Republic of the Congo are home to more than 600 tree species and 10,000 animal species. Forest loss puts all of them at risk.

◑ **DESERT CARAVAN.** Legendary Tuareg tribesmen lead their camels across the desert in northern Chad. The camels, loaded with trade goods such as salt, are destined for distant market towns.

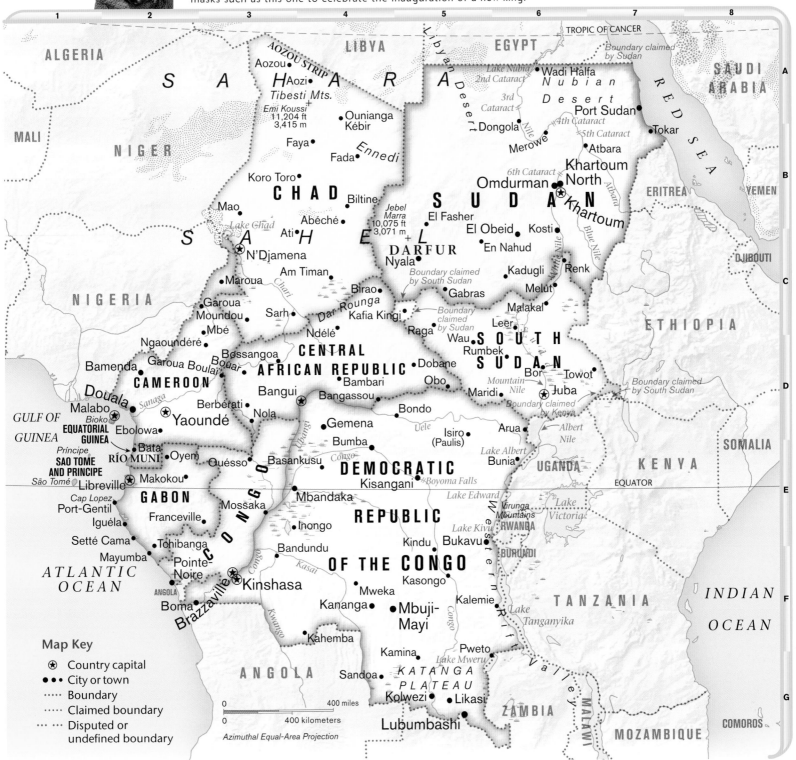

◗ **CELEBRATING A KING.** The Chokwe people of central Africa used masks such as this one to celebrate the inauguration of a new king.

ALGERIA

MALI

NIGER

LIBYA

EGYPT

TROPIC OF CANCER

SAUDI ARABIA

YEMEN

S A H A R A

AOZOU STRIP
Aozou
Aozi
Tibesti Mts.
Emi Koussi
11,204 ft
3,415 m
Ounianga Kébir
Faya

Libyan Desert

Lake Nubia
2nd Cataract
Wadi Halfa
N u b i a n
D e s e r t
Boundary claimed by Sudan
3rd Cataract
Dongola
Nile
4th Cataract
Merowe
5th Cataract
Port Sudan
Tokar

RED SEA

Ennedi
Fada

Koro Toro

CHAD

Biltine

Mao

Lake Chad

Abéché

Ati

N'Djamena

S A H E L

Jebel Marra
10,075 ft
3,071 m

El Fasher

DARFUR
Nyala

Boundary claimed by South Sudan

6th Cataract
Omdurman
Khartoum North
S U D A N
Khartoum

Atbara

El Obeid
En Nahud

Kosti

Kadugli

Renk

Blue Nile
Atbara

ERITREA

DJIBOUTI

Maroua

Am Timan

Chari

Birao
Dar Rounga
Kafia Kingi

Melut
Malakal
Leer

Boundary claimed by Sudan

Gabras

Melut

SOUTH SUDAN

ETHIOPIA

NIGERIA

Garoua
Moundou
Mbé
Ngaoundéré
Bamenda
Garoua Boulaï
CAMEROON

Sarh
Ndélé

Bossangoa
Bouar
CENTRAL
AFRICAN REPUBLIC
Bambari

Dobane
Obo

Raga
Wau
Rumbek

Bor

Mountain Nile

Towot

Boundary claimed by South Sudan

Douala
Malabo
Bioko
EQUATORIAL GUINEA
Príncipe
SAO TOME AND PRINCIPE
São Tomé

Berbérati
Yaoundé
Ebolowa
Bata
RÍO MUNI
Oyem
Makokou
Libreville

Bangui
Nola

Sanaga

Bangassou

Bondo

Uele

Gemena
Bumba
Basankusu

Isiro
(Paulis)

Maridi

Arua

Bunia

Albert Nile

Lake Albert

Boundary claimed by Kenya

UGANDA

SOMALIA

KENYA

Cap Lopez
Port-Gentil
Iguéla
GABON
Franceville
Tchibanga
Setté Cama
Mayumba
Pointe-Noire
Boma
Brazzaville
Kinshasa

CONGO

Ubangi
Congo

DEMOCRATIC
Kisangani
Boyoma Falls

Mbandaka
REPUBLIC
Inongo

Bandundu

Mossaka

Kasai

Kwango
Kahemba

OF THE CONGO

Mweka
Kananga
Mbuji-Mayi

Sandoa
KATANGA
PLATEAU
Kolwezi
Lubumbashi

Kindu
Kasongo

Kamina

Kolwezi
Likasi

Bukavu
RWANDA
Lake Kivu
BURUNDI

Kalemie

Pweto
Lake Mweru

ZAMBIA

Lake Edward
Virunga Mountains
Lake Victoria

EQUATOR

Western Rift Valley
Lake Tanganyika

TANZANIA

INDIAN OCEAN

ATLANTIC OCEAN

GULF OF GUINEA

ANGOLA

ANGOLA

MALAWI

MOZAMBIQUE

COMOROS

Map Key
⊛ Country capital
• • • City or town
· · · · Boundary
· · · · Claimed boundary
· · · Disputed or undefined boundary

0   400 miles
0   400 kilometers

Azimuthal Equal-Area Projection

◗ **FACING HUNGER.** Refugees fleeing civil unrest and hunger in South Sudan wait to receive food at the Khour Al-Waral refugee camp in neighboring Sudan. The camp is home to 50,000 people.

THE BASICS

STATS

Largest country
Angola 481,351 sq mi
(1,246,700 sq km)

Smallest country
Seychelles 176 sq mi
(455 sq km)

Most populous country
South Africa 54,842,000

Least populous country
Seychelles 94,000

Predominant languages
English, French, Portuguese,
indigenous languages

Predominant religions
Christianity, Islam,
indigenous beliefs

Highest GDP per capita
Seychelles $27,600

Lowest GDP per capita
Malawi $1,100

Highest life expectancy
Mauritius 76 years

Lowest life expectancy
Swaziland 52 years

GEO WHIZ

**South Africa's Kruger National
Park, the largest in Africa,
covers more area than the
country of Israel.**

**Great Zimbabwe National
Monument has the largest ancient
stone ruins south of the Sahara.**

**Treacherous crosscurrents off the
northwest coast of Namibia have
caused countless ships to wreck,
earning the area the nickname
Skeleton Coast.**

Southern Africa

⬤ **NATURAL WONDER.**
Victoria Falls, third largest
waterfall in the world, is
5,500 feet (1,676 m) wide
and 355 feet (108 m) high.

Ringed by uplands, the region's central basin holds the seasonally lush Okavango Delta and scorching Kalahari Desert. The mighty Zambezi thunders over Victoria Falls on its way to the Indian Ocean, where Madagascar is home to plants and animals found nowhere else in the world. Bantu and San are among the indigenous people who saw their hold on the land give way to Portuguese, Dutch, and British traders and colonists. The region offers a range of mineral resources and a variety of climates and soils that in some places yield bumper crops of grains, grapes, and citrus. Rich deposits of coal, diamonds, and gold have helped make South Africa the continent's economic powerhouse.

◐ **STARING EYES.**
This ring-tailed lemur rests
in the crook of a forest
tree branch. The ring-tail,
found only in Madagascar,
spends time both on the
ground and in trees. It eats
fruits, leaves, insects, small
birds, and even lizards.

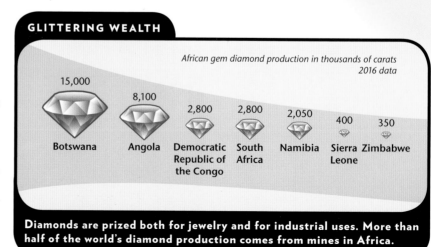

GLITTERING WEALTH

*African gem diamond production in thousands of carats
2016 data*

Botswana	Angola	Democratic Republic of the Congo	South Africa	Namibia	Sierra Leone	Zimbabwe
15,000	8,100	2,800	2,800	2,050	400	350

**Diamonds are prized both for jewelry and for industrial uses. More than
half of the world's diamond production comes from mines in Africa.**

◑ **EARLY MAN.** Dating back perhaps 70,000 years, this skull of "Broken Hill Man" was found in Zimbabwe.

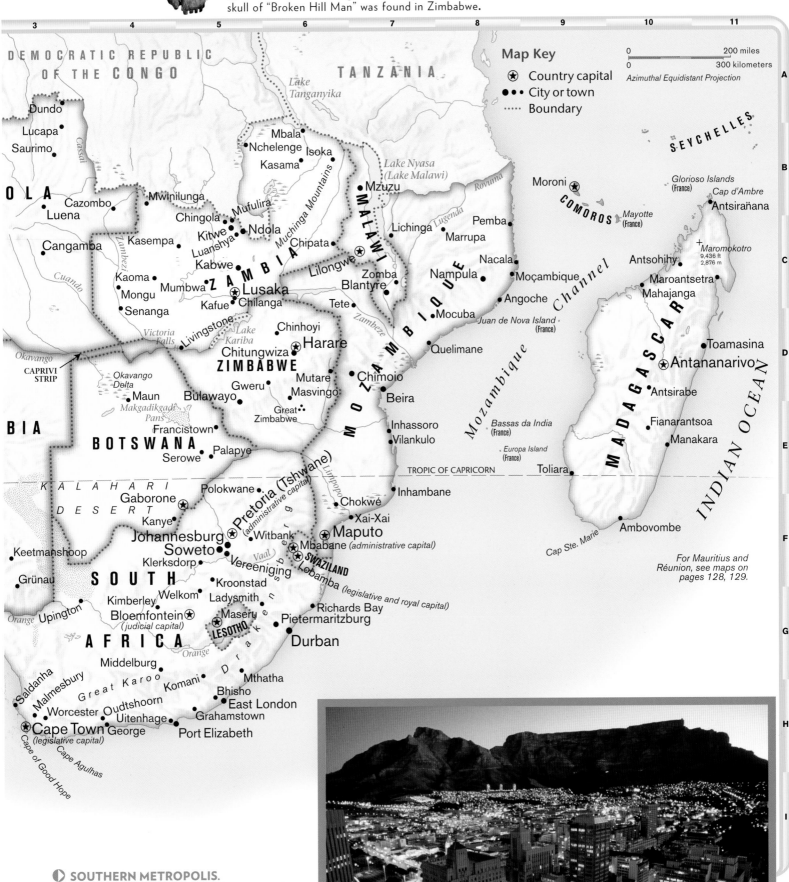

Map Key

★ Country capital
●●● City or town
∙∙∙∙ Boundary

0 ————— 200 miles
0 ————— 300 kilometers

Azimuthal Equidistant Projection

DEMOCRATIC REPUBLIC OF THE CONGO

TANZANIA

Lake Tanganyika

●Dundo
●Lucapa
●Saurimo

●Mbala
●Nchelenge   ●Isoka
●Kasama

*Lake Nyasa
(Lake Malawi)*

Rovuma

●Moroni ★

S E Y C H E L L E S

*Glorioso Islands
(France)*

Cap d'Ambre

OLA

●Cazombo
●Luena

●Mwinilunga

●Mzuzu

M A L A W I

●Lichinga

Lugenda

●Pemba
●Marrupa

C O M O R O S

*Mayotte
(France)*

●Antsiraňana

+ *Maromokotro
9,436 ft
2,876 m*

●Antsohihy

●Cangamba

●Mufulira
●Chingola ●Ndola
●Kitwe
●Luanshya
●Kasempa   ●Kabwe

●Chipata

★Lilongwe

●Zomba
●Blantyre

●Nacala
●Nampula

●Moçambique
●Angoche

Muchinga Mountains

M O Z A M B I Q U E

●Maroantsetra
●Mahajanga

M A D A G A S C A R

●Kaoma
●Mongu
●Mumbwa Z A M B I A ★Lusaka
●Chilanga
●Kafue
●Senanga

●Tete

●Mocuba
●Mucuba

*Juan de Nova Island
(France)*

●Chinhoyi

●Livingstone
Victoria Falls

Lake Kariba

★Harare
●Chitungwiza

Z I M B A B W E

●Quelimane

Zambeze

M O Z A M B I Q U E   C H A N N E L

●Toamasina

★Antananarivo
●Antsirabe

Cuando

Okavango

CAPRIVI
STRIP

*Okavango
Delta*

●Maun

*Makgadikgadi
Pans*

●Gweru
●Bulawayo

●Mutare
●Masvingo

●Chimoio

●Beira

M O Z A M B I Q U E

*Bassas da India
(France)*

*Europa Island
(France)*

●Fianarantsoa
●Manakara

BIA

●Francistown

B O T S W A N A

●Serowe ●Palapye

*Great
Zimbabwe*

●Inhassoro
●Vilankulo

I N D I A N   O C E A N

TROPIC OF CAPRICORN

●Toliara

●Ambovombe

K A L A H A R I
D E S E R T

●Polokwane
★Gaborone
●Kanye

●Pretoria (Tshwane)
(administrative capital)

●Chokwé
●Xai-Xai

●Inhambane

Limpopo

Cap Ste. Marie

*For Mauritius and
Réunion, see maps on
pages 128, 129.*

●Keetmanshoop

●Johannesburg
●Soweto
●Klerksdorp
●Vereeniging

●Witbank

★Maputo
●Mbabane *(administrative capital)*
SWAZILAND
★Lobamba *(legislative and royal capital)*

●Grünau

S O U T H

●Kroonstad
●Welkom
●Kimberley
●Bloemfontein
(judicial capital)
●Ladysmith

Vaal

●Richards Bay

Orange ●Upington

A F R I C A

●Maseru
★
LESOTHO

●Pietermaritzburg

Drakensberg

Durban

●Saldanha
●Malmesbury

●Middelburg

Orange

Great Karoo

●Komani
●Mthatha

●Worcester ●Oudtshoorn
★Cape Town ●Uitenhage
(legislative capital)
●George

●Bhisho
●East London
●Grahamstown

●Port Elizabeth

Cape of Good Hope

Cape Agulhas

◑ **SOUTHERN METROPOLIS.**
Cape Town, South Africa's second most populous metropolitan area and seat of the legislative capital, began as a Dutch supply station in 1652. Table Mountain rises in the background.

THE REGION:
AUSTRALIA, NEW ZEALAND & OCEANIA

PHYSICAL			POLITICAL	
Area and population totals are for the independent countries in the region only.	**HIGHEST POINT** Mount Wilhelm, Papua New Guinea 14,793 ft (4,509 m)	**LONGEST RIVER** Murray-Darling, Australia 2,310 mi (3,718 km)	**POPULATION** 37,139,000	**LARGEST COUNTRY** Australia 2,988,885 sq mi (7,741,220 sq km)
			LARGEST METROPOLITAN AREA Sydney, Australia Pop. 4,540,000	
LAND AREA 3,296,000 sq mi (8,537,000 sq km)	**LOWEST POINT** Lake Eyre, Australia -49 ft (-15 m)	**LARGEST LAKE** Lake Eyre, Australia 3,430 sq mi (8,884 sq km)		**MOST DENSELY POPULATED COUNTRY** Nauru 1,205.3 people per sq mi (459.1 per sq km)

AUSTRALIA, NEW ZEALAND & OCEANIA

Australia, New Zealand & Oceania

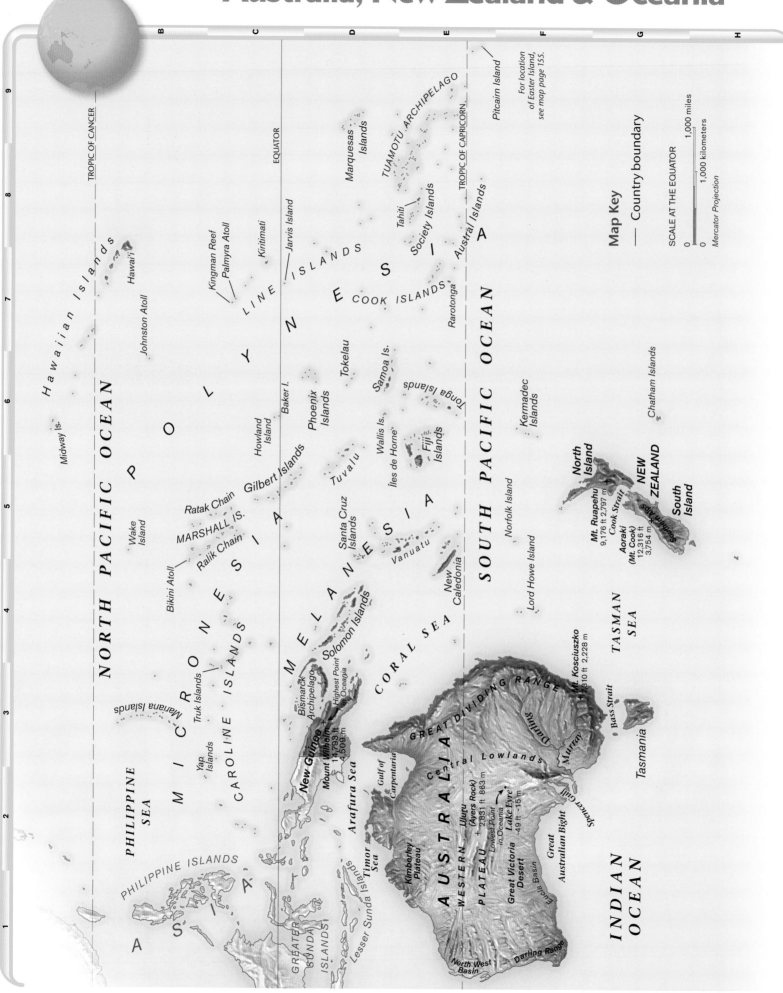

TROPIC OF CANCER

EQUATOR

TROPIC OF CAPRICORN

For location
of Easter Island,
see map page 155.

Pitcairn Island

Map Key

— Country boundary

SCALE AT THE EQUATOR

1,000 miles

1,000 kilometers

Mercator Projection

Hawaiian Islands

Hawai'i

Midway Is.

Johnston Atoll

Wake
Island

Kingman Reef
Palmyra Atoll
Kiritimati

Jarvis Island

LINE ISLANDS

Marquesas
Islands

TUAMOTU ARCHIPELAGO

Tahiti
Society Islands

Austral Islands

P O L Y N E S I A

COOK ISLANDS

Rarotonga

NORTH PACIFIC OCEAN

Tokelau

Baker I.

Howland
Island

Phoenix
Islands

Samoa Is.

Tonga Islands

SOUTH PACIFIC OCEAN

Ratak Chain
Gilbert Islands
MARSHALL IS.
Ralik Chain

Bikini Atoll

Santa Cruz
Islands

Tuvalu

Wallis Is.
Îles de Horne

Fiji
Islands

Vanuatu

Kermadec
Islands

Chatham Islands

Norfolk Island

North
Island

NEW
ZEALAND

Mt. Ruapehu
9,176 ft 2,797 m
Cook Strait
Aoraki
(Mt. Cook)
12,316 ft
3,754 m

Southern Alps

South
Island

M I C R O N E S I A

Mariana Islands

Yap
Islands

Truk Islands

CAROLINE ISLANDS

PHILIPPINE
SEA

M E L A N E S I A

Bismarck
Archipelago

New Guinea

Mount Wilhelm
14,793 ft
4,509 m
Highest Point
in Oceania

Solomon Islands

New
Caledonia

Lord Howe Island

CORAL SEA

TASMAN
SEA

Mt. Kosciuszko
7,310 ft 2,228 m

Bass Strait

Tasmania

GREAT DIVIDING RANGE

Darling

Murray

A S I A

PHILIPPINE ISLANDS

GREATER SUNDA ISLANDS

Lesser Sunda Islands

Timor
Sea

Arafura Sea

Gulf of
Carpentaria

A U S T R A L I A

Central Lowlands

WESTERN PLATEAU

Kimberley
Plateau

Great Victoria
Desert

Uluru
(Ayers Rock)
2,831 ft 863 m

Lake Eyre
Lowest Point
in Oceania
-49 ft -15 m

Eucla Basin

Great
Australian Bight

Spencer Gulf

North West
Basin

Darling Range

INDIAN
OCEAN

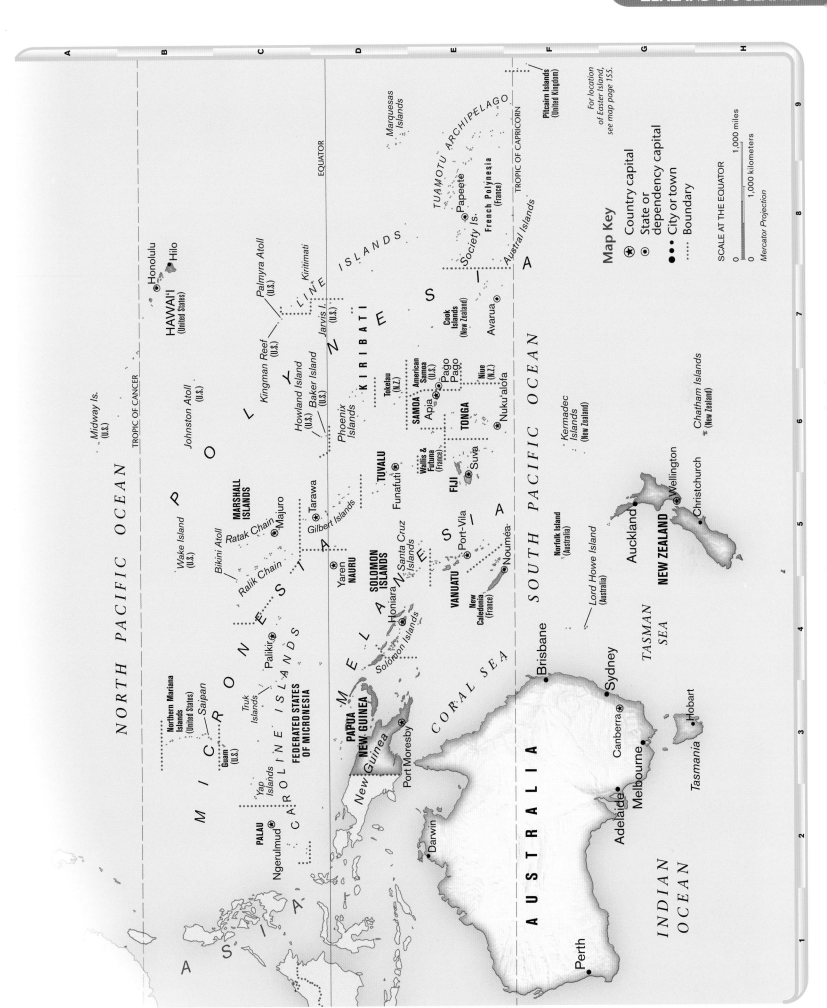

A B C D E F G H

9

Marquesas
Islands

TUAMOTU ARCHIPELAGO

EQUATOR

Pitcairn Islands
(United Kingdom)

For location
of Easter Island,
see map page 155.

8

Papeete
Society Is. French Polynesia
(France)

Australe Islands

TROPIC OF CAPRICORN

Map Key

★ Country capital
◉ State or
dependency capital
● City or town
····· Boundary

SCALE AT THE EQUATOR
0   1,000 miles
0   1,000 kilometers

Mercator Projection

7

Honolulu
◉   ● Hilo

HAWAI'I
(United States)

Palmyra Atoll
(U.S.)

LINE

Kiritimati

ISLANDS

P O L Y N E S I A

Cook
Islands
(New Zealand)   Avarua ◉

NORTH PACIFIC OCEAN

TROPIC OF CANCER

Midway Is.
(U.S.)

Johnston Atoll
(U.S.)

Kingman Reef
(U.S.)

Jarvis I.
(U.S.)

K I R I B A T I

Tokelau
(N.Z.)   American
Samoa
(U.S.)   Pago
Pago   Niue
(N.Z.)

6

Wake Island
(U.S.)

Howland Island
(U.S.)

Baker Island
(U.S.)

Phoenix
Islands

SAMOA
Apia
TONGA   Nuku'alofa ★

Kermadec
Islands
(New Zealand)

Chatham Islands
(New Zealand)

MARSHALL
ISLANDS

Bikini Atoll

Ratak Chain
Majuro ◉

Tarawa

Gilbert Islands

TUVALU
Funafuti ●

Wallis &
Futuna
(France)

FIJI   Suva ★

Norfolk Island
(Australia)

SOUTH PACIFIC OCEAN

Wellington
NEW ZEALAND
Christchurch

5

Yap
Islands

Ralik Chain

M I C R O N E S I A

Yaren ★
NAURU

SOLOMON
ISLANDS
Honiara ★   Santa Cruz
Islands

Port-Vila ●
VANUATU

New
Caledonia
(France)   Nouméa ●

Lord Howe Island
(Australia)

Auckland

4

Northern Mariana
Islands
(United States)

Saipan

Truk
Islands

Palikir ◉

FEDERATED STATES
OF MICRONESIA

CAROLINE ISLANDS

Solomon Islands

CORAL SEA

TASMAN
SEA

Brisbane

Sydney

3

Guam
(U.S.)

PAPUA
NEW GUINEA

New Guinea

Port Moresby ★

A U S T R A L I A

Canberra ★

Hobart

Tasmania

2

PALAU
Ngerulmud ★

Darwin

Adelaide
Melbourne

INDIAN
OCEAN

A S I A

Perth

1

Australia,
New Zealand & Oceania

WORLDS APART

○ **AUSTRALIAN TEDDY BEAR.** Koalas, which are not bears at all, are native to the eucalyptus forests of eastern Australia.

This vast region includes Australia—the world's smallest continent—New Zealand, and a fleet of mostly tiny island worlds scattered across the Pacific Ocean. Apart from Australia, New Zealand, and Papua New Guinea, Oceania's other 11 independent countries cover about 25,000 square miles (65,000 sq km), an area only slightly larger than half of New Zealand's North Island. Twenty-one other island groups are dependencies of the United States, France, Australia, New Zealand, or the United Kingdom. Long isolation has allowed the growth of diverse marine communities, such as Australia's Great Barrier Reef, and the evolution of platypuses, kangaroos, kiwis, and other land animals that live nowhere else on the planet.

◑ **ANCIENT VOYAGERS.** The Maoris are believed to have sailed to New Zealand from islands far to the northeast. Maori warriors traditionally adorned themselves with elaborate tattoos to frighten enemies.

PLACE OF LEGENDS. Once part of an ancient seabed, Uluru, also known as Ayers Rock, is sacred to native Aboriginals. This massive sandstone block was exposed by erosion.

TROPICAL HABITAT. Brilliantly colored fish swim among branching corals in the warm waters of the Vatu-i-Ra Channel in the Fiji Islands. The waters around Fiji have some of the richest and most diverse fish populations in the world.

NATIVE COWBOYS. Competition is fierce during a rodeo in Hope Vale, an Aboriginal community on Australia's Cape York Peninsula. Hope Vale is home to several Aboriginal clan groups.

more about
Australia, New Zealand & Oceania

BIG JUMPER. The red kangaroo, the largest living marsupial—an animal that carries its young in a pouch—is at home on the dry inland plains of Australia. It can cover 30 feet (9 m) in a single hop.

A WATER WORLD. Located just 7 degrees north of the Equator, the islands of the Republic of Palau were a United Nations Trust Territory until 1994, when they gained independence.

WOOLLY POPULATION. Sheep outnumber people in Australia and New Zealand. Wool production is an important part of the economies of these two countries.

FLYING HIGH. Prevailing winds lift adventurous tourists in a tandem parasail high above the waters of New Zealand's Bay of Islands. Rising up to 1,200 feet (366 m) above the water, visitors get a bird's-eye view of the islands.

WHERE THE PICTURES ARE

New Guinea tribesman
with painted face p. 155

Tropical islands of
Palau pp. 150–151

Ambrym volcano p. 154

Aborigine
cowboys p. 149

Catching octopus p. 155

Uluru
(Ayers Rock)
pp. 148–149

Parasailing p. 150
Lagoon p. 154

Easter Island statue
p. 155

Coral reef with fish pp. 148–149

Auckland skyline pp. 150–151
Maori man p. 148

Red kangaroo
p. 150

Great white
shark p. 152

Sheep in pasture p. 150

Koala p. 148

Aoraki (Mt. Cook) p. 151

Dingo p. 153

Jet boat with tourists p. 151

Sydney Opera House p. 152

Fiordland National Park p. 153

⬇ A WET RIDE. Tourists go for a wild ride in a jet boat
on the roaring waters of New Zealand's Shotover River.

⬇ MODERN METROPOLIS.
Modern buildings rise against
a twilight sky in Auckland, on
New Zealand's North Island. It is
home to almost one-third of the
country's population.

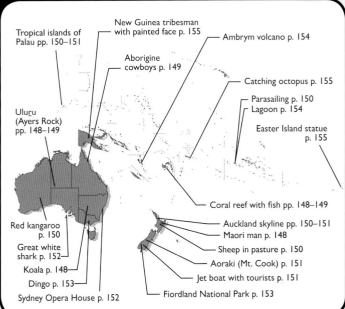

⬇ SNOWY PEAK. New Zealand's Aoraki (Mount
Cook) rises above the clouds. Legend says the peak is
a frozen Maori warrior.

THE BASICS

STATS

Largest country
Australia 2,998,885 sq mi
(7,741,220 sq km)

Smallest country
New Zealand 103,363 sq mi
(267,710 sq km)

Most populous country
Australia 23,232,000

Least populous country
New Zealand 4,510,000

Predominant languages
English, Maori

Predominant religion
Christianity

Highest GDP per capita
Australia $48,900

Lowest GDP per capita
New Zealand $37,300

Highest life expectancy
Australia 82 years

Lowest life expectancy
New Zealand 81 years

GEO WHIZ

A tree trunk hollowed out by termites is used by Australia's Aboriginals to make a musical instrument called a didgeridoo.

Wellington, in New Zealand, is the southernmost national capital city in the world.

Lake Eyre is Australia's largest lake, but it is very shallow. When filled to capacity, it is not quite 20 feet (6 m) deep.

In September 2010, a magnitude 7.1 earthquake, followed by a 6.3 aftershock in February 2011, caused widespread destruction in Christchurch, on New Zealand's South Island.

Australia & New Zealand

Most people in Australia live along the coast, far from the country's dry interior, known as the Outback. The most populous cities and the best croplands are in the southeast. This "Land Down Under" is increasingly linked by trade to Asia and to 4.5 million "neighbors" in New Zealand. Lying 1,200 miles (1,930 km) across the Tasman Sea, New Zealand is cooler, wetter, and more mountainous than Australia. Geologically active, it has ecosystems ranging from subtropical forests on North Island to snowy peaks on South Island. Both countries enjoy high standards of living and strong agricultural and mining outputs, including wool, wines, gold, coal, and iron ore.

[Map of Western Australia showing cities including Wyndham, Derby, Broome, Port Hedland, Perth, Kalgoorlie, Albany, and geographic features such as Great Sandy Desert, Gibson Desert, Great Victoria Desert, Nullarbor, Tropic of Capricorn, and Indian Ocean. Scale: 0–400 miles / 0–400 kilometers. Azimuthal Equidistant Projection.]

◑ SAILS AT SUNSET.
Reminiscent of a ship in full sail, the Sydney Opera House, in Sydney Harbor, has become a symbol of Australia that is recognized worldwide.

◐ KILLER OF THE DEEP.
Great white sharks inhabit the warm waters off the coast of southern Australia. These marine predators can grow up to 20 feet (6 m) in length.

◗ **DOG OF THE OUTBACK.** The dingo is a wild dog found throughout Australia except Tasmania. Unlike most domestic dogs, the dingo does not bark, although it howls.

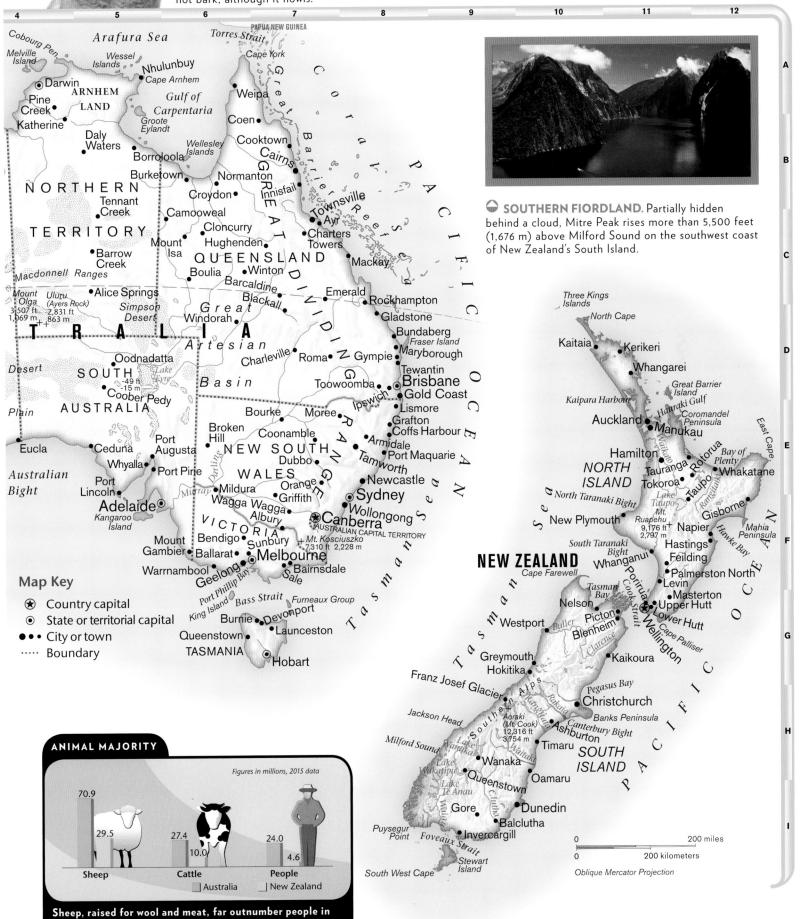

⬤ **SOUTHERN FIORDLAND.** Partially hidden behind a cloud, Mitre Peak rises more than 5,500 feet (1,676 m) above Milford Sound on the southwest coast of New Zealand's South Island.

Map Key

- ✪ Country capital
- ◉ State or territorial capital
- ●•• City or town
- ····· Boundary

ANIMAL MAJORITY

Figures in millions, 2015 data

	Sheep	Cattle	People
Australia	70.9	27.4	24.0
New Zealand	29.5	10.0	4.6

Sheep, raised for wool and meat, far outnumber people in both Australia and New Zealand. Beef and dairy cattle also surpass human population numbers.

200 miles
200 kilometers

Oblique Mercator Projection

THE BASICS

STATS

Largest country
Papua New Guinea
178,703 sq mi (462,840 sq km)

Smallest country
Nauru 8 sq mi (21 sq km)

Most populous country
Papua New Guinea 6,910,000

Least populous country
Nauru 10,000

Predominant languages
**English, indigenous
languages**

Predominant religions
Christianity, indigenous beliefs

Highest GDP per capita
Palau $15,400

Lowest GDP per capita
Kiribati $1,800

Highest life expectancy
Tonga 76 years

Lowest life expectancy
Kiribati 66 years

GEO WHIZ

Five uninhabited islands in the Solomon group have disappeared due to rising sea levels that may be related to climate change, and the inhabited island of Nuatambu has lost more than 50 percent of its land area.

For centuries Fiji's tribal officials would bring out their best utensils—not to serve guests, but to eat them. Cannibalism in Fiji ended when Christianity was adopted in the late 1800s.

The infamous mutiny aboard the British ship H.M.S. *Bounty* took place off Tonga in 1789.

Oceania

Although in its broadest sense Oceania includes Australia and New Zealand, more commonly it refers to some 25,000 islands that make up three large cultural regions in the Pacific Ocean. Melanesia, which extends from Papua New Guinea to Fiji, is closest to Australia. Micronesia lies mostly north of the Equator and includes Palau and the Federated States of Micronesia. New Zealand, Hawai'i, and Rapa Nui (Easter Island) mark the western, northern, and eastern limits of Polynesia, with Tahiti, Samoa, and Tonga near its heart. Oceania's people often face problems of limited living space and freshwater. Plantation agriculture, fishing, tourism, or mining form the economic base for most of the islands in this region.

TROPICAL PARADISE.
A reef separates an area of seawater from the ocean, forming a quiet lagoon around the island of Bora Bora in the Society Islands of French Polynesia.

LIVING EARTH. Ambrym volcano, in Vanuatu, is one of the most active volcanoes in Oceania. First observed by Britain's Captain Cook in 1774, Ambrym continues to erupt regularly, adding to the island's black sand beaches.

◑ **UNSOLVED MYSTERY.** Carved from volcanic rock, the giant stone heads, called *moai*, on Rapa Nui (Easter Island) remain a mystery.

3   4   5   6   7   8   9   10   11

◑ **LONG ARMS.** Octopuses live on coral reefs in the warm tropical waters of the South Pacific Ocean. They use the suckers on their tentacles to move around and to catch crustaceans and small fish.

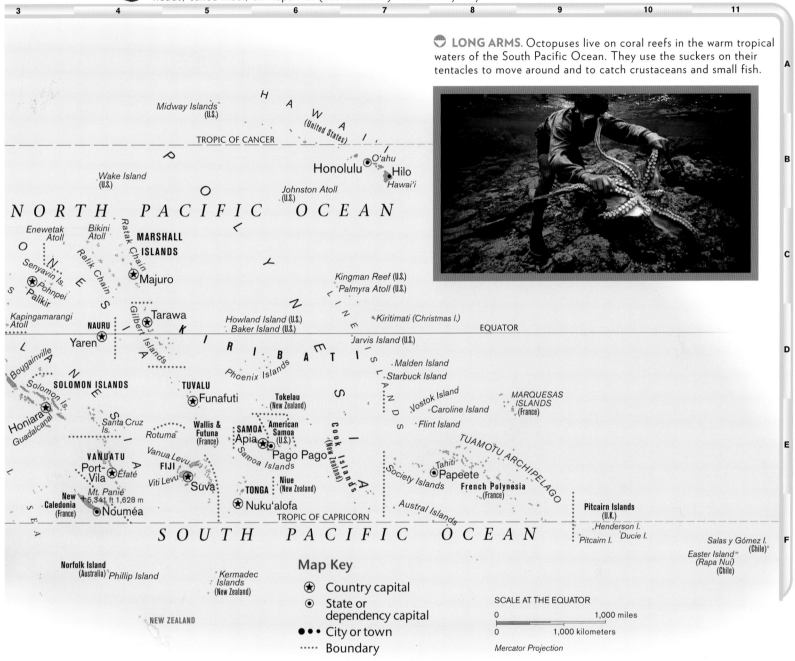

A

B

C

D

E

F

NORTH PACIFIC OCEAN

Midway Islands (U.S.)

TROPIC OF CANCER

Wake Island (U.S.)

Honolulu   O'ahu
Hilo
Hawai'i

Johnston Atoll (U.S.)

Enewetak Atoll
Bikini Atoll
Ratak Chain
MARSHALL ISLANDS
Ralik Chain

Senyavin Is.
Pohnpei
Palikir

★ Majuro

Kingman Reef (U.S.)
Palmyra Atoll (U.S.)

Kapingamarangi Atoll

Tarawa
NAURU
Gilbert Islands

Howland Island (U.S.)
Baker Island (U.S.)

Kiritimati (Christmas I.)

EQUATOR

Yaren ★

Jarvis Island (U.S.)

Bougainville

Malden Island
Starbuck Island

Solomon Is.
SOLOMON ISLANDS

TUVALU
★ Funafuti

Phoenix Islands

Vostok Island
Caroline Island

MARQUESAS ISLANDS (France)

Honiara ★
Guadalcanal

Santa Cruz Is.

Rotuma

Wallis & Futuna (France)

Tokelau (New Zealand)

SAMOA
Apia ★
American Samoa (U.S.)

Flint Island

VANUATU
Port-Vila ★ Éfaté

Vanua Levu
FIJI
Viti Levu

Samoa Islands

Pago Pago

Cook Islands (New Zealand)

Tahiti
Papeete
Society Islands
French Polynesia (France)

TUAMOTU ARCHIPELAGO

New Caledonia (France)
Mt. Panié
5,341 ft 1,628 m
★ Nouméa

Suva

TONGA
★ Nuku'alofa

Niue (New Zealand)

Austral Islands

Pitcairn Islands (U.K.)

TROPIC OF CAPRICORN

Henderson I.
Pitcairn I.   Ducie I.

Salas y Gómez I. (Chile)

SOUTH PACIFIC OCEAN

Easter Island (Rapa Nui) (Chile)

Norfolk Island (Australia)
Phillip Island

Kermadec Islands (New Zealand)

NEW ZEALAND

Map Key

★ Country capital

◉ State or dependency capital

●●● City or town

⋯⋯ Boundary

SCALE AT THE EQUATOR

0   1,000 miles
0   1,000 kilometers

Mercator Projection

◑ **MELANESIAN CUSTOM.** In the Huli culture of Papua New Guinea's Eastern Highlands, men adorn themselves with colorful paints, feathers, and grasses as they prepare to take part in festivals.

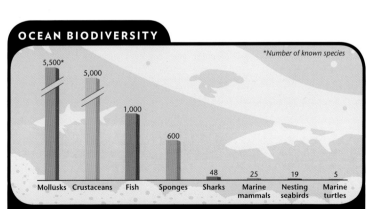

OCEAN BIODIVERSITY

*Number of known species

5,500*	5,000	1,000	600	48	25	19	5
Mollusks	Crustaceans	Fish	Sponges	Sharks	Marine mammals	Nesting seabirds	Marine turtles

The second longest double barrier reef in the world stretches 930 miles (1,500 km) along New Caledonia. The reef is habitat for a diversity of species—some still unclassified.

PHYSICAL

LAND AREA	LOWEST POINT	AVERAGE PRECIPITATION ON THE POLAR PLATEAU
5,100,000 sq mi (13,209,000 sq km)	Byrd Glacier (depression) -9,416 ft (-2,870 m)	Less than 2 in (5 cm) per year
HIGHEST POINT	**COLDEST PLACE**	
Vinson Massif 16,067 ft (4,897 m)	Ridge A Annual average temperature -94°F (-70°C)	

POLITICAL

POPULATION	NUMBER OF INDEPENDENT COUNTRIES	NUMBER OF COUNTRIES OPERATING YEAR-ROUND RESEARCH STATIONS
There are no indigenous inhabitants, but there are scientists and other staff at both permanent and summer-only research stations.	0	20
	NUMBER OF COUNTRIES CLAIMING LAND	**NUMBER OF YEAR-ROUND RESEARCH STATIONS**
	7	40

ANTARCTICA
THE FROZEN SOUTH

Antarctica is the coldest, windiest, and even driest continent. Though its immense ice sheet holds more than 60 percent of Earth's freshwater, its interior averages less than two inches (5 cm) of precipitation per year. Hidden beneath the ice is a continent of valleys, mountains, and lakes, but less than 2 percent of the land actually breaks through the ice cover. Like a finger pointing north toward South America, the Antarctic Peninsula is the most visited region of the continent, but scientists occupy a total of more than 70 permanent and seasonal research stations throughout the continent from which they study this frozen land.

⬤ **FORMAL DRESS.** Black-and-white gentoo penguins live in colonies year-round along the Antarctic Peninsula. These flightless birds dive to more than 300 feet (90 m) to catch fish and krill, their main food source.

DRIFTING RESEARCH. The U.S. Amundsen-Scott research station is located at the geographic South Pole. The station and the ice sheet on which it sits are drifting about 33 feet (10 m) each year.

WHERE THE PICTURES ARE

Researcher
p. 160

Leopard seal
p. 161

Tourists & whale
p. 160

Iceberg
p. 159

Gentoo
penguins
p. 158

Orcas
p. 161

Amundsen-
Scott
Station p. 159

BLUE WONDER. An iceberg drifts in the Lemaire Channel near the Antarctic Peninsula. The dense, compressed ice reflects only short wavelengths, giving the ice a blue tint.

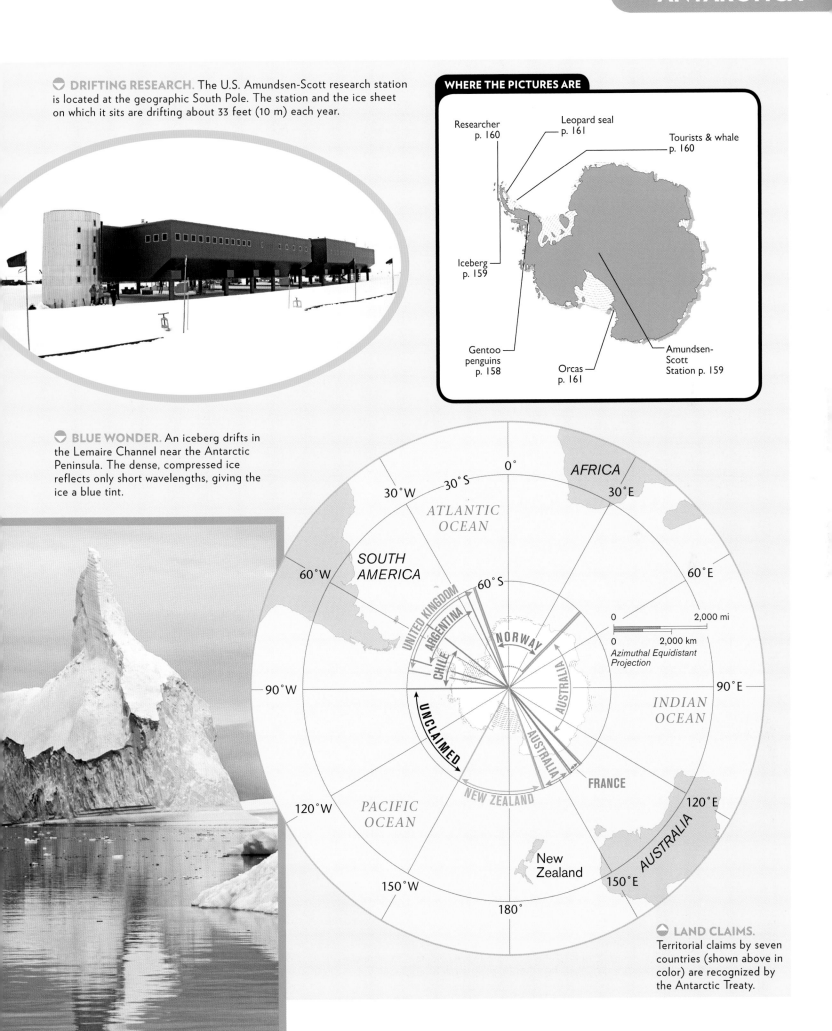

AFRICA

0°

30°W   30°S   30°E

ATLANTIC
OCEAN

SOUTH
AMERICA

60°W   60°E

UNITED KINGDOM
ARGENTINA
CHILE

60°S

NORWAY

AUSTRALIA

0   2,000 mi

0   2,000 km

Azimuthal Equidistant
Projection

90°W   90°E

UNCLAIMED

AUSTRALIA

INDIAN
OCEAN

AUSTRALIA

FRANCE

NEW ZEALAND

120°W   120°E

PACIFIC
OCEAN

New
Zealand

AUSTRALIA

150°W   150°E

180°

LAND CLAIMS.
Territorial claims by seven countries (shown above in color) are recognized by the Antarctic Treaty.

ANTARCTICA

Antarctica

THE BASICS

Antarctica is the only continent that has no political boundaries and no economy or permanent population. Seven countries claim portions of the landmass (map, page 159), but according to the Antarctic Treaty, which preserves the continent for peaceful use and scientific study, no country rules.

GEO WHIZ

The Antarctic Convergence, an area where the waters of Earth's four oceans meet the cold Antarctic Circumpolar Current, is one of the planet's richest marine ecosystems.

Krill, a tiny shrimplike creature that thrives in Antarctic waters, is important in the Antarctic food chain. Whales, seals, and penguins are among the creatures that depend on it for survival.

The tiny wingless midge—less than one-quarter inch (6 mm) long—is Antarctica's largest land animal. This insect is able to survive high levels of salt, freezing temperatures, and ultraviolet radiation in the continent's extreme climate.

Mount Erebus, named for a British explorer's ship, is the world's southernmost active volcano.

NATURE STUDY.
A researcher at Palmer Station examines penguin eggs attacked by skuas, birds that feed on penguin eggs.

Under the terms of the Antarctic Treaty, the region beyond 60° south latitude is set aside for peaceful scientific study and research. Antarctica was first visited by Europeans in 1821, but there has never been a permanent human population. Today, more than 4,000 scientists live at research stations during the southern summer (October to March) studying climate history that is preserved in the ice sheets that cover the continent and observing the effects of current climate change on plant and animal life. During the cold, dark southern winter, the research population drops to only a little over 1,000. In addition to scientists, almost 30,000 tourists visit Antarctica during the southern summer, mainly along the Antarctic Peninsula, where they view wildlife such as seals, whales, penguins, and other birds.

South Orkney Islands

South Shetland Islands

Joinville Island

Palmer Station (United States)

Bellingshausen Sea

DAY AND NIGHT

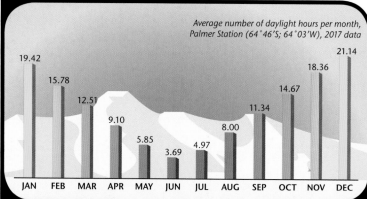

Average number of daylight hours per month, Palmer Station (64°46'S; 64°03'W), 2017 data

JAN	FEB	MAR	APR	MAY	JUN	JUL	AUG	SEP	OCT	NOV	DEC
19.42	15.78	12.51	9.10	5.85	3.69	4.97	8.00	11.34	14.67	18.36	21.14

Because of its very high southern latitude, Antarctica experiences extreme fluctuations in the length of daylight hours. At the South Pole (90° S) there are months of total darkness.

◐ **STANDING GUARD.** Leopard seals' preferred food is penguins, but they also eat other species of seals and have even been known to attack humans.

ATLANTIC OCEAN

ANTARCTIC CIRCLE

Fimbul Ice Shelf

Cape Norvegia

Riiser-Larsen Ice Shelf

Queen Maud Land

Riiser-Larsen Peninsula

Lützow-Holm Bay

INDIAN OCEAN

Enderby Land

Azimuthal Equidistant Projection

0   500 miles
0   500 kilometers

Weddell Sea

Larsen C iceberg detached July 12, 2017

Coats Land

Larsen Ice Shelf

Mt. Jackson
10,446 ft 3,184 m

Filchner Ice Shelf

tic Peninsula

Alexander Island

Ronne Ice Shelf

Berkner Island

Pensacola Mountains

Cape Darnley

Amery Ice Shelf

Coldest place in the world

RIDGE A

EAST ANTARCTICA

American Highland

Prydz Bay

West Ice Shelf

POLAR PLATEAU

Vinson Massif
16,067 ft
4,897 m

Highest point in Antarctica

Ellsworth Mts.

★ South Pole
■ Amundsen-Scott Station (United States)

Transantarctic Mountains

Ellsworth Land

WEST ANTARCTICA

Thurston Island

Amundsen Sea

Marie Byrd Land

Getz Ice Shelf

■ Vostok Station (Russia)

Shackleton Ice Shelf

Wilkes Land

Ross Ice Shelf

Roosevelt Island

Lowest point in Antarctica

Byrd Glacier
-9,416 ft
-2,870 m

Cape Poinsett

PACIFIC OCEAN

Ross Sea

Mt. Erebus
12,448 ft
3,794 m

Ross I.

Cape Crozier

McMurdo Sound

Victoria Land

Porpoise Bay

Map Key

★ Pole

■ Research station

Mt. Minto
13,665 ft
4,165 m

Cape Adare

ANTARCTIC CIRCLE

★ South Magnetic Pole

◐ **SOUTHERN EXPLORATION.** Adventurous tourists, riding in a Zodiac, get a close-up look at a humpback whale diving under the waters of the Weddell Sea. These motorized inflatable boats enable passengers to travel from their expedition ship, anchored in deep water, to the shores of the Antarctic Peninsula.

◑ **COLD SWIM.** A mother orca and her calf come up for air in the icy waters of McMurdo Sound. Orcas live in social groups called pods and work together to catch a meal of fish, seals, or sea lions.

THE OCEANS

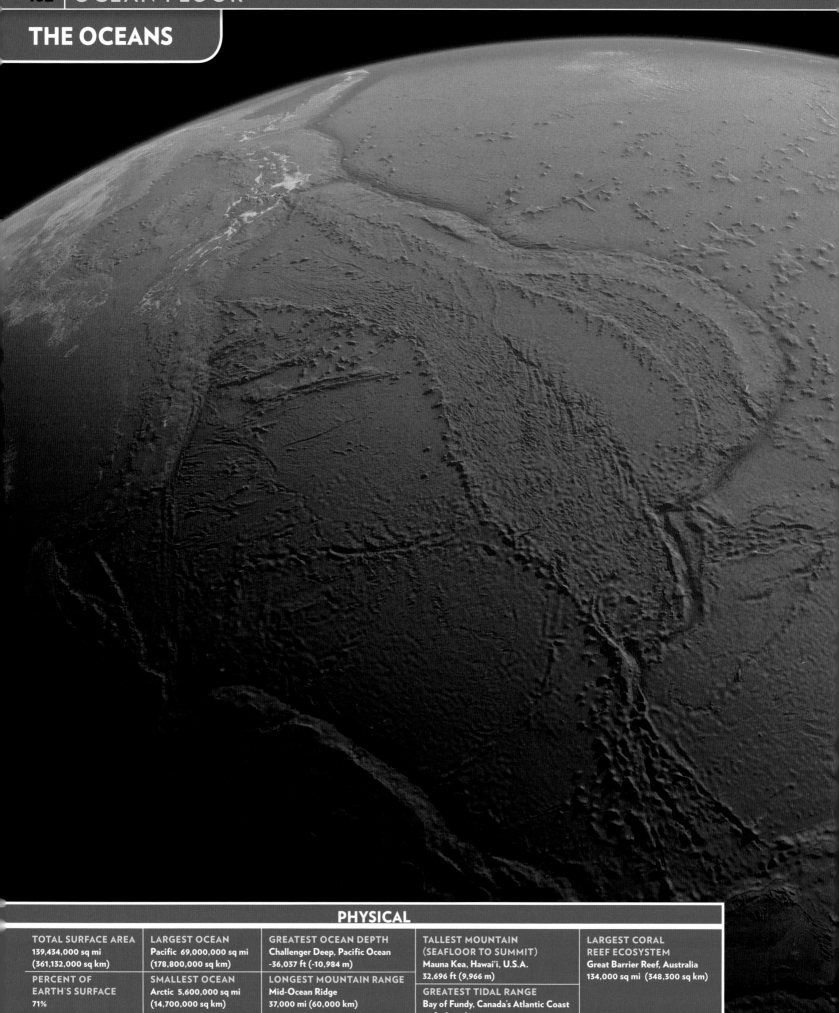

PHYSICAL

TOTAL SURFACE AREA	LARGEST OCEAN	GREATEST OCEAN DEPTH	TALLEST MOUNTAIN (SEAFLOOR TO SUMMIT)	LARGEST CORAL REEF ECOSYSTEM
139,434,000 sq mi (361,132,000 sq km)	Pacific 69,000,000 sq mi (178,800,000 sq km)	Challenger Deep, Pacific Ocean -36,037 ft (-10,984 m)	Mauna Kea, Hawai'i, U.S.A. 32,696 ft (9,966 m)	Great Barrier Reef, Australia 134,000 sq mi (348,300 sq km)
PERCENT OF EARTH'S SURFACE 71%	SMALLEST OCEAN Arctic 5,600,000 sq mi (14,700,000 sq km)	LONGEST MOUNTAIN RANGE Mid-Ocean Ridge 37,000 mi (60,000 km)	GREATEST TIDAL RANGE Bay of Fundy, Canada's Atlantic Coast 53 ft (16 m)	

THE OCEANS

Investigating the Oceans

The map at right shows that more than 70 percent of Earth's surface is underwater, mainly covered by four great oceans. There is growing support for recognizing a fifth ocean, called the Southern Ocean, in the area from Antarctica to 60° S latitude. The oceans are really inter-connected bodies of water that together form one global ocean.

The ocean floor is as varied as the surface of the continents, but mapping the oceans is challenging. Past explorers cut their way through jungles of the Amazon and conquered icy heights of the Himalaya, but explorers could not march across the floor of the Pacific Ocean, which in places descends to more than 36,000 feet (10,984 m) below the surface of the water.

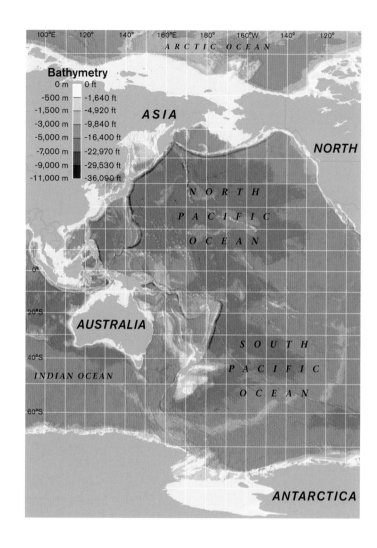

⬬ **UNDERWATER LANDSCAPE.** The landscape of the ocean floor is varied and constantly changing. A continental edge that slopes gently beneath the water is called a continental shelf (1). Mountain ranges, called mid-ocean ridges (2), rise where ocean plates are spreading and magma flows out to create new land. Elsewhere, plates plunge into trenches (3) more than six miles (10 km) deep. In addition, magma, rising through vents called hot spots, pushes through ocean plates, creating seamounts (4) and volcanoes (5).

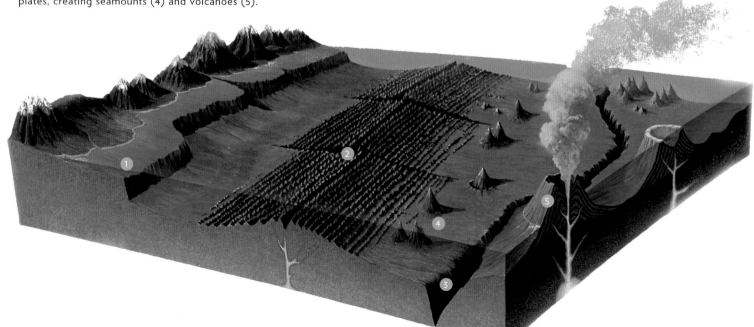

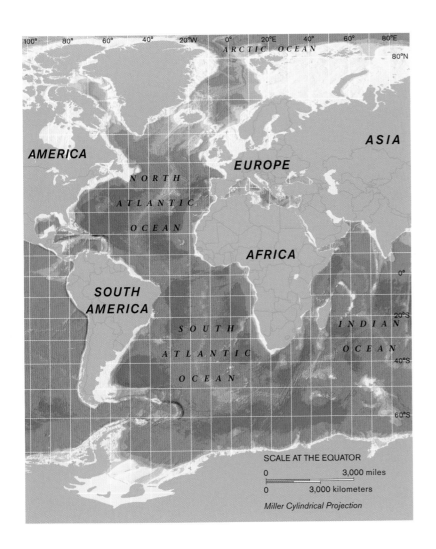

SCALE AT THE EQUATOR

0   3,000 miles

0   3,000 kilometers

Miller Cylindrical Projection

FROM OCEAN TO SATELLITE. In the 1990s, scientists developed the Argo Float to collect data from below the ocean surface. Argo Floats sink to a preset depth, often thousands of feet, where they gather data, such as temperature and salt content. At regular intervals, the floats rise to the surface (above) and transmit the data collected to a satellite. Then the cycle starts over again.

SEEING WITH YOUR EARS.
Special instruments, such as this acoustic buoy, use sound waves bounced off the ocean floor to record variations in water temperature. This technique, called Acoustic Thermometry of Ocean Climate (ATOC), may someday help monitor long-term climate changes.

EYE ON THE OCEAN. Satellites orbiting high above Earth's surface record digital images of ocean colors, sea surface temperatures, and salinity levels. These can be used to identify and follow plant and animal activity as well as changes in the ocean environment.

THE BASICS

STATS

Surface area
69,000,000 sq mi
(178,800,000 sq km)

Percent of Earth's water area
49.5%

Greatest depth
Challenger Deep
(in the Mariana Trench)
-36,037 ft (-10,984 m)

Tides
Highest: 30 ft (9 m)
near Korean peninsula
Lowest: 1 ft (0.3 m)
near Midway Islands

GEO WHIZ

The Pacific Ocean has more islands—tens of thousands of them—than any other ocean.

The ocean's name comes from the Latin *Mare Pacificum*, meaning "peaceful sea," but earthquakes and volcanic activity along the Ring of Fire generate powerful waves called tsunamis, which cause death and destruction when they slam ashore.

With the greatest area of tropical waters, the Pacific is also home to the largest number of coral reefs, including Earth's longest: Australia's Great Barrier Reef.

Only about 1,000 Hawaiian monk seals remain in the wild. Most live in protected waters of the Hawaiian archipelago.

Pacific Ocean

⬤ **IN THE MIDST OF DANGER.** A false-clown anemonefish swims among the tentacles of a sea anemone off the coast of the Philippines, in the western Pacific. This colorful fish is immune to the anemone's paralyzing sting.

The Pacific Ocean, largest of Earth's oceans, is more than 15 times larger than the United States and covers more than 30 percent of Earth's surface. The margins of the Pacific are often called the Ring of Fire because many active volcanoes and earthquakes occur where the ocean plate is moving under the edges of continental plates. The southwestern Pacific is dotted with many islands. Also in the western Pacific, Challenger Deep in the Mariana Trench plunges to 36,037 ft (10,984 m) below sea level. Most of the world's fish catch comes from the Pacific, and oil and gas reserves in the Pacific are an important energy source.

⬤ **CIRCLE OF LIFE.** Atolls, such as this one near Okinawa, Japan, are ocean landforms created by tiny marine animals called corals. These creatures live in warm tropical waters. The circular shapes of atolls often mark the coastlines of sunken volcanic islands.

SCALE AT THE EQUATOR
0 ____ 1,000 miles
0 ____ 1,000 kilometers
Mercator Projection

ASIA

Amur

Sea of Japan (East Sea)

Korea

Yellow Sea

East China Sea

Ryukyu Is.

Taiwan

Ryukyu Trench

South China Sea

Philippine Trench

PHILIPPINE ISLANDS

Sulu Basin

Celebes Basin

INDONESIA

Banda Sea

Weber Basin

North Australian Basin

Izu-Ogasawara Trench

Bonin Trench

Philippine Sea

Kyushu-Palau Ridge

West Mariana Basin

Mariana Trench

Palau Trench

Yap Trench

West Caroline Basin

New Guinea

Continental Shelf

TROPIC OF CAPRICORN

AUSTRALIA

South Australian Basin

INDIAN OCEAN

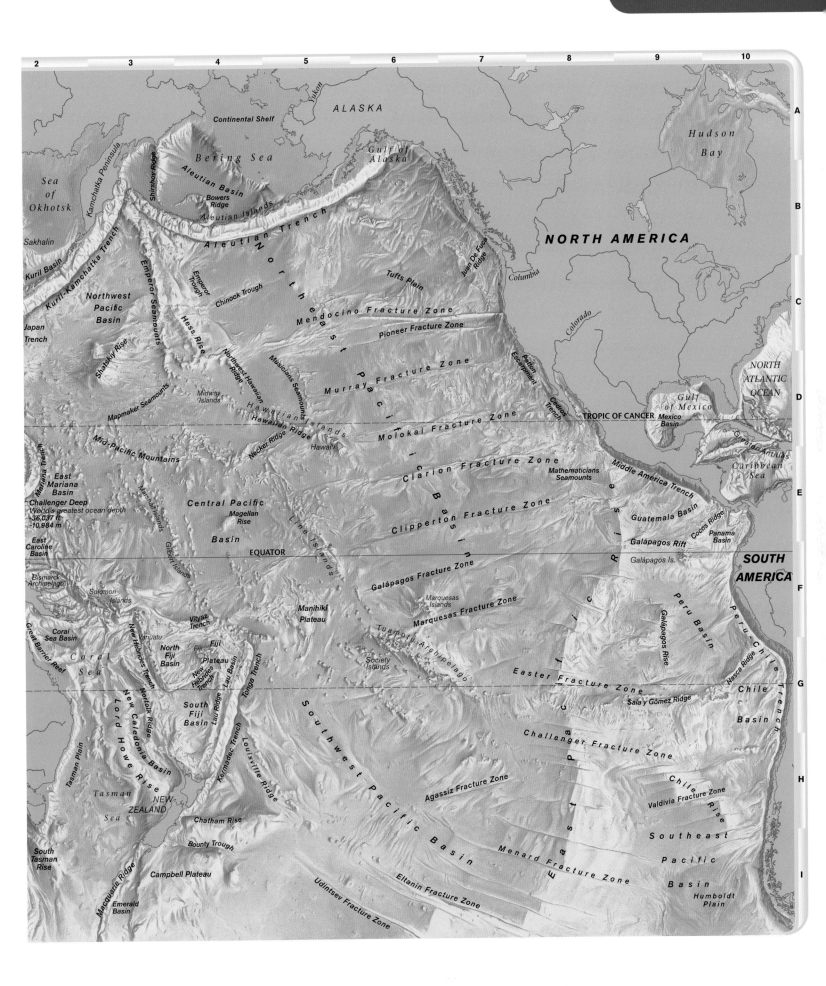

ALASKA

Hudson Bay

Bering Sea

Continental Shelf

Aleutian Basin

Bowers Ridge

Aleutian Islands

NORTH AMERICA

Sea of Okhotsk

Sakhalin

Kamchatka Peninsula

Shirshov Ridge

Emperor Trough

Gulf of Alaska

Kuril Basin

Kuril-Kamchatka Trench

Northwest Pacific Basin

Emperor Seamounts

Hess Rise

Chinook Trough

Tufts Plain

Juan De Fuca Ridge

Columbia

Japan Trench

Northwest Hawaiian Ridge

Mendocino Fracture Zone

Pioneer Fracture Zone

Patton Escarpment

NORTH ATLANTIC OCEAN

Shatsky Rise

Murray Fracture Zone

Cedros Trench

Mapmaker Seamounts

Midway Islands

Musicians Seamounts

Hawaiian Islands

Gulf of Mexico

Greater Antilles

Mid-Pacific Mountains

Hawaiian Ridge

Necker Ridge

Molokai Fracture Zone

TROPIC OF CANCER

Mexico Basin

Mariana Trench

East Mariana Basin

Hawai'i

Clarion Fracture Zone

Mathematicians Seamounts

Middle America Trench

Caribbean Sea

Challenger Deep
World's greatest ocean depth
-36,037 ft
-10,984 m

Central Pacific

Magellan Rise

Marshall Islands

Basin

Clipperton Fracture Zone

Guatemala Basin

Cocos Ridge

Panama Basin

East Caroline Basin

Gilbert Islands

EQUATOR

Line Islands

Galápagos Rift

SOUTH AMERICA

Bismarck Archipelago

Solomon Islands

Galápagos Fracture Zone

Galápagos Is.

Manihiki Plateau

Marquesas Islands

Marquesas Fracture Zone

Peru Basin

Galápagos Rise

Vityaz Trench

Tuamotu Archipelago

Vanuatu

Fiji

Coral Sea Basin

New Hebrides Trench

North Fiji Basin

Fiji Plateau

Society Islands

Peru-Chile Trench

Nasca Ridge

Great Barrier Reef

Coral Sea

New Hebrides Trench

Lau Ridge

Easter Fracture Zone

Chile Basin

South Fiji Basin

Lau Basin

Tonga Trench

Sala y Gómez Ridge

Norfolk Ridge

New Caledonia Basin

Kermadec Trench

Louisville Ridge

Southwest Pacific Basin

Challenger Fracture Zone

Chile Rise

Tasman Plain

Lord Howe Rise

Agassiz Fracture Zone

Valdivia Fracture Zone

Southeast

Tasman Sea

NEW ZEALAND

Chatham Rise

Menard Fracture Zone

Pacific

South Tasman Rise

Bounty Trough

Basin

Macquarie Ridge

Campbell Plateau

Eltanin Fracture Zone

Humboldt Plain

Emerald Basin

Udintsev Fracture Zone

THE BASICS

STATS

Surface area
35,400,000 sq mi
(91,700,000 sq km)

Percent of Earth's water area
25.4%

Greatest depth
Puerto Rico Trench
-28,232 ft (-8,605 m)

Tides
Highest: 53 ft (16 m)
Bay of Fundy, Canada
Lowest: 1.5 ft (0.5 m)
Gulf of Mexico and
Mediterranean Sea

GEO WHIZ

In 2005, the Atlantic Ocean experienced a record-setting 27 named tropical storms, including 14 hurricanes. Three hurricanes (Katrina, Rita, and Wilma) reached category 5 level, with sustained winds of at least 155 miles an hour (249 km/h).

The Atlantic Ocean is about half the size of the Pacific and growing. As molten rock from Earth's interior escapes where spreading occurs along the Mid-Atlantic Ridge, new ocean floor forms.

Each year, the amount of water that flows into the Atlantic Ocean from the Amazon River, in South America, is equal to 20 percent of Earth's available freshwater.

Atlantic Ocean

⬤ **CAMOUFLAGE ON ICE.** A young harp seal, called a pup, rests on the ice in Canada's Gulf of St. Lawrence. Pups are cared for by their mothers for only 12 days. After that, they must survive on their own.

Among Earth's great oceans, the Atlantic is second only to the Pacific in size. The floor of the Atlantic is split by the Mid-Atlantic Ridge, which is part of the Mid-Ocean Ridge—the longest mountain chain on Earth. The Atlantic poses many hazards to human activity. Tropical storms called hurricanes form in the warm tropical waters off the west coast of Africa and move across the ocean to bombard the islands of the Caribbean and coastal areas of North America with damaging winds, waves, and rain in the late summer and fall. In the cold waters of the North Atlantic, sea ice and icebergs pose risks to shipping, especially during winter and spring.

The Atlantic has rich deposits of oil and natural gas, but drilling has raised concerns about pollution. In addition, the Atlantic has important marine fisheries, but overfishing has put some species at risk. Sea lanes between Europe and the Americas are among the most heavily trafficked in the world.

◗ **HIDDEN DANGER.** Icebergs (right) are huge blocks of ice that break away, or calve, from the edges of glaciers. They pose a danger to ships because only about 10 percent of their bulk is visible above the waterline. A tragic disaster associated with an iceberg was the 1912 sinking of the R.M.S. *Titanic,* whose ghostly ruins lie below the waters of the North Atlantic Ocean (far right).

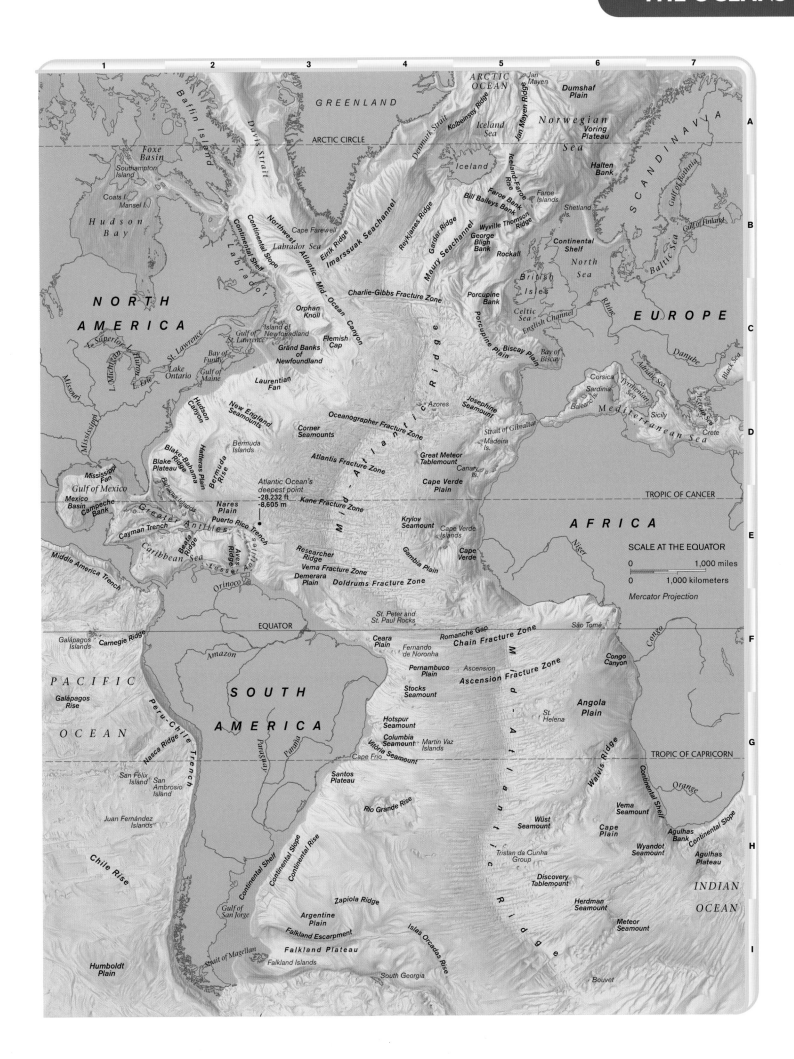

ARCTIC OCEAN

GREENLAND

ARCTIC CIRCLE

Jan Mayen
Dumshaf Plain
Norwegian Sea
Voring Plateau
SCANDINAVIA
Kolbeinsey Ridge
Iceland Sea
Jan Mayen Ridge
Denmark Strait
Iceland
Halten Bank
Gulf of Bothnia

Foxe Basin
Southampton Island
Coats I.
Mansel I.
Hudson Bay
Baffin Island
Davis Strait
Cape Farewell
Labrador Sea
Eirik Ridge
Atlantic Mid-Ocean Canyon
Imarssuak Seachannel
Reykjanes Ridge
Gardar Ridge
Maury Seachannel
Iceland-Faroe Rise
Faroe Bank
Bill Baileys Bank
Wyville Thomson Ridge
George Bligh Bank
Rockall
Faroe Islands
Shetland Is.
Continental Shelf
Baltic Sea
Gulf of Finland

NORTH AMERICA
Continental Slope
Labrador
Continental Shelf
Northwest
Charlie-Gibbs Fracture Zone
North Sea
British Isles
EUROPE
Rhine

Orphan Knoll
Island of Newfoundland
Gulf of St. Lawrence
Flemish Cap
Porcupine Bank
Celtic Sea
English Channel
Danube

L. Superior L. Huron
St. Lawrence
Bay of Fundy
Grand Banks of Newfoundland
Porcupine Plain
Biscay Plain
Bay of Biscay
Black Sea

L. Michigan
L. Erie
Lake Ontario
Gulf of Maine
Laurentian Fan
Mid-Atlantic Ridge
Azores
Josephine Seamount
Corsica
Sardinia
Balearic Is.
Tyrrhenian Sea
Adriatic Sea
Sicily
Crete
Mediterranean Sea

Missouri
Hudson Canyon
New England Seamounts
Oceanographer Fracture Zone
Great Meteor Tablemount
Strait of Gibraltar
Madeira Is.
Canary Is.
Madeira

Corner Seamounts
Atlantis Fracture Zone
Bermuda Islands
Blake-Bahama Ridge
Blake Plateau
Hatteras Plain
Bermuda Rise
Cape Verde Plain

Mississippi
Mississippi Fan
Gulf of Mexico
Mexico Basin
Campeche Bank
Bahama Islands
Nares Plain
Atlantic Ocean's deepest point
-28,232 ft
-8,605 m
Kane Fracture Zone
TROPIC OF CANCER
AFRICA
Niger

Greater Antilles
Puerto Rico Trench
Krylov Seamount
Cape Verde Islands
Cape Verde

Cayman Trench
Beata Ridge
Aves Ridge
Researcher Ridge
Gambia Plain
SCALE AT THE EQUATOR
0   1,000 miles
0   1,000 kilometers
Mercator Projection

Middle America Trench
Caribbean Sea
Lesser Antilles
Vema Fracture Zone
Demerara Plain
Doldrums Fracture Zone
Orinoco

St. Peter and St. Paul Rocks
EQUATOR
Ceara Plain
Romanche Gap
Chain Fracture Zone
São Tomé
Congo

Galápagos Islands
Carnegie Ridge
Amazon
Fernando de Noronha
Ascension Fracture Zone
Mid-Atlantic Ridge
Congo Canyon

PACIFIC OCEAN
Galápagos Rise
SOUTH AMERICA
Pernambuco Plain
Stocks Seamount
Ascension
St. Helena
Angola Plain

Peru-Chile Trench
Nasca Ridge
Paraguay
Paraná
Hotspur Seamount
Columbia Seamount
Vitória Seamount
Martin Vaz Islands
Cape Frio

San Félix Island
San Ambrosio Island
Santos Plateau
Walvis Ridge
Continental Shelf
Orange
TROPIC OF CAPRICORN

Juan Fernández Islands
Rio Grande Rise
Vema Seamount
Cape Plain
Agulhas Bank
Continental Slope
Agulhas Plateau

Chile Rise
Continental Shelf
Continental Slope
Continental Rise
Wüst Seamount
Wyandot Seamount
INDIAN OCEAN

Zapiola Ridge
Tristan da Cunha Group
Discovery Tablemount
Herdman Seamount
Meteor Seamount

Gulf of San Jorge
Argentine Plain
Falkland Escarpment
Islas Orcadas Rise
Mid-Atlantic Ridge

Strait of Magellan
Falkland Plateau
Falkland Islands
Humboldt Plain
South Georgia
Bouvet

THE OCEANS

THE BASICS
STATS

Surface area
29,400,000 sq mi
(76,200,000 sq km)

Percent of Earth's water area
21%

Greatest depth
Java Trench
-23,376 ft (-7,125 m)

Tides
Highest: 36 ft (11 m)
Lowest: 2 ft (0.6 m)
Both along Australia's west coast

GEO WHIZ

Some of the world's largest breeding grounds for humpback whales are in the Indian Ocean, the Arabian Sea, and off the east coast of Africa.

The Bay of Bengal is sometimes called Cyclone Alley because of the large number of tropical storms that occur there each year between May and November.

Sailors from what is now Indonesia used seasonal winds called monsoons to reach Africa's east coast. They arrived on the continent long before Europeans did.

A December 2004 earthquake caused a tsunami that killed more than 225,000 people in countries bordering the Indian Ocean. Waves reached as high as 49 feet (15 m).

Indian Ocean

The Indian Ocean stretches from Africa's east coast to the southern coast of Asia and the western coast of Australia. It is the third largest of Earth's great oceans. Changing air pressure systems over its warm waters trigger South Asia's famous monsoon climate—a weather pattern in which winds reverse directions seasonally. The Bay of Bengal, an arm of the Indian Ocean, experiences devastating tropical storms, similar to hurricanes, but called cyclones in this region. Islands along the eastern edge of the Indian Ocean plate experience earthquakes that sometimes cause destructive ocean waves called tsunamis.

The Arabian Sea, Persian Gulf, and Red Sea, extensions of the Indian Ocean, are important sources of oil and natural gas and account for more than half of Earth's offshore oil production. Sea routes of the Indian Ocean connect the Middle East to the rest of the world, carrying vital energy resources on huge tanker ships.

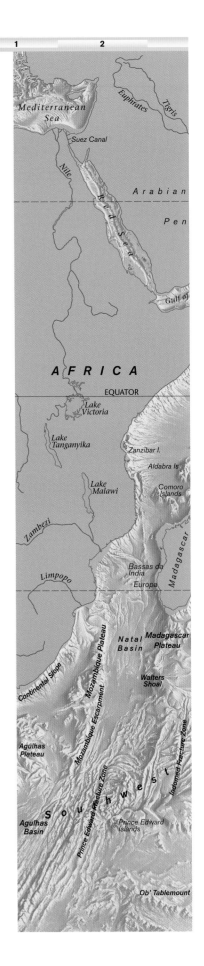

◑ LIVING FOSSIL.
A coelacanth swims in the warm waters of the western Indian Ocean off the Comoro Islands. Once thought to have become extinct 65 million years ago along with the dinosaurs, a living coelacanth was discovered in 1938.

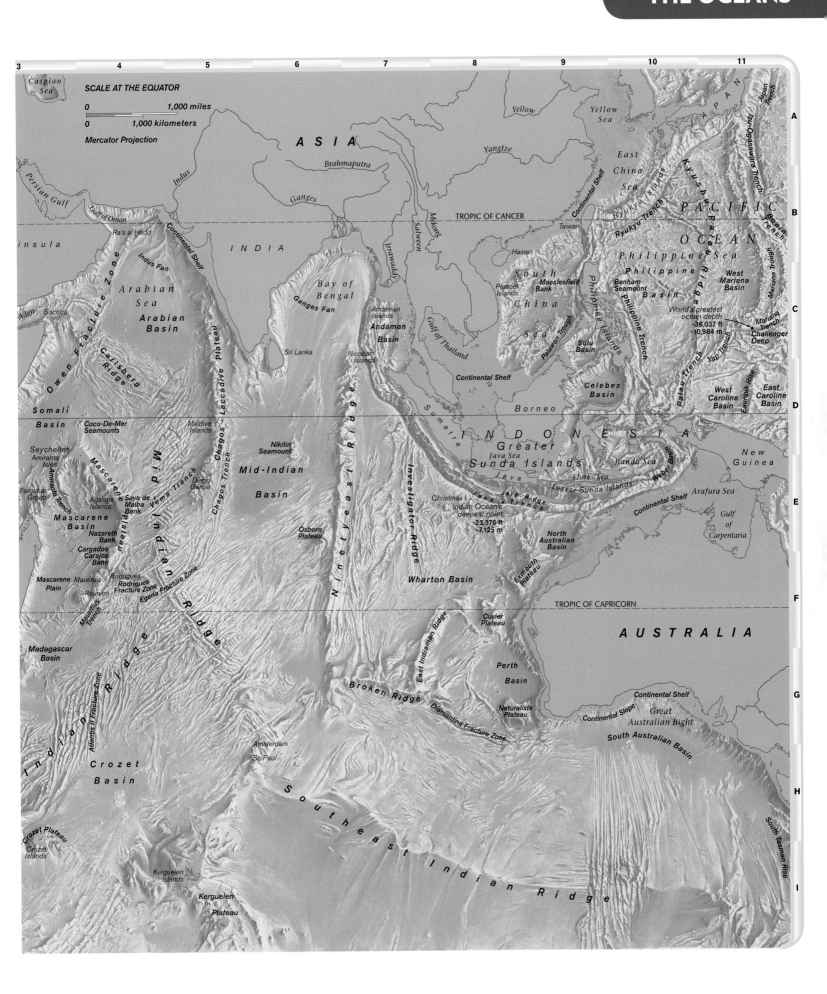

3   4   5   6   7   8   9   10   11

Caspian Sea

SCALE AT THE EQUATOR

0   1,000 miles
0   1,000 kilometers

Mercator Projection

ASIA

Yellow

Yellow Sea

JAPAN

Izu-Ogasawara Trench

A

Persian Gulf

Indus

Brahmaputra

Yangtze

East China Sea

PACIFIC

Bonin Trench

Gulf of Oman

Ganges

Salween

Mekong

TROPIC OF CANCER

Continental Shelf

Taiwan

Ryukyu Islands

Kyushu-Palau Ridge

OCEAN

Izu-Ogasawara Trench

B

insula

Ra's al Hadd

Continental Shelf

INDIA

Irrawaddy

Hainan

Ryukyu Trench

Philippine Sea

Philippine Islands

West Mariana Basin

Owen Fracture Zone

Indus Fan

Arabian Sea

Bay of Bengal

Ganges Fan

Andaman Islands

South China Sea

Paracel Islands

Macclesfield Bank

Benham Seamount

Philippine Basin

Mariana Trench

C

Aden

Socotra

Arabian Basin

Sri Lanka

Andaman Basin

Gulf of Thailand

Palawan Trough

Sulu Basin

Philippine Trench

World's greatest ocean depth −36,037 ft ~10,984 m

Yap Trench

Mariana Trench Challenger Deep

Carlsberg Ridge

Chagos-Laccadive Plateau

Nicobar Islands

Continental Shelf

Borneo

Celebes Basin

Palau Trench

West Caroline Basin

East Caroline Basin

D

Somali Basin

Coco-De-Mer Seamounts

Maldive Islands

Chagos Trench

Nikitin Seamount

Sumatra

INDONESIA

Greater Sunda Islands

Java Sea

Banda Sea

Weber Basin

Eauripik Rise

New Guinea

Seychelles Amirante Isles

Mascarene Plateau

Mid-Indian Basin

Diego Garcia

Mid-Indian Basin

Ninetyeast Ridge

Investigator Ridge

Java

Flores Sea

Lesser Sunda Islands

Continental Shelf

Arafura Sea

E

Farquhar Group

Amirante Trench

Agalega Islands

Saya de Malha Bank

Vema Trench

Java Ridge

Christmas I.

Indian Ocean's deepest point −23,376 ft −7,125 m

North Australian Basin

Gulf of Carpentaria

Mascarene Basin

Nazareth Bank

Cargados Carajos Bank

Osborn Plateau

Java Trench

Exmouth Plateau

Mascarene Plain

Mauritius

Réunion

Rodrigues

Rodrigues Fracture Zone

Egeria Fracture Zone

Wharton Basin

F

Mauritius Trench

Mid Indian Ridge

TROPIC OF CAPRICORN

Cuvier Plateau

AUSTRALIA

Madagascar Basin

Indian Ridge

Atlantis II Fracture Zone

East Indiaman Ridge

Perth Basin

G

Broken Ridge

Diamantina Fracture Zone

Naturaliste Plateau

Continental Slope

Continental Shelf

Great Australian Bight

South Australian Basin

Amsterdam

St. Paul

Crozet Basin

H

Crozet Plateau

Crozet Islands

Southeast Indian Ridge

South Tasman Rise

Kerguelen Islands

I

Kerguelen Plateau

THE OCEANS

THE BASICS

STATS

Surface area
5,600,000 sq mi
(14,700,000 sq km)

Percent of Earth's water area
4.1%

Greatest depth
Molloy Deep: -18,599 ft
(-5,669 m)

Tides
Less than a 1-ft (0.3-m) variation
throughout the ocean

GEO WHIZ

Satellite monitoring of Arctic
sea ice since the late 1970s shows
that the extent of the sea ice is
declining at a rate of 13.3 percent
every 10 years—possibly as a
result of climate change.

The geographic North Pole lies
roughly in the middle of the
Arctic Ocean under 13,000 feet
(3,962 m) of water.

In 1958, a submarine named the
U.S.S. *Nautilus* cruised beneath
the frozen surface of the Arctic
Ocean, proving that the enormous ice sheet rests on water,
not land.

Arctic Ocean

The Arctic Ocean lies mostly north
of the Arctic Circle, bounded by North
America, Europe, and Asia. Unlike the
other oceans, the Arctic is subject to
persistent cold throughout the year.
Also, because of its very high latitude,
the Arctic experiences winters of per-
petual night and summers of continual
daylight. Except for coastal margins, the
Arctic Ocean is covered by permanent
drifting pack ice that averages almost
10 feet (3 m) in thickness. Some scientists are concerned that the polar ice
may be melting due to climate change,
putting at risk the habitat of polar bears
and other arctic animals.

◑ **ARCTIC RESEARCH.** Scientists wearing cold
weather survival suits prepare to measure salt content,
nutrients, and plant and animal life in ice and meltwater.
They also record data related to climate change, such as
the shrinking of polar sea ice.

◑ **FREE RIDE.**
A baby polar bear
catches a ride as its
mother crosses the
frozen landscape of
Canada's Arctic. Polar
bear populations are
showing signs of stress
as sea ice shrinks.

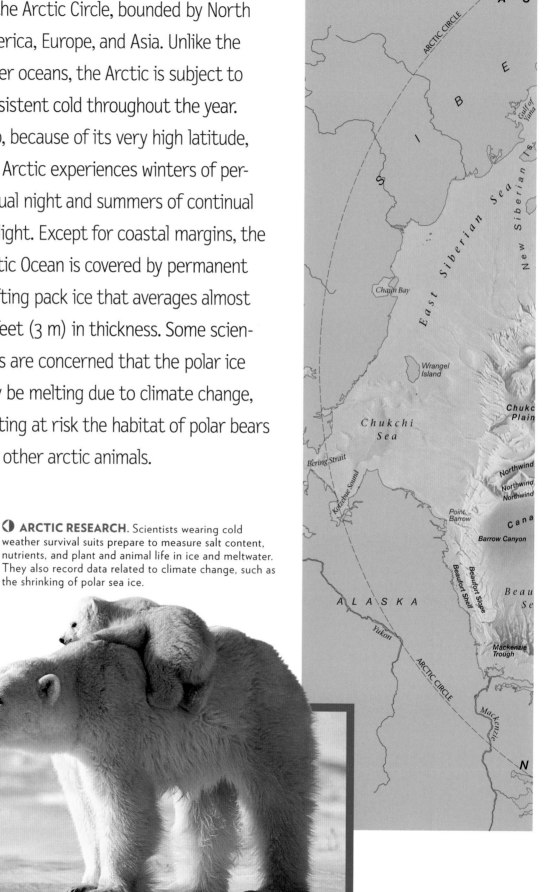

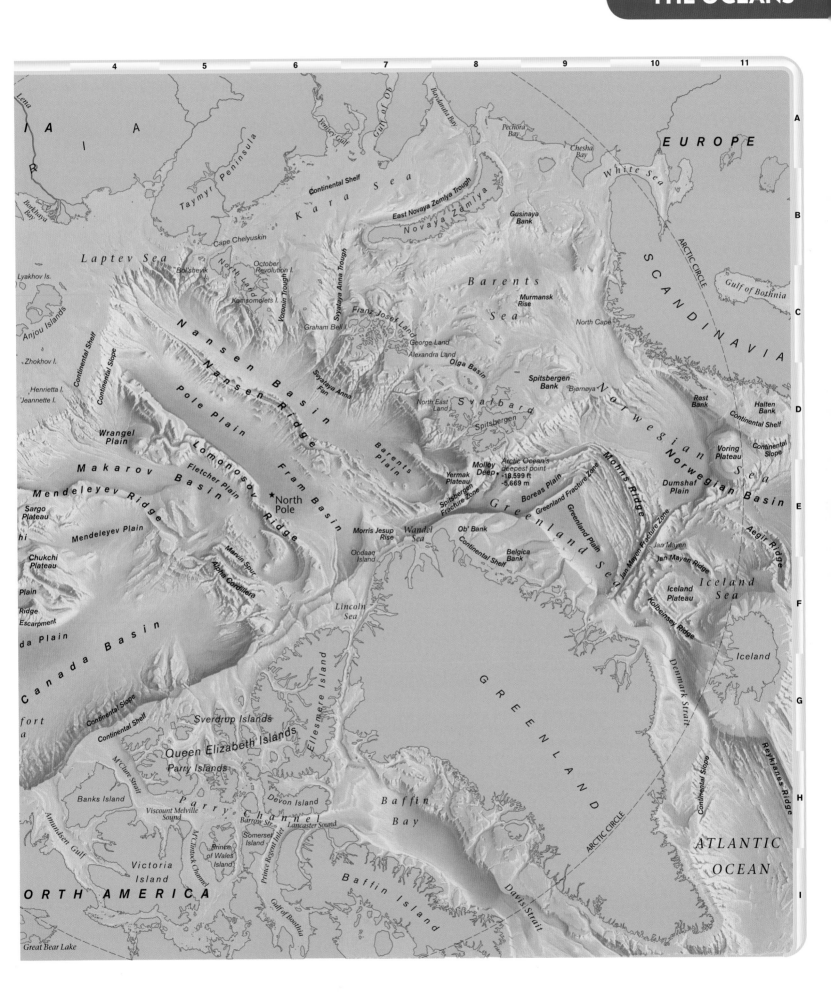

4 5 6 7 8 9 10 11

A S I A

R

Lena

Borkhaya
Bay

EUROPE

Gulf of Ob

Yenisey Gulf

Baydaratsa Bay

Pechora
Bay

Chesha
Bay

White Sea

ARCTIC CIRCLE

Taymyr Peninsula

Continental Shelf

Kara Sea

East Novaya Zemlya Trough

Novaya Zemlya

Gusinaya
Bank

SCANDINAVIA

Gulf of Bothnia

Cape Chelyuskin

Barents

Murmansk
Rise

Laptev Sea

North Land

October
Revolution I.

Voronin Trough

Svyataya Anna Trough

Franz Josef Land

Sea

North Cape

Lyakhov Is.

Bol'shevik

Komsomolets I.

Graham Bell I.

George Land

Anjou Islands

Continental Shelf

Nansen

Svyataya
Fan

Svyataya Anna

Alexandra Land

Olga Basin

Spitsbergen
Bank

Bjørnøya

Norwegian

Røst
Bank

Halten
Bank

Zhokhov I.

Continental Slope

Basin

North East
Land

Svalbard

Continental Shelf

Henrietta I.
Jeannette I.

Nansen Ridge

Pole Plain

Spitsbergen

Voring
Plateau

Continental
Slope

Wrangel
Plain

Lomonosov

Barents
Plain

Molloy
Deep

Arctic Ocean's
deepest point
-18,599 ft
-5,669 m

Mohns Ridge

Sea

Norwegian Basin

Makarov

Fletcher Plain

Basin

Fram Basin

Yermak
Plateau

Boreas Plain

Greenland Fracture Zone

Greenland Plain

Dumshaf
Plain

Mendeleyev Ridge

Ridge

North Pole

Spitsbergen
Fracture Zone

Greenland Fracture Zone

Aegir Ridge

Sargo
Plateau

Mendeleyev Plain

Marvin Spur

Morris Jesup
Rise

Wandel
Sea

Ob' Bank

Greenland Sea

Jan Mayen Fracture Zone

Jan Mayen

Iceland
Sea

hi

Chukchi
Plateau

Alpha Cordillera

Oodaaq
Island

Continental
Shelf

Belgica
Bank

Jan Mayen Ridge

Plain

Iceland
Plateau

Kolbeinsey Ridge

Iceland

Ridge
Escarpment

Lincoln
Sea

da Plain

Canada Basin

Ellesmere Island

GREENLAND

Continental Slope

fort
a

Continental Slope

Sverdrup Islands

Reykjanes Ridge

Continental Shelf

Queen Elizabeth Islands

Parry Islands

M'Clure Strait

Banks Island

Viscount Melville
Sound

Devon Island

Parry

Channel

Barrow Str.

Lancaster Sound

Baffin
Bay

Amundsen Gulf

M'Clintock Channel

Somerset
Island

Prince
of Wales
Island

Prince Regent Inlet

ATLANTIC

Victoria
Island

Gulf of Boothia

Baffin Island

OCEAN

ARCTIC CIRCLE

NORTH AMERICA

Davis Strait

Great Bear Lake

FLAGS & FACTS

These flags and factoids represent the world's 195 independent countries—those with national governments that are recognized as having the highest legal authority over the land and people within their boundaries. Data are based on the CIA's 2017 *World Factbook*. The flags shown are national flags recognized by the United Nations. Area figures include land and inland water bodies. Languages are those most commonly spoken within a country or official languages, which are marked with an asterisk (*). Only the most commonly practiced religions are listed. All GDP per capita figures are in U.S. dollars and are adjusted to reflect purchasing power parity (PPP).

NORTH AMERICA

Antigua and Barbuda
Area: 171 sq mi
(443 sq km)
Population: 95,000
Percent urban: 23%
Capital: St. John's
Language: English*, Creole
Religion: Christianity
GDP per capita: $25,200
Life expectancy: 77 years

Bahamas
Area: 5,359 sq mi
(13,880 sq km)
Population: 330,000
Percent urban: 83%
Capital: Nassau
Language: English*
Religion: Christianity
GDP per capita: $24,600
Life expectancy: 72 years

Barbados
Area: 166 sq mi
(430 sq km)
Population: 292,000
Percent urban: 31.4%
Capital: Bridgetown
Language: English*, Creole
Religion: Christianity
GDP per capita: $17,100
Life expectancy: 75 years

Belize
Area: 8,867 sq mi
(22,966 sq km)
Population: 360,000
Percent urban: 43.7%
Capital: Belmopan
Language: English*, Spanish, Creole, Mayan
Religion: Christianity
GDP per capita: $8,200
Life expectancy: 69 years

Canada
Area: 3,855,081 sq mi
(9,984,670 sq km)
Population: 35,624,000
Percent urban: 82.2%
Capital: Ottawa
Language: English*, French*
Religion: Christianity
GDP per capita: $46,400
Life expectancy: 82 years

Costa Rica
Area: 19,730 sq mi
(51,100 sq km)
Population: 4,930,000
Percent urban: 78.5%
Capital: San José
Language: Spanish*, English
Religion: Christianity
GDP per capita: $16,400
Life expectancy: 79 years

Cuba
Area: 42,803 sq mi
(110,860 sq km)
Population: 11,147,000
Percent urban: 77.3%
Capital: Havana
Language: Spanish*
Religion: Christianity
GDP per capita: $11,900
Life expectancy: 79 years

Dominica
Area: 290 sq mi
(751 sq km)
Population: 74,000
Percent urban: 70.1%
Capital: Roseau
Languages: English*, Creole
Religion: Christianity
GDP per capita: $11,300
Life expectancy: 77 years

Dominican Republic
Area: 18,791 sq mi
(48,670 sq km)
Population: 10,734,000
Percent urban: 80.6%
Capital: Santo Domingo
Language: Spanish*
Religion: Christianity
GDP per capita: $16,000
Life expectancy: 78 years

El Salvador
Area: 8,124 sq mi
(21,041 sq km)
Population: 6,172,000
Percent urban: 67.6%
Capital: San Salvador
Language: Spanish*
Religion: Christianity
GDP per capita: $8,900
Life expectancy: 75 years

Grenada
Area: 133 sq mi
(344 sq km)
Population: 112,000
Percent urban: 35.7%
Capital: St. George's
Language: English*, Creole
Religion: Christianity
GDP per capita: $14,100
Life expectancy: 74 years

Guatemala
Area: 42,042 sq mi
(108,889 sq km)
Population: 15,461,000
Percent urban: 52.5%
Capital: Guatemala City
Language: Spanish*, indigenous languages
Religion: Christianity, indigenous beliefs
GDP per capita: $7,900
Life expectancy: 72 years

Haiti
Area: 10,714 sq mi
(27,750 sq km)
Population: 10,647,000
Percent urban: 60.9%
Capital: Port-au-Prince
Language: French*, Creole*
Religion: Christianity, indigenous beliefs
GDP per capita: $1,800
Life expectancy: 64 years

Honduras
Area: 43,278 sq mi
(112,090 sq km)
Population: 9,039,000
Percent urban: 55.9%
Capital: Tegucigalpa
Language: Spanish*, indigenous languages
Religion: Christianity
GDP per capita: $5,300
Life expectancy: 71 years

Jamaica
Area: 4,244 sq mi
(10,991 sq km)
Population: 2,991,000
Percent urban: 55.3%
Capital: Kingston
Language: English*, Creole
Religion: Christianity
GDP per capita: $9,000
Life expectancy: 74 years

Mexico
Area: 758,445 sq mi
(1,964,375 sq km)
Population: 124,575,000
Percent urban: 79.8%
Capital: Mexico City
Language: Spanish
Religion: Christianity
GDP per capita: $18,900
Life expectancy: 76 years

Nicaragua
Area: 50,336 sq mi
(130,370 sq km)
Population: 6,026,000
Percent urban: 59.4%
Capital: Managua
Language: Spanish*
Religion: Christianity
GDP per capita: $5,500
Life expectancy: 73 years

Panama
Area: 29,120 sq mi
(75,420 sq km)
Population: 3,753,000
Percent urban: 67.2%
Capital: Panama City
Language: Spanish*, indigenous languages
Religion: Christianity
GDP per capita: $23,000
Life expectancy: 79 years

St. Kitts and Nevis
Area: 101 sq mi
(261 sq km)
Population: 53,000
Percent urban: 32.3%
Capital: Basseterre
Language: English*
Religion: Christianity
GDP per capita: $26,100
Life expectancy: 76 years

St. Lucia
Area: 238 sq mi
(616 sq km)
Population: 165,000
Percent urban: 18.6%
Capital: Castries
Language: English*, Creole
Religion: Christianity
GDP per capita: $11,800
Life expectancy: 78 years

St. Vincent and the Grenadines
Area: 150 sq mi
(389 sq km)
Population: 102,000
Percent urban: 51.2%
Capital: Kingstown
Language: English*, Creole
Religion: Christianity
GDP per capita: $11,300
Life expectancy: 75 years

Trinidad and Tobago
Area: 1,980 sq mi
(5,128 sq km)
Population: 1,218,000
Percent urban: 8.3%
Capital: Port of Spain
Language: English*, Creole
Religion: Christianity, Hinduism
GDP per capita: $31,900
Life expectancy: 73 years

United States
Area: 3,794,079 sq mi
(9,826,675 sq km)
Population: 326,626,000
Percent urban: 82%
Capital: Washington, D.C.
Language: English, Spanish
Religion: Christianity
GDP per capita: $57,400
Life expectancy: 80 years

SOUTH AMERICA

Argentina
Area: 1,073,512 sq mi
(2,780,400 sq km)
Population: 44,293,000
Percent urban: 92%
Capital: Buenos Aires
Language: Spanish*, English, Italian,
German, French
Religion: Christianity
GDP per capita: $20,000
Life expectancy: 77 years

Bolivia
Area: 424,162 sq mi
(1,098,581 sq km)
Population: 11,138,000
Percent urban: 69.3%
Capital: La Paz (administrative),
Sucre (constitutional)
Language: Spanish*, Quechua*,
Aymara*, other indigenous
languages*
Religion: Christianity
GDP per capita: $7,200
Life expectancy: 69 years

Brazil
Area: 3,287,594 sq mi
(8,514,877 sq km)
Population: 207,353,000
Percent urban: 86.2%
Capital: Brasília
Language: Portuguese*
Religion: Christianity
GDP per capita: $15,200
Life expectancy: 74 years

Chile
Area: 291,931 sq mi
(756,102 sq km)
Population: 17,789,000
Percent urban: 89.9%
Capital: Santiago
Language: Spanish*, English
Religion: Christianity
GDP per capita: $24,100
Life expectancy: 79 years

Colombia
Area: 439,733 sq mi
(1,138,910 sq km)
Population: 47,699,000
Percent urban: 77%
Capital: Bogotá
Language: Spanish*
Religion: Christianity
GDP per capita: $14,100
Life expectancy: 76 years

Ecuador
Area: 109,483 sq mi
(283,561 sq km)
Population: 16,291,000
Percent urban: 64.2%
Capital: Quito
Language: Spanish*, indigenous
languages
Religion: Christianity
GDP per capita: $11,100
Life expectancy: 77 years

Guyana
Area: 83,000 sq mi
(214,969 sq km)
Population: 738,000
Percent urban: 28.8%
Capital: Georgetown
Language: English*, Creole
Religion: Christianity, Hinduism
GDP per capita: $7,900
Life expectancy: 68 years

Paraguay
Area: 157,047 sq mi
(406,752 sq km)
Population: 6,944,000
Percent urban: 60.2%
Capital: Asunción
Language: Spanish*, Guaraní*
Religion: Christianity
GDP per capita: $9,400
Life expectancy: 77 years

Peru
Area: 496,222 sq mi
(1,285,216 sq km)
Population: 31,037,000
Percent urban: 79.2%
Capital: Lima
Language: Spanish*, Quechua*,
Aymara*
Religion: Christianity
GDP per capita: $12,900
Life expectancy: 74 years

Suriname
Area: 63,251 sq mi
(163,820 sq km)
Population: 592,000
Percent urban: 66%
Capital: Paramaribo
Language: Dutch*, Sranan, English
Religion: Christianity, Hinduism,
Islam
GDP per capita: $14,000
Life expectancy: 72 years

Uruguay
Area: 68,037 sq mi
(176,215 sq km)
Population: 3,360,000
Percent urban: 95.6%
Capital: Montevideo
Language: Spanish*
Religion: Christianity
GDP per capita: $21,500
Life expectancy: 77 years

Venezuela
Area: 352,143 sq mi
(912,050 sq km)
Population: 31,304,000
Percent urban: 89.1%
Capital: Caracas
Language: Spanish*, indigenous
languages
Religion: Christianity
GDP per capita: $13,800
Life expectancy: 76 years

EUROPE

Albania
Area: 11,100 sq mi
(28,748 sq km)
Population: 3,048,000
Percent urban: 59.3%
Capital: Tirana
Language: Albanian*
Religion: Islam, Christianity
GDP per capita: $11,800
Life expectancy: 78 years

Andorra
Area: 181 sq mi
(468 sq km)
Population: 86,000
Percent urban: 84.1%
Capital: Andorra la Vella
Language: Catalan*, French,
Spanish, Portuguese
Religion: Christianity
GDP per capita: $49,900
Life expectancy: 83 years

Austria
Area: 32,383 sq mi
(83,871 sq km)
Population: 8,754,000
Percent urban: 66.1%
Capital: Vienna
Language: German*
Religion: Christianity
GDP per capita: $48,000
Life expectancy: 82 years

FLAGS & FACTS

Belarus
Area: 80,154 sq mi
(207,600 sq km)
Population: 9,550,000
Percent urban: 77.4%
Capital: Minsk
Language: Russian*, Belarusian*
Religion: Christianity
GDP per capita: $18,000
Life expectancy: 73 years

Belgium
Area: 11,787 sq mi
(30,528 sq km)
Population: 11,491,000
Percent urban: 97.9%
Capital: Brussels
Language: Dutch*, French*, German*
Religion: Christianity
GDP per capita: $45,000
Life expectancy: 81 years

Bosnia and Herzegovina
Area: 19,767 sq mi
(51,197 sq km)
Population: 3,856,000
Percent urban: 40.1%
Capital: Sarajevo
Language: Bosnian*, Serbian*, Croatian*
Religion: Islam, Christianity
GDP per capita: $11,000
Life expectancy: 77 years

Bulgaria
Area: 42,810 sq mi
(110,879 sq km)
Population: 7,102,000
Percent urban: 74.6%
Capital: Sofia
Language: Bulgarian*
Religion: Christianity
GDP per capita: $20,300
Life expectancy: 75 years

Croatia
Area: 21,851 sq mi
(56,594 sq km)
Population: 4,292,000
Percent urban: 59.6%
Capital: Zagreb
Language: Croatian*
Religion: Christianity
GDP per capita: $22,800
Life expectancy: 76 years

Cyprus
Area: 3,572 sq mi
(9,251 sq km)
Population: 1,222,000
Percent urban: 66.8%
Capital: Nicosia
Language: Greek*, Turkish*
Religion: Christianity, Islam
GDP per capita: $35,000
Life expectancy: 79 years

Czechia (Czech Republic)
Area: 30,451 sq mi
(78,867 sq km)
Population: 10,675,000
Percent urban: 73%
Capital: Prague
Language: Czech*
Religion: Christianity
GDP per capita: $33,200
Life expectancy: 79 years

Denmark
Area: 16,639 sq mi
(43,094 sq km)
Population: 5,606,000
Percent urban: 88%
Capital: Copenhagen
Language: Danish, English
Religion: Christianity
GDP per capita: $48,000
Life expectancy: 79 years

Estonia
Area: 17,463 sq mi
(45,228 sq km)
Population: 1,252,000
Percent urban: 67.4%
Capital: Tallinn
Language: Estonian*, Russian
Religion: Christianity
GDP per capita: $29,300
Life expectancy: 77 years

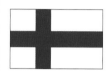

Finland
Area: 130,558 sq mi
(338,145 sq km)
Population: 5,518,000
Percent urban: 84.5%
Capital: Helsinki
Language: Finnish*, Swedish*
Religion: Christianity
GDP per capita: $42,200
Life expectancy: 81 years

France
Area: 248,572 sq mi
(643,801 sq km)
Population: 67,106,000
Percent urban: 80%
Capital: Paris
Language: French*
Religion: Christianity
GDP per capita: $42,300
Life expectancy: 82 years

Germany
Area: 137,846 sq mi
(357,022 sq km)
Population: 80,594,000
Percent urban: 75.7%
Capital: Berlin
Language: German*
Religion: Christianity
GDP per capita: $48,100
Life expectancy: 81 years

Greece
Area: 50,949 sq mi
(131,957 sq km)
Population: 10,768,000
Percent urban: 78.6%
Capital: Athens
Language: Greek*
Religion: Christianity
GDP per capita: $26,700
Life expectancy: 81 years

Hungary
Area: 35,918 sq mi
(93,028 sq km)
Population: 9,851,000
Percent urban: 72.1%
Capital: Budapest
Language: Hungarian*, English, German
Religion: Christianity
GDP per capita: $27,500
Life expectancy: 76 years

Iceland
Area: 39,768 sq mi
(103,000 sq km)
Population: 340,000
Percent urban: 94.3%
Capital: Reykjavik
Language: Icelandic, English, Nordic languages
Religion: Christianity
GDP per capita: $49,200
Life expectancy: 83 years

Ireland
Area: 27,132 sq mi
(70,273 sq km)
Population: 5,011,000
Percent urban: 63.8%
Capital: Dublin
Language: English*, Irish (Gaelic)*
Religion: Christianity
GDP per capita: $69,200
Life expectancy: 81 years

Italy
Area: 116,347 sq mi
(301,340 sq km)
Population: 62,138,000
Percent urban: 69.3%
Capital: Rome
Language: Italian*
Religion: Christianity
GDP per capita: $36,800
Life expectancy: 82 years

Kosovo
Area: 4,203 sq mi
(10,887 sq km)
Population: 1,895,000
Percent urban: NA
Capital: Pristina
Language: Albanian*, Serbian*
Religion: Islam
GDP per capita: $9,600
Life expectancy: NA

Latvia
Area: 24,938 sq mi
(64,589 sq km)
Population: 1,945,000
Percent urban: 67.4%
Capital: Riga
Language: Latvian*, Russian
Religion: Christianity
GDP per capita: $25,700
Life expectancy: 75 years

Liechtenstein
Area: 62 sq mi
(160 sq km)
Population: 38,000
Percent urban: 14.3%
Capital: Vaduz
Language: German*
Religion: Christianity
GDP per capita: $139,100
Life expectancy: 82 years

Lithuania
Area: 25,212 sq mi
(65,300 sq km)
Population: 2,824,000
Percent urban: 66.5%
Capital: Vilnius
Language: Lithuanian*
Religion: Christianity
GDP per capita: $30,000
Life expectancy: 75 years

Luxembourg
Area: 998 sq mi
(2,586 sq km)
Population: 594,000
Percent urban: 90.7%
Capital: Luxembourg
Language: Luxembourgish*, French*,
German*
Religion: Christianity
GDP per capita: $104,000
Life expectancy: 82 years

Macedonia
Area: 9,928 sq mi
(25,713 sq km)
Population: 2,104,000
Percent urban: 57.3%
Capital: Skopje
Language: Macedonian*, Albanian*
Religion: Christianity, Islam
GDP per capita: $14,600
Life expectancy: 76 years

Malta
Area: 122 sq mi
(316 sq km)
Population: 416,000
Percent urban: 95.6%
Capital: Valletta
Language: Maltese*, English*
Religion: Christianity
GDP per capita: $39,900
Life expectancy: 80 years

Moldova
Area: 13,070 sq mi
(33,851 sq km)
Population: 3,474,000
Percent urban: 45.2%
Capital: Chisinau
Language: Romanian (Moldovan)*,
Russian
Religion: Christianity
GDP per capita: $5,300
Life expectancy: 71 years

Monaco
Area: 0.8 sq mi
(2.0 sq km)
Population: 31,000
Percent urban: 100%
Capital: Monaco
Language: French*, English, Italian,
Monégasque
Religion: Christianity
GDP per capita: $115,700
Life expectancy: 90 years

Montenegro
Area: 5,333 sq mi
(13,812 sq km)
Population: 643,000
Percent urban: 64.4%
Capital: Podgorica
Language: Serbian, Montenegrin*
Religion: Christianity, Islam
GDP per capita: $16,600
Life expectancy: NA

Netherlands
Area: 16,040 sq mi
(41,543 sq km)
Population: 17,085,000
Percent urban: 91.5%
Capital: Amsterdam
Language: Dutch*
Religion: Christianity
GDP per capita: $51,000
Life expectancy: 81 years

Norway
Area: 125,020 sq mi
(323,802 sq km)
Population: 5,320,000
Percent urban: 81%
Capital: Oslo
Language: Norwegian*, Sami
Religion: Christianity
GDP per capita: $69,200
Life expectancy: 82 years

Poland
Area: 120,728 sq mi
(312,685 sq km)
Population: 38,476,000
Percent urban: 60.5%
Capital: Warsaw
Language: Polish*
Religion: Christianity
GDP per capita: $27,800
Life expectancy: 78 years

Portugal
Area: 35,556 sq mi
(92,090 sq km)
Population: 10,840,000
Percent urban: 64.6%
Capital: Lisbon
Language: Portuguese*,
Mirandese*
Religion: Christianity
GDP per capita: $28,900
Life expectancy: 79 years

Romania
Area: 92,043 sq mi
(238,391 sq km)
Population: 21,530,000
Percent urban: 54.9%
Capital: Bucharest
Language: Romanian*
Religion: Christianity
GDP per capita: $22,300
Life expectancy: 75 years

Russia
Area: 6,601,631 sq mi
(17,098,242 sq km)
Population: 142,258,000
Percent urban: 74.2%
Capital: Moscow
Language: Russian*
Religion: Christianity, Islam
GDP per capita: $26,500
Life expectancy: 71 years

San Marino
Area: 24 sq mi
(61 sq km)
Population: 34,000
Percent urban: 94.2%
Capital: San Marino
Language: Italian
Religion: Christianity
GDP per capita: $59,500
Life expectancy: 83 years

Serbia
Area: 29,913 sq mi
(77,474 sq km)
Population: 7,111,000
Percent urban: 55.8%
Capital: Belgrade
Language: Serbian*
Religion: Christianity
GDP per capita: $14,500
Life expectancy: 76 years

Slovakia
Area: 18,932 sq mi
(49,035 km)
Population: 5,446,000
Percent urban: 53.4%
Capital: Bratislava
Language: Slovak*
Religion: Christianity
GDP per capita: $31,300
Life expectancy: 77 years

Slovenia
Area: 7,827 sq mi
(20,273 sq km)
Population: 1,972,000
Percent urban: 49.6%
Capital: Ljubljana
Language: Slovenian*
Religion: Christianity
GDP per capita: $32,100
Life expectancy: 78 years

Spain
Area: 195,123 sq mi
(505,370 sq km)
Population: 48,958,000
Percent urban: 80%
Capital: Madrid
Language: Spanish*, Catalan,
Galician, Basque
Religion: Christianity
GDP per capita: $36,400
Life expectancy: 82 years

Sweden
Area: 173,859 sq mi
(450,295 sq km)
Population: 9,960,000
Percent urban: 83.1%
Capital: Stockholm
Language: Swedish*
Religion: Christianity
GDP per capita: $49,800
Life expectancy: 82 years

Switzerland
Area: 15,937 sq mi
(41,277 sq km)
Population: 8,236,000
Percent urban: 74.1%
Capital: Bern
Language: German*, French*,
Italian*, Romansch*
Religion: Christianity
GDP per capita: $59,600
Life expectancy: 83 years

FLAGS & FACTS

Ukraine
Area: 233,031 sq mi
(603,550 sq km)
Population: 44,034,000
Percent urban: 70.1%
Capital: Kiev
Language: Ukrainian*, Russian
Religion: Christianity
GDP per capita: $8,300
Life expectancy: 72 years

United Kingdom
Area: 94,058 sq mi
(243,610 sq km)
Population: 64,769,000
Percent urban: 83.1%
Capital: London
Language: English, regional
languages
Religion: Christianity
GDP per capita: $42,500
Life expectancy: 81 years

Vatican City (Holy See)
Area: 0.2 sq mi
(0.4 sq km)
Population: 1,000
Percent urban: 100%
Capital: Vatican City
Language: Italian, Latin, French
Religion: Christianity
GDP per capita: NA
Life expectancy: NA

ASIA

Afghanistan
Area: 251,826 sq mi
(652,230 sq km)
Population: 34,125,000
Percent urban: 27.6%
Capital: Kabul
Language: Dari*, Pashto*, Turkic
languages
Religion: Islam
GDP per capita: $1,900
Life expectancy: 51 years

Armenia
Area: 11,484 sq mi
(29,743 sq km)
Population: 3,045,000
Percent urban: 62.5%
Capital: Yerevan
Language: Armenian*
Religion: Christianity
GDP per capita: $8,600
Life expectancy: 75 years

Azerbaijan
Area: 33,436 sq mi
(86,600 sq km)
Population: 9,961,000
Percent urban: 55.2%
Capital: Baku
Language: Azerbaijani*
Religion: Islam
GDP per capita: $17,400
Life expectancy: 73 years

Bahrain
Area: 293 sq mi
(760 sq km)
Population: 1,411,000
Percent urban: 88.9%
Capital: Manama
Language: Arabic*, English
Religion: Islam, Christianity
GDP per capita: $50,700
Life expectancy: 79 years

Bangladesh
Area: 55,598 sq mi
(143,998 sq km)
Population: 157,827,000
Percent urban: 35.8%
Capital: Dhaka
Language: Bengali*
Religion: Islam, Hinduism
GDP per capita: $3,900
Life expectancy: 73 years

Bhutan
Area: 14,824 sq mi
(38,394 sq km)
Population: 758,000
Percent urban: 40.1%
Capital: Thimphu
Language: Sharchhopka, Dzongkha*,
Lhotshamkha
Religion: Buddhism, Hinduism
GDP per capita: $8,200
Life expectancy: 70 years

Brunei
Area: 2,226 sq mi
(5,765 sq km)
Population: 444,000
Percent urban: 77.8%
Capital: Bandar Seri Begawan
Language: Malay*, English
Religion: Islam
GDP per capita: $76,900
Life expectancy: 77 years

Cambodia
Area: 69,898 sq mi
(181,035 sq km)
Population: 16,204,000
Percent urban: 21.2%
Capital: Phnom Penh
Language: Khmer*
Religion: Buddhism
GDP per capita: $3,700
Life expectancy: 65 years

China
Area: 3,705,386 sq mi
(9,596,960 sq km)
Population: 1,379,303,000
Percent urban: 57.9%
Capital: Beijing
Language: Mandarin*
Religion: Officially atheist;
Buddhism, Christianity,
indigenous beliefs
GDP per capita: $15,400
Life expectancy: 76 years

Georgia
Area: 26,911 sq mi
(69,700 sq km)
Population: 4,926,000
Percent urban: 54%
Capital: Tbilisi
Language: Georgian*
Religion: Christianity, Islam
GDP per capita: $10,000
Life expectancy: 76 years

India
Area: 1,269,212 sq mi
(3,287,263 sq km)
Population: 1,281,936,000
Percent urban: 33.5%
Capital: New Delhi
Language: Hindi*, English*, state
languages
Religion: Hinduism, Islam
GDP per capita: $6,600
Life expectancy: 69 years

Indonesia
Area: 735,354 sq mi
(1,904,569 sq km)
Population: 260,581,000
Percent urban: 55.2%
Capital: Jakarta
Language: Indonesian*, indigenous
languages
Religion: Islam, Christianity
GDP per capita: $11,700
Life expectancy: 73 years

Iran
Area: 636,368 sq mi
(1,648,195 sq km)
Population: 82,022,000
Percent urban: 74.4%
Capital: Tehran
Language: Persian (Farsi)*
Religion: Islam
GDP per capita: $18,100
Life expectancy: 71 years

Iraq
Area: 169,234 sq mi
(438,317 sq km)
Population: 39,192,000
Percent urban: 69.7%
Capital: Baghdad
Language: Arabic*, Kurdish*
Religion: Islam
GDP per capita: $17,900
Life expectancy: 75 years

Israel
Area: 8,019 sq mi
(20,770 sq km)
Population: 8,300,000
Percent urban: 92.3%
Capital: Jerusalem
Language: Hebrew*, Arabic, English
Religion: Judaism, Islam
GDP per capita: $35,200
Life expectancy: 82 years

Japan
Area: 145,913 sq mi
(377,915 sq km)
Population: 126,451,000
Percent urban: 94.3%
Capital: Tokyo
Language: Japanese
Religion: Shintoism, Buddhism
GDP per capita: $41,300
Life expectancy: 85 years

Jordan
Area: 34,495 sq mi
(89,342 sq km)
Population: 10,248,000
Percent urban: 84.1%
Capital: Amman
Language: Arabic*, English
Religion: Islam
GDP per capita: $12,300
Life expectancy: 75 years

Kazakhstan
Area: 1,052,084 sq mi
(2,724,900 sq km)
Population: 18,557,000
Percent urban: 53.2%
Capital: Astana
Language: Kazakh*, Russian*
Religion: Islam, Christianity
GDP per capita: $25,100
Life expectancy: 71 years

Kuwait
Area: 6,880 sq mi
(17,818 sq km)
Population: 2,875,000
Percent urban: 98.4%
Capital: Kuwait City
Language: Arabic*, English
Religion: Islam, Christianity
GDP per capita: $71,900
Life expectancy: 78 years

Kyrgyzstan
Area: 77,201 sq mi
(199,951 sq km)
Population: 5,789,000
Percent urban: 36%
Capital: Bishkek
Language: Kyrgyz*, Uzbek, Russian*
Religion: Islam, Christianity
GDP per capita: $3,500
Life expectancy: 71 years

Laos
Area: 91,428 sq mi
(236,800 sq km)
Population: 7,127,000
Percent urban: 40.7%
Capital: Vientiane
Language: Lao*, French, indigenous languages
Religion: Buddhism
GDP per capita: $5,700
Life expectancy: 64 years

Lebanon
Area: 4,015 sq mi
(10,400 sq km)
Population: 6,230,000
Percent urban: 88%
Capital: Beirut
Language: Arabic*, French, English
Religion: Islam, Christianity
GDP per capita: $18,500
Life expectancy: 78 years

Malaysia
Area: 127,354 sq mi
(329,847 sq km)
Population: 31,382,000
Percent urban: 76%
Capital: Kuala Lumpur
Language: Malaysian*, English
Religion: Islam, Buddhism, Christianity
GDP per capita: $27,300
Life expectancy: 75 years

Maldives
Area: 115 sq mi
(298 sq km)
Population: 393,000
Percent urban: 47.5%
Capital: Male
Language: Dhivehi*, English
Religion: Islam
GDP per capita: $15,500
Life expectancy: 76 years

Mongolia
Area: 603,905 sq mi
(1,564,116 sq km)
Population: 3,068,000
Percent urban: 73.6%
Capital: Ulaanbaatar
Language: Mongolian*
Religion: Buddhism
GDP per capita: $12,300
Life expectancy: 70 years

Myanmar (Burma)
Area: 261,227 sq mi
(676,578 sq km)
Population: 55,124,000
Percent urban: 35.2%
Capital: Nay Pyi Taw (administrative), Yangon (Rangoon) (legislative)
Language: Burmese*
Religion: Buddhism, Christianity, Islam
GDP per capita: $5,800
Life expectancy: 67 years

Nepal
Area: 56,827 sq mi
(147,181 sq km)
Population: 29,384,000
Percent urban: 19.4%
Capital: Kathmandu
Language: Nepali*, Maithali
Religion: Hinduism, Buddhism
GDP per capita: $2,500
Life expectancy: 71 years

North Korea
Area: 46,540 sq mi
(120,538 sq km)
Population: 25,248,000
Percent urban: 61.2%
Capital: Pyongyang
Language: Korean
Religion: Mainly atheist; Buddhism, Confucianism, indigenous beliefs
GDP per capita: $1,700
Life expectancy: 70 years

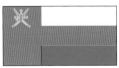

Oman
Area: 119,498 sq mi
(309,500 sq km)
Population: 3,424,000
Percent urban: 78.5%
Capital: Muscat
Language: Arabic*, English
Religion: Islam
GDP per capita: $46,700
Life expectancy: 76 years

Pakistan
Area: 307,372 sq mi
(796,095 sq km)
Population: 204,925,000
Percent urban: 39.7%
Capital: Islamabad
Language: Punjabi, Sindhi, Saraiki, Pashto, Urdu*, English*
Religion: Islam
GDP per capita: $5,100
Life expectancy: 68 years

Philippines
Area: 115,830 sq mi
(300,000 sq km)
Population: 104,256,000
Percent urban: 44.2%
Capital: Manila
Language: Filipino (Tagalog)*, English*, indigenous languages
Religion: Christianity
GDP per capita: $7,700
Life expectancy: 69 years

Qatar
Area: 4,473 sq mi
(11,586 sq km)
Population: 2,314,000
Percent urban: 99.4%
Capital: Doha
Language: Arabic*, English
Religion: Islam, Christianity, Hinduism
GDP per capita: $127,700
Life expectancy: 79 years

Saudi Arabia
Area: 829,995 sq mi
(2,149,690 sq km)
Population: 28,572,000
Percent urban: 83.5%
Capital: Riyadh
Language: Arabic*
Religion: Islam
GDP per capita: $55,200
Life expectancy: 75 years

Singapore
Area: 269 sq mi
(697 sq km)
Population: 5,889,000
Percent urban: 100%
Capital: Singapore
Language: Mandarin*, English*, Malay*, Tamil*
Religion: Buddhism, Islam, Taoism, Christianity
GDP per capita: $87,900
Life expectancy: 85 years

South Korea
Area: 38,502 sq mi
(99,720 sq km)
Population: 51,181,000
Percent urban: 82.7%
Capital: Seoul
Language: Korean, English
Religion: Christianity, Buddhism
GDP per capita: $37,700
Life expectancy: 82 years

Sri Lanka
Area: 25,332 sq mi
(65,610 sq km)
Population: 22,409,000
Percent urban: 18.5%
Capital: Colombo (administrative), Sri Jayewardenepura Kotta (legislative)
Language: Sinhala*, Tamil*, English
Religion: Buddhism, Hinduism, Islam, Christianity
GDP per capita: $12,300
Life expectancy: 77 years

Syria
Area: 71,498 sq mi
(185,180 sq km)
Population: 18,029,000
Percent urban: 58.5%
Capital: Damascus
Language: Arabic*, Kurdish, English, French
Religion: Islam, Christianity
GDP per capita: $2,900
Life expectancy: 75 years

FLAGS & FACTS

Tajikistan
Area: 55,251 sq mi
(143,100 sq km)
Population: 8,469,000
Percent urban: 27%
Capital: Dushanbe
Language: Tajik*, Russian
Religion: Islam
GDP per capita: $3,000
Life expectancy: 68 years

Thailand
Area: 198,116 sq mi
(513,120 sq km)
Population: 68,414,000
Percent urban: 52.7%
Capital: Bangkok
Language: Thai*
Religion: Buddhism
GDP per capita: $16,900
Life expectancy: 75 years

Timor-Leste (East Timor)
Area: 5,743 sq mi
(14,874 sq km)
Population: 1,291,000
Percent urban: 34%
Capital: Dili
Language: Tetum*, Portuguese*,
Indonesian, English
Religion: Christianity
GDP per capita: $4,200
Life expectancy: 68 years

Turkey
Area: 302,533 sq mi
(783,562 sq km)
Population: 80,845,000
Percent urban: 74.4%
Capital: Ankara
Language: Turkish*, Kurdish
Religion: Islam
GDP per capita: $24,900
Life expectancy: 75 years

Turkmenistan
Area: 188,455 sq mi
(488,100 sq km)
Population: 5,351,000
Percent urban: 50.8%
Capital: Ashgabat
Language: Turkmen*, Russian
Religion: Islam, Christianity
GDP per capita: $17,500
Life expectancy: 70 years

United Arab Emirates
Area: 32,278 sq mi
(83,600 sq km)
Population: 6,072,000
Percent urban: 86.1%
Capital: Abu Dhabi
Language: Arabic*, Persian, English
Religion: Islam, Christianity
GDP per capita: $67,900
Life expectancy: 78 years

Uzbekistan
Area: 172,741 sq mi
(447,400 sq km)
Population: 29,749,000
Percent urban: 36.6%
Capital: Tashkent
Language: Uzbek*, Russian
Religion: Islam, Christianity
GDP per capita: $6,600
Life expectancy: 74 years

Vietnam
Area: 127,880 sq mi
(331,210 sq km)
Population: 96,160,000
Percent urban: 34.9%
Capital: Hanoi
Language: Vietnamese*, English
Religion: Buddhism, Christianity
GDP per capita: $6,400
Life expectancy: 73 years

Yemen
Area: 203,848 sq mi
(527,968 sq km)
Population: 28,037,000
Percent urban: 35.8%
Capital: Sanaa
Language: Arabic*
Religion: Islam
GDP per capita: $2,400
Life expectancy: 66 years

AFRICA

Algeria
Area: 919,590 sq mi
(2,381,741 sq km)
Population: 40,969,000
Percent urban: 71.9%
Capital: Algiers
Language: Arabic*, French, Berber*
Religion: Islam
GDP per capita: $15,000
Life expectancy: 77 years

Angola
Area: 481,351 sq mi
(1,246,700 sq km)
Population: 29,310,000
Percent urban: 45.6%
Capital: Luanda
Language: Portuguese*, Bantu,
other indigenous languages
Religion: Christianity
GDP per capita: $6,800
Life expectancy: 56 years

Benin
Area: 43,483 sq mi
(112,622 sq km)
Population: 11,039,000
Percent urban: 44.8%
Capital: Porto-Novo (constitutional),
Cotonou (seat of government)
Language: French*, Fon, Yoruba
Religion: Christianity, Islam,
indigenous beliefs
GDP per capita: $2,100
Life expectancy: 62 years

Botswana
Area: 224,606 sq mi
(581,730 sq km)
Population: 2,215,000
Percent urban: 58%
Capital: Gaborone
Language: Setswana, English*
Religion: Christianity
GDP per capita: $17,000
Life expectancy: 55 years

Burkina Faso
Area: 105,869 sq mi
(274,200 sq km)
Population: 20,108,000
Percent urban: 31.5%
Capital: Ouagadougou
Language: French*, indigenous
languages
Religion: Islam, Christianity
GDP per capita: $1,800
Life expectancy: 56 years

Burundi
Area: 10,745 sq mi
(27,830 sq km)
Population: 11,467,000
Percent urban: 12.7%
Capital: Bujumbura
Language: Kirundi*, French*,
English*
Religion: Christianity
GDP per capita: $800
Life expectancy: 61 years

Cabo Verde
Area: 1,557 sq mi
(4,033 sq km)
Population: 561,000
Percent urban: 66.8%
Capital: Praia
Language: Portuguese*, Creole
Religion: Christianity
GDP per capita: $6,700
Life expectancy: 72 years

Cameroon
Area: 183,567 sq mi
(475,440 sq km)
Population: 24,995,000
Percent urban: 55.5%
Capital: Yaoundé
Language: English*, French*,
indigenous languages
Religion: Christianity, Islam
GDP per capita: $3,200
Life expectancy: 59 years

Central African Republic
Area: 240,534 sq mi
(622,984 sq km)
Population: 5,625,000
Percent urban: 40.6%
Capital: Bangui
Language: French*, Sangho
Religion: Christianity, indigenous
beliefs, Islam
GDP per capita: $700
Life expectancy: 52 years

Chad
Area: 495,752 sq mi
(1,284,000 sq km)
Population: 12,076,000
Percent urban: 22.8%
Capital: N'Djamena
Language: French*, Arabic*,
indigenous languages
Religion: Islam, Christianity
GDP per capita: $2,400
Life expectancy: 50 years

Comoros
Area: 863 sq mi
(2,235 sq km)
Population: 808,000
Percent urban: 28.5%
Capital: Moroni
Language: Arabic*, French*,
Shikomoro*
Religion: Islam
GDP per capita: $1,500
Life expectancy: 64 years

Congo
Area: 132,046 sq mi
(342,000 sq km)
Population: 4,955,000
Percent urban: 66.2%
Capital: Brazzaville
Language: French*, Lingala,
Monokutuba, other indigenous
languages
Religion: Christianity, indigenous
beliefs
GDP per capita: $6,700
Life expectancy: 59 years

**Congo, Democratic
Republic of the**
Area: 905,350 sq mi
(2,344,858 sq km)
Population: 83,301,000
Percent urban: 43.5%
Capital: Kinshasa
Language: French*, Lingala, other
indigenous languages
Religion: Christianity, indigenous
beliefs, Islam
GDP per capita: $800
Life expectancy: 57 years

Côte d'Ivoire (Ivory Coast)
Area: 124,503 sq mi
(322,463 sq km)
Population: 24,185,000
Percent urban: 55.5%
Capitals: Abidjan (administrative),
Yamoussoukro (legislative)
Language: French*, Dioula, other
indigenous languages
Religion: Islam, Christianity
GDP per capita: $3,600
Life expectancy: 59 years

Djibouti
Area: 8,958 sq mi
(23,200 sq km)
Population: 865,000
Percent urban: 77.5%
Capital: Djibouti
Language: French*, Arabic*, Somali,
Afar
Religion: Islam
GDP per capita: $3,400
Life expectancy: 63 years

Egypt
Area: 386,660 sq mi
(1,001,450 sq km)
Population: 97,041,000
Percent urban: 43.3%
Capital: Cairo
Language: Arabic*, English, French
Religion: Islam, Christianity
GDP per capita: $12,600
Life expectancy: 73 years

Equatorial Guinea
Area: 10,830 sq mi
(28,051 sq km)
Population: 778,000
Percent urban: 40.3%
Capital: Malabo
Language: Spanish*, French*,
Portuguese*, indigenous languages
Religion: Christianity, indigenous
beliefs
GDP per capita: $38,600
Life expectancy: 64 years

Eritrea
Area: 45,405 sq mi
(117,600 sq km)
Population: 5,919,000
Percent urban: 23.6%
Capital: Asmara
Language: Tigrinya*, Arabic*,
English*, indigenous languages
Religion: Islam, Christianity
GDP per capita: $1,400
Life expectancy: 65 years

Ethiopia
Area: 426,370 sq mi
(1,104,300 sq km)
Population: 105,350,000
Percent urban: 20.4%
Capital: Addis Ababa
Language: Oromo, Amharic*, Somali,
Tigrinya, Afar
Religion: Christianity, Islam
GDP per capita: $1,900
Life expectancy: 62 years

Gabon
Area: 103,346 sq mi
(267,667 sq km)
Population: 1,772,000
Percent urban: 87.6%
Capital: Libreville
Language: French*, indigenous
languages
Religion: Christianity
GDP per capita: $19,100
Life expectancy: 52 years

Gambia
Area: 4,361 sq mi
(11,295 sq km)
Population: 2,051,000
Percent urban: 60.8%
Capital: Banjul
Language: English*, indigenous
languages
Religion: Islam
GDP per capita: $1,700
Life expectancy: 65 years

Ghana
Area: 92,098 sq mi
(238,533 sq km)
Population: 27,500,000
Percent urban: 55.3%
Capital: Accra
Language: Assanta, Ewe, Fante,
English*
Religion: Christianity, Islam
GDP per capita: $4,400
Life expectancy: 67 years

Guinea
Area: 94,925 sq mi
(245,857 sq km)
Population: 12,414,000
Percent urban: 38.2%
Capital: Conakry
Language: French*, indigenous
languages
Religion: Islam
GDP per capita: $1,300
Life expectancy: 61 years

Guinea-Bissau
Area: 13,948 sq mi
(36,125 sq km)
Population: 1,792,000
Percent urban: 50.8%
Capital: Bissau
Language: Creole, Portuguese*
Religion: Islam, Christianity,
animism
GDP per capita: $1,700
Life expectancy: 51 years

Kenya
Area: 224,080 sq mi
(580,367 sq km)
Population: 47,616,000
Percent urban: 26.5%
Capital: Nairobi
Language: English*, Kiswahili*,
indigenous languages
Religion: Christianity, Islam
GDP per capita: $3,400
Life expectancy: 64 years

Lesotho
Area: 11,720 sq mi
(30,355 sq km)
Population: 1,958,000
Percent urban: 28.4%
Capital: Maseru
Language: Sesotho*, English*
Religion: Christianity, indigenous
beliefs
GDP per capita: $3,600
Life expectancy: 53 years

Liberia
Area: 43,000 sq mi
(111,369 sq km)
Population: 4,689,000
Percent urban: 50.5%
Capital: Monrovia
Language: English*, indigenous
languages
Religion: Christianity, Islam
GDP per capita: $900
Life expectancy: 59 years

Libya
Area: 679,358 sq mi
(1,759,540 sq km)
Population: 6,653,000
Percent urban: 79%
Capital: Tripoli
Language: Arabic*, Italian, English
Religion: Islam
GDP per capita: $8,700
Life expectancy: 77 years

Madagascar
Area: 226,657 sq mi
(587,041 sq km)
Population: 25,054,000
Percent urban: 36.4%
Capital: Antananarivo
Language: French*, Malagasy*
Religion: Christianity, indigenous
beliefs, Islam
GDP per capita: $1,500
Life expectancy: 66 years

Malawi
Area: 45,747 sq mi
(118,484 sq km)
Population: 19,196,000
Percent urban: 16.6%
Capital: Lilongwe
Language: English*, Chichewa, other
indigenous languages
Religion: Christianity, Islam
GDP per capita: $1,100
Life expectancy: 61 years

Mali
Area: 478,838 sq mi
(1,240,192 sq km)
Population: 17,885,000
Percent urban: 41.4%
Capital: Bamako
Language: French*, Bambara, other
indigenous languages
Religion: Islam
GDP per capita: $2,300
Life expectancy: 56 years

FLAGS & FACTS

Mauritania
Area: 397,953 sq mi
(1,030,700 sq km)
Population: 3,759,000
Percent urban: 61%
Capital: Nouakchott
Language: Arabic*, indigenous
languages
Religion: Islam
GDP per capita: $4,300
Life expectancy: 63 years

Mauritius
Area: 788 sq mi
(2,040 sq km)
Population: 1,356,000
Percent urban: 39.4%
Capital: Port Louis
Language: Creole, English*
Religion: Hinduism, Christianity,
Islam
GDP per capita: $20,400
Life expectancy: 76 years

Morocco
Area: 172,413 sq mi
(446,550 sq km)
Population: 33,987,000
Percent urban: 61.2%
Capital: Rabat
Language: Arabic*, Tamazight*,
French
Religion: Islam
GDP per capita: $8,300
Life expectancy: 77 years

Mozambique
Area: 308,641 sq mi
(799,380 sq km)
Population: 26,574,000
Percent urban: 32.8%
Capital: Maputo
Language: Emakhuwa, Portuguese*,
Xichangana, other indigenous
languages
Religion: Christianity, Islam
GDP per capita: $1,200
Life expectancy: 53 years

Namibia
Area: 318,259 sq mi
(824,292 sq km)
Population: 2,485,000
Percent urban: 48.6%
Capital: Windhoek
Language: Indigenous languages,
Afrikaans, English*
Religion: Christianity, indigenous
beliefs
GDP per capita: $11,300
Life expectancy: 64 years

Niger
Area: 489,189 sq mi
(1,267,000 sq km)
Population: 19,245,000
Percent urban: 19.3%
Capital: Niamey
Language: French*, indigenous
languages
Religion: Islam, indigenous beliefs,
Christianity
GDP per capita: $1,100
Life expectancy: 56 years

Nigeria
Area: 356,667 sq mi
(923,768 sq km)
Population: 190,632,000
Percent urban: 49.4%
Capital: Abuja
Language: English*, indigenous
languages
Religion: Islam, Christianity,
indigenous beliefs
GDP per capita: $5,900
Life expectancy: 53 years

Rwanda
Area: 10,169 sq mi
(26,338 sq km)
Population: 11,901,000
Percent urban: 30.7%
Capital: Kigali
Language: Kinyarwanda*, Kiswahili,
French*, English*
Religion: Christianity
GDP per capita: $2,000
Life expectancy: 60 years

Sao Tome and Principe
Area: 372 sq mi
(964 sq km)
Population: 201,000
Percent urban: 66.2%
Capital: São Tomé
Language: Portuguese*, Forro
Religion: Christianity
GDP per capita: $3,100
Life expectancy: 65 years

Senegal
Area: 75,954 sq mi
(196,722 sq km)
Population: 14,669,000
Percent urban: 44.4%
Capital: Dakar
Language: French*, Wolof, other
indigenous languages
Religion: Islam
GDP per capita: $2,600
Life expectancy: 62 years

Seychelles
Area: 176 sq mi
(455 sq km)
Population: 94,000
Percent urban: 54.5%
Capital: Victoria
Language: Creole*, English*,
French*
Religion: Christianity
GDP per capita: $27,600
Life expectancy: 75 years

Sierra Leone
Area: 27,699 sq mi
(71,740 sq km)
Population: 6,163,000
Percent urban: 40.7%
Capital: Freetown
Language: English*, Mende, Temne,
Krio
Religion: Islam, indigenous beliefs,
Christianity
GDP per capita: $1,700
Life expectancy: 58 years

Somalia
Area: 246,199 sq mi
(637,657 sq km)
Population: 11,031,000
Percent urban: 40.5%
Capital: Mogadishu
Language: Somali*, Arabic*, Italian,
English
Religion: Islam
GDP per capita: $400
Life expectancy: 52 years

South Africa
Area: 470,691 sq mi
(1,219,090 sq km)
Population: 54,842,000
Percent urban: 65.8%
Capital: Pretoria (Tshwane)
(administrative), Cape Town
(legislative), Bloemfontein (judicial)
Language: IsiZulu*, IsiXhosa*, other
indigenous languages*, Afrikaans*,
English*
Religion: Christianity
GDP per capita: $13,200
Life expectancy: 63 years

South Sudan
Area: 248,775 sq mi
(644,329 sq km)
Population: 13,026,000
Percent urban: 19.3%
Capital: Juba
Language: English*, Arabic,
indigenous languages
Religion: Animism, Christianity
GDP per capita: $1,700
Life expectancy: NA

Sudan
Area: 718,719 sq mi
(1,861,484 sq km)
Population: 37,346,000
Percent urban: 34.2%
Capital: Khartoum
Language: Arabic*, English*
Religion: Islam
GDP per capita: $4,400
Life expectancy: 64 years

Swaziland
Area: 6,704 sq mi
(17,364 sq km)
Population: 1,467,000
Percent urban: 21.3%
Capital: Mbabane (administrative),
Lobamba (legislative and royal)
Language: English*, siSwati*
Religion: Christianity
GDP per capita: $9,800
Life expectancy: 52 years

Tanzania
Area: 365,753 sq mi
(947,300 sq km)
Population: 53,951,000
Percent urban: 33%
Capital: Dar es Salaam
(administrative), Dodoma (legislative)
Language: Kiswahili*, English*,
indigenous languages
Religion: Christianity, Islam
GDP per capita: $3,100
Life expectancy: 62 years

Togo
Area: 21,925 sq mi
(56,785 sq km)
Population: 7,965,000
Percent urban: 41%
Capital: Lomé
Language: French*, Ewe, Mina,
Kabye, Dagomba
Religion: Indigenous beliefs,
Christianity, Islam
GDP per capita: $1,600
Life expectancy: 65 years

Tunisia
Area: 63,170 sq mi
(163,610 sq km)
Population: 11,404,000
Percent urban: 67.3%
Capital: Tunis
Language: Arabic*, French, Berber
Religion: Islam
GDP per capita: $11,600
Life expectancy: 76 years

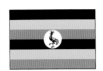

Uganda
Area: 93,065 sq mi
(241,038 sq km)
Population: 39,570,000
Percent urban: 16.8%
Capital: Kampala
Language: English*, Swahili*, Ganda
(Luganda)
Religion: Christianity, Islam
GDP per capita: $2,100
Life expectancy: 55 years

Zambia
Area: 290,586 sq mi
(752,618 sq km)
Population: 15,972,000
Percent urban: 41.8%
Capital: Lusaka
Language: Bembe, Nyanja, Tonga,
other indigenous languages,
English*
Religion: Christianity
GDP per capita: $3,900
Life expectancy: 53 years

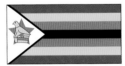

Zimbabwe
Area: 150,871 sq mi
(390,757 sq km)
Population: 13,805,000
Percent urban: 32.2%
Capital: Harare
Language: Shona*, Ndebele*, English*,
indigenous languages*
Religion: Christianity, indigenous
beliefs
GDP per capita: $2,000
Life expectancy: 58 years

**AUSTRALIA,
NEW ZEALAND & OCEANIA**

Australia
Area: 2,988,885 sq mi
(7,741,220 sq km)
Population: 23,232,000
Percent urban: 89.7%
Capital: Canberra
Language: English
Religion: Christianity
GDP per capita: $48,900
Life expectancy: 82 years

Fiji
Area: 7,056 sq mi
(18,274 sq km)
Population: 921,000
Percent urban: 54.5%
Capital: Suva
Language: English*, Fijian*, Hindi
Religion: Christianity, Hinduism
GDP per capita: $9,300
Life expectancy: 73 years

Kiribati
Area: 313 sq mi
(811 sq km)
Population: 108,000
Percent urban: 44.6%
Capital: Tarawa
Language: I-Kiribati, English*
Religion: Christianity
GDP per capita: $1,800
Life expectancy: 66 years

Marshall Islands
Area: 70 sq mi
(181 sq km)
Population: 75,000
Percent urban: 73.2%
Capital: Majuro
Language: Marshallese*, English*
Religion: Christianity
GDP per capita: $3,300
Life expectancy: 73 years

Micronesia, Federated States of
Area: 271 sq mi
(702 sq km)
Population: 104,000
Percent urban: 22.5%
Capital: Palikir
Language: English*, indigenous
languages
Religion: Christianity
GDP per capita: $3,200
Life expectancy: 73 years

Nauru
Area: 8 sq mi
(21 sq km)
Population: 10,000
Percent urban: 100%
Capital: Yaren
Language: Nauruan*, English
Religion: Christianity
GDP per capita: $11,600
Life expectancy: 67 years

New Zealand
Area: 103,363 sq mi
(267,710 sq km)
Population: 4,510,000
Percent urban: 86.4%
Capital: Wellington
Language: English*, Maori*
Religion: Christianity
GDP per capita: $37,300
Life expectancy: 81 years

Palau
Area: 177 sq mi
(459 sq km)
Population: 21,000
Percent urban: 88.2%
Capital: Ngerulmud
Language: Palauan*, English*,
Filipino
Religion: Christianity
GDP per capita: $15,400
Life expectancy: 73 years

Papua New Guinea
Area: 178,703 sq mi
(462,840 sq km)
Population: 6,910,000
Percent urban: 13.1%
Capital: Port Moresby
Language: Tok Pisin*, English*, Hiri
Motu*, other indigenous languages
Religion: Christianity
GDP per capita: $3,500
Life expectancy: 67 years

Samoa
Area: 1,093 sq mi
(2,831 sq km)
Population: 200,000
Percent urban: 18.8%
Capital: Apia
Language: Samoan*, English
Religion: Christianity
GDP per capita: $5,500
Life expectancy: 74 years

Solomon Islands
Area: 11,157 sq mi
(28,896 sq km)
Population: 648,000
Percent urban: 23.2%
Capital: Honiara
Language: Melanesian pidgin,
English*, indigenous languages
Religion: Christianity
GDP per capita: $2,000
Life expectancy: 75 years

Tonga
Area: 288 sq mi
(747 sq km)
Population: 106,000
Percent urban: 23.9%
Capital: Nuku'alofa
Language: Tongan*, English*
Religion: Christianity
GDP per capita: $5,400
Life expectancy: 76 years

Tuvalu
Area: 10 sq mi
(26 sq km)
Population: 11,000
Percent urban: 61.5%
Capital: Funafuti
Language: Tuvaluan*, English*
Religion: Christianity
GDP per capita: $3,500
Life expectancy: 67 years

Vanuatu
Area: 4,706 sq mi
(12,189 sq km)
Population: 283,000
Percent urban: 26.8%
Capital: Port-Vila
Language: Bislama*, English*,
French*, indigenous languages
Religion: Christianity
GDP per capita: $2,600
Life expectancy: 73 years

Glossary

acid rain precipitation containing acid droplets resulting from the mixture of moisture in the air with carbon dioxide, nitrogen oxide, sulfur dioxide, and hydrocarbons released by factories and motor vehicles

archipelago group or chain of islands

atheist person or group that does not believe in any deity

basin area of land that is lower at the center than at the rim

bathymetry measurement of depth at various places in the ocean or other body of water

bay body of water, usually smaller than a gulf, that is partially surrounded by land

biomass total volume of organic material in a certain area or ecosystem that can be used as a renewable energy source (a biofuel)

border area along each side of the boundary that separates one country from another

boundary most commonly, a line that has been established by people to mark the limit of one political unit, such as a country or state, and the beginning of another; geographical features such as mountains sometimes act as boundaries.

caloric supply measure of the amount of food available to a particular person, household, or community

canal human-made waterway that is used by ships or to carry water for irrigation

canyon deep, narrow valley that has steep sides

carat unit of weight for precious stones equal to 200 milligrams

cliff very steep rock face, usually along a coast or on the side of a mountain

climate change change in typical climate patterns, including temperature or precipitation; may result from natural cycles or from human activities such as use of fossil fuels

continent one of the seven main landmasses on Earth's surface

continental climate interior areas found only in the Northern Hemisphere north of mild climate regions; summer to winter temperature extremes

country territory with a government that is the highest legal authority over the land and people within its boundaries

Creole language formed from a mixture of different languages, such as French and an indigenous language

delta lowland formed by silt, sand, and gravel deposited by a river at its mouth

desert hot or cold region that receives 10 inches (25 cm) or less of rain or other forms of precipitation a year

desertification spread of desertlike conditions in semiarid regions that is the result of human pressures, such as overgrazing, removal of natural vegetation, and cultivation of land, as well as climatic changes

divide elevated boundary line separating river systems from which rivers flow in different directions

dry climate areas experiencing low annual precipitation and day to night temperature extremes

earthquake sudden movement or shaking of Earth's crust, often resulting in damage on the surface

elevation distance above sea level, usually measured in feet or meters

escarpment cliff that separates two nearly flat land areas that lie at different elevations

fault break in Earth's crust along which movement up, down, or sideways occurs

fjord/fiord long narrow coastal inlet associated with past glaciation, as in Norway and Chile

fork place where a river splits into two smaller streams

geographic pole 90° N or 90° S latitude; location of the ends of Earth's axis

glacier large, slow-moving mass of ice

greenhouse gases gases, such as carbon dioxide and methane, that contribute to atmospheric warming

gross domestic product (GDP) per capita total value of goods and services produced by a country's economy in a year divided by the country's total population; figures in this atlas are in U.S. dollars and based on **purchasing power parity (PPP),** an economic calculation for comparing the value of different currencies that takes into account the cost of living in each country.

gulf portion of the ocean that cuts into the land; usually larger than a bay

harbor body of water, sheltered by natural or artificial barriers, that is deep enough for ships

hemisphere half a sphere; Earth can be divided into Northern and Southern Hemispheres, or Eastern and Western Hemispheres.

highland climate areas associated with mountains where elevation is the main factor in determining temperature and precipitation

highlands an elevated area or the more mountainous region of a country

hybrid car a car that is powered by gasoline and electricity

ice cap thick layer of ice and snow covering less than 19,300 square miles (50,000 sq km)

ice sheet thick layer of ice and snow covering more than 19,300 square miles (50,000 sq km)

indigenous naturally occurring in a particular area or region, as with people, languages, or religions

inlet narrow opening in the land that is filled with water flowing from an ocean, a lake, or a river

island landmass, smaller than a continent, that is completely surrounded by water

lagoon shallow body of water that is open to the sea but also protected from it by a reef or sandbar

lake body of water that is surrounded by land; large lakes are sometimes called seas.

landform physical feature shaped by tectonic activity, weathering, and erosion; Earth's four major kinds are plains, mountains, plateaus, and hills.

landmass large area of Earth's crust that lies above sea level, such as a continent

large-scale map map, such as a street map, that shows a small area in great detail

Latin America cultural region generally considered to include Mexico, Central America, South America, and the West Indies; Spanish and Portuguese are the principal languages.

latitude measurement in degrees north or south of 0° (Equator) to 90°

leeward side away from or sheltered from the wind

life expectancy average number of years a person can expect to live

lingua franca language not native to the local population that is used as a common or commercial language

longitude measurement in degrees east or west from 0° (prime meridian) to 180°

magma molten rock in Earth's mantle

magnetic pole point at which the axis of Earth's magnetic field intersects Earth's surface; compass needles align with Earth's magnetic field so that one end points to the north magnetic pole, the other to the south magnetic pole.

mesa eroded plateau, broader than it is high, found in arid or semiarid regions

metropolitan area a city and its surrounding suburbs or communities

Middle East term commonly used for the countries of southwestern Asia, but which can also include northern Africa from Morocco to Egypt

molten liquefied by heat; melted

mountain landform, higher than a hill, that rises at least 1,000 feet (300 m) above the surrounding land and is wider at its base than at its top, or peak; a series of mountains is called a range.

nation people who share a common culture or sense of history; often used as another word for "country," although people within a country may be of many cultures

ocean the large body of salt water that surrounds the continents and covers more than two-thirds of Earth's surface

pack ice large blocks of ice that form on the surface of the sea, pushed together by wind and currents

peninsula extension of land that is surrounded by water on three sides

pidgin simplified form of speech that allows speakers of different languages to communicate

plain large area of relatively flat land that is often covered with grasses

plantation agriculture type of commercial agriculture specializing in one or two crops, such as coffee or bananas

plate tectonics theory that Earth's crust is broken into large sections, or plates, that slowly move over the mantle (diagram, p. 16)

plateau relatively flat area, larger than a mesa, that rises above the surrounding landscape

poaching illegal killing or taking of animals from their natural habitats

polar climate area north of the Arctic Circle and south of the Antarctic Circle where temperatures remain cold year-round and precipitation is low

population density in a country, the average number of people living on each square mile or square kilometer of land (calculated by dividing population by land area)

Prairie Provinces popular name for the Canadian provinces of Manitoba, Saskatchewan, and Alberta

prime meridian imaginary line that runs through Greenwich, England, and is accepted as the line of 0° longitude

projection process of representing the round Earth on a flat surface, such as a map

Glossary

rain shadow dry region on the leeward side of a mountain range

reef offshore ridge made of coral, rocks, or sand; a reef that lies parallel to a coastline and is separated from it by a lagoon is called a barrier reef.

renewable resources resources that are replenished naturally, but the supply of which can be endangered by over-use and pollution

revolution movement of Earth in its orbit around the sun (365 days/1 year)

rotation movement of Earth on its axis (24 hours/1 day)

rural relating to an area outside a city and its surrounding suburbs with low population density and an agricultural economy

Sahel semiarid grassland in Africa along the Sahara's southern border

savanna tropical grassland with scattered trees

scale on a map, a means of explaining the relationship between distances on the map and actual distances on Earth's surface

sea ocean or a partially enclosed body of salt water that is connected to the ocean; completely enclosed bodies of salt water, such as the Dead Sea, are really lakes.

sea level average surface level of Earth's oceans from which the height of land areas can be measured

Silk Road ancient trade route stretching from China to the Mediterranean

slot canyon very narrow, deep canyon formed by water and wind erosion

small-scale map map, such as a country map, that shows a large area without much detail

sound long, broad inlet of the ocean that lies parallel to the coast and often separates an island and the mainland

Soviet Union shortened name for the Union of Soviet Socialist Republics (U.S.S.R.), a former Communist republic (1920–1991) in eastern Europe and northern and central Asia, made up of 15 republics, of which Russia was the largest

staple chief food of a people's diet

steppe Slavic word referring to relatively flat, mostly treeless temperate grasslands that stretch across much of the central parts of Europe and Asia

strait narrow passage of water that connects two larger bodies of water

Sunbelt U.S. region made up of southern and western states that are experiencing major population in-migration and economic growth

territory land that is under the jurisdiction of a country but is not a state or a province

topography features, such as mountains and valleys, that are evident on Earth's surface

tornado violently rotating column of air associated with thunderstorms

transshipment movement of goods or containers to one location before moving on, often by a different form of transportation, to a final destination

tributary stream that flows into a larger river

tropical cyclone large weather system that forms over warm tropical water; with sustained winds of at least 74 miles an hour (119 km/h), it is called a hurricane in the Atlantic Ocean and eastern Pacific; a cyclone in the Bay of Bengal, Indian Ocean, and South Pacific, and a typhoon in the western Pacific.

tropics region lying within $23\frac{1}{2}°$ north and south of the Equator that experiences warm temperatures year-round

tsunami very large ocean wave caused by an earthquake or other powerful underwater disturbance, such as a volcanic eruption

urban relating to a city and its densely populated surrounding area with a non-agricultural economy

valley long depression, usually created by a river, that is bordered by higher land

virgin forest forest made up of trees that have never been cut down by humans

volcano opening in Earth's crust through which molten rock erupts; a volcano that has not erupted in the past 10,000 years but is expected to erupt again is said to be dormant.

wat Buddhist monastery or temple in southeastern Asia

windward side or direction that faces the wind

Geo Facts & Figures

PLANET EARTH

Mass:
   6,584,800,000,000,000,000,000 tons
   (5,973,600,000,000,000,000,000
   metric tons)
Distance around the Equator: 24,902 mi
   (40,075 km)
Area: 196,940,000 sq mi
   (510,072,000 sq km)
Land area: 57,506,000 sq mi
   (148,940,000 sq km)
Water area: 139,434,000 sq mi
   (361,132,000 sq km))

The Continents

Asia: 17,208,000 sq mi
   (44,570,000 sq km)
Africa: 11,608,000 sq mi
   (30,065,000 sq km)
North America: 9,449,000 sq mi
   (24,474,000 sq km)
South America: 6,880,000 sq mi
   (17,819,000 sq km)
Antarctica: 5,100,000 sq mi
   (13,209,000 sq km)
Europe: 3,841,000 sq mi
   (9,947,000 sq km)
Australia: 2,989,000 sq mi
   (7,741,000 sq km)

Highest Mountain on Each Continent

Everest, Asia: 29,035 ft (8,850 m)
Aconcagua, South America: 22,831 ft
   (6,959 m)
Denali (McKinley), North America:
   20,210 ft (6,194 m)
Kilimanjaro, Africa: 19,340 ft
   (5,895 m)
El'brus, Europe: 18,510 ft (5,642 m)
Vinson Massif, Antarctica: 16,067 ft
   (4,897 m)
Kosciuszko, Australia: 7,310 ft
   (2,228 m)

Lowest Point on Each Continent

Byrd Glacier (depression), Antarctica:
   −9,416 ft (−2,870 m)
Dead Sea, Asia: −1,388 ft (−423 m)
Lake Assal, Africa: −509 ft (−155 m)
Laguna del Carbón, South America:
   −344 ft (−105 m)
Death Valley, North America:
   −282 ft (−86 m)
Caspian Sea, Europe: −92 ft (−28 m)
Lake Eyre, Australia: −49 ft (−15 m)

Longest Rivers

Nile, Africa: 4,400 mi (7,081 km)
Amazon, South America: 4,150 mi
   (6,679 km)
Yangtze (Chang), Asia: 3,880 mi
   (6,244 km)
Mississippi-Missouri, North America:
   3,780 mi (6,083 km)
Yenisey-Angara, Asia: 3,610 mi
   (5,536 km)
Yellow (Huang), Asia: 3,590 mi (5,778 km)
Ob-Irtysh, Asia: 3,430 mi (5,520 km)
Amur, Asia: 3,420 mi (5,504 km)
Lena, Asia: 3,200 mi (5,150 km)
Congo, Africa: 3,180 mi (5,118 km)

Largest Islands

Greenland: 836,000 sq mi
   (2,166,000 sq km)
New Guinea: 306,000 sq mi
   (792,500 sq km)
Borneo: 280,100 sq mi (725,500 sq km)
Madagascar: 226,600 sq mi
   (587,000 sq km)
Baffin: 196,000 sq mi (507,500 sq km)
Sumatra: 165,000 sq mi
   (427,300 sq km)
Honshu: 87,800 sq mi (227,400 sq km)
Great Britain: 84,200 sq mi
   (218,100 sq km)
Victoria: 83,900 sq mi (217,300 sq km)
Ellesmere: 75,800 sq mi
   (196,200 sq km)

Oceans

Pacific: 69,000,000 sq mi
   (178,800,000 sq km)
Atlantic: 35,400,000 sq mi
   (91,700,000 sq km)
Indian: 29,400,000 sq mi
   (76,200,000 sq km)
Arctic: 5,600,000 sq mi
   (14,700,000 sq km)

Largest Seas (by area)

Coral: 1,615,500 sq mi
   (4,184,000 sq km)
South China: 1,388,400 sq mi
   (3,596,000 sq km)
Caribbean: 1,094,200 sq mi
   (2,834,000 sq km)
Bering: 973,000 sq mi
   (2,520,000 sq km)
Mediterranean: 953,300 sq mi
   (2,469,000 sq km)
Okhotsk: 627,400 sq mi
   (1,625,000 sq km)
Gulf of Mexico: 591,500 sq mi
   (1,532,000 sq km)
Norwegian: 550,200 sq mi
   (1,425,000 sq km)
Greenland: 447,100 sq mi
   (1,158,000 sq km)
Japan (East Sea): 389,200 sq mi
   (1,008,000 sq km)

Largest Lakes (by area)

Caspian Sea, Europe-Asia: 143,200 sq mi
   (371,000 sq km)
Superior, North America: 31,700 sq mi
   (82,100 sq km)
Victoria, Africa: 26,800 sq mi
   (69,500 sq km)
Huron, North America: 23,000 sq mi
   (59,600 sq km)
Michigan, North America: 22,300 sq mi
   (57,800 sq km)
Tanganyika, Africa: 12,600 sq mi
   (32,600 sq km)
Baikal, Asia: 12,200 sq mi
   (31,500 sq km)

Geo Facts & Figures

Largest Lakes (cont'd)

Great Bear, North America: 12,100 sq mi
(31,300 sq km)

Malawi (Nyasa), Africa: 11,200 sq mi
(28,900 sq km)

Great Slave, North America: 11,000 sq mi
(28,600 sq km)

GEOGRAPHIC EXTREMES

Highest Mountain
Everest, China/Nepal:
29,035 ft (8,850 m)

Deepest Point in the Ocean
Challenger Deep, Mariana Trench, Pacific:
-36,037 ft (-10,984 m)

Hottest Place
Dalol, Danakil Depression, Ethiopia:
annual average temperature 93°F
(34°C)

Coldest Place
Ridge A, Antarctica:
annual average temperature -94°F
(-70°C)

Wettest Place
Mawsynram, Meghalaya, India: annual
average rainfall 467 in (1,187 cm)

Driest Place
Arica, Atacama Desert, Chile: barely
measurable rainfall

Largest Hot Desert
Sahara, Africa: 3,475,000 sq mi
(9,000,000 sq km)

Largest Cold Desert
Antarctica: 5,100,000 sq mi
(13,209,000 sq km)

PEOPLE

Most Populous Continent
Asia   4,405,052,000

Least Populous Continent
Antarctica   no permanent population
Australia   23,232,000

Population Density by Continent (highest to lowest)

Asia   256.0 people/sq mi
                    98.8 people /sq km
Europe   178.1 people/sq mi
                    68.7 people /sq km
Africa   104.7 people/sq mi
                    40.4 people /sq km
North America   67.7 people/sq mi
                    26.1 people /sq km
South America   60.8 people/sq mi
                    23.5 people /sq km
Austr/NZ/Oceania 11.5 people/sq mi
                    4.4 people /sq km

Most Populous Country
China   1,379,303,000

Least Populous Country
Vatican City   1,000

Most Densely Populated Countries

Monaco   30,645.0 people/sq mi
                    (15,322.5 people/sq km)
Singapore   21,891.9 people/sq mi
                    (8,449.0 people/sq km)
Bahrain   4,815.5 people/sq mi
                    (1,856.5 people/sq km)
Maldives   3,414.9 people/sq mi
                    (1,317.8 people/sq km)
Malta   3,412.6 people/sq mi
                    (1,317.5 people/sq km)
Bangladesh   2,838.7 people/sq mi
                    (1,096.0 people/sq km)
Barbados   1,761.1 people/sq mi
                    (679.9 people/sq km)

Mauritius   1,721.3 people/sq mi
                    (664.9 people/sq km)
Lebanon   1,551.6 people/sq mi
                    (599.0 people/sq km)
San Marino   1,397.4 people/sq mi
                    (549.8 people/sq km)

Least Densely Populated Countries

Mongolia   5.1 people/sq mi
                    (2.0 people/sq km)
Australia   7.8 people/sq mi
                    (3.0 people/sq km)
Namibia   7.8 people/sq mi
                    (3.0 people/sq km)
Iceland   8.5 people/sq mi
                    (3.3 people/sq km)
Guyana   8.9 people/sq mi
                    (3.4 people/sq km)
Canada   9.2 people/sq mi
                    (3.6 people/sq km)
Mauritania   9.4 people/sq mi
                    (3.6 people/sq km)
Suriname   9.4 people/sq mi
                    (3.6 people/sq km)
Libya   9.8 people/sq mi
                    (3.8 people/sq km)
Botswana   10.0 people/sq mi
                    (3.8 people/sq km)

Most Populous Metropolitan Areas

Tokyo, Japan	38,140,000
Delhi, India	26,454,000
Shanghai, China	24,484,000
Mumbai (Bombay), India	21,357,000
São Paulo, Brazil	21,297,000
Beijing, China	21,240,000
Mexico City, Mexico	21,157,000
Osaka, Japan	20,337,000
Cairo, Egypt	19,128,000
New York, U.S.A.	18,604,000

Countries With the Highest Population Growth Rate

South Sudan	3.83%
Angola	3.52%
Malawi	3.31%
Burundi	3.25%
Uganda	3.20%
Niger	3.19%
Mali	3.02%
Burkina Faso	3.00%
Zambia	2.93%
Ethiopia	2.85%

Countries With the Lowest Population Growth Rate

Lebanon	-1.1%
Latvia	-1.08%
Lithuania	-1.08%
Moldova	-1.05%
Bulgaria	-0.61%
Estonia	-0.57%
Federated States of Micronesia	-0.52%
Croatia	-0.5%
Serbia	-0.46%
Ukraine	-0.41%

Countries With the Highest Life Expectancy

Monaco	90 years
Japan	85 years
Singapore	85 years
Iceland	83 years
San Marino	83 years
Switzerland	83 years
Australia	82 years
Austria	82 years
Canada	82 years
France	82 years
Israel	82 years
Italy	82 years
Liechtenstein	82 years
Luxembourg	82 years
Norway	82 years
South Korea	82 years
Spain	82 years
Sweden	82 years

Countries With the Lowest Life Expectancy

Chad	50 years
Afghanistan	51 years
Guinea-Bissau	51 years
Central African Republic	52 years
Gabon	52 years
Somalia	52 years
Swaziland	52 years
Lesotho	53 years
Mozambique	53 years
Nigeria	53 years
Zambia	53 years

Countries With the Highest Percent Urban Population

Monaco	100%
Nauru	100%
Singapore	100%
Vatican City	100%
Qatar	99.4%
Kuwait	98.4%
Belgium	97.9%
Malta	95.6%
Uruguay	95.6%
Iceland	94.3%
Japan	94.3%
San Marino	94.2%

Countries With the Lowest Percent Urban Population

Trinidad & Tobago	8.3%
Burundi	12.7%
Papua New Guinea	13.1%
Liechtenstein	14.3%
Malawi	16.6%
Uganda	16.8%
Sri Lanka	18.5%
St. Lucia	18.6%
Samoa	18.8%
Niger	19.3%
South Sudan	19.3%
Nepal	19.4%

Countries With the Highest Gross Domestic Product per Person (PPP)

Liechtenstein	$139,100
Qatar	$127,700
Monaco	$115,700
Luxembourg	$104,000
Singapore	$87,900
Brunei	$76,900
Kuwait	$71,900
Ireland	$69,200
Norway	$69,200
United Arab Emirates	$67,900

Countries With the Lowest Gross Domestic Product per Person (PPP)

Somalia	$400
Central African Republic	$700
Burundi	$800
Dem. Rep. of the Congo	$800
Liberia	$900
Malawi	$1,100
Niger	$1,100
Mozambique	$1,200
Guinea	$1,300
Eritrea	$1,400

Outside Websites

With an adult's help, check out these websites for more information about various topics discussed in this atlas.

Antarctica
www.coolantarctica.com

Biomes
www.blueplanetbiomes.org

Climate change
climate.nasa.gov

Climates
www.worldclimate.com

Countries of the world (statistics)
www.cia.gov/library/publications/
resources/the-world-factbook

Endangered species
www.iucnredlist.org

Extreme facts about the world
www.extremescience.com

Flags of the world
www.crwflags.com/fotw/flags

Languages: "Say Hello"
www.ipl.org/div/hello

Mapping the world
www.google.com/earth

National anthems
www.nationalanthems.info

Natural disasters
Earthquakes: earthquake.usgs.gov/
earthquakes
Hurricanes: www.nhc.noaa.gov
Tsunamis: www.tsunami.noaa.gov
Volcanoes: volcanoes.usgs.gov/
index.html

Population
Population clock: www.census.gov/
popclock
World population: www.prb.org/pdf17/
2017_World_Population.pdf

Religions of the world
www.adherents.com

Solar system
solarsystem.nasa.gov/planets

Time
Time around the world: www.world
timeserver.com
Time zones: worldtimezone.com

Weather around the world
weather.com

World Heritage sites
whc.unesco.org/en/list

Abbreviations

°E	degrees East	L.	Lake	N.Z.	New Zealand
°N	degrees North	LA.	Louisiana	OKLA.	Oklahoma
°S	degrees South	LIECH.	Liechtenstein	OREG.	Oregon
°W	degrees West	LUX.	Luxembourg	P.E.I.	Prince Edward Island
°C	degrees Celsius	m	meters	p.	page
°F	degrees Fahrenheit	MASS.	Massachusetts	pp.	pages
AFGHAN.	Afghanistan	MD.	Maryland	PA.	Pennsylvania
ALA.	Alabama	ME.	Maine	Pen.	Peninsula
ARK.	Arkansas	mi	miles	R.I.	Rhode Island
B.&H.	Bosnia and Herzegovina	MICH.	Michigan	Rep.	Republic
BELG.	Belgium	MINN.	Minnesota	S	South
COLO.	Colorado	MISS.	Mississippi	S. DAK.	South Dakota
CONN.	Connecticut	MO.	Missouri	S.C.	South Carolina
D.C.	District of Columbia	MONT.	Montana	sq km	square kilometers
DEL.	Delaware	MONT.	Montenegro	sq mi	square miles
DEM.	Democratic	Mt.	Mount, Mountain	St., Ste.	Saint, Sainte
E	East	Mts.	Mountains	Str.	Strait
FLA.	Florida	N	North	SWITZ.	Switzerland
ft	feet	N. DAK.	North Dakota	TENN.	Tennessee
GA.	Georgia	N. MEX.	New Mexico	U.A.E.	United Arab Emirates
GDP	Gross Domestic Product	N.B.	New Brunswick	U.K.	United Kingdom
I.	Island	N.C.	North Carolina	U.S./U.S.A.	United States
ILL.	Illinois	N.H.	New Hampshire	VA.	Virginia
IND.	Indiana	N.J.	New Jersey	VT.	Vermont
Is.	Islands	N.P.	National Park	W	West
KANS.	Kansas	N.Y.	New York	W. VA.	West Virginia
km	kilometers	NEBR.	Nebraska	WASH.	Washington
KY.	Kentucky	NETH.	Netherlands	WIS.	Wisconsin
KYRG.	Kyrgyzstan	NEV.	Nevada	WYO.	Wyoming

Index

Map references are in boldface (**50**) *type. Letters and numbers following in lightface* (D12) *locate the place-names using the map grid. (Refer to page 7 for more details.)*

PLACE-NAMES

A

1st Cataract (falls), Egypt **135** C10
2nd Cataract (falls), Sudan **141** A6
3rd Cataract (falls), Sudan **141** A6
4th Cataract (falls), Sudan **141** A6
5th Cataract (falls), Sudan **141** B6
6th Cataract (falls), Sudan **141** B6
Aba as Saud, Saudi Arabia **119** G3
Abaco Island, Bahamas **69** A3
Abadan, Iran **119** D4
Abéché, Chad **141** B4
Aberdeen, United Kingdom **95** B3
Abidjan, Côte d'Ivoire **137** E3
Abilene, Texas (U.S.) **65** E5
Abkhazia (region), Georgia **117** A7
Abu Dhabi, United Arab Emirates **119** E6
Abuja, Nigeria **137** E6
Acapulco, Mexico **67** E3
Accra, Ghana **137** E4
Acklins Island, Bahamas **69** B3
Aconcagua, Cerro, Argentina **83** D1
A Coruña, Spain **95** G1
Adana, Turkey **117** D4
Adapazarı, Turkey **117** B3
Adare, Cape, Antarctica **161** G5
Ad Dahna (region), Saudi Arabia **119** E4
Ad Dakhla, Western Sahara (Morocco) **132** C1
Ad Dammam, Saudi Arabia **119** E5
Addis Ababa, Ethiopia **139** C4
Adelaide, Australia **153** F5
Aden, Yemen **119** I4
Admiralty Gulf, Australia **152** A3
Admiralty Islands, Papua New Guinea **154** D2
Adrar des Ifôghas (range), Mali **137** C5
Adriatic Sea, Europe **86** F4
Aegean Sea, Europe **86** G6
Afghanistan (country), Asia **105** E3
Agadez, Niger **137** C6
Agadir, Morocco **132** B2
Agra, India **121** C4
Agulhas, Cape, South Africa **143** H3
Ahaggar Mountains, Algeria **135** D5
Ahmadabad, India **121** D3
Ahvaz, Iran **119** D4
Aïr Massif (range), Niger **137** C6
Ajaccio, France **95** G6

Ajdābiyā, Libya **135** B7
Ajmer, India **121** C3
Akimiski Island, Nunavut, Canada **63** F6
Akita, Japan **115** B10
Ak'ordat, Eritrea **139** 4A
Akureyri, Iceland **93** A2
Alabama (state), U.S. **65** E8
Alajuela, Costa Rica **67** G7
Al Amarah, Iraq **119** C4
Aland Islands, Finland **93** F5
Alaska (state), U.S. **64** G2
Alaska, Gulf of, U.S. **56** C1
Alaska Peninsula, Alaska (U.S.) **64** GS
Alaska Range, Alaska (U.S.) **64** G2
Albania (country), Europe **87** G5
Albany, Australia **152** F2
Albany, New York (U.S.) **65** B10
Albert, Lake, Africa **139** D2
Alberta (province), Canada **63** E3
Albert Nile (river), Uganda **139** D2
Alboran Sea, Europe **95** I2
Albuquerque, New Mexico (U.S.) **65** E4
Aldan (river), Russia **104** C6
Aleppo, Syria **117** D5
Ålesund, Norway **93** E2
Aleutian Islands, Alaska (U.S.) **64** G1
Aleutian Range, Alaska (U.S.) **56** B1
Alexander Archipelago, Alaska (U.S.) **56** C2
Alexander Island, Antarctica **161** C8
Alexandria, Egypt **135** B9
Al Farciya, Western Sahara (Morocco) **132** C2
Algeria (country), Africa **135** C3
Alghiena, Eritrea **139** A4
Algiers, Algeria **135** A4
Al Hadidah (crater), Saudi Arabia **119** F5
Al Hijaz (region), Saudi Arabia **119** E2
Al Hillah, Iraq **119** C3
Al Hillah, Saudi Arabia **119** F4
Al Hudaydah, Yemen **119** H3
Alice Springs, Australia **153** C5
Al Jawf, Libya **125** D9
Al Jawf, Saudi Arabia **135** D9
Allahabad, India **121** D5
Almaty, Kazakhstan **113** D6
Al Mukalla, Yemen **119** H4
Alps (range), Europe **86** F3
Al Qamishli, Syria **117** D6
Al Qunfudhah, Saudi Arabia **119** G2
Altay Mountains, Asia **104** D5
Altiplano (region), South America **79** H4
Altun Ha (ruins), Belize **67** E6
Altun Shan (range), China **114** D3

Amarillo, Texas (U.S.) **65** E5
Amazon (Solimões) (river), South America **72** B6
Amazon Basin, South America **72** B4
Ambon, Indonesia **125** D8
Ambovombe, Madagascar **143** F10
Ambre, Cap d', Madagascar **143** B11
Ambriz, Angola **142** A1
American Highland, Antarctica **161** C8
American Samoa (islands), U.S. **155** E6
Amery Ice Shelf, Antarctica **161** C8
Amman, Jordan **117** G4
Amritsar, India **121** B3
Amsterdam, Netherlands **95** D5
Am Timan, Chad **141** C4
Amu Darya (river), Asia **113** D4
Amundsen Gulf, Northwest Territories (Canada) **63** C3
Amundsen-Scott Station, Antarctica **161** D5
Amundsen Sea, Antarctica **161** E2
Amur (river), Asia **104** C7
Anadyr, Russia **105** A7
Anadyr, Gulf of, Russia **105** A7
Anambas Islands, Indonesia **124** B2
Anatolia (Asia Minor) (region), Turkey **117** C3
Anchorage, Alaska (U.S.) **64** G3
Andaman Islands, India **121** F8
Andaman Sea, Asia **104** G5
Andes (range), South America **72** C2
Andorra, Andorra **95** G4
Andorra (country), Europe **87** G2
Andros Island, Bahamas **69** B2
Anefis i-n-Darane, Mali **137** C5
Angara (river), Russia **111** E6
Angarsk, Russia **105** D5
Angel Falls, Venezuela **79** B6
Ångermanälven (river), Sweden **93** D4
Angoche, Mozambique **143** C8
Angohran, Iran **119** E7
Angola (country), Africa **127** G5
Angora, see Ankara, Turkey **117** C3
Anguilla (island), United Kingdom **69** C6
Ankara (Angora), Turkey **117** C3
Annaba, Algeria **135** A5
An Nafud (region), Saudi Arabia **119** D3
An Najaf, Iraq **119** C3
Annapolis, Maryland (U.S.) **65** C10
Anshan, China **115** C8
Antalya, Turkey **117** D2
Antananarivo, Madagascar **143** D10

Antarctic Peninsula, Antarctica **161** C2
Anticosti Island, Quebec (Canada) **63** F9
Anticosti Island, see Anticosti, Île de, Quebec (Canada) **63** F9
Antigua and Barbuda (country), North America **57** H8
Antioch, see Hatay, Turkey **117** D4
Antofagasta, Chile **83** B1
Antsirabe, Madagascar **143** D10
Antsiranana, Madagascar **143** B11
Antsohihy, Madagascar **143** C10
Antwerp, Belgium **95** D4
Aomori, Japan **115** B10
Aoraki (Mount Cook), New Zealand **153** H9
Aoulef, Algeria **135** C4
Aozi, Chad **141** A4
Aozou, Chad **141** A3
Aozou Strip (region), Chad **141** A3
Apennines (range), Italy **95** G7
Apia, Samoa **155** E6
Appalachian Mountains, U.S. **65** D9
Apurímac (river), Peru **79** G3
Aqaba, Gulf of, Asia **135** B11
Aqaba, Jordan **117** H4
Aqtöbe, Kazakhstan **113** C2
Arabian Peninsula, Asia **104** E1
Arabian Sea, Asia **104** F2
Aracaju, Brazil **81** D7
Arad, Romania **99** B5
Arafura Sea, Asia **125** E9
Araguaia (river), Brazil **81** E5
Arak, Algeria **135** D5
Arak, Iran **119** C5
Aral Sea, Asia **113** C3
Araouane, Mali **137** C4
Ararat, Mount, Turkey **117** C8
Aras (river), Asia **117** C9
Àrba Minch', Ethiopia **139** C3
Ardabil, Iran **119** B4
Åre, Sweden **87** C4
Arequipa, Peru **79** H3
Argentina (country), South America **73** G4
Århus, Denmark **93** H3
Arica, Chile **83** A1
Arizona (state), U.S. **64** E3
Arkansas (river), U.S. **65** D5
Arkansas (state), U.S. **65** E7
Arkhangel'sk, Russia **101** C4
Armenia (country), Asia **105** D2
Armidale, Australia **153** E8
Arnhem, Cape, Australia **153** A5
Arnhem Land, Australia **153** A5
Ar Ramadi, Iraq **119** C3
Ar Raqqah, Syria **117** E6
Arua, Dem. Rep. of the Congo **141** D6
Aruba (island), Netherlands **69** E5
Aru Islands, Indonesia **125** D9
Arusha, Tanzania **139** F3
Asansol, India **121** D6

Ascension (island), United Kingdom **128** F1
Ashburton, New Zealand **153** H10
Ashgabat, Turkmenistan **113** D3
Ashmore Islands, Australia **152** A3
Ash Shihr, Yemen **119** H4
Asia Minor (region), see Anatolia, Turkey **117** C3
Asmara, Eritrea **139** 4A
Assab, Eritrea **139** B5
As Sulaymaniyah, Iraq **119** B4
Astana, Kazakhstan **113** B5
Astrakhan', Russia **101** H6
Asunción, Paraguay **83** B4
Aswân, Egypt **135** D10
Aswan High Dam, Egypt **135** D10
Asyût, Egypt **135** C10
Atacama Desert, Chile **83** A1
Atar, Mauritania **137** B2
Atbara, Sudan **141** B6
Atbara (river), Sudan **141** B7
Athabasca (river), Alberta (Canada) **56** D3
Athabasca, Lake, Canada **63** E3
Athens, Greece **99** G6
Ati, Chad **141** C3
Atlanta, Georgia (U.S.) **65** E9
Atlas Mountains, Africa **128** C2
At Ta'if, Saudi Arabia **119** F2
Atyrau, Kazakhstan **113** B2
Auckland, New Zealand **153** E11
Augusta, Australia **152** F2
Augusta, Maine (U.S.) **65** B11
Austin, Texas (U.S.) **65** F6
Australia (country), Oceania **147** F2
Australian Capital Territory, Australia **153** F7
Austral Islands, French Polynesia, France **155** F7
Austria (country), Europe **87** F4
Avalon Peninsula, Newfoundland & Labrador (Canada) **56** D7
Avarua, Cook Islands, N.Z. **147** E7
Avignon, France **95** G5
Awjilah, Libya **135** C8
Axel Heiberg Island, Nunavut (Canada) **56** A4
Ayers Rock (peak), see Uluru, Australia **152** D4
Ayr, Australia **153** C7
Azerbaijan (country), Asia **105** D2
Azores (islands), Portugal **128** B1
Azov, Sea of, Europe **86** F7
Az Zarqa', Jordan **117** F4

B

Bab el Mandeb (strait), Djibouti **139** B5
Babruysk, Belarus **97** C7

Babuyan Islands — Cagliari

Babuyan Islands, Philippines **123** B7
Bacolod City, Philippines **123** D7
Baetic Mountains, Spain **86** G1
Baffin Bay, North America **63** B7
Baffin Island, Nunavut (Canada) **63** C6
Bagan, Myanmar **121** D8
Baghdad, Iraq **119** C4
Baguio, Philippines **123** C7
Bagzane, Mont, Niger **137** C7
Bahamas (country), North America **57** G6
Bahia, see Salvador, Brazil **81** E7
Bahía Blanca, Argentina **83** F3
Bahir Dar, Ethiopia **139** B3
Bahrain (country), Asia **105** E2
Baia Mare, Romania **99** A6
Baidoa, Somalia **139** D6
Baikal, Lake, Russia **111** E7
Baikonur Cosmodrome, Kazakhstan **113** C4
Baja California (peninsula), Mexico **66** B1
Baker Island, U.S. **155** D5
Bakersfield, California (U.S.) **64** D2
Baku, Azerbaijan **117** B10
Balclutha, New Zealand **153** I9
Balearic Islands, Spain **95** H4
Balearic Sea, Spain **95** H4
Bali (island), Indonesia **125** E4
Balıkesir, Turkey **117** B2
Balikpapan, Indonesia **125** C5
Balkanabat, Turkmenistan, **113** D2
Balkan Mountains, Bulgaria **99** D6
Balkan Peninsula, Europe **99** D5
Balkhash, Lake, Kazakhstan **113** C5
Ballarat, Australia **153** F6
Balsas (river), Mexico **67** E3
Balti, Moldova **97** F6
Baltic Sea, Europe **86** D5
Baltimore, Maryland (U.S.) **65** C10
Baluchistan (region), Iran **119** E8
Bam, Iran **119** D7
Bamako, Mali **137** D2
Bambari, Central African Rep. **141** D4
Bamenda, Cameroon **141** D2
Banaras, see Varanasi, India **121** D5
Banda Aceh, Indonesia **124** A1
Bandar-e Abbas, Iran **119** E6
Bandar-e Bushehr, Iran **119** D5
Bandar Seri Begawan, Brunei **123** E5
Banda Sea, Indonesia **125** D8
Bandundu, Dem. Rep. of the Congo **141** F3
Bandung, Indonesia **124** D2
Banff National Park, Alberta (Canada) **62** F2
Bangassou, Central African Rep. **141** D4
Bangkok, Thailand **123** C2
Bangladesh (country), Asia **105** F4

Bangui, Central African Rep. **141** D4
Banja Luka, Bosnia & Herzegovina **99** C3
Banjarmasin, Indonesia **125** D4
Banjul, Gambia **137** D1
Banks Island, Northwest Territories (Canada) **63** B3
Banks Peninsula, New Zealand **153** H10
Baotou, China **115** C6
Baranavichy, Belarus **97** C6
Barat Daya Islands, Indonesia **125** E7
Barbados (country), North America **57** H8
Barcaldine, Australia **153** C7
Barcelona, Spain **95** G4
Bareilly, India **121** C4
Barents Sea, Europe **86** A6
Bargaal, Somalia **139** B7
Bari, Italy **95** G8
Barisan Mountains, Indonesia **124** C1
Barnaul, Russia **111** F5
Barquisimeto, Venezuela **79** A4
Barranquilla, Colombia **79** A2
Barrow, Point, Alaska (U.S.) **56** B2
Barrow Creek, Australia **153** C5
Barrow Island, Australia **152** C1
Barú, Volcán, Panama **67** G7
Basankusu, Dem. Rep. of the Congo **141** E4
Basel, Switzerland **95** E5
Basra, Iraq **119** D4
Bassas da India (islands), France **143** E8
Basseterre, St. Kitts & Nevis **69** C7
Bass Strait, Australia **153** G7
Bata, Equatorial Guinea **141** E2
Batan Islands, Philippines **123** B7
Batanme (island), Indonesia **125** C8
Bathurst Island, Nunavut (Canada) **63** B5
Baton Rouge, Louisiana (U.S.) **65** F7
Battambang, Cambodia **123** C2
Batumi, Georgia **117** B7
Bawku, Ghana **137** D4
Beaufort Sea, North America **56** B3
Beaumont, Texas, (U.S.) **65** F7
Béchar, Algeria **135** B4
Beersheba, Israel **117** G4
Beijing, China **115** C7
Beira, Mozambique **143** D7
Beirut, Lebanon **117** F4
Belarus (country), Europe **87** E6
Belaya (river), Russia **101** F7
Belcher Islands, Nunavut (Canada) **63** F7
Beledweyne, Somalia **139** D5
Belém, Brazil **81** C5
Belfast, United Kingdom **95** C2
Belgavi, India **121** E3
Belgium (country), Europe **87** E3
Belgorod, Russia **101** G3
Belgrade, Serbia **99** C4

Belize (country), North America **57** H5
Belize City, Belize **67** E6
Bellingshausen Sea, Antarctica **160** D1
Belmopan, Belize **67** E6
Belo Horizonte, Brazil **81** F6
Bendigo, Australia **153** F6
Bengal, Bay of, Asia **104** F4
Bengaluru (Bangalore), India **121** F4
Benghazi, Libya **135** B7
Benguela, Angola **142** C1
Beni Abbès, Algeria **135** B4
Benin (country), Africa **137** D5
Benin, Bight of, Africa **137** E5
Bentley Subglacial Trench, Antarctica **161** E3
Benue (river), Africa **137** E6
Berbera, Somalia **139** B5
Berbérati, Central African Rep. **141** D3
Berdyans'k, Ukraine **97** F10
Berezniki, Russia **101** D7
Bergen, Norway **93** F2
Bering Sea, Asia/North America **104** A7
Bering Strait, Asia/North America **104** A7
Berkner Island, Antarctica **161** C3
Berlin, Germany **95** D6
Bermuda Islands, United Kingdom **56** F7
Bern, Switzerland **95** F5
Beyla, Guinea **137** E3
Bhisho, South Africa **143** H5
Bhopal, India **121** D4
Bhutan (country), Asia **105** F5
Biak (island), Indonesia **125** C10
Bialystok, Poland **97** C5
Bikini Atoll, Marshall Islands **155** C4
Bila Tserkva, Ukraine **97** D7
Bilbao, Spain **95** G3
Billings, Montana (U.S.) **65** B4
Bilma, Niger **137** C7
Biloxi, Mississippi (U.S.) **65** F8
Biltine, Chad **141** B4
Bioko (island), Equatorial Guinea **141** D2
Birao, Central African Rep. **141** C4
Birjand, Iran **119** C7
Birmingham, Alabama (U.S.) **65** E8
Birmingham, United Kingdom **95** D3
Bîr Mogreïn (Fort Trinquet), Mauritania **137** A3
Biscay, Bay of, Europe **95** F2
Bishkek, Kyrgyzstan **113** D5
Biskra, Algeria **135** B5
Bismarck, North Dakota (U.S.) **65** B5
Bismarck Archipelago, Papua New Guinea **154** D2
Bissagos Islands, Guinea-Bissau **137** D1
Bissau, Guinea-Bissau **137** D1
Bitola, Macedonia **99** E4
Bizerte, Tunisia **135** A6
Black (river), Vietnam **123** A3
Blackall, Australia **153** D7
Black Sea, Europe/Asia **86** F7

Black Volta (river), Africa **137** D4
Blagoveshchensk, Russia **111** E9
Blanc, Mont, Europe **95** F5
Blantyre, Malawi **143** C7
Blenheim, New Zealand **153** G11
Bloemfontein, South Africa **143** G5
Bluefields, Nicaragua **67** F8
Blue Nile (river), Africa **141** C7
Bo, Sierra Leone **137** E2
Boa Vista, Brazil **81** B3
Bobo Dioulasso, Burkina Faso **137** D3
Bodø, Norway **93** C4
Bogor, Indonesia **124** D2
Bogotá, Colombia **79** C3
Bohol (island), Philippines **123** D8
Boise, Idaho (U.S.) **64** B3
Boké, Guinea **137** D2
Bolívar, Pico, Venezuela **79** B4
Bolivia (country), South America **73** D4
Bologna, Italy **95** F6
Boma, Dem. Rep. of the Congo **141** F2
Bombay, see Mumbai, India **121** E3
Bonaire (island), Netherlands Antilles (Netherlands) **69** E5
Bondo, Dem. Rep. of the Congo **141** D5
Bonin Islands, Japan **154** A2
Bonn, Germany **95** D5
Boothia, Gulf of, Nunavut (Canada) **63** C5
Boothia Peninsula, Nunavut (Canada) **63** C5
Bor, South Sudan **141** D6
Borås, Sweden **93** H4
Bordeaux, France **95** F3
Borden Island, Canada **56** B4
Borneo (island), Asia **104** G7
Bornholm (island), Denmark **93** I4
Borroloola, Australia **153** B5
Bosnia and Herzegovina (country), Europe **87** F4
Bosporus (strait), Turkey **117** B2
Bossangoa, Central African Rep. **141** D3
Boston, Massachusetts (U.S.) **65** B11
Bothnia, Gulf of, Europe **93** E6
Botosani, Romania **99** A7
Botswana (country), Africa **127** H5
Bouaké, Côte d'Ivoire **137** E3
Bouar, Central African Rep. **141** D3
Bougainville (island), Papua New Guinea **155** D3
Boulder, Colorado (U.S.) **65** C4
Boulia, Australia **153** C6
Bourke, Australia **153** E7
Boyoma Falls, Dem. Rep. of the Congo **141** E5
Brahmaputra (river), Asia **121** C7
Braila, Romania **99** B7
Brasília, Brazil **81** E5
Brasov, Romania **99** B6

Bratislava, Slovakia **96** E2
Bratsk, Russia **111** E7
Brazil (country), South America **73** D6
Brazilian Highlands, Brazil **81** E5
Brazos (river), Texas (U.S.) **65** E6
Brazzaville, Congo **141** F3
Bremen, Germany **95** C5
Brest, Belarus **97** C5
Brest, France **95** E2
Bridgetown, Barbados **69** D8
Brisbane, Australia **153** D8
Bristol, United Kingdom **95** D3
Bristol Bay, Alaska (U.S.) **56** B1
British Columbia (province), Canada **62** F2
British Isles, Europe **86** C2
Brittany (region), France **86** E2
Brno, Czech Republic **96** D2
Broken Hill, Australia **153** E6
Brooks Range, Alaska (U.S.) **64** F2
Broome, Australia **152** B3
Brownsville, Texas (U.S.) **65** G6
Brussels, Belgium **95** D4
Bryansk, Russia **101** F3
Bucaramanga, Colombia **79** B3
Buchanan, Liberia **137** E2
Bucharest, Romania **99** C7
Budapest, Hungary **97** F3
Buenos Aires, Argentina **83** E4
Buffalo, New York (U.S.) **65** B9
Bujumbura, Burundi **139** F2
Bukavu, Dem. Rep. of the Congo **141** E5
Bukhara, Uzbekistan **113** D4
Bulawayo, Zimbabwe **143** E5
Bulgaria (country), Europe **87** G5
Buller (river), New Zealand **153** G10
Bumba, Dem. Rep. of the Congo **141** E4
Bunbury, Australia **152** E2
Bundaberg, Australia **153** D8
Bunia, Dem. Rep. of the Congo **141** E6
Bura, Kenya **139** E4
Buraydah, Saudi Arabia **119** E3
Burgas, Bulgaria **99** D7
Burketown, Australia **153** B6
Burkina Faso (country), Africa **137** D4
Burlington, Vermont (U.S.) **65** B10
Burma (country), see Myanmar, Asia **105** F5
Burnie, Australia **153** G7
Bursa, Turkey **117** B2
Buru (island), Indonesia **125** D7
Burundi (country), Africa **139** E2
Busan, South Korea **115** D9
Butte, Montana (U.S.) **65** B3
Bydgoszcz, Poland **97** B3
Bytom, Poland **97** D3

C
Cabot Strait, Canada **63** G10
Cabo Verde (country) **129** D1
Cádiz, Spain **95** I1
Cagayan de Oro, Philippines **123** D8
Cagliari, Italy **95** H6

Caicos Islands, Turks & Caicos Islands (U.K.) **69** B4
Cairns, Australia **153** B7
Cairo, Egypt **135** B10
Cajamarca, Peru **79** F2
Calcutta, see Kolkata, India **121** D6
Cali, Colombia **79** C2
California (state), U.S. **64** D2
California, Gulf of, Mexico **66** B1
Callao, Peru **79** G2
Camagüey, Cuba **69** C2
Cambodia (country), Asia **105** G6
Cambridge Bay, Nunavut (Canada) **63** C4
Cameroon (country), Africa **141** D2
Camooweal, Australia **153** C6
Campeche, Mexico **67** E5
Campo Grande, Brazil **81** F4
Canada (country), North America **57** C3
Canadian Shield, Canada **56** D4
Canary Islands, Spain **132** B1
Canaveral, Cape, Florida (U.S.) **65** F10
Canberra, Australia **153** F7
Cancún Island, Mexico **67** D6
Cangamba, Angola **143** C3
Cantabrian Mountains, Spain **86** F1
Canterbury Bight, New Zealand **153** H10
Can Tho, Vietnam **123** D3
Cap Barbas (cape), Western Sahara (Morocco) **132** D1
Cape Breton Island, Nova Scotia (Canada) **63** G9
Cape Dorset, Nunavut (Canada) **63** D6
Cape Palmas, Côte d'Ivoire **137** F3
Cape Town, South Africa **143** H3
Caprivi Strip, Namibia **143** D3
Caracas, Venezuela **79** A5
Carbón, Laguna del, Argentina **83** H2
Cardiff, United Kingdom **95** D3
Caribbean Sea, North America **56** H6
Carnarvon, Australia **152** D1
Carolina Island, French Polynesia (France) **155** E8
Caroline Islands, Federated States of Micronesia **154** C2
Carpathian Mountains, Europe **86** E5
Carpentaria, Gulf of, Australia **153** A6
Carson City, Nevada (U.S.) **64** C2
Cartagena, Colombia **79** A2
Cartagena, Spain **95** I3
Cartier Island, Australia **152** A3
Casablanca, Morocco **132** B2
Cascade Range, U.S. **64** B1
Casper, Wyoming (U.S.) **65** C4
Caspian Depression, Europe/Asia **113** B2
Caspian Sea, Europe/Asia **104** D2

Cassai (river), Africa **143** B3
Castries, St. Lucia **69** D7
Catania, Italy **95** I8
Cat Island, Bahamas **69** B3
Cauca (river), Colombia **79** B2
Caucasus Mountains, Europe/Asia **117** A7
Caxito, Angola **142** B1
Cayambe, Ecuador **79** D2
Cayman Islands, United Kingdom **56** H6
Cazombo, Angola **143** B4
Cebu City (island), Philippines **123** D8
Cebu, Philippines **123** D8
Cedar Rapids, Iowa (U.S.) **65** C7
Ceduna, Australia **153** E5
Celebes Sea, Asia **125** B6
Celtic Sea, Europe **95** D2
Central African Republic (country), Africa **141** D4
Central America, North America **56** I5
Central Lowland, U.S. **56** F5
Central Lowlands, Australia **146** E3
Central Range, Russia **111** C11
Central Russian Upland, Russia **101** F3
Central Siberian Plateau, Russia **111** D7
Ceram (island), Indonesia **125** D8
Ceram Sea, Indonesia **125** C8
Ceuta, Spain **132** A3
Chabahar, Iran **119** E8
Chad (country), Africa **141** B4
Chad, Lake, Africa **141** B3
Chagos Archipelago, British Indian Ocean Territory, U.K. **105** H3
Champlain, Lake, U.S. **65** B10
Changchun, China **115** C8
Changsha, China **115** F7
Channel Islands, California (U.S.) **64** D1
Channel Islands, United Kingdom **95** E3
Chao Phraya (river), Thailand **123** C2
Chaozhou, China **115** F8
Chapala, Lake, Mexico **67** D2
Chari (river), Africa **141** C3
Charleston, South Carolina (U.S.) **65** E10
Charleston, West Virginia (U.S.) **65** D9
Charleville, Australia **153** D7
Charlotte, North Carolina (U.S.) **65** D9
Charlottetown, Prince Edward Island (Canada) **63** G9
Charters Towers, Australia **153** C7
Chatham Island, New Zealand **146** G6
Chattanooga, Tennessee (U.S.) **65** E8
Chechnya (region), Russia **101** I5
Chelyabinsk, Russia **110** E3
Chengdu, China **115** E5
Chennai (Madras), India **121** F5
Cherepovets, Russia **101** D4
Cherkasy, Ukraine **97** E8
Chernihiv, Ukraine **97** C8

Chernivtsi, Ukraine **97** E6
Cherskiy Range, Russia **104** B6
Chesapeake Bay, U.S. **65** D11
Cheyenne, Wyoming (U.S.) **65** C4
Chiang Mai, Thailand **123** B2
Chicago, Illinois (U.S.) **65** C8
Chichén Itza (ruins), Mexico **67** D6
Chiclayo, Peru **79** F1
Chihuahua, Mexico **67** B2
Chilanga, Zambia **143** C5
Chile (country), South America **73** G4
Chiloé Island, Chile **83** G1
Chimborazo (peak), Ecuador **79** D1
Chimbote, Peru **79** F1
China (country), Asia **105** E5
Chinandega, Nicaragua **67** F6
Chingola, Zambia **143** C5
Chinhoyi, Zimbabwe **143** D6
Chios (island), Greece **99** G7
Chirripó, Cerro, Costa Rica **67** G7
Chisasibi, Quebec (Canada) **63** F7
Chisinau, Moldova **97** F7
Chita, Russia **111** F8
Chittagong, Bangladesh **121** D7
Chokwé, Mozambique **143** F6
Choluteca, Honduras **67** F6
Ch'ongjin, North Korea **115** C9
Chongqing, China **115** E6
Chornobyl', Ukraine **97** D7
Chott Melrhir (dry salt lake), Algeria **135** B5
Choybalsan, Mongolia **115** B6
Christchurch, New Zealand **153** H10
Christmas Island, see Kirimati, Kiribati **155** D7
Chukchi Peninsula, Russia **104** A7
Chukchi Sea, Asia/North America **104** A6
Chuquicamata, Chile **83** B2
Churchill (river), Manitoba (Canada) **63** F5
Churchill, Manitoba (Canada) **63** E5
Cincinnati, Ohio (U.S.) **65** D9
Cirebon, Indonesia **124** D3
Ciudad Bolívar, Venezuela **79** B6
Ciudad del Este, Paraguay **83** B5
Ciudad Guayana, Venezuela **79** B6
Ciudad Juárez, Mexico **67** A2
Ciudad Obregón, Mexico **66** B1
Ciudad Victoria, Mexico **67** D4
Clarence (river), New Zealand **153** G10
Cleveland, Ohio (U.S.) **65** C9
Clipperton (island), France **56** I2
Cloncurry, Australia **153** C6
Cluj-Napoca, Romania **99** B5
Clutha (river), New Zealand **153** I9
Coastal Plain, U.S. **56** G4
Coast Mountains, North America **56** D2
Coast Ranges, U.S. **64** B1

Coats Island, Nunavut (Canada) **63** E6
Coats Land, Antarctica **161** B4
Cobourg Peninsula, Australia **153** A4
Cochabamba, Bolivia **79** H5
Coco (river), North River **67** F7
Cocos Island, Costa Rica **56** I5
Cod, Cape, Massachusetts (U.S.) **56** E6
Coen, Australia **153** B7
Coiba Island, Panama **67** H8
Coimbatore, India **121** G4
Coimbra, Portugal **95** H1
Collier Bay, Australia **152** B3
Colombia (country), South America **73** B3
Colombo, Sri Lanka **121** G4
Colón, Panama **67** G8
Colorado (river), Argentina **83** F3
Colorado (river), U.S. **64** E2
Colorado (state), U.S. **65** D4
Colorado Plateau, U.S. **56** F3
Colorado Springs, Colorado (U.S.) **65** D4
Columbia (river), North America **56** E2
Columbia, South Carolina (U.S.) **65** E9
Columbia Mountains, Canada **56** D2
Columbia Plateau, U.S. **56** E2
Columbus, Georgia (U.S.) **65** E9
Columbus, Ohio (U.S.) **65** C9
Commander Islands, Russia **111** C11
Comodoro Rivadavia, Argentina **83** G2
Comoros (country), Africa **127** G7
Conakry, Guinea **137** E1
Concepción, Chile **83** E1
Concepción, Paraguay **83** B4
Conception, Point, California (U.S.) **64** D1
Conchos (river), Mexico **67** B2
Concord, New Hampshire (U.S.) **65** B11
Congo (country), Africa **141** E3
Congo (river), Africa **141** E4
Congo Basin, Africa **128** F5
Connecticut (river), U.S. **65** B11
Connecticut (state), U.S. **65** C11
Constanta, Romania **99** C8
Constantine, Algeria **135** A5
Coober Pedy, Australia **153** D5
Cook Islands, New Zealand **155** E7
Cook Strait, New Zealand **153** G11
Cooktown, Australia **153** B7
Coonamble, Australia **153** E7
Copán (ruins), Honduras **67** F6
Copenhagen, Denmark **93** I3
Coral Sea, Oceania **146** E4
Córdoba, Argentina **83** D3
Córdoba, Spain **95** I2
Corfu (island), Greece **99** F4
Corinth, Greece **99** G5
Cork, Ireland **95** D2
Corn Islands, Nicaragua **67** F8
Coromandel Peninsula, New Zealand **153** E11
Corpus Christi, Texas (U.S.) **65** F6

Corrientes, Argentina **83** C4
Corsica (island), France **95** G6
Costa Rica (country), North America **57** I5
Cotabato City, Philippines **123** E8
Côte d'Ivoire (Ivory Coast) (country), Africa **137** E3
Cotonou, Benin **137** E5
Cozumel Island, Mexico **67** D6
Craiova, Romania **99** C6
Crater Lake, Oregon (U.S.) **64** B1
Crete (island), Greece **99** I6
Crete, Sea of, Greece **99** H6
Crimea (region), Ukraine **97** G9
Croatia (country), Europe **87** F4
Croydon, Australia **153** B6
Crozier, Cape, Antarctica **161** F5
Cuando (river), Africa **143** C3
Cuango (river), Africa **142** A2
Cuba (country), North America **57** H6
Cúcuta, Colombia **79** B3
Cuenca, Ecuador **79** E1
Cuiabá, Brazil **81** E4
Culiacán, Mexico **67** C2
Cumaná, Venezuela **79** A5
Curaçao (island), Netherlands Antilles (Netherlands) **69** E5
Curitiba, Brazil **81** G5
Cusco, Peru **79** G3
Cyclades (islands), Greece **99** G6
Cyrenaica (region), Libya **135** B8
Czech Republic (country), Europe **87** E4

D
Daegu, South Korea **115** D9
Dakar, Senegal **137** C1
Dalian, China **115** D8
Dallas, Texas (U.S.) **65** E6
Dalmatia (region), Europe **99** C2
Daly Waters, Australia **153** B5
Damascus, Syria **117** F5
Damavand, Mount, Iran **119** B5
Dampier, Australia **152** C2
Dampier Land, Australia **152** B3
Danakil (region), Ethiopia **139** B4
Da Nang, Vietnam **123** C4
Dangrek Range, Thailand **123** C2
Danube (river), Europe **86** F6
Dardanelles (strait), Turkey **116** B1
Dar es Salaam, Tanzania **139** F4
Darfur (region), Sudan **141** C5
Darhad Valley, Mongolia **115** B5
Darhan, Mongolia **115** B5
Darling (river), Australia **153** E6
Darling Range, Australia **146** F1
Darnah, Libya **135** B8
Darnley, Cape, Antarctica **161** C8
Dar Rounga, Central African Rep. **141** C4
Darwin, Australia **153** A4

Dasht-e Kavīr (Kavir Desert) (region), Iran **119** C6
Dasht-e Lut (region), Iran **119** C7
Datong, China **115** C7
Daugava (river), Europe **86** D6
Daugavpils, Latvia **93** H7
Davao City, Philippines **123** E8
David, Panama **67** G7
Davis Strait, Canada **63** C8
Dawei, Myanmar **121** F9
Dawson Creek, British Columbia (Canada) **62** E2
Dayr az Zawr, Syria **117** E6
Dead Sea, Asia **117** G4
Death Valley, California (U.S.) **64** D2
Deccan Plateau, India **121** E4
Dehra Dun, India **121** C4
Delaware (state), U.S. **65** C10
Delhi, India **121** C4
Democratic Republic of the Congo (country), Africa **141** E4
Denali (Mount McKinley), Alaska (U.S.) **64** F2
Denizli, Turkey **117** C2
Denmark (country), Europe **87** D4
Denpasar, Indonesia **125** E4
Denver, Colorado (U.S.) **65** C4
Derby, Australia **152** B3
Desē, Ethiopia **139** B4
Des Moines, Iowa (U.S.) **65** C7
Detroit, Michigan (U.S.) **65** C9
Devon Island, Nunavut (Canada) **63** B5
Devonport, Australia **153** G7
Dezful, Iran **119** C4
Dhaka, Bangladesh **121** D7
Dibrugarh, India **121** C8
Dif, Kenya **139** E4
Dijon, France **95** E5
Dili, East Timor **125** E7
Dinaric Alps (range), Europe **99** C3
Dindigul, India **121** G4
Dire Dawa, Ethiopia **139** C4
District of Columbia, U.S. **65** D11
Diyarbakır, Turkey **117** D6
Djado, Niger **137** B7
Djanet, Algeria **135** D6
Djelfa, Algeria **135** B5
Djibouti (country), Africa **139** B5
Djibouti (city), Djibouti **139** B5
Dnieper (river), Europe **97** F9
Dniester (river), Europe **97** E6
Dnipro, Ukraine **97** E9
Dniprodzerzhyns'k, Ukraine **97** E9
Dobane, Central African Rep. **141** D5
Dodecanese (islands), Greece **99** H7
Dodge City, Kansas (U.S.) **65** D5
Dodoma, Tanzania **139** F3
Doha, Qatar **119** E5
Dolak (island), Indonesia **125** D10
Dolo Bay, Ethiopia **139** D5
Dominica (country), North America **57** H8
Dominican Republic (country), North America **57** H7

Don (river), Russia **101** G4
Donets'k, Ukraine **97** E10
Dongara, Australia **152** E1
Dongola, Sudan **141** A6
Donostia-San Sebastián, Spain **95** G3
Dosso, Niger **137** D5
Douala, Cameroon **141** D2
Douro (river), Portugal **95** G1
Dover, Delaware (U.S.) **65** C10
Dover, Strait of, Europe **95** D4
Drakensberg (range), South Africa **143** G5
Drammen, Norway **93** F3
Drava (river), Europe **86** F5
Dresden, Germany **95** D7
Dubai, United Arab Emirates **119** E6
Dubbo, Australia **153** E7
Dublin, Ireland **95** C2
Dubrovnik, Croatia **99** D3
Ducie Island, United Kingdom **155** F10
Duero (river), Spain **95** G3
Duluth, Minnesota (U.S.) **65** B7
Dundo, Angola **143** A3
Dunedin, New Zealand **153** I10
Duqm, Oman **119** G7
Durango, Mexico **67** C2
Durban, South Africa **143** G6
Durrës, Albania **99** E4
Dushanbe, Tajikistan **113** E4
Dzhugdzhur Range, Russia **111** D9

E

East Antarctica, Antarctica **161** D7
East Cape, New Zealand **153** E12
East China Sea, Asia **104** E7
Easter Island, see Rapa Nui, Chile **155** F11
Eastern Desert, Egypt **135** B10
Eastern Ghats (range), India **121** F4
Eastern Rift Valley, Africa **139** E3
East London, South Africa **143** H5
East Sea, see Japan, Sea of, Asia **104** D7
East Siberian Sea, Russia **104** A6
East Timor (country), see Timor-Leste, Asia **125** E7
Ebolowa, Cameroon **141** D2
Ebro (river), Spain **95** G3
Ecuador (country), South America **73** C2
Edge Island, Norway **93** A3
Edinburgh, United Kingdom **95** B3
Edmonton, Alberta (Canada) **63** F3
Edward, Lake, Africa **139** E2
Éfaté (island), Vanuatu **155** E4
Egmont, Mount, see Taranaki, Mount, N.Z. **153** F11
Egypt (country), Africa **135** C9
Elazığ, Turkey **117** C6
Elbasan, Albania **99** E4
Elbe (river), Europe **95** C6
El'brus (peak), Russia **101** I4
Elburz Mountains, Iran **119** B5
El Djouf, Mauritania **137** B3

Eleuthera Island, Bahamas **69** B3
El Fasher, Sudan **141** B5
El Gîza, Egypt **135** C9
El Golea, Libya **135** B5
El Khârga, Egypt **135** C9
Ellesmere Island, Nunavut (Canada) **63** A6
Ellsworth Land, Antarctica **161** D2
Ellsworth Mountains, Antarctica **161** D3
El Minya, Egypt **135** C9
El Obeid, Sudan **141** C6
El Paso, Texas (U.S.) **65** E4
El Salvador (country), North America **57** I5
Emerald, Australia **153** C7
Emi Koussi (peak), Chad **141** A4
Empty Quarter, see Rub' al Khali, Saudi Arabia **119** G5
Enderby Land, Antarctica **161** B8
Enewetak Atoll, Marshall Islands **155** C3
England (country), United Kingdom **95** D4
English Channel, Europe **95** E3
En Nahud, Sudan **141** C5
Ennedi (range), Chad **141** B4
Enugu, Nigeria **137** E6
Equatorial Guinea (country), Africa **141** E2
Erbil, Iraq **119** B3
Erebus, Mount, Antarctica **161** F5
Eritrea (country), Africa **139** A4
Erg Chech (desert), Algeria **132** D3
Erg Iguidi (desert), Algeria **132** C3
Erie, Pennsylvania (U.S.) **65** C9
Erie, Lake, North America **56** F5
Ertis (river), Kazakhstan **113** B6
Ertix (river), China **113** C6
Erzurum, Turkey **117** C7
Esbjerg, Denmark **93** I2
Eskisehir, Turkey **117** B3
Esperance, Australia **152** E3
Essen, Germany **95** D5
Estonia (country), Europe **87** D5
Ethiopia (country), Africa **139** C4
Ethiopian Highlands (region), Africa **139** C3
Etna, Mount (peak), Italy **95** H7
Etosha Pan, Namibia **142** D2
Eucla Basin, Australia **146** F1
Eucla, Australia **153** E4
Eugene, Oregon (U.S.) **64** B1
Eugenia Point, Mexico **56** G2
Euphrates (river), Asia **104** D2
Eureka, California (U.S.) **64** C1
Europa, Île, France **143** E8
Evansville, Indiana (U.S.) **65** D8
Everest, Mount, Asia **104** E4
Everglades, The, Florida (U.S.) **65** G10
Exmouth, Australia **152** C1
Eyl, Somalia **139** C6
Eyre, Lake, Australia **153** D5

F

Fada, Chad **141** B4
Fairbanks, Alaska (U.S.) **64** F3
Faisalabad, Pakistan **121** B3
Falkland Islands (Islas Malvinas), United Kingdom **83** H4
Falun, Sweden **93** F4
Farewell, Cape, Greenland (Denmark) **56** C7
Farewell, Cape, N.Z. **153** F10
Fargo, North Dakota (U.S.) **65** B6
Faroe Islands, Denmark **86** B2
Fars (region), Iran **119** D6
Faya, Chad **141** B4
Feilding, New Zealand **153** F11
Feira de Santana, Brazil **81** E7
Fez, Morocco **132** B3
Fezzan (region), Libya **135** C6
Fianarantsoa, Madagascar **143** E10
Fiji (country), Oceania **147** E6
Filchner Ice Shelf, Antarctica **161** C4
Fimbul Ice Shelf, Antarctica **161** A5
Finland (country), Europe **87** C5
Finland, Gulf of, Europe **86** C5
Fitzroy (river), Australia **152** B3
Fitzroy Crossing, Australia **152** B3
Flagstaff, Arizona (U.S.) **64** D3
Flattery, Cape, Washington (U.S.) **64** A1
Flint Island, French Polynesia (France) **155** E7
Florence, Italy **95** G6
Florencia, Colombia **79** C2
Flores (island), Indonesia **125** E6
Flores Sea, Indonesia **125** D6
Florida (state), U.S. **65** F9
Florida, Straits of, North America **56** G6
Florida Keys, Florida (U.S.) **65** G10
Fly (river), Papua New Guinea **154** D2
Formosa, Argentina **83** C4
Fort Albany, Ontario (Canada) **63** F6
Fortaleza, Brazil **81** C7
Fort Collins, Colorado (U.S.) **65** C4
Fort Severn, Ontario (Canada) **63** F6
Fort Smith, Arkansas (U.S.) **65** E7
Fort Smith, Northwest Territories (Canada) **63** E3
Fort Wayne, Indiana (U.S.) **65** C8
Fort Worth, Texas (U.S.) **65** E6
Foshan, China **115** F7
Foveaux Strait, New Zealand **153** I9
Foxe Basin, Nunavut (Canada) **63** C6
France (country), Europe **87** F2
Franceville, Gabon **141** E3
Frankfort, Kentucky (U.S.) **65** D8
Frankfurt, Germany **95** D5

Franz Josef Glacier, New Zealand **153** H9
Franz Josef Land (islands), Russia **111** B5
Fraser (river), British Columbia (Canada) **62** F2
Fraser Island, Australia **153** D8
Fraser Plateau, Canada **56** D2
Fredericton, New Brunswick (Canada) **63** G9
Freetown, Sierra Leone **137** E1
French Guiana, France **73** B6
French Polynesia (islands), France **155** E8
Frisian Islands, Europe **95** C5
Fua Mulaku (island), Maldives **121** I3
Fuji (peak), Japan **115** C11
Fukuoka, Japan **115** D9
Funafuti, Tuvalu **155** E5
Fundy, Bay of, Canada **63** G9
Furneaux Group (islands), Australia **153** G7
Fushun, China **115** C8
Fuzhou, China **115** F8
Fyn (island), Denmark **93** I3

G

Gaalkacyo, Somalia **139** C6
Gabès, Tunisia **135** B6
Gabes, Gulf of, Tunisia **135** B6
Gabon (country), Africa **141** E2
Gaborone, Botswana **143** F5
Gabras, Sudan **141** C5
Galápagos Islands, Ecuador **72** C1
Galati, Romania **99** B7
Galdhøpiggen (peak), Norway **93** E3
Galilee, Sea of, Israel **117** F4
Gambia (country), Africa **137** D1
Gan (island), Maldives **121** I3
Ganges (river), Asia **121** C4
Ganges, Mouths of the, Bangladesh **121** D7
Gao, Mali **137** C5
Garagum (desert), Turkmenistan **113** D3
Garonne (river), France **95** F3
Garoua, Cameroon **141** C3
Garoua Boulaï, Cameroon **141** D3
Gary, Indiana (U.S.) **65** C8
Gaspé Peninsula, Quebec (Canada) **63** G9
Gaza, Gaza Strip **117** G4
Gaza Strip, Asia **117** G4
Gaziantep, Turkey **117** D5
Gdansk, Poland **97** B3
Gdynia, Poland **97** B3
Geelong, Australia **153** F6
Gemena, Dem. Rep. of the Congo **141** D4
Gemsa, Egypt **135** C10
Gǝncǝ, Azerbaijan **117** B8
General Santos, Philippines **123** E8
Geneva, Switzerland **95** F5
Genoa, Italy **95** F6
Geographe Bay, Australia **152** E2
George Town, Malaysia **123** E1
Georgetown, Guyana **81** A3
Georgia (country), Asia **105** D2
Georgia (state), U.S. **65** E9

Geraldton, Australia **152** E1
Germany (country), Europe **87** E4
Getz Ice Shelf, Antarctica **161** F2
Ghadāmis, Libya **135** C6
Ghana (country), Africa **137** E4
Ghardaïa, Algeria **135** B4
Ghāt, Libya **135** D6
Gibraltar (country), United Kingdom **95** I2
Gibson Desert, Australia **152** C3
Gilbert Islands, Kiribati **155** D4
Gisborne, New Zealand **153** F12
Glacier Bay, Alaska (U.S.) **56** C2
Gladstone, Australia **153** D8
Glåma (river), Norway **93** F3
Glasgow, United Kingdom **95** B3
Glorioso Islands, France **143** B10
Goba, Ethiopia **139** C4
Gobi (desert), Asia **104** D6
Godavari (river), India **121** E4
Godthåb, see Nuuk, Greenland (Denmark) **57** C6
Godwin Austen (peak), see K2, Pakistan **121** A4
Goiânia, Brazil **81** E5
Gold Coast, Africa **137** F4
Gold Coast, Australia **153** D8
Gonabad, Iran **119** C7
Gonder, Ethiopia **139** B3
Gongga Shan (peak), China **104** E5
Good Hope, Cape of, South Africa **143** H3
Gorē, Ethiopia **139** C3
Gore, New Zealand **153** I9
Gorgan, Iran **119** B6
Gorontalo, Indonesia **125** C6
Götaland (region), Sweden **93** H4
Göteborg, Sweden **93** H3
Gotland (island), Sweden **93** H5
Governador Valadares, Brazil **81** F6
Grafton, Australia **153** E8
Grahamstown, South Africa **143** H5
Grain Coast, Africa **137** E2
Granada, Nicaragua **67** F7
Gran Chaco (region), South America **83** B3
Grand Bahama Island, Bahamas **69** A2
Grand Canal (river), China **115** D7
Grand Canyon, Arizona (U.S.) **64** D3
Grand Cayman (island), Cayman Islands (U.K.) **69** C2
Grand Junction, Colorado (U.S.) **65** C4
Grand Rapids, Michigan (U.S.) **65** C8
Graz, Austria **95** E7
Great Artesian Basin, Australia **153** D6
Great Australian Bight, Australia **152** E4
Great Barrier Island, New Zealand **153** D11
Great Barrier Reef, Australia **153** B7

Great Basin, U.S. **64** C2
Great Bear Lake, Northwest Territories (Canada) **63** C3
Great Britain (island), United Kingdom **95** C3
Great Dividing Range, Australia **153** C7
Great Eastern Erg (dunes), Algeria **135** C5
Great Falls, Montana (U.S.) **65** A4
Great Inagua Island, Bahamas **69** C4
Great Indian Desert, Asia **121** C3
Great Karoo (range), South Africa **143** H4
Great Plains, North America **56** E3
Great Rift Valley, Africa **128** F6
Great Salt Lake, Utah (U.S.) **64** C3
Great Sandy Desert, Australia **152** C3
Great Slave Lake, Northwest Territories (Canada) **63** D3
Great Victoria Desert, Australia **152** D4
Great Western Erg (dunes), Algeria **135** C4
Great Zimbabwe (ruins), Zimbabwe **143** E6
Greater Antilles (islands), North America **69** C2
Greater Khingan Range, China **115** B7
Greater Sunda Islands, Indonesia **125** D4
Greece (country), Europe **87** G5
Green Bay, Wisconsin (U.S.) **65** B8
Greenland (Kalaallit Nunaat), Denmark **57** A6
Greenland Sea, Atlantic Ocean **56** A6
Greensboro, North Carolina (U.S.) **65** D10
Greenville, Liberia **137** E2
Grenada (country), North America **57** H8
Greymouth, New Zealand **153** G10
Grijalva (river), Mexico **67** E5
Groote Eylandt (island), Australia **153** A5
Groznyy, Russia **101** I5
Grünau, Namibia **143** F3
Guadalajara, Mexico **67** D2
Guadalcanal (island), Solomon Islands **155** E3
Guadalupe Island, Mexico **56** G2
Guadeloupe (island), France **69** C7
Guadiana (river), Europe **95** H2
Guam (island), U.S. **154** C2
Guangzhou, China **115** F7
Guantánamo, Cuba **69** C3
Guaporé (river), South America **79** G5
Guatemala (country), North America **57** H5
Guayaquil, Ecuador **79** D1
Guelmim, Morocco **132** B2
Guiana Highlands, South America **72** B5

Guilin, China **115** F6
Guinea (country), Africa **137** D2
Guinea-Bissau (country), Africa **137** D2
Guinea, Gulf of, Africa **137** F4
Guiyang, China **137** F6
Gujranwala, Pakistan **121** B3
Gulu, Uganda **139** D5
Gunnbjørn (peak), Greenland (Denmark) **56** B6
Guntur, India **121** E5
Gusau, Nigeria **137** D6
Guyana (country), South America **73** A5
Gwalior, India **121** C4
Gwangju, South Korea **115** D9
Gwardafuy, Cape, Somalia **139** B7
Gyor, Hungary **96** E2
Gyumri, Armenia **117** B8

H

Hadramawt (region), Yemen **119** H5
Haida Gwaii, British Columbia (Canada) **62** E1
Haifa, Israel **117** F4
Haig, Australia **152** E3
Haikou, China **115** G6
Ha'il, Saudi Arabia **119** E3
Hailar, China **115** B7
Hainan (island), China **115** G6
Haines Junction, Yukon (Canada) **62** D1
Haiphong, Vietnam **123** B3
Haiti (country), North America **57** H7
Halayeb, Egypt **135** D11
Halifax, Nova Scotia (Canada) **63** G9
Halls Creek, Australia **152** B4
Halmahera (island), Indonesia **125** C8
Hama, Syria **117** E5
Hamada de Tinrhert (plateau), Africa **135** C5
Hamadan, Iran **119** C4
Hamburg, Germany **95** C6
Hami, China **115** C4
Hamilton, New Zealand **153** E11
Hamilton, Ontario (Canada) **63** H7
Hammerfest, Norway **93** A6
Hangayn Mountains, Mongolia **115** B5
Hangzhou, China **115** E8
Hannover, Germany **95** D6
Hanoi, Vietnam **123** B3
Happy Valley-Goose Bay, Newfoundland & Labrador (Canada) **63** F9
Harare, Zimbabwe **143** D6
Harbin, China **115** B8
Hargeysa, Somalia **139** C5
Harirud (river), Asia **121** A2
Harper, Liberia **137** F3
Harrisburg, Pennsylvania (U.S.) **65** C10
Hartford, Connecticut (U.S.) **65** C11
Hastings, New Zealand **153** F12
Hatay (Antioch), Turkey **117** D4
Hatteras, Cape, North Carolina (U.S.) **65** D11
Hat Yai, Thailand **123** D1

Haugesund, Norway **93** F2
Hauraki Gulf, New Zealand **153** E11
Havana, Cuba **69** B1
Hawai'i (island), Hawai'i (U.S.) **65** G5
Hawai'i (state), U.S. **65** G4
Hawaiian Islands, U.S. **146** A7
Hawf, Yemen **119** G6
Hawke Bay, New Zealand **153** F12
Hayes Peninsula, Greenland (Denmark) **56** B5
Hay River, Northwest Territories (Canada) **63** E3
Hefei, China **115** E7
Heilong Jiang (Amur) (river), Asia **115** A8
Helena, Montana (U.S.) **65** B3
Helmand (river), Afghanistan **121** B1
Helsingborg, Sweden **93** H3
Helsinki, Finland **93** F7
Henderson Island, United Kingdom **155** F9
Hengyang, China **115** F7
Herat, Afghanistan **121** A1
Herlen (river), **115** B6
Hermosillo, Mexico **66** B1
Highlands, United Kingdom **86** C2
High Plains, U.S. **56** F3
Hiiumaa (island), Estonia **93** G6
Hilalaye, Somalia **139** C6
Hilo, Hawai'i (U.S.) **65** G5
Himalaya (range), Asia **104** E4
Hindu Kush (range), Asia **121** A3
Hiroshima, Japan **115** D10
Hispaniola (island), North America **69** C4
Hobart, Australia **153** G7
Ho Chi Minh City (Saigon), Vietnam **123** D3
Höfn, Iceland **87** B2
Hofuf, Saudi Arabia **119** E5
Hohhot, China **115** C6
Hokitika, New Zealand **153** G10
Hokkaido (island), Japan **115** B11
Homs, Syria **117** E5
Homyel', Belarus **97** C7
Honduras (country), North America **57** H5
Hong Kong, China **115** G7
Hongshui (river), China **115** F6
Honiara, Solomon Island **155** E3
Honolulu, Hawai'i (U.S.) **65** G4
Honshu (island), Japan **115** C11
Hopetoun, Australia **152** E3
Horlivka, Ukraine **97** E10
Hormuz, Strait of, Asia **119** E6
Horn, Cape, Chile **72** I5
Hotan, China **114** D2
Houston, Texas (U.S.) **65** F6
Hovd, Mongolia **115** B4
Howland Island, U.S. **155** D5
Hrodna, Belarus **97** B5
Huambo, Angola **142** C2
Huancayo, Peru **79** G2
Huánuco, Peru **79** F2
Huascarán, Nevado, Peru **79** F2
Hubballi, India **121** F3
Hudson Bay, Canada **63** E6
Hudson Strait, Canada **63** D7

Hue, Vietnam **123** C3
Hughenden, Australia **153** C7
Hungary (country), Europe **87** F5
Hūn, Libya **135** C7
Huntsville, Alabama (U.S.) **65** E8
Huron, Lake, North America **56** E5
Hustai National Park, Mongolia **115** B5
Hyderabad, India **121** E4
Hyderabad, Pakistan **121** C2

I

Iasi, Romania **99** A7
Ibadan, Nigeria **137** E5
Ibagué, Colombia **79** C2
Iberian Peninsula, Europe **86** F1
Ica, Peru **79** G2
Iceland (country), Europe **87** B2
Idaho (state), U.S. **64** B3
Idaho Falls, Idaho (U.S.) **65** B3
Ife, Nigeria **137** E6
Iferouâne, Niger **137** C6
Igloolik, Nunavut (Canada) **63** C6
Iguazú Falls, South America **72** E6
Iguéla, Gabon **141** E2
Ikaría (island), Greece **99** G7
Îles de Horne (islands), Oceania **146** D6
Illinois (state), U.S. **65** C7
Illizi, Algeria **135** C6
Iloilo City, Philippines **123** D7
Īm ī, Ethiopia **139** C5
Imperatriz, Brazil **81** C5
Imphal, India **121** D8
I-n-Amenas, Algeria **135** C5
Incheon, South Korea **115** D9
India (country), Asia **105** F4
Indiana (state), U.S. **65** C8
Indianapolis, Indiana (U.S.) **65** C8
Indonesia (country), Asia **105** H6
Indore, India **121** D4
Indus (river), Asia **121** C2
Indus, Mouths of the, Pakistan **121** D2
Ingal, Niger **137** C6
Inhambane, Mozambique **143** E7
Inhassoro, Mozambique **143** E7
Inland Niger Delta, Mali **137** C4
Inongo, Dem. Rep. of the Congo **141** E3
Inner Hebrides (islands), United Kingdom **95** B2
Inner Mongolia, China **115** C6
Innisfail, Australia **153** B7
Innsbruck, Austria **95** E6
I-n-Salah, Algeria **135** C5
Inscription, Cape, Australia **152** D1
International Falls, Minnesota (U.S.) **65** A7
Inuvik, Northwest Territories (Canada) **62** C2
Invercargill, New Zealand **153** I9
Inverness, United Kingdom **87** C2
Ionian Islands, Greece **99** G4

Ionian Sea — Laccadive Sea

Ionian Sea, Europe **86** G5
Iowa (state), U.S. **65** C7
Iqaluit, Nunavut (Canada) **63** D7
Iquique, Chile **83** A1
Iquitos, Peru **79** E3
Irákleio, Greece **99** H6
Iran (country), Asia **105** E2
Iraq (country), Asia **105** D2
Ireland (island), Europe **87** D2
Ireland (Éire) (country), Europe **87** D2
Irian Jaya (province), Indonesia **125** C10
Iringa, Tanzania **139** G3
Irish Sea, Europe **86** D2
Irkutsk, Russia **111** F7
Iron Gate Dam, Europe **99** C5
Irrawaddy (river), Myanmar **121** D8
Irtysh (river), Russia **111** E4
Ísafjördur, Iceland **87** A2
Isfahan, Iran **119** C5
Isiro (Paulis), Dem. Rep. of the Congo **141** D5
Iskenderun, Turkey **117** D5
Islamabad, Pakistan **121** B3
Isoka, Zambia **143** B6
Israel (country), Asia **105** D1
Istanbul, Turkey **117** B2
Italy (country), Europe **87** G4
Ivalo, Finland **87** B5
Ivanovo, Russia **101** E4
Ivory Coast (country), see Côte d'Ivoire, Africa **137** F3
Ivujivik, Quebec (Canada) **63** D6
Izhevsk, Russia **101** E6
Izmir, Turkey **116** C1
İzmit, Turkey **117** B2

J

Jabalpur, India **121** D4
Jabal Tuwayq (region), Saudi Arabia **119** G4
Jackson, Mississippi (U.S.) **65** E7
Jackson, Mount, Antarctica **161** C2
Jackson Head (cape), New Zealand **153** H9
Jacksonville, Florida (U.S.) **65** F9
Jaffna, Sri Lanka **121** G4
Jaipur, India **121** C4
Jakarta, Indonesia **124** D2
Jamaica (country), North America **57** H6
Jambi, Indonesia **124** C2
James Bay, Canada **63** F6
Jammu, India **121** B4
Jamshedpur, India **121** D6
Jan Mayen (island), Norway **86** A3
Japan (country), Asia **105** D8
Japan, Sea of, (East Sea), Asia **104** D7
Jarvis Island, U.S. **155** D7
Java (island), Indonesia **124** D3
Java Sea, Indonesia **125** D4
Jayapura, Indonesia **125** C11
Jebel Marra (peak), Sudan **141** C5
Jebel Toubkal (peak), Morocco **132** B2
Jeddah, Saudi Arabia **119** F2

Jefferson City, Missouri (U.S.) **65** D7
Jelgava, Latvia **93** H7
Jerba Island, Tunisia **135** B6
Jerusalem, Israel **117** G4
Jilin, China **115** B8
Jinan, China **115** D7
Jinja, Uganda **139** E3
Jizan, Saudi Arabia **119** G3
João Pessoa, Brazil **81** D8
Jodhpur, India **121** C3
Joensuu, Finland **93** E8
Johannesburg, South Africa **143** F5
Johnston Atoll, U.S. **155** B6
Johor Bahru, Malaysia **123** F2
Joinvile, Brazil **81** G5
Joinville Island, Antarctica **160** B1
Jönköping, Sweden **93** H4
Jordan (country), Asia **105** D1
Jordan (river), Asia **117** F4
Jos, Nigeria **137** D6
Joseph Bonaparte Gulf, Australia **152** A4
Juan De Nova Island, France **143** D9
Juan Fernández Islands, Chile **72** G3
Juazeiro, Brazil **81** D7
Juba, South Sudan **141** D6
Juiz de Fora, Brazil **81** F6
Juneau, Alaska (U.S.) **64** G3
Juruena (river), Brazil **81** D3
Jutland (region), Denmark **93** H2
Jyväskylä, Finland **93** E7

K

K2 (Godwin Austen) (peak), Pakistan **121** A4
Kaambooni, Somalia **139** E4
Kabala, Sierra Leone **137** D2
Kabul, Afghanistan **121** B2
Kabwe, Zambia **143** C5
Kadugli, Sudan **141** C6
Kaduna, Nigeria **137** D6
Kaédi, Mauritania **137** C2
Kafia Kingi, South Sudan **141** C5
Kafue, Zambia **143** C5
Kahemba, Dem. Rep. of the Congo **141** F4
Kaho'olawe (island), Hawai'i (U.S.) **65** G4
Kaikoura, New Zealand **153** G11
Kaipara Harbour, New Zealand **153** E11
Kaitaia, New Zealand **153** D10
Kalaallit Nunaat, see Greenland (Denmark) **57** A6
Kalahari Desert, Africa **143** E4
Kalamáta, Greece **87** H5
Kalemie, Dem. Rep. of the Congo **141** F5
Kalgoorlie, Australia **152** E3
Kaliningrad Oblast (region), Russia **101** E1
Kalisz, Poland **96** C3
Kaluga, Russia **101** F4
Kama (river), Russia **101** E7
Kamchatka Peninsula, Russia **111** C11
Kamina, Dem. Rep. of the Congo **141** G5
Kampala, Uganda **139** E2

Kam'yanets'-Podil's'kyy, Ukraine **97** E6
Kananga, Dem. Rep. of the Congo **141** F4
Kandahar, Afghanistan **121** B2
Kandi, Benin **137** D5
Kandy, Sri Lanka **121** G5
Kangaroo Island, Australia **153** F5
Kanin Peninsula, Russia **101** B5
Kankan, Guinea **137** D2
Kano, Nigeria **137** D7
Kanpur, India **121** C5
Kansas (state), U.S. **65** D6
Kansas City, Missouri (U.S.) **65** D7
Kansk, Russia **111** E6
Kanye, Botswana **143** F4
Kaohsiung, Taiwan **115** F8
Kaokoland (region), Namibia **142** D1
Kaolack, Senegal **137** D1
Kaoma, Zambia **143** C4
Kapingamarangi Atoll, Federated States of Micronesia **155** D3
Karachi, Pakistan **121** C2
Kara Sea, Russia **104** B4
Karbala, Iraq **119** C3
Kariba, Lake, Africa **143** D5
Karlstad, Sweden **93** G4
Kasai (river), Africa **141** F4
Kasempa, Zambia **143** C5
Kashi, China **114** C1
Kashmir (region), Asia **105** E4
Kasongo, Dem. Rep. of the Congo **141** F5
Katanga Plateau, Africa **128** G5
Kathmandu, Nepal **121** C6
Katsina, Nigeria **137** D6
Kattegat (strait), Europe **93** H3
Kaua'i (island), Hawai'i (U.S.) **65** F4
Kaunas, Lithuania **93** I7
Kaválа, Greece **99** E6
Kayes, Mali **137** D2
Kayseri, Turkey **117** C4
Kazakhstan (country), Asia **105** D3
Kazakh Uplands, Kazakhstan **113** C5
Kazan', Russia **101** E6
Kebnekaise (peak), Sweden **93** B5
Kédougou, Senegal **137** D2
Keetmanshoop, Namibia **143** F3
Keflavík, Iceland **93** A1
Kem', Russia **87** B6
Kemerovo, Russia **111** E5
Kemi, Finland **93** C6
Kenai Peninsula, Alaska (U.S.) **56** C1
Kentucky (state), U.S. **65** D8
Kenya (country), Africa **139** E4
Kenya (peak), Mount, Kenya **139** E3
Kerch, Ukraine **97** G10
Kerikeri, New Zealand **153** D11
Kermadec Islands, New Zealand **155** F5
Kerman, Iran **119** D7
Kermanshah, Iran **119** C4
Khabarovsk, Russia **111** E10
Khaluf, Oman **119** F7
Kharkiv, Ukraine **97** D9

Khartoum, Sudan **141** B6
Khartoum North, Sudan **141** B6
Kherson, Ukraine **97** F8
Khmel'nyts'kyy, Ukraine **97** E6
Khorasan (region), Asia **119** C7
Khulna, Bangladesh **121** D7
Khvoy, Iran **119** B4
Kiel, Germany **95** C6
Kielce, Poland **97** D4
Kiev, Ukraine **97** D7
Kiffa, Mauritania **137** C2
Kigali, Rwanda **139** E2
Kigoma, Tanzania **139** F2
Kilimanjaro (peak), Tanzania **139** E3
Kilwa Kivinje, Tanzania **139** G4
Kimberley, South Africa **143** G4
Kimberley Plateau, Australia **146** E2
Kindia, Guinea **137** D2
Kindu, Dem. Rep. of the Congo **141** F5
King Island, Australia **153** G6
King Sound, Australia **152** B3
King William Island, Nunavut (Canada) **63** C5
Kingman Reef, U.S. **155** C6
Kingston, Jamaica **69** C3
Kingston, Ontario (Canada) **63** H7
Kingston upon Hull, United Kingdom **95** C4
Kingstown, St. Vincent & the Grenadines **69** D7
Kinshasa, Dem. Rep. of the Congo **141** F3
Kiribati (country), Oceania **147** D7
Kiritimati (Christmas Island), Kiribati **155** D7
Kirkenes, Norway **87** A6
Kirkuk, Iraq **119** C3
Kirov, Russia **101** D6
Kirovohrad, Ukraine **97** E8
Kirovsk, Russia **87** B6
Kiruna, Sweden **93** B5
Kisangani, Dem. Rep. of the Congo **141** E5
Kismaayo, Somalia **139** E5
Kisumu, Kenya **139** E3
Kitakyushu, Japan **115** D10
Kitwe, Zambia **143** C5
Kivu, Lake, Africa **139** E2
Kızılırmak (river), Turkey **117** B4
Klaipeda, Lithuania **93** I6
Klarälven (river), Europe **93** F4
Klerksdorp, South Africa **143** F5
Knoxville, Tennessee (U.S.) **65** D9
Knud Rasmussen Land, Greenland (Denmark) **56** A5
Kobe, Japan **115** D10
Kochi, India **121** G4
Kodiak Island, Alaska (U.S.) **56** C1
Kökshetau, Kazakhstan **113** B5
Kola Peninsula, Russia **101** B4
Kolguyev Island, Russia **101** A5
Kolhapur, India **121** E3
Kolkata (Calcutta), India **121** D6
Köln, Germany **95** D5

Kolwezi, Dem. Rep. of the Congo **141** G5
Kolyma (river), Russia **111** B9
Kolyma Range, Russia **111** C10
Komani, South Africa **143** G5
Kôm Ombo, Egypt **135** C10
Komsomol'sk na Amure, Russia **111** E10
Konya, Turkey **117** C3
Kópavogur, Iceland **93** A1
Korhogo, Côte d'Ivoire **137** E3
Koro Toro, Chad **141** B4
Kosciuszko, Mount, Australia **153** F7
Kosice, Slovakia **97** E4
Kosovo (country), Europe **99** D4
Kosti, Sudan **141** C6
Kostroma, Russia **101** E4
Koszalin, Poland **96** B2
Kota Baharu, Malaysia **123** E2
Kota Kinabalu, Malaysia **123** E5
Kotka, Finland **93** F7
Kozhikode, India **121** F3
Kra, Isthmus of, Asia **121** F9
Kragujevac, Serbia **99** C4
Kraków, Poland **97** D3
Kramators'k, Ukraine **97** E10
Krasnodar, Russia **101** H4
Krasnoyarsk, Russia **111** E6
Kremenchuk, Ukraine **97** E8
Krishna (river), India **121** E4
Kristiansand, Norway **93** G2
Kroonstad, South Africa **143** F5
Kryvyy Rih, Ukraine **97** E8
Kuala Lumpur, Malaysia **123** E2
Kuala Terengganu, Malaysia **123** E2
Kuching, Malaysia **123** F4
Kugluktuk, Nunavut (Canada) **63** C3
Kumasi, Ghana **137** E4
Kunlun Shan (range), China **114** D2
Kunming, China **115** F5
Kuopio, Finland **93** E7
Kupang, Indonesia **125** E6
Kura (river), Asia **117** B8
Kurdistan (region), Asia **119** B3
Kurgan, Russia **111** E4
Kuril Islands, Russia **104** C8
Kursk, Russia **101** F3
Kuskokwim (river), Alaska (U.S.) **56** B1
Kuujjuaq, Quebec (Canada) **63** E8
Kuwait (country), Asia **105** E2
Kuwait City, Kuwait **119** D4
Kuzey Anadolu Daglari (range), Turkey **117** B5
Kwango (river), Africa **141** F3
Kyoto, Japan **115** C10
Kyrgyzstan (country), Asia **105** D4
Kyushu (island), Japan **115** D10

L

Laayoune, Western Sahara (Morocco) **132** C1
Labé, Guinea **137** D2
Labrador (region), Newfoundland & Labrador (Canada) **63** E9
Labrador Sea, North America **56** C6
Laccadive Sea, Asia **104** G3

La Ceiba, Honduras **67** F6
Ladoga, Lake, Russia **101** D3
Ladysmith, South Africa **143** G5
La Esmeralda, Paraguay **83** B3
Laghouat, Algeria **135** B4
Lagos, Nigeria **137** E6
Lahij, Yemen **119** H3
Lahore, Pakistan **121** B3
Lahti, Finland **93** F7
Lake Region, Finland **93** E7
Lakshadweep (islands), India **121** G3
Lamu, Kenya **139** E4
Lana'i (island), Hawai'i (U.S.) **65** G4
L'Anse aux Meadows, Newfoundland & Labrador (Canada) **63** F9
Lansing, Michigan (U.S.) **65** C8
Lanzhou, China **115** D5
Laoag, Philippines **123** B7
Laos (country), Asia **105** F6
La Paz, Bolivia **79** H4
La Paz, Mexico **66** C1
Lapland (region), Europe **93** B6
La Plata, Argentina **83** E4
Lappeenranta, Finland **93** F8
Laptev Sea, Russia **104** B5
Laramie, Wyoming (U.S.) **65** C4
Laredo, Texas (U.S.) **65** G5
Lárissa, Greece **99** F5
La Rochelle, France **87** F2
Larsen Ice Shelf, Antarctica **161** B1
La Serena, Chile **83** D1
Las Vegas, Nevada (U.S.) **64** D2
Latakia, Syria **117** E4
Latvia (country), Europe **87** D5
Launceston, Australia **153** G7
Laurentide Scarp, Canada **56** D6
Lausanne, Switzerland **95** F5
Laverton, Australia **152** D3
Lebanon (country), Asia **105** D1
Leeds, United Kingdom **95** C3
Leeuwin, Cape, Australia **152** F2
Leeward Islands, North America **69** C8
Legnica, Poland **96** C2
Le Havre, France **95** E3
Leipzig, Germany **95** D6
Lemnos (island), Greece **99** F6
Lena (river), Russia **111** C7
León, Mexico **67** D3
León, Nicaragua **67** F6
Leer, South Sudan **141** C6
Lerwick, United Kingdom **87** C3
Lesbos (island), Greece **99** F7
Lesotho (country), Africa **127** H5
Lesser Antilles (islands), North America **69** D6
Lesser Sunda Islands, Asia **125** E5
Lethbridge, Alberta (Canada) **63** G3
Leveque, Cape, Australia **152** B3
Levin, New Zealand **153** F11
Lewiston, Idaho (U.S.) **64** B3
Leyte (island), Philippines **123** D8
Lhasa, China **115** E3
Liberec, Czech Republic **96** D2

Liberia (country), Africa **137** E3
Libreville, Gabon **141** E2
Libya (country), Africa **135** C7
Libyan Desert, Africa **128** C5
Liechtenstein (country), Europe **87** F3
Liepaja, Latvia **93** H6
Ligurian Sea, Europe **95** G6
Likasi, Dem. Rep. of the Congo **141** G5
Lille, France **95** D4
Lilongwe, Malawi **143** C7
Lima, Peru **79** G2
Limerick, Ireland **95** C2
Limoges, France **87** F2
Limpopo (river), Africa **143** E6
Lincoln, Nebraska (U.S.) **65** C6
Lincoln Sea, North America **56** A5
Lindi, Tanzania **139** G4
Line Islands, Kiribati **155** D7
Linköping, Sweden **93** G4
Linz, Austria **87** F4
Lipetsk, Russia **101** F4
Lisbon, Portugal **95** H1
Lismore, Australia **153** E8
Lithuania (country), Europe **87** D5
Little Cayman (island), United Kingdom **69** C2
Little Rock, Arkansas (U.S.) **65** E7
Liverpool, United Kingdom **95** C3
Livingstone, Zambia **143** D5
Ljubljana, Slovenia **99** B2
Ljusnan (river), Sweden **93** F4
Llanos (region), South America **79** B4
Lobamba, Swaziland **143** F6
Lobito, Angola **142** C1
Lódz, Poland **97** C3
Lofoten (islands), Norway **93** B4
Logan, Mount, Yukon (Canada) **62** D1
Loire (river), France **95** E3
Lokitaung, Kenya **139** D3
Lombok (island), Indonesia **125** E5
Lomé, Togo **137** E5
London, Ontario (Canada) **63** H7
London, United Kingdom **95** D3
Londonderry, United Kingdom **95** C2
Londrina, Brazil **81** G5
Long Beach, California (U.S.) **64** E2
Long Island, Bahamas **69** B3
Long Island, New York (U.S.) **65** C11
Long Xuyen, Vietnam **123** D3
Longyearbyen, Norway **93** A3
Lopez, Cap, (cape), Gabon **141** E2
Lop Nur (lake), China **115** C3
Lord Howe Island, Australia **146** F4
Los Angeles, California (U.S.) **64** D2
Louangphabang, Laos **123** B2
Louisiana (state), U.S. **65** F7
Louisville, Kentucky (U.S.) **65** D8

Lower Guinea (region), Africa **128** F4
Lower Hutt, New Zealand **153** G11
Luanda, Angola **142** B1
Lubango, Angola **142** C1
Lubbock, Texas (U.S.) **65** E5
Lüderitz, Namibia **142** F2
Lublin, Poland **97** D4
Lubumbashi, Dem. Rep. of the Congo **141** G5
Lucapa, Angola **143** A3
Lucknow, India **121** C5
Ludhiana, India **121** B4
Luena, Angola **143** B3
Luhans'k, Ukraine **97** E11
Luleå, Sweden **93** D6
Luoyang, China **115** D7
Lusaka, Zambia **143** C5
Luts'k, Ukraine **97** D5
Lützow-Holm Bay, Antarctica **161** A7
Luxembourg (country), Europe **87** E3
Luxembourg, Luxembourg **95** E5
Luxor, Egypt **135** C10
Luzhou, China **115** F5
Luzon (island), Philippines **123** C7
L'viv, Ukraine **97** D5
Lyon, France **95** F5

M

Macapá, Brazil **81** B5
Macau, China **115** G7
Macdonnell Ranges, Australia **153** C4
Macedonia (country), Europe **87** G5
Maceió, Brazil **81** D8
Machala, Ecuador **79** E1
Machu Picchu (ruins), Peru **79** G3
Mackay, Australia **153** C8
Mackenzie (river), Northwest Territories (Canada) **63** D3
Mackenzie King Island, Canada **56** B4
Mackenzie Mountains, Canada **62** D2
Macon, Georgia (U.S.) **65** E9
Madagascar (country), Africa **127** H7
Madeira (river), Brazil **81** C3
Madeira Islands, Portugal **132** A1
Madison, Wisconsin (U.S.) **65** C7
Madras, see Chennai, India **121** F5
Madre de Dios (river), Bolivia **79** G4
Madrid, Spain **95** H2
Madurai, India **121** G4
Magadan, Russia **111** C10
Magdalena (river), Colombia **79** B3
Magdeburg, Germany **95** D6
Magellan, Strait of, Chile **83** I2
Magnitogorsk, Russia **101** F7
Mahajanga, Madagascar **143** C10
Mahia Peninsula, New Zealand **153** F12
Mahilyow, Belarus **97** B7
Maiduguri, Nigeria **137** D7

Maine (state), U.S. **65** A11
Maine, Gulf of, U.S. **56** E6
Maji, Ethiopia **139** C3
Majorca (island), Spain **95** H4
Majuro, Marshall Islands **155** C4
Makassar, Indonesia **125** D5
Makassar Strait, Indonesia **125** C5
Makgadikgadi Pans, Botswana **143** E4
Makhachkala, Russia **101** I6
Makiyivka, Ukraine **97** E10
Makokou, Gabon **141** E2
Makurdi, Nigeria **137** E6
Malabo, Equatorial Guinea **141** D2
Malacca, Malaysia **123** E2
Malacca, Strait of, Asia **124** B1
Málaga, Spain **95** I2
Malakal, South Sudan **141** C6
Malang, Indonesia **125** E4
Malanje, Angola **142** B2
Mälaren (lake), Sweden **93** G5
Malatya, Turkey **117** C5
Malawi (country), Africa **127** G6
Malay Peninsula, Asia **104** G5
Malaysia (country), Asia **105** G6
Malden Island, Kiribati **155** D7
Maldive Islands, Maldives **121** H3
Maldives (country), Asia **105** G3
Male, Maldives **121** H3
Mali (country), Africa **137** D4
Malindi, Kenya **139** E4
Malmesbury, South Africa **143** H3
Malmö, Sweden **93** I3
Malpelo Island, Colombia **72** B2
Malta (country), Europe **95** I7
Malvinas, Islas, see Falkland Islands, U.K. **83** H4
Mamoré (river), Bolivia **79** H5
Manado, Indonesia **125** C7
Managua, Nicaragua **67** F6
Manakara, Madagascar **143** E10
Manama, Bahrain **119** E5
Manaus, Brazil **81** C3
Manchester, United Kingdom **95** C3
Manchurian Plain, China **115** B8
Mandalay, Myanmar **121** D8
Mangaluru, India **121** F3
Manicouagan, Réservoir, Quebec (Canada) **63** G4
Manila, Philippines **123** C7
Manitoba (province), Canada **63** F5
Manitoba, Lake, Manitoba (Canada) **63** G4
Mannheim, Germany **95** E5
Manukau, New Zealand **153** E11
Mao, Chad **141** B3
Maoke Mountains, Indonesia **125** C10
Maputo, Mozambique **143** F6
Marabá, Brazil **81** C5
Maracaibo, Venezuela **79** A3
Maracaibo, Lake, Venezuela **72** A3
Maradi, Niger **137** D6
Marajó Island, Brazil **81** C5
Maralal, Kenya **139** E6
Marañón (river), Peru **79** E2
Marble Bar, Australia **152** C2

Mar del Plata, Argentina **83** E4
Mariana Islands, Oceania **146** B3
Maribor, Slovenia **99** B2
Maridi, South Sudan **141** D6
Marie Byrd Land, Antarctica **161** E3
Marie-Galante (island), Guadeloupe (France) **69** C7
Mariupol', Ukraine **97** F10
Marka, Somalia **139** D5
Marmara, Sea of, Turkey **117** B2
Maroantsetra, Madagascar **143** C11
Maromokotro (peak), Madagascar **143** C11
Maroua, Cameroon **141** C3
Marquesas Islands, French Polynesia (France) **155** E8
Marquette, Michigan (U.S.) **65** B8
Marrakech, Morocco **132** B2
Marrupa, Mozambique **143** C8
Marseille, France **95** G5
Marshall Islands (country), Oceania **147** C5
Martinique (island), France **69** D7
Mary, Turkmenistan **113** D3
Maryborough, Australia **153** D8
Maryland (state), U.S. **65** C10
Marzūq, Libya **135** C7
Maseru, Lesotho **143** G5
Mashhad, Iran **119** B7
Masira (island), Oman **119** F7
Massachusetts (state), U.S. **65** B11
Massif Central, France **95** F4
Masterton, New Zealand **153** G11
Masvingo, Zimbabwe **143** D6
Matala, Angola **142** C2
Matamoros, Mexico **67** C4
Matterhorn (peak), Europe **95** F5
Maui (island), Hawai'i (U.S.) **65** G5
Maun, Botswana **143** D4
Mauritania (country, Africa **137** C2
Mauritius (country), Africa **127** H8
Mauritius (island), Mauritius **128** H8
Mawlamyine, Myanmar **121** E9
Mayotte (possession), France **143** C10
Mayumba, Gabon **141** F2
Mazar-e Sharif, Afghanistan **121** A2
Mazatlán, Mexico **67** C2
Mazyr, Belarus **97** C7
Mbabane, Swaziland **143** F6
Mbala, Zambia **143** B6
Mbandaka, Dem. Rep. of the Congo **141** E3
Mbarara, Uganda **139** E2
Mbé, Cameroon **141** C3
Mbeya, Tanzania **139** G3
Mbuji-Mayi (Bakwanga), Dem. Rep. of the Congo **141** F4
McMurdo Sound, Antarctica **161** F5
Mead, Lake, U.S. **64** D3
Mecca, Saudi Arabia **119** F2

Medan — Northern European Plain

Medan, Indonesia **124** B1
Medellín, Colombia **79** B2
Medford, Oregon (U.S.) **64** B1
Medicine Hat, Alberta (Canada) **63** G3
Medina, Saudi Arabia **119** E2
Meekatharra, Australia **152** D2
Meerut, India **121** C4
Mēga, Ethiopia **139** D4
Mekele, Ethiopia **139** B4
Meknès, Morocco **132** B3
Mekong (river), Asia **104** F6
Melanesia (islands), Oceania **155** D4
Melbourne, Australia **153** F7
Melekeiok, Palau **154** C1
Melilla, Spain **135** A4
Melitopol', Ukraine **97** F9
Melut, South Sudan **141** C6
Melville Island, Australia **153** A4
Melville Island, Canada **63** B4
Melville Peninsula, Nunavut (Canada) **63** C6
Memphis, Tennessee (U.S.) **65** E7
Ménaka, Mali **137** C5
Mendocino, Cape, California (U.S.) **64** C1
Mendoza, Argentina **83** D2
Menzies, Australia **152** E3
Merauke, Indonesia **125** D11
Mereeg, Somalia **139** D6
Mérida, Mexico **67** D6
Mérida, Venezuela **79** B4
Merowe, Sudan **141** B6
Mersin, Turkey **117** D4
Mesa, Arizona (U.S.) **64** E3
Mesa Verde National Park, Colorado (U.S.) **65** D4
Mesopotamia (region), Asia **104** D2
Messina, Italy **95** H8
Messinia, Gulf of, Greece **99** H5
Meta (river), Colombia **79** B4
Metz, France **95** E5
Mexicali, Mexico **66** A1
Mexico (country), North America **57** G3
Mexico City, Mexico **67** E3
Mexico, Gulf of, North America **56** G5
Miami, Florida (U.S.) **65** G10
Michigan (state), U.S. **65** B8
Michigan, Lake, U.S. **65** B8
Micronesia (islands), Oceania **154** C3
Micronesia, Federated States of (country), Oceania **147** C3
Midway Islands, U.S. **155** A5
Mikkeli, Finland **93** E7
Milan, Italy **95** F6
Mildura, Australia **153** E6
Milford Sound, New Zealand **153** H9
Milwaukee, Wisconsin (U.S.) **65** C8
Minami Tori Shima, Japan **154** B3
Mindanao (island), Philippines **123** D8
Mindoro (island), Philippines **123** C7
Minicoy (island), India **121** G3

Minneapolis, Minnesota (U.S.) **65** B7
Minnesota (state), U.S. **65** B6
Minorca (island), Spain **95** H4
Minot, North Dakota (U.S.) **65** A5
Minsk, Belarus **97** B6
Minto, Mount, Antarctica **161** G5
Mirbat, Oman **119** G6
Mirnyy, Russia **105** C5
Miskolc, Hungary **97** E4
Mişrātah, Libya **135** B7
Mississippi (river), U.S. **65** E7
Mississippi (state), U.S. **65** E8
Mississippi River Delta, Louisiana (U.S.) **65** F8
Missouri (river), U.S. **65** C6
Missouri (state), U.S. **65** D7
Mitilíni (island), see Lesbos, Greece **99** F7
Mobile, Alabama (U.S.) **65** F8
Mobile Bay, Alabama (U.S.) **65** F8
Moçambique, Mozambique **143** C8
Mocuba, Mozambique **143** D7
Mogadishu, Somalia **139** D5
Mojave Desert, U.S. **64** D2
Moldova (country), Europe **87** F6
Moloka'i (island), Hawai'i (U.S.) **65** G4
Moluccas (islands), Indonesia **125** C8
Molucca Sea, Indonesia **125** C7
Mombasa, Kenya **139** F4
Monaco (country), Europe **87** G3
Mongolia (country), Asia **105** D4
Mongu, Zambia **143** C4
Monrovia, Liberia **137** E2
Montana (state), U.S. **65** B4
Monte Bello Islands, Australia **152** C1
Montego Bay, Jamaica **69** C3
Montenegro (country), Europe **87** G5
Montería, Colombia **79** B2
Monterrey, Mexico **67** C3
Montevideo, Uruguay **83** E4
Montgomery, Alabama (U.S.) **65** E8
Montpelier, Vermont (U.S.) **65** B11
Montréal, Quebec (Canada) **63** G8
Montserrat (island), United Kingdom **69** C7
Monywa, Myanmar **121** D8
Moose Jaw, Saskatchewan (Canada) **63** G3
Mopti, Mali **137** D4
Moree, Australia **153** E7
Morocco (country), Africa **134** B3
Moroni, Comoros **143** B9
Morotai (island), Indonesia **125** B8
Moscow, Russia **101** E4
Moshi, Tanzania **139** F3
Mosquito Cays, Nicaragua **67** F7
Mosquito Coast, Nicaragua **67** F7

Mossaka, Congo **141** E3
Mostar, Bosnia & Herzegovina **99** D3
Mosul, Iraq **119** B3
Moundou, Chad **141** C3
Mountain Nile (river), South Sudan **141** D6
Mount Gambier, Australia **153** F6
Mount Isa, Australia **153** C6
Mount Magnet, Australia **152** D2
Mozambique (country), Africa **129** G6
Mozambique Channel, Africa **128** G7
Mthatha, South Africa **143** G5
Mtwara, Tanzania **139** G4
Mubi, Nigeria **137** D7
Muchinga Mountains, Zambia **143** B6
Mufulira, Zambia **143** C5
Multan, Pakistan **121** C3
Mumbai (Bombay), India **121** E3
Mumbwa, Zambia **143** C5
Munich, Germany **95** E6
Murat (river), Turkey **117** C7
Murcia, Spain **95** I3
Murmansk, Russia **101** A4
Murray (river), Australia **153** E6
Muscat, Oman **119** F7
Mwanza, Tanzania **139** E2
Mweka, Dem. Rep. of the Congo **141** F4
Mweru, Lake, Africa **141** G5
Mwinilunga, Zambia **143** B4
Myanmar (Burma) (country), Asia **105** F5
Myeik, Myanmar **121** F9
Myitkyina, Myanmar **121** C8
Mykolayiv, Ukraine **97** F8
Mysuru, India **121** F4

N
Nagasaki, Japan **115** D9
Nagorno-Karabakh (region), Azerbaijan **117** C9
Nagoya, Japan **115** C10
Naha, Japan **115** E9
Nairobi, Kenya **139** E3
Najd (region), Saudi Arabia **119** E3
Nakhon Ratchasima, Thailand **123** C2
Namangan, Uzbekistan **113** D5
Nam Dinh, Vietnam **123** B3
Namib Desert, Namibia **142** E2
Namibe, Angola **142** C1
Namibia (country), Africa **129** H4
Nampo Shoto (islands), Japan **104** D8
Nampula, Mozambique **143** C8
Namsos, Norway **87** B4
Nanchang, China **115** E7
Nanjing, China **115** E8
Nanning, China **115** G6
Nantes, France **95** E3
Napier, New Zealand **153** F12
Naples, Italy **95** G7
Nara, Mali **137** C3
Narmada (river), India **121** D4
Narrogin, Australia **152** E2
Narva, Estonia **93** G8
Narvik, Norway **87** B5

Nashville, Tennessee (U.S.) **65** D8
Nassau, Bahamas **69** B3
Nasser, Lake, Egypt **135** D10
Natal, Brazil **81** D8
Natchez, Mississippi (U.S.) **65** F7
Natuna Islands, Indonesia **125** B3
Naturaliste, Cape, Australia **152** E2
Nauru (country), Oceania **147** D5
Naxçivan, Azerbaijan **117** C8
Náxos (island), Greece **99** G7
Nay Pyi Taw, Myanmar **121** E8
Nazwa, Oman **119** F7
Nchelenge, Zambia **143** B5
Ndélé, Central African Rep. **141** C4
N'Djamena, Chad **141** C3
Ndola, Zambia **143** C5
Neblina, Pico da, South America **81** B2
Nebraska (state), U.S. **65** C5
Negēlē, Ethiopia **139** D6
Negev (region), Israel **117** G4
Negro (river), Argentina **83** F2
Negro (river), Brazil **81** B2
Negros (island), Philippines **123** D7
Neijiang, China **115** E5
Neiva, Colombia **79** C2
Nelson (river), Manitoba (Canada) **63** F5
Nelson, New Zealand **153** G10
Néma, Mauritania **137** C3
Neman (river), Europe **93** I6
Nepal (country), Asia **105** F4
Netherlands (country), Europe **87** E3
Neuquén, Argentina **83** F2
Nevada (state), U.S. **64** C2
Newark, New Jersey (U.S.) **65** C10
New Britain (island), Papua New Guinea **154** D3
New Brunswick (province), Canada **63** G9
New Caledonia (island), France **155** F4
Newcastle, Australia **153** E8
Newcastle, United Kingdom **95** C3
New Delhi, India **121** C4
Newfoundland, Island of, Newfoundland & Labrador (Canada) **63** F10
Newfoundland and Labrador (province), Canada **63** E9
New Guinea (island), Asia/Oceania **154** D2
New Hampshire (state), U.S. **65** B11
New Ireland (island), Papua New Guinea **154** D3
New Jersey (state), U.S. **65** C10
New Mexico (state), U.S. **65** E4
New Orleans, Louisiana (U.S.) **65** F8
New Plymouth, New Zealand **153** F11
New Siberian Islands, Russia **111** B7
New South Wales (state), Australia **153** E7

New York, New York (U.S.) **65** C11
New York (state), U.S. **65** B10
New Zealand (country), Oceania **147** G5
Ngaoundéré, Cameroon **141** D3
Nguigmi, Niger **137** D7
Nha Trang, Vietnam **123** C4
Niagara Falls (waterfall), North America **65** B9
Niagara Falls, Ontario (Canada) **63** H7
Niamey, Niger **137** D5
Nicaragua (country), North America **57** I5
Nicaragua, Lake, Nicaragua **67** G7
Nice, France **95** G5
Nicobar Islands, India **121** G8
Nicosia, Cyprus **99** I8
Niger (country), Africa **137** C6
Niger (river), Africa **137** C4
Niger Delta, Nigeria **137** F6
Nigeria (country), Africa **137** E6
Niigata, Japan **115** C10
Ni'ihau (island), Hawai'i (U.S.) **65** F4
Nile (river), Africa **128** D6
Nile River Delta, Egypt **135** B10
Nimba, Mont, Guinea **137** E3
Nineveh (ruins), Iraq **119** B3
Ningbo, China **115** E8
Nioro, Mali **137** C3
Nipigon, Lake, Ontario (Canada) **63** G6
Nippur (ruins), Iraq **119** C4
Nis, Serbia **99** D5
Nishtun, Yemen **119** H6
Niue (island), New Zealand **147** E6
Nizhniy Novgorod, Russia **101** E5
Nizhniy Tagil, Russia **110** E3
Nogáles, Mexico **66** A1
Nola, Central African Rep. **141** D3
Norfolk, Virginia (U.S.) **65** D10
Norfolk Island, Australia **155** F4
Noril'sk, Russia **111** D6
Normanton, Australia **153** B6
Norrköping, Sweden **93** G4
Norrland (region), Sweden **93** D4
Norseman, Australia **152** E3
Northam, Australia **152** E2
North Cape, New Zealand **153** D10
North Cape, Norway **93** A6
North Carolina (state), U.S. **65** D10
North China Plain, China **104** E6
North Dakota (state), U.S. **65** B5
North East Land (island), Norway **93** A3
Northern Cyprus (region), Cyprus **99** I8
Northern Dvina (river), Russia **101** C5
Northern European Plain, Europe **86** E4

Northern Ireland (country), United Kingdom **95** C2
Northern Mariana Islands, U.S. **154** B2
Northern Territory, Australia **153** B5
North Island, New Zealand **153** E11
North Korea (country), Asia **105** D7
North Land (Severnaya Zemlya) (islands), Russia **111** B6
North Magnetic Pole, Arctic Ocean **104** A5
North Platte (river), U.S. **65** C4
North Pole, Arctic Ocean **104** A5
North Saskatchewan (river), Canada **63** F3
North Sea, Europe **86** D3
North Slope, Alaska (U.S.) **64** F2
North Taranaki Bight, New Zealand **153** F11
North West Basin, Australia **146** E1
North West Cape, Australia **152** C1
Northwest Territories, Canada **63** C3
Norvegia, Cape, Antarctica **161** A4
Norway (country), Europe **87** B4
Norwegian Sea, Europe **86** A3
Nottingham, United Kingdom **95** C3
Nouakchott, Mauritania **137** C1
Nouâmghâr, Mauritania **137** C1
Nouméa, New Caledonia (France) **155** F4
Nova Scotia (province), Canada **63** G9
Novaya Zemlya (island), Russia **111** C4
Novi Sad, Serbia **99** B4
Novokuznetsk, Russia **111** F5
Novosibirsk, Russia **111** E5
Nubia, Lake, Africa **141** A6
Nubian Desert, Sudan **141** A6
Nuevo Laredo, Mexico **67** C3
Nuku'alofa, Tonga **155** F5
Nullarbor Plain, Australia **152** E4
Nunavut (territory), Canada **63** D5
Nunivak Island, Alaska (U.S.) **56** B1
Nuremberg, Germany **95** E6
Nuuk (Godthåb), Greenland (Denmark) **57** C6
Nyala, Sudan **141** C5
Nyasa, Lake (Lake Malawi), Africa **139** G5
N'Zérékoré, Guinea **137** E2

O

O'ahu (island), Hawai'i (U.S.) **65** F4
Oakland, California (U.S.) **64** C1
Oamaru, New Zealand **153** H10
Oaxaca, Mexico **67** E4
Ob' (river), Russia **111** D4
Ob', Gulf of, Russia **111** C5
Obo, Central African Rep. **141** D5

Odense, Denmark **93** I3
Oder (river), Europe **86** E4
Odesa, Ukraine **97** F7
Ogbomosho, Nigeria **137** E5
Ogden, Utah (U.S.) **65** C3
Ohio (river), U.S. **65** D8
Ohio (state), U.S. **65** C9
Oka (river), Russia **101** E5
Okavango (river), Africa **143** D3
Okavango Delta, Botswana **143** D4
Okeechobee, Lake, Florida (U.S.) **65** F10
Okhotsk, Sea of, Asia **104** B7
Okinawa (island), Japan **115** E10
Oklahoma (state), U.S. **65** D6
Oklahoma City, Oklahoma (U.S.) **65** E6
Öland (island), Sweden **93** H5
Oleksandriya, Ukraine **97** E8
Olga, Mount, Australia **152** D4
Olsztyn, Poland **97** B4
Olympia (ruins), Greece **99** G5
Olympia, Washington (U.S.) **64** A2
Olympic Peninsula, Washington (U.S.) **56** E2
Olympus (peak), Greece **99** F5
Omaha, Nebraska (U.S.) **65** C6
Oman (country), Asia **105** F2
Oman, Gulf of, Asia **119** E7
Omdurman, Sudan **141** B6
Omsk, Russia **111** E4
Ondjiva, Angola **143** D2
Onega, Lake, Russia **101** D4
Onslow, Australia **152** C1
Ontario (province), Canada **63** G6
Ontario, Lake, North America **56** E5
Oodaaq Island, Greenland (Denmark) **56** A5
Oodnadatta, Australia **153** D5
Opole, Poland **96** D3
Oporto, Portugal **95** G1
Oradea, Romania **99** B5
Oral, Kazakhstan **113** B3
Oran, Algeria **135** A4
Orange (river), Africa **143** G3
Orange, Australia **153** E7
Ord (river), Australia **152** B4
Örebro, Sweden **93** G4
Oregon (state), U.S. **64** B2
Orel, Russia **101** F3
Orenburg, Russia **101** F7
Orinoco (river), Venezuela **79** B6
Orizaba, Pico de, Mexico **67** E4
Orkney Islands, United Kingdom **95** A3
Orlando, Florida (U.S.) **65** F10
Orléans, France **95** E4
Örnsköldsvik, Sweden **93** E5
Orsha, Belarus **97** B7
Orsk, Russia **101** F7
Oruro, Bolivia **79** H4
Osaka, Japan **115** D10
Osa Peninsula, Costa Rica **67** G7
Osijek, Croatia **99** B3
Öskemen, Kazakhstan **113** C7
Oslo, Norway **93** F3
Östersund, Sweden **93** E4
Ostrava, Czech Republic **96** D3
Otavi, Namibia **142** D2

Otranto, Strait of, Europe **99** E3
Ottawa (river), Canada **63** G7
Ottawa, Ontario (Canada) **63** H7
Ouadâne, Mauritania **137** B2
Ouagadougou, Burkina Faso **137** D3
Ouargla, Algeria **135** B5
Oudtshoorn, South Africa **143** H4
Oujda, Morocco **135** B4
Oulu (river), Finland **93** D7
Oulu, Finland **93** D7
Ounianga Kébir, Chad **141** A4
Outer Hebrides (islands), United Kingdom **95** B2
Oyem, Gabon **141** E2
Ozark Plateau, U.S. **56** F4

P

Padang, Indonesia **124** C1
Paducah, Kentucky (U.S.) **65** D8
Pago Pago, American Samoa (U.S.) **155** E6
Pakistan (country), Asia **105** E3
Palangkaraya, Indonesia **125** C4
Palapye, Botswana **143** E5
Palau (country), Oceania **147** C2
Palawan (island), Philippines **123** D6
Palembang, Indonesia **124** C2
Palermo, Italy **95** H7
Palikir, Federated States of Micronesia **155** C3
Palliser, Cape, New Zealand **153** G11
Palma, Spain **95** H4
Palmas, Cape, Côte d'Ivoire **137** F3
Palmerston North, New Zealand **153** F11
Palmyra Atoll, U.S. **155** C7
Pamirs (range), Tajikistan **113** E5
Pampas (region), Argentina **83** E2
Panama (country), North America **57** I6
Panama City, Panama **67** G8
Panama, Gulf of, Panama **67** G8
Panama, Isthmus of, Panama **56** I6
Panama Canal, Panama **67** G8
Panay (island), Philippines **123** D7
Panié, Mount, New Caledonia (France) **155** F4
Pantanal (region), Brazil **81** E4
Pánuco (river), Mexico **67** D4
Papeete, French Polynesia (France) **155** E8
Papua New Guinea (country), Oceania **147** D3
Paragominas, Brazil **81** C5
Paraguay (country), South America **73** E5
Paraguay (river), South America **72** E5
Parakou, Benin **137** E5
Paramaribo, Suriname **81** A4
Paraná, Argentina **83** D3
Paraná (river), South America **72** F5

Parece Vela (island), Japan **105** E8
Parepare, Indonesia **125** D5
Paris, France **95** E4
Parnaíba, Brazil **81** C7
Pärnu, Estonia **93** G7
Parry Channel, Canada **63** B5
Parry Islands, Canada **63** B4
Pasley, Cape, Australia **152** E3
Pasto, Colombia **79** C2
Patagonia (region), Argentina **83** G2
Pathein, Myanmar **121** E8
Patna, India **121** D6
Patos Lagoon, Brazil **81** H4
Pátrai, Greece **99** G5
Patuca (river), Honduras **67** F7
Pavlodar, Kazakhstan **113** B6
Peace (river), Canada **56** D3
Peary Land, Greenland (Denmark) **56** A5
Pec, Serbia **99** D4
Pechenga, Russia **87** A6
Pechora (river), Russia **101** B6
Pechora, Russia **101** B6
Pécs, Hungary **96** F3
Pegasus Bay, New Zealand **153** H10
Peipus, Lake, Europe **93** G8
Pekanbaru, Indonesia **124** C1
Peloponnesus (peninsula), Greece **99** G5
Pelotas, Brazil **81** H4
Pematangsiantar, Indonesia **124** B1
Pemba, Mozambique **143** C8
Pemba Island, Tanzania **139** F4
Pennines, The, (range), United Kingdom **86** D2
Pennsylvania (state), U.S. **65** C9
Pensacola Mountains, Antarctica **161** C4
Penza, Russia **101** F5
Peoria, Illinois (U.S.) **65** C7
Pereira, Colombia **79** C2
Perm', Russia **101** D7
Persepolis (ruins), Iran **119** D6
Persian Gulf, Asia **119** E5
Perth, Australia **152** E2
Peru (country), South America **73** C3
Peshawar, Pakistan **121** B3
Petra (ruins), Jordan **117** G4
Petropavlovsk, Kazakhstan **113** B5
Petropavlovsk-Kamchatsky, Russia **111** C11
Petrozavodsk, Russia **101** C4
Philadelphia, Pennsylvania (U.S.) **65** C10
Philippine Islands, Philippines **104** F7
Philippines (country), Asia **105** F7
Philippine Sea, Asia **104** F8
Phillip Island, Australia **155** F4
Phnom Penh, Cambodia **123** D3
Phoenix, Arizona (U.S.) **64** E3
Phoenix Islands, Kiribati **155** D6
Picton, New Zealand **153** G11
Pierre, South Dakota (U.S.) **65** B5
Pietermaritzburg, South Africa **143** G6
Polokwane, South Africa **143** E5

Pilsen, Czech Republic **96** D1
Pine Creek, Australia **153** A4
Pinsk, Belarus **97** C6
Pinsk Marshes, Belarus **97** C6
Pitcairn Island, United Kingdom **155** F9
Pitcairn Islands, United Kingdom **155** F10
Pittsburgh, Pennsylvania (U.S.) **65** C9
Piura, Peru **79** E1
Plate, River, South America **83** E4
Plateau Station, Antarctica **161** C6
Platte (river), U.S. **65** C5
Plenty, Bay of, New Zealand **153** E12
Pleven, Bulgaria **99** D6
Ploiesti, Romania **99** C7
Plovdiv, Bulgaria **99** D6
Plymouth, United Kingdom **95** D3
Po (river), Italy **95** F6
Pocatello, Idaho (U.S.) **64** C3
Podgorica, Montenegro **99** D3
Pohnpei (island), Federated States of Micronesia **155** C3
Poinsett, Cape, Antarctica **161** F9
Pointe-Noire, Congo **141** F2
Poland (country), Europe **87** E5
Polar Plateau, Antarctica **161** D5
Polokwane, South Africa **143** E5
Poltava, Ukraine **97** D9
Polynesia (islands), Oceania **155** C6
Pontianak, Indonesia **125** C3
Popayán, Colombia **79** C2
Popocatépetl (peak), Mexico **67** E3
Pori, Finland **93** F6
Porirua, New Zealand **153** G11
Porpoise Bay, Antarctica **161** G8
Port Augusta, Australia **153** E5
Port-au-Prince, Haiti **69** C4
Port Elizabeth, South Africa **143** H4
Port-Gentil, Gabon **141** E2
Port Harcourt, Nigeria **137** E6
Port Hedland, Australia **152** C2
Portland, Maine (U.S.) **65** B11
Portland, Oregon (U.S.) **64** A2
Port Lincoln, Australia **153** E5
Port Louis, Mauritius **129** H8
Port Moresby, Papua New Guinea **154** E2
Porto Alegre, Brazil **81** H5
Port of Spain, Trinidad & Tobago **69** E7
Porto-Novo, Benin **137** F5
Porto Velho, Brazil **81** D2
Portoviejo, Ecuador **79** D1
Port Phillip Bay, Australia **153** F6
Port Pirie, Australia **153** E5
Port Said, Egypt **135** B10
Port Sudan, Sudan **141** A7
Portugal (country), Europe **87** G1
Port-Vila, Vanuatu **155** E4
Posadas, Argentina **83** C4

BACK OF
THE BOOK

Potiskum — San José del Guaviare

Potiskum, Nigeria **137** D7
Potosí, Bolivia **79** I5
Powell, Lake, U.S. **65** D3
Poza Rica, Mexico **67** D4
Poznan, Poland **96** C3
Prague, Czech Republic **96** D1
Pretoria (Tshwane), South
　Africa **143** F5
Prince Albert, Saskatchewan
　(Canada) **63** F4
Prince Charles Island, Nunavut
　(Canada) **56** C5
Prince Edward Island
　(province), Canada **63** G9
Prince George, British
　Columbia (Canada) **62** F2
Prince of Wales Island, Nunavut
　(Canada) **63** C5
Prince Patrick Island,
　Northwest Territories
　(Canada) **63** B4
Prince Rupert, British
　Columbia (Canada) **62** E1
Príncipe (island), São Tomé &
　Principe **141** E1
Pristina, Kosovo **99** D4
Prokop'yevsk, Russia **111** F5
Providence, Rhode Island (U.S.)
　65 B11
Provo, Utah (U.S.) **65** C3
Prut (river), Europe **97** F7
Prydz Bay, Antarctica **161** C8
Pskov, Russia **101** D2
Pucallpa, Peru **79** F2
Puducherry, India **121** E4
Puebla, Mexico **67** E4
Pueblo, Colorado (U.S.) **65** D4
Puerto Barrios, Guatemala
　67 F6
Puerto Esperanza, Paraguay
　83 A4
Puerto La Cruz, Venezuela
　79 A5
Puerto Limón, Costa Rica
　67 G7
Puerto Montt, Chile **83** F1
Puerto Rico (island), U.S. **56** H7
Puerto Vallarta, Mexico **67** D2
Puncak Jaya (peak), Indonesia
　125 D10
Pune, India **121** E3
Punta Arenas, Chile **83** I2
Purus (river), Brazil **81** D2
Putumayo (river), South
　America **79** D3
Puysegur Point, New Zealand
　153 I8
Pweto, Dem. Rep. of the Congo
　141 G5
Pyinmana, Myanmar **121** E8
Pyongyang, North Korea **115**
　C8
Pyrenees (range), Europe **95** G3

Q

Qaidam Basin, China **104** E5
Qalat Bishah, Saudi Arabia
　119 G3
Qaraghandy, Kazakhstan **113**
　C5
Qardho, Somalia **139** C6
Qatar (country), Asia **105** E2
Qattara Depression, Egypt
　135 C9
Qazvin, Iran **119** B5

Qeqertarsuaq (island),
　Greenland (Denmark) **56** B6
Qeshm (island), Iran **119** E6
Qingdao, China **115** D8
Qinghai Hu (lake), China **115** D5
Qiqihar, China **115** B8
Qizilqum (desert), Uzbekistan
　113 D3
Qom, Iran **119** C5
Qomsheh, Iran **119** C5
Quebec (province), Canada
　63 G8
Québec, Quebec (Canada) **63**
　G8
Queen Elizabeth Islands,
　Canada **63** A5
Queen Maud Land, Antarctica
　161 B5
Queensland (state), Australia
　153 C6
Queenstown, Australia **153** G6
Queenstown, New Zealand
　153 H9
Quelimane, Mozambique **143**
　D7
Querétaro, Mexico **67** D3
Quetta, Pakistan **121** B2
Quetzaltenango, Guatemala
　67 F5
Quezon City, Philippines **123** C7
Quito, Ecuador **79** D2
Qullai Somoniyon, Tajikistan
　113 E5
Qurayyat, Oman **119** F7
Quy Nhon, Vietnam **123** C4

R

Raba, Indonesia **125** E5
Rabat, Morocco **134** A3
Race, Cape, Newfoundland &
　Labrador (Canada) **63** F10
Raga, South Sudan **141** C5
Raipur, India **121** D5
Rajkot, India **121** D2
Rakaia (river), New Zealand
　153 F10
Raleigh, North Carolina (U.S.)
　65 D10
Ralik Chain (islands), Marshall
　Islands **155** C4
Rangitaiki (river), New Zealand
　153 E12
Rangitata (river), New Zealand
　153 H10
Rangoon, see Yangon, Myanmar
　121 E8
Rangpur, Bangladesh **121** C7
Rankin Inlet, Nunavut (Canada)
　63 E5
Rapa Nui (Easter Island), Chile
　155 F11
Rapid City, South Dakota (U.S.)
　65 B5
Ras Dejen (peak), Ethiopia
　139 B4
Rasht, Iran **119** B5
Ratak Chain (islands), Marshall
　Islands **155** C4
Rawalpindi, Pakistan **121** B3
Recife, Brazil **81** D8
Red (river), U.S. **65** E7
Red (river), Vietnam **123** A3
Redding, California (U.S.) **64** C1
Redwood National Park,
　California (U.S.) **64** B1
Reggane, Algeria **135** C4

Regina, Saskatchewan (Canada)
　63 G4
Reindeer Lake, Canada **63** E4
Renk, South Sudan **141** C6
Rennes, France **87** E2
Reno, Nevada (U.S.) **64** C2
Resistencia, Argentina **83** C4
Resita, Romania **99** B5
Resolute, Nunavut (Canada)
　63 B5
Réunion (island), France **128**
　H8
Revillagigedo Islands, Mexico
　56 H2
Reykjavík, Iceland **93** A1
Rhine (river), Europe **95** D5
Rhode Island (state), U.S. **65**
　B11
Rhodes (island), Greece **99** H8
Rhodes, Greece **99** H8
Rhodope Mountains, Bulgaria
　99 E6
Rhône (river), France **95** F5
Ribeirão Preto, Brazil **81** F5
Richmond, Virginia (U.S.) **65**
　D10
Rida, Yemen **119** H4
Riga, Latvia **93** H7
Riga, Gulf of, Latvia **93** H7
Riiser-Larsen Ice Shelf,
　Antarctica **161** A4
Riiser-Larsen Peninsula,
　Antarctica **161** A7
Rijeka, Croatia **99** B2
Rimouski, Quebec (Canada)
　63 G8
Río Azul (ruins), Guatemala
　67 E6
Rio Branco, Brazil **81** D2
Rio Bravo del Norte (river), see
　Rio Grande, North America
　67 B3
Rio de Janeiro, Brazil **81** G6
Río Gallegos, Argentina **83** I2
Rio Grande (river), North
　America **56** G3
Río Muni (region), Equatorial
　Guinea **141** E2
Rivera, Uruguay **83** D4
Riviera (region), Europe **86** F3
Rivne, Ukraine **97** D6
Riyadh, Saudi Arabia **119** E4
Rochester, New York (U.S.) **65**
　B10
Rockall (island), United
　Kingdom **95** A1
Rockford, Illinois (U.S.) **65** C8
Rockhampton, Australia **153**
　C8
Rocky Mountains, North
　America **56** D3
Roma, Australia **153** D7
Romania (country), Europe
　87 F5
Rome, Italy **95** G7
Ronne Ice Shelf, Antarctica
　161 C3
Roosevelt Island, Antarctica
　161 F4
Roraima, Mount, South
　America **79** C6
Rosario, Argentina **83** D3
Roseau, Dominica **69** C7
Ross Ice Shelf, Antarctica
　161 E5
Ross Island, Antarctica **161** F5

Rosso, Mauritania **137** C1
Ross Sea, Antarctica **161** F4
Rostock, Germany **95** C6
Rostov, Russia **101** H4
Roswell, New Mexico (U.S.)
　65 E4
Rotorua, New Zealand **153** E11
Rotterdam, Netherlands **95** D4
Rotuma (island), Fiji **155** E5
Rouen, France **95** E4
Rovaniemi, Finland **93** C7
Rovuma (river), Africa **143** B8
Royale, Isle, Michigan (U.S.)
　65 A7
Ruapehu, Mount, New Zealand
　153 F11
Rub' al Khali (Empty Quarter)
　(desert), Saudi Arabia **119**
　G5
Rubtsovsk, Russia **111** F5
Rukwa, Lake, Tanzania **139** G2
Rumbek, South Sudan **141** D6
Ruse, Bulgaria **99** C7
Russia (country), Europe/Asia
　105 C4
Rustavi, Georgia **117** B8
Rwanda (country), Africa **139**
　E2
Ryazan', Russia **101** F4
Rybinsk, Russia **101** E4
Rybinsk Reservoir, Russia
　101 D4
Ryukyu Islands, Japan **115** E9
Rzeszów, Poland **97** D4

S

Saaremaa (island), Estonia
　93 G6
Saba (island), Netherlands
　Antilles (Netherlands) **69** C6
Sabah (state), Malaysia **123** E6
Sabhā, Libya **135** C7
Sable, Cape, Nova Scotia
　(Canada) **63** H9
Sable Island, Nova Scotia
　(Canada) **63** G10
Sabzevar, Iran **119** B7
Sacramento, California (U.S.)
　64 C1
Safi, Morocco **134** B2
Saguenay, Quebec (Canada)
　63 G8
Sahara (desert), Africa **128** D2
Sahel (region), Africa **128** D3
Saidabad, Iran **119** D6
Saigon, see Ho Chi Minh City,
　Vietnam **123** D3
St.-Barthélemy (island), France
　69 C7
St. Elias Mountains, North
　America **62** D1
Ste. Marie, Cap, Madagascar
　143 F9
St. Eustatius (island),
　Netherlands Antilles
　(Netherlands) **69** C7
St. George's, Grenada **69** D7
St. Helena (island), United
　Kingdom **128** G2
St. John's, Antigua & Barbuda
　69 C7
St. John's, Newfoundland &
　Labrador (Canada) **63** F10
St. Kitts and Nevis (country),
　North America **57** H8

St. Lawrence (river), North
　America **63** G8
St. Lawrence, Gulf of, Canada
　63 F9
St. Lawrence Island, Alaska
　(U.S.) **56** A1
Saint-Louis, Senegal **137** C1
St. Lucia (country), North
　America **57** H8
St.-Martin (France), **69** C6
St. Marys, Australia **153** G7
St. Petersburg, Russia **101** D3
St.-Pierre and Miquelon (island),
　France **63** F10
St. Vincent and the Grenadines
　(country), North America
　57 H8
Saipan (island), Northern
　Mariana Islands (U.S.) **147**
　B3
Saipan, Northern Mariana
　Islands (U.S.) **154** C2
Sajama, Nevado, Bolivia **79** H4
Sakarya (river), Turkey **117** B3
Sakhalin (island), Russia **111**
　E10
Şalālah, Oman **119** G6
Salamanca, Spain **95** G2
Salas y Gómez Island, Chile
　155 F11
Saldanha, South Africa **143** H3
Salem, India **121** F4
Salem, Oregon (U.S.) **64** B1
Salta, Argentina **83** B2
Saltillo, Mexico **67** C3
Salt Lake City, Utah (U.S.) **65** C3
Salto, Uruguay **83** D4
Salton Sea, California (U.S.)
　64 E2
Salvador (Bahia), Brazil **81** E7
Salwe150en (river), Asia **104** F5
Salzburg, Austria **95** E7
Samar (island), Philippines
　123 C8
Samara, Russia **101** F6
Samarinda, Indonesia **125** C5
Samarqand, Uzbekistan **113** D4
Samoa (country), Oceania
　147 E6
Samoa Islands, Oceania **155** E6
Sámso (island), Greece **99** G7
Samsun, Turkey **117** B5
Sanaa, Yemen **119** H3
Sanaga (river), Cameroon **141**
　D2
San Ambrosio Island, Chile
　72 F3
Sanandaj, Iran **119** C4
San Antonio, Texas (U.S.) **65** F6
San Bernardino, California (U.S.)
　64 D2
San Cristóbal, Venezuela **79** B3
Sandakan, Malaysia **123** E6
San Diego, California (U.S.)
　64 E2
Sandoa, Dem. Rep. of the Congo
　141 G4
San Félix Island, Chile **72** F2
San Francisco, California (U.S.)
　64 C1
San Jorge, Gulf of, Argentina
　83 G2
San Jose, California (U.S.) **64** C1
San José, Costa Rica **67** G7
San José del Guaviare,
　Colombia **79** C3

San Juan, Argentina **83** D2
San Juan (river), North
    America **67** G7
San Juan, Puerto Rico **69** C6
San Justo, Argentina **83** E4
Sanlıurfa, Turkey **117** D6
San Lucas, Cape, Mexico **66** C1
San Luis Potosí, Mexico **67** D3
San Marino (country), Europe
    87 G4
San Matías Gulf, Argentina
    83 F3
San Miguel, El Salvador **67** F6
San Miguel de Tucumán,
    Argentina **83** C2
San Pedro Sula, Honduras
    67 F6
San Salvador (island), Bahamas
    69 B3
San Salvador, El Salvador **67** F6
Santa Ana, El Salvador **67** F6
Santa Clara, Cuba **69** B2
Santa Cruz, Bolivia **79** H5
Santa Cruz Islands, Solomon
    Islands **155** E4
Santa Fe, Argentina **83** D3
Santa Fe, New Mexico (U.S.)
    65 D4
Santa Maria, Brazil **81** H4
Santa Marta, Colombia **79** A3
Santander, Spain **95** G2
Santarém, Brazil **81** C4
Santiago, Chile **83** D1
Santiago, Dominican Republic
    69 C4
Santiago de Cuba, Cuba **69** C3
Santiago del Estero, Argentina
    83 C3
Santo Domingo, Dominican
    Republic **69** C5
Santorini (island), see Thíra,
    Greece **99** H6
Santos, Brazil **81** G5
São Francisco (river), Brazil
    81 E6
São José do Rio Preto, Brazil
    81 F5
São José dos Campos, Brazil
    81 G6
São Luís, Brazil **81** C6
São Paulo, Brazil **81** G5
São Tomé (island), São Tomé
    and Principe **141** E1
São Tomé & Principe (country),
    Africa **141** E1
Sapporo, Japan **115** B10
Sarajevo, Bosnia & Herzegovina
    99 C3
Saransk, Russia **101** F5
Saratov, Russia **101** F5
Sarawak (state), Malaysia
    123 F5
Sardinia (island), Italy **95** H6
Sarh, Chad **141** C3
Sari, Iran **119** B5
Saskatchewan (province),
    Canada **63** F4
Saskatchewan (river), Canada
    56 D3
Saskatoon, Saskatchewan
    (Canada) **63** F3
Satu Mare, Romania **99** A5
Saudi Arabia (country), Asia
    105 E1
Sault Ste. Marie, Ontario
    (Canada) **63** G6

Saurimo, Angola **143** B3
Sava (river), Europe **99** C4
Savannah, Georgia (U.S.) **65** E10
Savannah (river), U.S. **65** E9
Savannakhét, Laos **123** C3
Sawkanah, Libya **135** C7
Scandinavia (region), Europe
    86 B5
Schefferville, Quebec (Canada)
    63 F8
Scotland (country), United
    Kingdom **95** B3
Seattle, Washington (U.S.)
    64 A2
Ségou, Mali **137** D4
Seine (river), France **95** E4
Selenga (river), Mongolia **115**
    B5
Selvas (region), Brazil **81** C2
Selwyn Mountains, Yukon
    (Canada) **62** D2
Semarang, Indonesia **125** D3
Semey, Kazakhstan **113** B6
Senanga, Zambia **143** C4
Sendai, Japan **115** C11
Senegal (country), Africa **137**
    C2
Sénégal (river), Africa **137** C2
Senyavin Islands, Federated
    States of Micronesia **155**
    C3
Seoul, South Korea **115** C9
Sept-Îles, Quebec (Canada)
    63 F8
Serbia (country), Europe **87** G5
Serowe, Botswana **143** E5
Sétif, Algeria **135** A5
Setté Cama, Gabon **141** E2
Sevastopol', Ukraine **97** G9
Severn (river), Ontario (Canada)
    63 F5
Severnaya Zemlya (islands), see
    North Land, Russia **111** B6
Severodvinsk, Russia **101** C4
Seville, Spain **95** I2
Seward Peninsula, Alaska (U.S.)
    56 B1
Seychelles (country), Africa
    129 F8
Sfax, Tunisia **135** B6
Shackleton Ice Shelf,
    Antarctica **161** E9
Shanghai, China **115** E8
Shantou, China **105** F6
Shark Bay, Australia **152** D1
Shebele (river), Africa **139** D5
Sheffield, United Kingdom
    95 C3
Shenyang, China **115** C8
Sherbro Island, Sierra Leone
    137 E2
Shetland Islands, United
    Kingdom **95** A4
Shijiazhuang, China **115** D7
Shikoku (island), Japan **115**
    D10
Shiraz, Iran **119** D5
Shkodër, Albania **99** D4
Shott el Jerid (dry salt lake),
    Tunisia **135** B5
Shreveport, Louisiana (U.S.)
    65 E7
Shymkent, Kazakhstan **113** D5
Šiauliai, Lithuania **93** H7
Siberia (region), Russia **111** D5
Sibiu, Romania **99** B6

Sibu, Malaysia **123** F4
Sichuan Basin, China **104** E6
Sicily (island), Italy **95** I7
Sîdi Barrâni, Egypt **135** B8
Sidon, Lebanon **117** F4
Sidra, Gulf of, Libya **135** B7
Siem Reap, Cambodia **123** C3
Sierra Leone (country), Africa
    137 E2
Sierra Madre (range), North
    America **56** H4
Sierra Madre del Sur (range),
    Mexico **67** E3
Sierra Madre Occidental
    (range), Mexico **67** C2
Sierra Madre Oriental (range),
    Mexico **67** D3
Sierra Morena (range), Spain
    95 H2
Sierra Nevada (range),
    California (U.S.) **64** C2
Sikasso, Mali **137** D3
Sikhote Alin Range, Russia
    111 E10
Silet, Algeria **135** D5
Simferopol', Ukraine **97** G9
Simla, India **121** B4
Sinai (region), Egypt **135** B10
Sinai, Mount, Egypt **135** C11
Singapore, Singapore **123** F2
Singapore (country), Asia **105**
    H6
Sinkiang (region), China **114** C2
Sinop, Turkey **117** B4
Sint Maarten (Netherlands),
    69 C6
Sioux Falls, South Dakota (U.S.)
    65 C6
Sittwe, Myanmar **121** D7
Sivas, Turkey **117** C5
Sīwah, Egypt **135** C9
Skagerrak (strait), Europe
    93 G2
Skellefteå, Sweden **93** D6
Skien, Norway **93** G3
Skopje, Macedonia **99** D4
Slave (river), Canada **56** D3
Slave Coast (region), Africa
    137 F5
Sliven, Bulgaria **99** D7
Slovakia (country), Europe
    87 F5
Slovenia (country), Europe
    87 F4
Slov"yans'k, Ukraine **97** E10
Smolensk, Russia **101** E3
Snake (river), U.S. **64** B3
Sochi, Russia **101** I4
Society Islands, French
    Polynesia (France) **119** I6
Sofia, Bulgaria **99** D5
Sokoto, Nigeria **137** D5
Sokhumi, Georgia **117** A6
Solimões (river), see Amazon,
    South America **81** C2
Solomon Islands, Oceania
    155 D3
Solomon Islands (country),
    Oceania **147** D4
Solomon Sea, Oceania **154** E3
Somali Peninsula, Africa **139**
    C5
Somalia (country), Africa **139**
    D6
Somaliland (region), Somalia
    139 C5

Somerset Island, Nunavut
    (Canada) **63** C5
Songea, Tanzania **139** G3
Songkhla, Thailand **123** D1
Sonoran Desert, U.S. **56** F3
Sorong, Indonesia **125** C8
South Africa (country), Africa
    129 H5
Southampton, United Kingdom
    87 E2
Southampton Island, Nunavut
    (Canada) **63** D6
South Australia (state),
    Australia **153** D5
South Carolina (state), U.S.
    65 E9
South China Sea, Asia **104** F7
South Dakota (state), U.S.
    65 B5
Southern Alps (range), New
    Zealand **153** H9
South Georgia (island), United
    Kingdom **72** I7
South Island, New Zealand
    153 H10
South Korea (country), Asia
    105 D7
South Magnetic Pole,
    Antarctica **161** G8
South Orkney Islands,
    Antarctica **160** A1
South Ossetia (region), Georgia
    117 B8
South Pole, Antarctica **161** D5
South Saskatchewan (river),
    Canada **63** G3
South Shetland Islands,
    Antarctica **160** A1
South Sudan (country), Africa
    141 D6
South Taranaki Bight, New
    Zealand **153** F11
South West Cape, New Zealand
    153 I9
Spain (country), Europe **87** G1
Sparta, Greece **99** G5
Spencer Gulf, Australia **146** F2
Spitsbergen (island), Norway
    93 A3
Split, Croatia **99** C2
Spokane, Washington (U.S.)
    64 A3
Springfield, Illinois (U.S.) **65** C7
Springfield, Missouri (U.S.)
    65 D7
Sri Jayewardenepura Kotte, Sri
    Lanka **121** G6
Sri Lanka (country), Asia **105**
    G4
Srinagar, India **121** B4
St. Louis, Missouri (U.S.) **65** D7
St. Paul, Minnesota (U.S.) **65** B7
St. Petersburg, Florida (U.S.)
    65 F9
Stanley, Falkland Islands (U.K.)
    83 I4
Stara Zagora, Bulgaria **99** D6
Starbuck Island, Kiribati **155**
    D7
Stavanger, Norway **93** G2
Stavropol', Russia **101** H4
Steppes, The, Kazakhstan
    113 B4
Sterlitamak, Russia **101** F7
Stewart Island, New Zealand
    153 I9

Stockholm, Sweden **93** G5
Strasbourg, France **95** E5
Stuttgart, Germany **95** E6
Subotica, Serbia **99** B4
Sucre, Bolivia **79** I5
Sudan (country), Africa **141** B6
Sudbury, Ontario (Canada)
    63 G7
Sudd (marsh), South Sudan
    141 D6
Suez Canal, Egypt **135** B10
Suez, Gulf of, Egypt **135** B10
Sukhona (river), Russia **101** D5
Sukkur, Pakistan **121** C2
Sula Islands, Indonesia **125** C7
Sulawesi (island), Indonesia
    125 C6
Sulu Archipelago, Philippines
    123 E7
Sulu Sea, Asia **123** D6
Sumatra (island), Indonesia
    124 C1
Sumba (island), Indonesia
    125 E5
Sumbawa (island), Indonesia
    125 E5
Sumbe, Angola **142** B1
Sumqayt, Azerbaijan **117** B10
Sumy, Ukraine **97** D9
Sundsvall, Sweden **93** E5
Superior, Wisconsin (U.S.) **65** B7
Superior, Lake, North America
    56 E5
Sur, Oman **119** F7
Surabaya, Indonesia **125** D4
Surakarta, Indonesia **125** E3
Surat, India **121** D3
Surgut, Russia **111** E4
Suriname (country), South
    America **73** B5
Surt, Libya **135** B7
Suva, Fiji **155** E5
Svealand (region), Sweden
    93 F4
Sverdrup Islands, Nunavut
    (Canada) **63** A5
Swakopmund, Namibia **142** E2
Swaziland (country), Africa
    129 H6
Sweden (country), Europe
    87 C4
Switzerland (country), Europe
    87 F3
Sydney, Australia **153** E8
Syktyvkar, Russia **101** D6
Syracuse, Italy **95** I8
Syr Darya (river), Kazakhstan
    113 C4
Syria (country), Asia **105** D1
Syrian Desert, Asia **104** D1
Szczecin, Poland **96** B2
Szeged, Hungary **97** F3
Székesfehérvár, Hungary **96** F3

T

Tabelbala, Algeria **134** C4
Tabora, Tanzania **139** F2
Tabriz, Iran **119** B4
Tabuk, Saudi Arabia **119** D1
Tacloban, Philippines **123** D8
Tacoma, Washington (U.S.)
    64 A2
Tademaït Plateau, Algeria
    135 C4
Taganrog, Russia **101** H4
Tagus (river), Europe **95** H2

Tahat, Libya **135** D5
Tahiti (island), French Polynesia
　(France) **155** E8
Tahoe, Lake, U.S. **64** C2
Tahoua, Niger **137** C6
Tainan, Taiwan **115** F8
Taipei, Taiwan **115** F8
Taitao Peninsula, Chile **72** H4
Taiwan (island), China **104** F7
Taiwan Strait, Asia **115** F8
Taiyuan, China **115** D7
Taizz, Yemen **119** H3
Tajikistan (country), Asia **105**
　E3
Tajumulco, Volcán, Guatemala
　67 F5
Taklimakan Desert, China
　114 D2
Talara, Peru **79** E1
Talaud Islands, Indonesia
　125 B7
Talbot, Cape, Australia **152** A3
Talca, Chile **83** E1
Taldyqorghan, Kazakhstan
　113 C6
Tallahassee, Florida (U.S.) **65** F9
Tallinn, Estonia **93** G7
Tamale, Ghana **137** E4
Tambov, Russia **101** F4
Tampa, Florida (U.S.) **65** F9
Tampere, Finland **93** F6
Tampico, Mexico **67** D4
Tamworth, Australia **153** E8
Tana, Lake, Ethiopia **139** B3
Tanga, Tanzania **139** F6
Tanganyika, Lake, Africa **139**
　F2
Tangshan, China **115** C7
Tangier, Morocco **134** A3
Tanimbar Islands, Indonesia
　125 D8
Tanjungkarang-Telukbetung,
　Indonesia **124** D2
Tânout, Niger **137** C6
Tanzania (country), Africa
　139 F3
Taormina, Italy **95** H8
Taoudenni, Mali **137** B3
Tapajós (river), Brazil **81** C4
Taranto, Gulf of, Italy **95** H8
Tarawa, Kiribati **155** D4
Taraz, Kazakhstan **113** D5
Tarfaya, Morocco **134** C1
Târgu-Mures, Romania **99** B6
Tarija, Bolivia **79** I5
Tarim (river), China **114** C2
Tarim Basin, China **114** C2
Tarom, Iran **119** D6
Tarsus, Turkey **117** D4
Tartu, Estonia **93** G7
Tashkent, Uzbekistan **113** D4
Tasman Bay, New Zealand **153**
　G10
Tasmania (state), Australia
　153 G7
Tasman Sea, Oceania **146** G4
Taunggyi, Myanmar **121** D8
Taupo, New Zealand **153** F11
Taupo, Lake, New Zealand
　153 F11
Tauranga, New Zealand **153** E11
Taurus Mountains, Turkey
　117 D3
Taymyr Peninsula, Russia **111**
　C6
Tbilisi, Georgia **117** B8

Tchibanga, Gabon **141** E2
Te Anau, Lake, New Zealand
　153 I9
Techla, Western Sahara
　(Morocco) **134** D1
Tegucigalpa, Honduras **67** F6
Tehran, Iran **119** C5
Tehuantepec, Gulf of, Mexico
　56 I4
Tehuantepec, Isthmus of,
　Mexico **56** H4
Tel Aviv-Yafo, Israel **117** F4
Teles Pires (river), Brazil **81** D4
Temirtaū, Kazakhstan, **113** B5
Temuco, Chile **83** F1
Ténéré (desert), Niger **137** B7
Tennant Creek, Australia **153**
　C5
Tennessee (river), U.S. **65** E8
Tennessee (state), U.S. **65** D8
Tepic, Mexico **67** D2
Teresina, Brazil **81** C6
Ternate, Indonesia **125** C8
Tessalit, Mali **137** B5
Tete, Mozambique **143** C7
Tetovo, Macedonia **99** D4
Texas (state), U.S. **65** F5
Thailand (country), Asia **105** F5
Thailand, Gulf of, Asia **123** D2
Thames (river), United Kingdom
　95 D3
Thebes (ruins), Egypt **135** C10
The Hague, Netherlands **95** D4
The Pas, Manitoba (Canada)
　63 F4
Thessaloníki, Greece **99** E5
Thiès, Senegal **137** C1
Thimphu, Bhutan **121** C7
Thíra (Santoríni) (island),
　Greece **99** H6
Thiruvananthapuram, India
　121 G4
Three Gorges Dam, China
　115 E6
Three Kings Islands, New
　Zealand **153** D10
Thunder Bay, Ontario (Canada)
　63 G6
Thurston Island, Antarctica
　161 E2
Tianjin, China **115** D7
Tian Shan (range), Asia **104** D4
Tibesti Mountains, Chad **141**
　A4
Tibet (region), China **114** E3
Tibet, Plateau of, China **114** D2
Tidjikdja, Mauritania **137** C2
Tierra del Fuego (island), South
　America **83** I2
Tigris (river), Asia **104** D2
Tijuana, Mexico **66** A1
Tikal (ruins), Guatemala **67** E6
Timaru, New Zealand **153** H10
Timbuktu (Tombouctou), Mali
　137 C4
Timimoun, Algeria **135** C4
Timisoara, Romania **99** B5
Timmins, Ontario (Canada)
　63 G7
Timor (island), Asia **125** E7
Timor-Leste, see East Timor
　(country), Asia **125** E7
Timor Sea, Asia/Australia
　125 E7
Tindouf, Algeria **134** C3
Ti-n-Zaouâtene, Algeria **135** E5

Tirana, Albania **99** E3
Tiraspol, Moldova **97** F7
Ţisza (river), Europe **86** F5
Titicaca, Lake, South America
　79 H4
Tmassah, Libya **135** C7
Toamasina, Madagascar **143**
　D11
Tobruk, Libya **135** B8
Tobseda, Russia **87** A7
Tocantins (river), Brazil **81** D5
Togo (country), Africa **137** E5
Tokar, Sudan **141** B7
Tokelau (islands), New Zealand
　155 E6
Tokyo, Japan **115** C11
Toledo, Ohio (U.S.) **65** C9
Toledo, Spain **95** H2
Toliara, Madagascar **143** E9
Tomini, Gulf of, Indonesia
　125 C6
Tomsk, Russia **111** E5
Tonga (country), Oceania **147**
　E6
Tonga Islands, Tonga **146** E6
Tonkin, Gulf of, Asia **123** B4
Tonle Sap (lake), Cambodia
　123 C3
Toowoomba, Australia **153** D8
Topeka, Kansas (U.S.) **65** D6
Torneälven (river), Europe
　93 C6
Toronto, Ontario (Canada)
　63 H7
Torreón, Mexico **67** C3
Torres Strait, Australia/
　Oceania **154** E2
Tórshavn, Denmark **87** B2
Touggourt, Algeria **135** B5
Toulouse, France **95** G4
Toummo, Libya **135** D7
Tours, France **95** E4
Townsville, Australia **153** C7
Towot, South Sudan **141** D7
Trabzon, Turkey **117** B6
Transantarctic Mountains,
　Antarctica **161** D4
Transylvania (region), Romania
　99 A6
Transylvanian Alps (range),
　Romania **99** B6
Trenton, New Jersey (U.S.)
　65 C10
Trieste, Italy **95** F7
Trinidad, Bolivia **79** G5
Trinidad (island), Trinidad &
　Tobago **56** H8
Trinidad & Tobago (country),
　North America **57** H8
Tripoli, Lebanon **117** E4
Tripoli, Libya **135** B7
Tripolitania (region), Libya
　135 B6
Tromsø, Norway **93** A5
Trondheim, Norway **93** E3
Trondheimsfjorden (bay),
　Norway **93** E3
Trujillo, Peru **79** F1
Truk Islands, Federated States
　of Micronesia **146** C3
Tshwane, see Pretoria, South
　Africa **143** F5
Tual, Indonesia **125** D9
Tuamotu Archipelago, French
　Polynesia, France **155** E8
Tucson, Arizona (U.S.) **64** E3

Tukangbesi Islands, Indonesia
　125 D6
Tuktoyaktuk, Northwest
　Territories (Canada) **62** C2
Tula, Russia **101** F4
Tulcea, Romania **99** C8
Tulsa, Oklahoma (U.S.) **65** D6
Tunis, Tunisia **135** A6
Tunisia (country), Africa **135**
　A6
Tunja, Colombia **79** B3
Turan Lowland, Asia **113** C4
Turaybīl, Iraq **119** C2
Turin, Italy **95** F5
Turkana, Lake (Lake Rudolf),
　Kenya **139** D3
Turkey (country), Asia/Europe
　105 C1
Turkmenistan (country), Asia
　105 D3
Turks Islands, Turks & Caicos
　Islands (U.K.) **69** B4
Turku, Finland **93** F6
Turpan Depression, China
　115 C3
Tuvalu (country), Oceania
　147 D6
Tuz, Lake, Turkey **117** C4
Tver', Russia **101** E4
Tyre, Lebanon **117** F4
Tyrrhenian Sea, Italy **86** G4
Tyumen', Russia **111** E4

U
Ubangi (river), Africa **141** D4
Uberlândia, Brazil **81** F5
Ubon Ratchathani, Thailand
　123 C3
Ucayali (river), Peru **79** E2
Udon Thani, Thailand **123** B2
Uele (river), Dem. Rep. of the
　Congo **141** D5
Ufa, Russia **101** E7
Uganda (country), Africa **139**
　D2
Ukraine (country), Europe
　87 E6
Ulaanbaatar, Mongolia **115** B6
Ulan-Ude, Russia **111** F7
Uluru (Ayers Rock) (peak),
　Australia **153** D4
Ul'yanovsk, Russia **101** F6
Umba, Russia **87** B6
Umeå, Sweden **93** D5
Umeälven (river), Sweden **93**
　D5
Umm al 'Abīd, Libya **135** C7
Ungava Bay, Canada **63** E8
Ungava Peninsula, Quebec
　(Canada) **63** E7
United Arab Emirates
　(country), Asia **105** E2
United Kingdom (country),
　Europe **87** D2
United States (country), North
　America **57** F3
Upington, South Africa **143** G3
Upper Guinea (region), Africa
　128 E3
Upper Hutt, New Zealand **153**
　G11
Uppsala, Sweden **93** F5
Ur (ruins), Iraq **119** D4
Ural (river), Europe/Asia **104**
　C3

Ural Mountains, Europe/Asia
　104 C3
Uranium City, Saskatchewan
　(Canada) **63** E4
Urmia, Iran **119** B4
Urmia, Lake, Iran **119** B4
Uruguay (country), South
　America **73** G5
Uruguay (river), South America
　72 F5
Ürümqi, China **115** C3
Ushuaia, Argentina **83** I2
Ussuriysk, Russia **111** F10
Ust' Ilimsk, Russia **111** E7
Ustyurt Plateau, Asia **113** C3
Usumacinta (river), North
　America **67** E5
Utah (state), U.S. **64** C3
Utrecht, Netherlands **95** D5
Uxmal (ruins), Mexico **67** D6
Uyuni, Salar de, Bolivia **79** I4
Uzbekistan (country), Asia
　105 D3
Uzhhorod, Ukraine **97** E4

V
Vaal (river), South Africa **143**
　F6
Vaasa, Finland **93** E6
Vadsø, Norway **87** A5
Valdés Peninsula, Argentina
　83 F3
Valencia, Spain **95** H3
Valencia, Venezuela **79** A4
Valladolid, Spain **95** G2
Valletta, Malta **95** I7
Valparaíso, Chile **83** D1
Van, Turkey **117** D7
Van, Lake, Turkey **117** C7
Vancouver, British Columbia
　(Canada) **62** F1
Vancouver Island, British
　Columbia (Canada) **62** F1
Vänern (lake), Sweden **93** G3
Vanua Levu (island), Fiji **155** E5
Vanuatu (country), Oceania
　147 E5
Varna, Bulgaria **99** D7
Västerås, Sweden **93** G5
Vatican City (country), Europe
　87 G4
Vatnajökull (glacier), Iceland
　93 A2
Vättern (lake), Sweden **93** G4
Velikiy Novgorod, Russia **101**
　D3
Venezuela (country), South
　America **73** A4
Venezuela, Gulf of, South
　America **79** A4
Venice, Italy **95** F6
Venice, Gulf of, Europe **99** B1
Veracruz, Mexico **67** E4
Verde, Cape, Senegal **128** D1
Verkhoyansk Range, Russia
　111 C8
Vermont (state), U.S. **65** B10
Verona, Italy **95** F6
Vesterålen (islands), Norway
　93 B4
Vestfjorden (bay), Norway
　93 B4
Vesuvius, Mount, Italy **95** G7
Vichy, France **95** F4
Victoria (state), Australia
　153 F6

Victoria, British Columbia
(Canada) **62** F1
Victoria Island, Canada **63** C4
Victoria, Lake, Africa **139** E2
Victoria Land, Antarctica
161 G6
Victoria Nile (river), Uganda
139 D2
Victory Peak, Asia **113** D6
Vienna, Austria **95** E7
Vientiane, Laos **123** B2
Vietnam (country), Asia **105** F6
Vigo, Spain **95** G1
Vijayawada, India **121** E5
Vilankulo, Mozambique **143** E7
Villahermosa, Mexico **67** E5
Villarrica, Paraguay **83** C4
Vilnius, Lithuania **93** I7
Vinh, Vietnam **123** B3
Vinnytsya, Ukraine **97** E7
Vinson Massif (peak),
Antarctica **161** D3
Virgin Islands, North America
69 C6
Virginia (state), U.S. **65** D10
Virginia Beach, Virginia (U.S.)
65 D10
Virunga Mountains, Africa
128 F6
Visby, Sweden **93** H5
Vishakhapatnam, India **121** E5
Vistula (river), Poland **97** B3
Viti Levu (island), Fiji **155** E5
Vitória, Brazil **81** F7
Vitória da Conquista, Brazil
81 E7
Vitsyebsk, Belarus **97** A7
Vladikavkaz, Russia **101** I5
Vladimir, Russia **101** E4
Vladivostok, Russia **111** F10
Vlorë, Albania **99** E4
Volcano Islands, Japan **154** B2
Volga (river), Russia **101** G5
Volgograd, Russia **101** G5
Vologda, Russia **101** D4
Volta, Lake, Ghana **137** E4
Vopnafjördur, Iceland **87** A2
Vorkuta, Russia **101** B7
Voronezh, Russia **101** F4
Vostok Island, French Polynesia
(France) **155** E7
Vostok Station, Antarctica
161 E7

W

Wabash (river), U.S. **65** D8
Waco, Texas (U.S.) **65** F6
Wadi Halfa, Sudan **141** A6
Wagga Wagga, Australia **153** F7
Waiau (river), New Zealand
153 I9
Waikato (river), New Zealand
153 E11
Waitaki (river), New Zealand
153 H10
Wajir, Kenya **139** D4
Wakatipu, Lake, New Zealand
153 H9
Wake Island, U.S. **155** B4
Walbrzych, Poland **96** D2
Wales (country), United
Kingdom **95** D3
Wallis and Futuna (islands),
France **155** E5
Wallis Islands, Oceania **146** D6
Walvis Bay, Namibia **142** E2

Wanaka, New Zealand **153** H9
Wanaka, Lake, New Zealand
153 H9
Wandel Sea, Greenland
(Denmark) **56** A5
Warrnambool, Australia **153** F6
Warsaw, Poland **97** C4
Washington, District of
Columbia (U.S.) **65** C10
Washington (state), U.S. **64** A2
Waterford, Ireland **95** D2
Wau, South Sudan **141** D5
Webi Shabeelle (river), Africa
137 F5
Weddel Sea, Antarctica **161** B3
Weipa, Australia **153** A6
Welkom, South Africa **143** G5
Wellesley Islands, Australia
153 B6
Wellington, New Zealand **153**
G11
Wellington Island, Chile **83** H1
Wessel Islands, Australia **153**
A5
West Antarctica, Antarctica
161 E3
West Bank (region), Asia **117** F4
West Cape Howe, Australia
152 F2
Western Australia (state),
Australia **152** D2
Western Desert, Egypt **135** C9
Western Ghats (range), India
121 F3
Western Plateau, Australia
146 E1
Western Rift Valley, Africa
141 F6
Western Sahara (Morocco),
Africa **134** C1
West Ice Shelf, Antarctica
161 D9
West Indies (islands), North
America **56** H7
Westport, New Zealand **153**
G10
West Siberian Plain, Russia
111 D5
West Virginia (state), U.S. **65** C9
Whakatane, New Zealand **153**
E12
Whanganui, New Zealand **153**
F11
Whangarei, New Zealand **153**
D11
Whitehorse, Yukon (Canada)
62 D1
White Nile (river), Africa **141**
C6
White Sea, Russia **86** B6
White Volta (river), Africa
137 E4
Whitney, Mount, California (U.S.)
64 D2
Whyalla, Australia **153** E5
Wichita, Kansas (U.S.) **65** D6
Wilhelm, Mount, Papua New
Guinea **154** D2
Wilkes Land, Antarctica **161** F8
Wiluna, Australia **152** D2
Windhoek, Namibia **142** E2
Windorah, Australia **153** D6
Windsor, Ontario (Canada)
63 H7
Windward Islands, North
America **69** D8

Winnipeg, Manitoba (Canada)
63 G5
Winnipeg, Lake, Manitoba
(Canada) **63** F5
Winton, Australia **153** C6
Wisconsin (state), U.S. **65** B7
Witbank, South Africa **143** F5
Wollongong, Australia **153** F8
Wonsan, North Korea **115** C9
Woods, Lake of the, North
America **65** A6
Worcester, South Africa **143**
H3
Wrangel Island, Russia **111** A9
Wroclaw, Poland **96** C2
Wuhan, China **115** E7
Wuwei, China **105** E5
Wyndham, Australia **152** B4
Wyoming (state), U.S. **65** C4

X

Xai-Xai, Mozambique **143** F7
Xiamen, China **115** F8
Xi'an, China **115** E6
Xingu (river), Brazil **81** D4
Xining, China **115** D5
Xuzhou, China **115** D7

Y

Yablonovyy Range, Russia
104 C6
Yakutsk, Russia **111** D8
Yalta, Ukraine **97** G9
Yamal Peninsula, Russia **111** C5
Yamoussoukro, Côte d'Ivoire
137 E3
Yanbu al Bahr, Saudi Arabia
119 E2
Yangon (Rangoon), Myanmar
121 E8
Yangtze (river), China **115** E6
Yangtze Gorges, China **104** E6
Yaoundé, Cameroon **141** D2
Yap Islands, Federated States
of Micronesia **154** C1
Yaqui (river), Mexico **66** B1
Yaren, Nauru **155** D4
Yarlung Zangbo (river), China
115 E3
Yaroslavl', Russia **101** E4
Yazd, Iran **119** C6
Yekaterinburg, Russia **110** E3
Yellow (river), China **115** D7
Yellowknife, Northwest
Territories (Canada) **63** D3
Yellow Sea, Asia **115** D8
Yellowstone Lake, Wyoming
(U.S.) **65** B4
Yellowstone National Park, U.S.
65 B4
Yemen (country), Asia **105** F1
Yenisey (river), Russia **111** D5
Yerevan, Armenia **97** H7
Yevpatoriya, Ukraine **97** G9
Yogyakarta, Indonesia **125** E3
Yokohama, Japan **115** C11
Yola, Nigeria **137** E7
York, Cape, Australia **153** A6
Ysyk-Köl (lake), Kyrgyzstan
113 D6
Yucatán Peninsula, Mexico
67 E6
Yukon (territory), Canada
62 C2
Yukon (river), North America
56 B2

Yukon Plateau, Canada **56** C2
Yuma, Arizona (U.S.) **64** E2
Yumen, China **115** D4
Yuzhno Sakhalinsk, Russia
111 E11

Z

Zabol, Iran **119** D8
Zadar, Croatia **99** C2
Zagreb, Croatia **99** B2
Zagros Mountains, Iran **119** C5
Zahedan, Iran **119** D7
Zambeze (river), Africa **143** D7
Zambia (country), Africa **129** G6
Zamboanga City, Philippines
123 E7
Zanjan, Iran **119** B4
Zanzibar, Tanzania **139** F4
Zanzibar Island, Tanzania
139 F4
Zaporizhzhya, Ukraine **97** E9
Zaragoza, Spain **95** G3
Zealand (island), Denmark **93** I3
Zenica, Bosnia & Herzegovina
99 C3
Zhengzhou, China **115** D7
Zhytomyr, Ukraine **97** D7
Zibo, China **115** D7
Ziguinchor, Senegal **137** D1
Zimbabwe (country), Africa
129 G6
Zinder, Niger **137** D7
Zonguldak, Turkey **117** B3
Zouerate, Mauritania **137** B2
Zufar (region), Oman **119** G6
Zürich, Switzerland **95** E5

OCEAN FEATURES

A

Aden, Gulf of, Indian Ocean
170 C3
Adriatic Sea, Mediterranean
Sea **169** C7
Aegean Sea, Mediterranean
Sea **169** D7
Aegir Ridge, Atlantic Ocean
173 E11
Agalega Islands, Indian Ocean
171 E4
Agassiz Fracture Zone, Pacific
Ocean **167** H7
Agulhas Bank, Atlantic Ocean
169 H7
Agulhas Basin, Indian Ocean
170 H1
Agulhas Seamount, Atlantic
Ocean **169** H7
Alaska, Gulf of, Pacific Ocean
167 B6
Aldabra Islands, Indian Ocean
170 E3
Aleutian Basin, Pacific Ocean
167 B4
Aleutian Trench, Pacific Ocean
167 B4
Alexandra Land, Arctic Ocean
173 C7
Alpha Cordillera, Arctic Ocean
173 F5

Amirante Isles, Indian Ocean
171 E3
Amirante Trench, Indian Ocean
171 E3
Amsterdam (island), Indian
Ocean **171** G5
Amundsen Gulf, Arctic Ocean
173 H3
Andaman Basin, Indian Ocean
171 C7
Angola Plain, Atlantic Ocean
169 G6
Anjou Islands, Arctic Ocean
173 C3
Arabian Basin, Indian Ocean
171 C4
Arabian Sea, Indian Ocean
171 C4
Arafura Sea, Indian Ocean
171 E11
Argentine Plain, Atlantic Ocean
169 I3
Ascension (island), Atlantic
Ocean **169** F5
Ascension Fracture Zone,
Atlantic Ocean **169** F5
Atlantic-Indian Ridge, Indian
Ocean **170** I1
Atlantis Fracture Zone, Atlantic
Ocean **169** D3
Atlantis II Fracture Zone,
Indian Ocean **171** G4
Aves Ridge, Atlantic Ocean
169 E2

B

Baffin Bay, Atlantic Ocean
173 H7
Baltic Sea, Atlantic Ocean
169 B7
Banda Sea, Pacific Ocean
166 F1
Barents Plain, Arctic Ocean
173 D7
Barents Sea, Arctic Ocean
173 C8
Barrow Canyon, Arctic Ocean
172 G2
Barrow Strait, Arctic Ocean
173 H6
Baydarata Bay, Arctic Ocean
173 A8
Beata Ridge, Atlantic Ocean
169 E2
Beaufort Sea, Arctic Ocean
172 G3
Beaufort Shelf, Arctic Ocean
172 G2
Beaufort Slope, Arctic Ocean
172 G2
Belgica Bank, Arctic Ocean
173 E8
Bengal, Bay of, Indian Ocean
171 C6
Benham Seamount, Pacific
Ocean **171** C10
Bering Sea, Pacific Ocean
166 A4
Bering Strait, Arctic Ocean
172 F1
Bermuda Rise, Atlantic Ocean
169 D2
Bill Baileys Bank, Atlantic
Ocean **169** B5
Biscay, Bay of, Atlantic Ocean
169 C5

Biscay Plain — Maine, Gulf of

Biscay Plain, Atlantic Ocean **169** C5
Bjørnøya (island), Arctic Ocean **173** D9
Black Sea, Europe/Asia **169** C7
Blake-Bahama Ridge, Atlantic Ocean **169** D2
Blake Plateau, Atlantic Ocean **169** D1
Bol'shevik Islands, Arctic Ocean **173** B5
Bonin Trench, Pacific Ocean **166** D2
Boothia, Gulf of, Arctic Ocean **173** I6
Boreas Plain, Arctic Ocean **173** E9
Borkhaya Bay, Arctic Ocean **173** B3
Bothnia, Gulf of, Atlantic Ocean **169** B7
Bounty Trough, Pacific Ocean **167** I4
Bouvet (island), Atlantic Ocean **169** I6
Bowers Ridge, Pacific Ocean **167** B4
Broken Ridge, Indian Ocean **171** G7
Bylot Island, Arctic Ocean **173** H6

C
Campbell Plateau, Pacific Ocean **166** I3
Campeche Bank, Atlantic Ocean **169** E1
Canada Basin, Arctic Ocean **173** G3
Canada Plain, Arctic Ocean **172** F3
Cape Verde Islands, Atlantic Ocean **169** E4
Cargados Carajos Bank, Indian Ocean **171** E4
Caribbean Sea, Atlantic Ocean **169** E1
Carlsberg Ridge, Indian Ocean **171** D4
Carnegie Ridge, Pacific Ocean **169** F1
Carpentaria, Gulf of, Pacific Ocean **171** E11
Cayman Trench, Atlantic Ocean **169** E1
Cedros Trench, Pacific Ocean **167** D8
Celebes Basin, Pacific Ocean **166** E1
Celtic Sea, Atlantic Ocean **169** C5
Central Pacific Basin, Pacific Ocean **167** E44
Chagos Trench, Indian Ocean **171** E5
Chain Fracture Zone, Atlantic Ocean **169** F5
Challenger Deep, Pacific Ocean **166** E2
Chatham Rise, Pacific Ocean **167** H4
Chaun Bay, Arctic Ocean **172** D1
Chelyuskin, Cape, Arctic Ocean **173** B5

Chesha Bay, Arctic Ocean **173** A9
Chile Basin, Pacific Ocean **167** G9
Chile Rise, Pacific Ocean **167** H9
Chinook Trough, Pacific Ocean **167** C4
Christmas Island, Indian Ocean **171** E8
Chukchi Plain, Arctic Ocean **172** E3
Chukchi Plateau, Arctic Ocean **173** E3
Chukchi Sea, Arctic Ocean **172** E1
Clarion Fracture Zone, Pacific Ocean **167** E7
Clipperton Fracture Zone, Pacific Ocean **167** E7
Coco-De-Mer Seamounts, Indian Ocean **171** D4
Cocos Ridge, Pacific Ocean **167** E9
Columbia Seamount, Atlantic Ocean **169** G4
Comoro Islands, Indian Ocean **170** E3
Congo Canyon, Atlantic Ocean **169** F6
Coral Sea, Pacific Ocean **167** G3
Coral Sea Basin, Pacific Ocean **167** F2
Corner Seamounts, Atlantic Ocean **169** D3
Cornwallis Island, Arctic Ocean **173** H5
Crozet Basin, Indian Ocean **171** H4
Crozet Islands, Indian Ocean **171** H3
Cuvier Plateau, Indian Ocean **171** F8

D
Davis Strait, Atlantic Ocean **169** A2
Demerara Plain, Atlantic Ocean **169** E3
Denmark Strait, Atlantic Ocean **169** A4
Diamantina Fracture Zone, Indian Ocean **171** G8
Diego Garcia (island), Indian Ocean **171** E5
Discovery Tablemount, Atlantic Ocean **169** H6
Disko (island), see Qeqertarsuak, Arctic Ocean **173** H8
Doldrums Fracture Zone, Atlantic Ocean **169** E4
Dumshaf Plain, Atlantic Ocean **169** A6

E
East Caroline Basin, Pacific Ocean **167** E2
East China Sea, Pacific Ocean **166** D1
Easter Fracture Zone, Pacific Ocean **167** G8
East Indiaman Ridge, Indian Ocean **171** F7

East Mariana Basin, Pacific Ocean **167** E2
East Novaya Zemlya Trough, Arctic Ocean **173** B7
East Pacific Rise, Pacific Ocean **167** G8
East Sea, see Japan, Sea of, Pacific Ocean **166** C1
East Siberian Sea, Arctic Ocean **172** D2
Eauripik Rise, Pacific Ocean **171** D11
Egeria Fracture Zone, Indian Ocean **171** F4
Eirik Ridge, Atlantic Ocean **169** B3
Ellef Ringnes Island, Arctic Ocean **173** G5
Eltanin Fracture Zone, Pacific Ocean **167** I6
Emerald Basin, Pacific Ocean **166** I3
Emperor Seamounts, Pacific Ocean **167** C3
Emperor Trough, Pacific Ocean **167** C4
English Channel, Atlantic Ocean **169** C6
Europa (island), Indian Ocean **170** F2
Exmouth Plateau, Indian Ocean **171** F9

F
Falkland Escarpment, Atlantic Ocean **169** I3
Falkland Plateau, Atlantic Ocean **169** I3
Farewell, Cape, Atlantic Ocean **169** B3
Faroe Bank, Atlantic Ocean **169** B5
Farquhar Group, Indian Ocean **171** E3
Fiji Islands Plateau, Pacific Ocean **167** G4
Finland, Gulf of, Atlantic Ocean **169** B7
Flemish Cap, Atlantic Ocean **169** C3
Fletcher Plain, Arctic Ocean **173** E5
Flores Sea, Pacific Ocean **171** E9
Foxe Basin, Atlantic Ocean **169** A1
Fram Basin, Arctic Ocean **173** E6
Frio, Cape, Atlantic Ocean **169** G3
Fundy, Bay of, Atlantic Ocean **169** C2

G
Galápagos Fracture Zone, Pacific Ocean **167** F6
Galápagos Rift, Pacific Ocean **167** E9
Galápagos Rise, Pacific Ocean **167** F9
Gambia Plain, Atlantic Ocean **169** E4
Ganges Fan, Indianv **171** C6
Gardar Ridge, Atlantic Ocean **169** B4

George Bligh Bank, Atlantic Ocean **169** B5
George Land, Arctic Ocean **173** C7
Gibraltar, Strait of, Atlantic Ocean **169** D5
Gilbert Islands, Pacific Ocean **167** F3
Graham Bell Island, Arctic Ocean **173** C7
Grand Banks of Newfoundland, Atlantic Ocean **169** C3
Great Australian Bight, Indian Ocean **171** G10
Great Meteor Tablemount, Atlantic Ocean **169** D4
Greenland Fracture Zone, Arctic Ocean **173** E9
Greenland Plain, Arctic Ocean **173** E9
Greenland Sea, Arctic Ocean **173** E9
Guatemala Basin, Pacific Ocean **167** E9
Gusinaya Bank, Arctic Ocean **173** B9

H
Halten Bank, Atlantic **169** A6
Hatteras Plain, Atlantic Ocean **169** D2
Hawaiian Ridge, Pacific Ocean **167** D5
Henrietta Island, Arctic Ocean **173** D3
Herdman Seamount, Atlantic Ocean **169** I6
Hess Rise, Pacific Ocean **167** C4
Hope, Point, Arctic Ocean **172** F1
Hotspur Seamount, Atlantic Ocean **169** G4
Hudson Bay, Atlantic Ocean **169** B1
Hudson Canyon, Atlantic Ocean **169** D2
Humboldt Plain, Pacific Ocean **167** I10

I
Iceland-Faroe Rise, Atlantic Ocean **169** B5
Iceland Plateau, Atlantic Ocean **173** F10
Iceland Sea, Atlantic Ocean **169** A5
Imarssuak Seachannel, Atlantic Ocean **169** B3
Indomed Fracture Zone, Indian Ocean **170** H3
Indus Fan, Indian Ocean **171** B4
Investigator Ridge, Indian Ocean **171** E7
Islas Orcadas Rise, Atlantic Ocean **169** I4
Izu-Ogasawara Trench, Pacific Ocean **166** D2

J
Jan Mayen Fracture Zone, Arctic Ocean **173** E10
Jan Mayen Ridge, Atlantic Ocean **169** A5
Japan, Sea of (East Sea), Pacific Ocean **166** C1
Japan Trench, Pacific Ocean **167** C2

Java Ridge, Indian Ocean **171** E8
Java Sea, Pacific Ocean **171** D8
Java Trench, Indian Ocean **171** E8
Jeannette Island, Arctic Ocean **173** D3
Josephine Seamount, Atlantic Ocean **169** D5
Juan De Fuca Ridge, Pacific Ocean **167** B7

K
Kane Fracture Zone, Atlantic Ocean **169** E3
Kara Sea, Arctic Ocean **173** B6
Kerguélen Islands, Indian Ocean **171** I5
Kerguélen Plateau, Indian Ocean **171** I5
Kermadec Trench, Pacific Ocean **167** H4
Kolbeinsey Ridge, Atlantic Ocean **169** A5
Komsomolets Island, Arctic Ocean **173** C5
Kotzebue Sound, Arctic Ocean **172** F1
Krylov Seamount, Atlantic Ocean **169** E4
Kuril Basin, Pacific Ocean **167** C2
Kuril-Kamchatka Trench, Pacific Ocean **166** C2
Kyushu-Palau Ridge, Pacific Ocean **166** E1

L
Lancaster Sound, Arctic Ocean **173** H6
Laptev Sea, Arctic Ocean **173** B4
Lau Basin, Pacific Ocean **167** G4
Laurentian Fan, Atlantic Ocean **169** C3
Lau Ridge, Pacific Ocean **167** G4
Lincoln Sea, Arctic Ocean **173** F7
Line Islands, Pacific Ocean **167** E5
Lomonosov Ridge, Arctic Ocean **173** E5
Lord Howe Rise, Pacific Ocean **166** H3
Louisville Ridge, Pacific Ocean **167** H4
Lyakhov Islands, Arctic Ocean **173** C3

M
Macclesfield Bank, Pacific Ocean **171** C9
Mackenzie Trough, Arctic Ocean **172** H3
Macquarie Ridge, Pacific Ocean **166** I3
Madagascar Basin, Indian Ocean **170** F3
Madagascar Plateau, Indian Ocean **170** G3
Magellan, Strait of, Atlantic Ocean **169** I2
Magellan Rise, Pacific Ocean **167** E4
Maine, Gulf of, Atlantic Ocean **169** C2

Makarov Basin, Arctic Ocean **173** E4

Manihiki Plateau, Pacific Ocean **167** F5

Mapmaker Seamounts, Pacific Ocean **167** D3

Mariana Trench, Pacific Ocean **167** E2

Mariana Trough, Pacific Ocean **166** E2

Marquesas Fracture Zone, Pacific Ocean **167** F7

Martin Vaz Islands, Atlantic Ocean **169** G4

Marvin Spur, Arctic Ocean **173** E5

Mascarene Basin, Indian Ocean **171** E4

Mascarene Plain, Indian Ocean **171** F3

Mascarene Plateau, Indian Ocean **171** E4

Mathematicians Seamounts, Pacific Ocean **167** E8

Mauritius Trench, Indian Ocean **171** F4

Maury Seachannel, Atlantic Ocean **169** B4

M'Clintock Channel, Arctic Ocean **173** I5

M'Clure Strait, Arctic Ocean **173** H4

Mediterranean Sea, Europe/Asia/Africa **169** D6

Menard Fracture Zone, Pacific Ocean **167** I8

Mendeleyev Plain, Arctic Ocean **173** E4

Mendeleyev Ridge, Arctic Ocean **173** E4

Mendocino Fracture Zone, Pacific Ocean **167** C6

Meteor Seamount, Atlantic Ocean **169** I6

Mexico, Gulf of, Atlantic Ocean **169** E1

Mexico Basin, Atlantic Ocean **169** E1

Mid-Atlantic Ridge, Atlantic Ocean **169** D4

Middle America Trench, Pacific Ocean **167** E9

Mid-Indian Basin, Indian Ocean **171** E6

Mid-Indian Ridge, Indian Ocean **171** E4

Mid-Pacific Mountains, Pacific Ocean **167** D3

Mississippi Fan, Atlantic Ocean **169** D1

Mohns Ridge, Arctic Ocean **173** E10

Molloy Deep, Arctic Ocean **173** E8

Molokai Fracture Zone, Pacific Ocean **167** D6

Morris Jessup Rise, Arctic Ocean **173** E7

Mozambique Escarpment, Indian Ocean **170** G2

Mozambique Plateau, Indian Ocean **170** G2

Murmansk Rise, Arctic Ocean **173** C8

Murray Fracture Zone, Pacific Ocean **167** D6

Musicians Seamounts, Pacific Ocean **167** D5

N

Nansen Basin, Arctic Ocean **173** C5

Nansen Ridge, Arctic Ocean **173** D6

Nares Plain, Atlantic Ocean **169** E2

Natal Basin, Indian Ocean **170** G2

Naturaliste Plateau, Indian Ocean **171** G8

Nazareth Bank, Indian Ocean **171** E4

Nazca Ridge, Pacific Ocean **167** G9

Necker Ridge, Pacific Ocean **167** D5

New Caledonia Basin, Pacific Ocean **167** G3

New England Seamounts, Atlantic Ocean **169** D2

New Hebrides Trench, Pacific Ocean **167** G4

Nikitin Seamount, Indian Ocean **171** D6

Ninetyeast Ridge, Indian Ocean **171** E7

Norfolk Ridge, Pacific Ocean **167** G3

North Australian Basin, Indian Ocean **171** E9

Northeast Pacific Basin, Pacific Ocean **167** D6

North Fiji Basin, Pacific Ocean **167** G3

North Sea, Atlantic Ocean **169** B6

Northwest Atlantic Mid-Ocean Canyon, Atlantic Ocean **169** B3

Northwest Hawaiian Ridge, Pacific Ocean **167** D4

Northwest Pacific Basin, Pacific Ocean **167** C3

Northwind Escarpment, Arctic Ocean **172** F3

Northwind Plain, Arctic Ocean **172** F3

Northwind Ridge, Arctic Ocean **172** F3

Norwegian Basin, Atlantic Ocean **173** E11

Norwegian Sea, Atlantic Ocean **169** A6

O

Ob, Gulf of, Arctic Ocean **173** A7

Ob' Bank, Arctic Ocean **173** E8

Ob' Tablemount, Indian Ocean **170** I2

Oceanographer Fracture Zone, Atlantic Ocean **169** D4

October Revolution Island, Arctic Ocean **173** C5

Okhotsk, Sea of, Pacific Ocean **167** B2

Olga Basin, Arctic Ocean **173** D8

Oman, Gulf of, Indian Ocean **171** B4

Orphan Knoll, Atlantic Ocean **169** C3

Osborn Plateau, Indian Ocean **171** E6

Owen Fracture Zone, Indian Ocean **171** C4

P

Palau Trench, Pacific Ocean **166** E1

Palawan Trough, Pacific Ocean **171** C9

Panama Basin, Pacific Ocean **167** E10

Paracel Islands, Indian Ocean **171** C8

Parry Channel, Arctic Ocean **173** H5

Patton Escarpment, Pacific Ocean **167** D8

Pechora Bay, Arctic Ocean **173** A8

Pernambuco Plain, Atlantic Ocean **169** F4

Persian Gulf, Indian Ocean **171** B3

Perth Basin, Indian Ocean **171** G8

Peru Basin, Pacific Ocean **167** F9

Peru-Chile Trench, Pacific Ocean **167** G9

Philippine Basin, Pacific Ocean **171** C10

Philippine Sea, Pacific Ocean **166** D1

Philippine Trench, Pacific Ocean **166** E1

Pioneer Fracture Zone, Pacific Ocean **167** C6

Pole Plain, Arctic Ocean **173** D5

Porcupine Bank, Atlantic Ocean **169** C5

Porcupine Plain, Atlantic Ocean **169** C5

Prince Edward Fracture Zone, Indian Ocean **170** H2

Prince Edward Islands, Indian Ocean **170** H2

Prince Regent Inlet, Arctic Ocean **173** I6

Puerto Rico Trench, Atlantic Ocean **169** E2

Q

Qeqertarsuaq (Disko), Atlantic Ocean **173** H8

R

Ra's al Hadd (cape), Indian Ocean **171** B4

Red Sea, Indian Ocean **170** B2

Researcher Ridge, Atlantic Ocean **169** E3

Reykjanes Ridge, Atlantic Ocean **169** B4

Rio Grande Rise, Atlantic Ocean **169** G4

Rodrigues (island), Indian Ocean **171** F4

Rodrigues Fracture Zone, Indian Ocean **171** F4

Romanche Gap, Atlantic Ocean **169** F5

Røst Bank, Atlantic Ocean **173** D11

Ryukyu Trench, Pacific Ocean **166** D1

S

St. Lawrence, Gulf of, Atlantic Ocean **169** C2

St. Paul (island), Indian Ocean **171** H5

St. Peter and St. Paul Rocks, Atlantic Ocean **169** F4

Sala y Gómez Ridge, Pacific Ocean **167** G9

San Jorge, Gulf of, Atlantic Ocean **169** I2

Santos Plateau, Atlantic Ocean **169** G3

Sargo Plateau, Arctic Ocean **173** E3

Saya de Malha Bank, Indian Ocean **171** E4

Shatskiy Rise, Pacific Ocean **167** D3

Shirshov Ridge, Pacific Ocean **167** B3

Somali Basin, Indian Ocean **171** D3

South Australian Basin, Indian Ocean **171** G10

South China Sea, Pacific Ocean **171** C9

Southeast Indian Ridge, Indian Ocean **171** H7

Southeast Pacific Basin, Pacific Ocean **167** I9

South Fiji Basin, Pacific Ocean **167** G4

South Tasman Rise, Pacific Ocean **166** I2

Southwest Indian Ridge, Indian Ocean **170** H3

Southwest Pacific Basin, Pacific Ocean **167** H6

Spitsbergen (island), Arctic Ocean **173** D8

Spitsbergen Bank, Arctic Ocean **173** D9

Spitsbergen Fracture Zone, Arctic Ocean **173** E8

Stocks Seamount, Atlantic Ocean **169** G4

Sulu Basin, Pacific Ocean **166** E1

Surtsey (island), Atlantic Ocean **169** B5

Svalbard (island), Arctic Ocean **173** D8

Svyataya Anna Fan, Arctic Ocean **173** D6

Svyataya Anna Trough, Arctic Ocean **173** C6

T

Tasman Plain, Pacific Ocean **166** H2

Tasman Sea, Pacific Ocean **166** H3

Thailand, Gulf of, Pacific Ocean **171** C8

Tonga Trench, Pacific Ocean **167** G4

Tristan da Cunha Group, Atlantic Ocean **169** H5

Tufts Plain, Pacific Ocean **167** C6

Tyrrhenian Sea, Mediterranean **169** D6

U

Udintsev Fracture Zone, Pacific Ocean **167** I5

V

Valdivia Fracture Zone, Pacific Ocean **167** H9

Vema Seamount, Atlantic Ocean **169** H6

Vema Trench, Indian Ocean **171** E5

Viscount Melville Sound, Arctic Ocean **173** H5

Vitória Seamount, Atlantic Ocean **169** G4

Vityaz Trench, Pacific Ocean **167** F4

Voring Plateau, Atlantic Ocean **169** A6

Voronin Trough, Arctic Ocean **173** C6

W

Walters Shoal, Indian Ocean **170** G3

Walvis Ridge, Atlantic Ocean **169** G6

Wandel Sea, Arctic Ocean **173** E7

Weber Basin, Pacific Ocean **166** F1

West Caroline Basin, Pacific Ocean **166** E2

West Mariana Basin, Pacific Ocean **166** E2

Wharton Basin, Indian Ocean **171** F8

White Sea, Arctic Ocean **173** B10

Wrangel Plain, Arctic Ocean **173** D4

Wüst Seamount, Atlantic Ocean **169** H5

Wyandot Seamount, Atlantic Ocean **169** H7

Wyville Thomson Ridge, Atlantic Ocean **169** B5

Y

Yana, Gulf of, Arctic Ocean **173** B3

Yap Trench, Pacific Ocean **166** E2

Yellow Sea, Pacific Ocean **166** C1

Yenisey Gulf, Arctic Ocean **173** A6

Yermak Plateau, Arctic Ocean **173** E8

Z

Zanzibar Island, Indian Ocean **170** E2

Zapiola Ridge, Atlantic Ocean **169** I3

Zhokhov Island, Arctic Ocean **173** C3

Map Data Sources

8 (Find Your House) SkylineGlobe. www.skylineglobe.com; 17 (Tectonic Features), USGS Earthquake Hazards Program and USGS National Earthquake Information Center (NEIC). earthquake.usgs.gov; Smithsonian Institution, Global Volcanism Program. volcano.si.edu; USGS and the International Association of Volcanology and Chemistry of the Earth's Interior. vulcan.wr.usgs.gov; 22 (Climatic Zones), © H.J. de Blij, P.O. Muller, and John Wiley & Sons, Inc.; 25 (Land and Ocean Temperature Averages), NOAA National Centers for Environmental Information, State of the Climate: Global Climate Report for July 2017. Published online August 2017. www.ncdc.noaa.gov/sotc/global/201707; 26 (Vegetation Zones), *Biodiversity*. NG Maps for *National Geographic* magazine (February 1999); 28 (Human Footprint), Venter, O., E.W. Sanderson, A. Magrach, J.R. Allan, J. Beher, K.R. Jones, H.P. Possingham, W.F. Laurance, P. Wood, B.M. Fekete, M.A. Levy, and J.E.M. Watson. "Sixteen years of change in the global terrestrial human footprint and implications for biodiversity conservation." *Nature Communications* 2016. doi:10.1038/ncomms12558; Watson, J.E.M., D.F. Shanahan, M. Di Marco, J. Allan, W.F. Laurance, E.W. Sanderson, B. Mackey, and O. Venter. "Catastrophic declines in wilderness areas undermine global environment targets." *Current Biology* 26, 2016. doi:10.1016/j.cub.2016.08.049; 28 (Environmental Stresses), Halpern, B. S. et al. "Spatial and temporal changes in cumulative human impacts on the world's ocean." *Nature Communications* 6:7615. 2015. doi: 10.1038/ncomms8615; Millennium Ecosystem Assessment. *Ecosystems and Human Well-Being, Synthesis*; NASA's Goddard Space Flight Center; van Donkelaar, A., R.V. Martin, M. Brauer, R. Kahn, R. Levy, C. Verduzco, and P.J. Villeneuve. "Global estimates of exposure to fine particulate matter concentrations from satellite-based aerosol optical dept." *Environmental Health Perspective* 118(6), 2010. doi:10.1289/ehp.0901623; 30 (Number of Threatened Species, 2016), IUCN 2017. The IUCN Red List of Threatened Species. Version 2016-3. www.iucnredlist.org; 32 (Natural Disasters), USGS Earthquake Hazards Program and USGS National Earthquake Information Center (NEIC). earthquake.usgs.gov; Smithsonian Institution, Global Volcanism Program. volcano.si.edu; USGS and the International Association of Volcanology and Chemistry of the Earth's Interior. vulcan .wr.usgs.gov; National Geophysical Data Center/World Data Service (NGDC/WDS): Global Historical Tsunami Database. National Geophysical Data Center, NOAA, 36 (Population Density), Landscan 2014 Population Dataset created by UT-Battelle, LLC, the management and operating contractor of the Oak Ridge National Laboratory acting on behalf of the U.S. Department of Energy under Contract No. DE-AC05-00OR22725. Distributed by East View Geospatial: geospatial.com and East View Information Services: eastview .com/online/landscan; 36 (Urban Area Population), United Nations, Department of Economic and Social Affairs, Population Division (2016). *The World's Cities in 2016—Data Booklet*; 26 (Urban Population Growth, 1950–2015, and Population Graph), United Nations Department of Economic and Social Affairs Population Division. *World Urbanization Prospects: The 2014 Revision*; *World Population Prospects: The 2012 Revision*; and *Trends in International Migrant Stock: The 2013 Revision*; 38 (Projected Population Change (%), 2015–2050), CIA. *The World Factbook*. cia.gov; Population Reference Bureau. prb.org/DataFinder; 38 (Population Pyramids) U.S. Census Bureau; 40 (Major Language Families Today), Global Mapping International (GMI) and SIL International. World Language Mapping System, version 3.2.1; 42 (Dominant Religion), Johnson, Todd M., and Brian J. Grim, eds. World Religion Database. worldreligiondatabase.org. Leiden/Boston: Brill; 44 (Dominant Economic Sector), CIA. *The World Factbook*. cia.gov; 46 (World Economies), World Bank. data.worldbank.org; 46 (Single-Commodity-Dependent Economies), International Trade Centre. intracen.org; 47 (Major Regional Trade Agreements), APEC (apec.org); ASEAN (asean.org); COMESA (about.comesa.int); ECOWAS (comm.ecowas.int); EU (europa.eu); MERCOSUR (mercosur.int); NAFTA (ustr.gov); SAFTA (saarc-sec.org); 48 (Renewable Freshwater Resources per Capita), Food and Agriculture Organization. AQUASTAT data; 50 (Crop Allocation), Global Landscapes Initiative, Institute on the Environment, University of Minnesota. Hooke, Roger LeB., and José F. Martín-Duque. "Land Transformation by Humans: A Review." *GSA Today* (2012), Volume 22 (12): 4–10; 52 (Total Energy Consumption, Major Energy Deposit), EIA (U.S. Energy Information Administration); 137 (Changing the Land), UN Food and Agricultural Organization. www.fao.org/docrep/008/ y5744e/y5744e04.htm.

Illustrations Credits

Cover
(Empire State Building), Cedric Weber/Shutterstock; (Indian girl), Bartosz Hadyniak/E+/Getty Images; (red-eyed tree frog), Jeffrey Mcgraw/Dreamstime; (dolphin), tubuceo/ Shutterstock; back cover (Arches National Park), Lunamarina/Dreamstime; (Volga River), Iakov Filimonov/Shutterstock; back cover (tiger), estima/iStockphoto; (African girl), Blend Images/Getty Images

Front of Book
1, Premium Stock/Corbis; 2, Premium Stock/Corbis; 2 (FAR LE), Roy Toft/NG Creative; 2 (LE), Tom Murphy/NG Creative; 2 (RT), Cary Wolinsky/NG Creative; 2 (FAR RT), Richard Nowitz/NG Creative; 3 (FAR LE), Ron Kimball Stock; 3 (LE), Jose Fuste Raga/Corbis; 3 (RT), Barbara Schneider/scxh; 3 (FAR RT), Brand X; 4 (UP RT), Todd Gipstein/NG Creative; 4 (LO), Richard Nowitz/NG Creative; 4 (UP LE), Tomasz Tomaszewski/NG Creative; 5 (LO RT), Cary Wolinsky/NG Creative; 5 (UP LE), Frans Lanting/NG Creative; 5 (UP RT), Gordon Wiltsie/NG Creative; 5 (LO LE), Taylor S. Kennedy/NG Creative; 10, Mark Theissen & Becky Hale/NG Staff; 11, NASA-JPL/Caltech; 14-15, David Aguilar; 20 (FAR LE), Maria Stenzel/ NG Creative; 20 (LE), Bill Hatcher/NG Creative; 20 (RT), Carsten Peter/NG Creative; 20 (FAR RT), Carsten Peter/NG Creative; 21 (FAR LE), Gordon Wiltsie/NG Creative; 21 (LE), James P. Blair/NG Creative; 21 (RT), Thomas J. Abercrombie/NG Creative; 21 (FAR RT), Anne Keiser/NG Creative; 24-25, NG Creative; 25 (UP), Kevin Rivoli/Associated Press; 25 (LO BOTH), Weiss and Overpeck, The University of Arizona; 26 (FAR LE), Raymond Gehman/NG Creative; 26 (LE), George F. Mobley/NG Creative; 26 (RT), Paul Nicklen/NG Creative; 26 (FAR RT), Raymond Gehman/NG Creative; 27 (FAR LE), Annie Griffiths Belt/NG Creative; 27 (LE), Beverly Joubert/NG Creative; 27 (RT), Michael Melford/NG Creative; 27 (FAR RT), Maria Stenzel/NG Creative; 28, James P. Blair/NG Creative; 29 (LE), William Thompson/NG Creative; 29 (CTR), Steve Mccurry/NG Creative; 29 (RT), Seyllou/AFP/Getty Images; 31 (A), Nature Picture Library/Alamy Stock Photo; 31 (B), Martin Harvey/Photolibrary RM/Getty Images; 31 (C), Martin Willis/Minden Pictures; 31 (D), Mike Bowie, Lincoln University, NZ; 31 (E), Suzi Eszterhas/Minden Pictures; 31 (F), Christophe Courteau/Nature Picture Library; 31 (G), Danita Delimont/Getty Images; 31 (H), Zoonar GmbH/ Alamy Stock Photo; 32 (UP), Ron Gravelle/National Geographic My Shot; 32 (LO), Gemma Handy/AFP/Getty Images; 33 (UP), Pablo Hidalgo/Shutterstock; 33 (LO RT), Jiji Press/ AFP/Getty Images; 33 (LO LE), Pacific Press/Alamy Stock Photo; 37, Justin Guariglia/NG Creative; 40, Maria Stenzel/NG Creative; 41 (LE), Justin Guariglia/NG Creative; 41 (RT), Phillipe Lissac/Godong/Corbis; 42 (LE), Martin Gray/NG Creative; 42 (CTR), Randy Olson/NG Creative; 42 (RT), Amit Dave/Reuters/Corbis; 43 (LE), Reza/NG Creative; 43 (RT), Richard Nowitz/NG Creative; 44 (LE), Jon Parker Lee/Alamy; 44 (RT), Justin Guariglia/NG Creative; 45 (LE), Mike Goldwater/Alamy Stock Photo; 45 (RT), Phil Schermeister/NG Creative; 46, hxdyl/Shutterstock; 48, Jodi Cobb/NG Creative; 50, Monty Rakusen/Cultura RF/Getty Images; 51 (LE), James P. Blair/NG Creative; 51 (UP RT), Stephen St. John/NG Creative; 51 (CTR RT), Joel Sartore/NG Creative; 51 (LO RT), Michael Nichols/NG Creative; 53 (FAR LE), Walter Rawlings/Robert Harding World Imagery/Corbis; 53 (LE), Richard Nowitz/NG Creative; 53 (RT), Sarah Leen/NG Creative; 53 (FAR RT), Priit Vesilind/NG Creative

North America
58 (UP), Lonely Planet Images/Getty Images; 58 (LO LE), Tomasz Tomaszewski/NG Creative; 58 (LO RT), Rex Stucky/NG Creative; 59 (UP), Michael Melford/NG Creative; 59 (LO), Jeff Vanuga/Corbis; 60 (UP LE), Ira Block/NG Creative; 60 (UP RT), NG Creative; 60 (LO LE), George F. Mobley/NG Creative; 60 (LO RT), Martin Gray/NG Creative; 61 (UP), vilainecrevette/iStockphoto; 61 (LO RT), Brad Mitchell/Alamy; 61 (LO LE), Glen Allison/The Image Bank/Getty Images; 62 (LO), Richard Nowitz/NG Creative; 62 (UP), Alaska Stock/NG Creative; 63 (LO), Michael S. Yamashita/NG Creative; 63 (UP), Tim Laman/NG Creative; 64 (UP), Zeljko Radojko/Shutterstock; 64 (LO), Todd Gipstein/NG Creative; 64-65, Norbert Rosing/NG Creative; 65 (UP), Brooks Walker/NG Creative; 66 (UP), Chris Jenner/Shutterstock; 66 (LO), Kenneth Garrett/NG Creative; 67 (UP LE), Macduff Everton/NG Creative; 67 (UP RT), worldswildlifewonders/Shutterstock; 68 (UP), Pablo Corral Vega/Corbis; 68 (LO), Steve Raymer/NG Creative; 68-69, Bill Curtsinger/NG Creative; 69 (UP), Michael Melford/NG Creative; 69 (LO), Jose Fuste Raga/Corbis

South America
74 (UP), Tim Laman/NG Creative; 74 (LO), Pablo Corral Vega/NG Creative; 75 (UP), Stephanie Maze/NG Creative; 75 (LO LE), Anne Keiser/NG Creative; 75 (LO RT), Todd Gipstein/NG Creative; 76 (UP LE), Jimmy Chin/NG Creative; 76 (UP RT), Catarina Belova/Shutterstock; 76 (LO RT), Pablo Corral Vega/NG Creative; 76 (LO LE), Ed George/NG Creative; 77 (UP), Richard Nowitz/NG Creative; 77 (LO LE), Joel Sartore/NG Creative; 77 (LO RT), Melissa Farlow/NG Creative; 78 (UP), William Albert Allard/NG Creative; 78 (LO), Pablo Corral Vega/NG Creative; 78-79, Meredith Davenport/NG Creative; 79 (UP), O. Louis Mazzatenta/NG Creative; 80 (UP), Macduff Everton/NG Creative; 80 (LO), Priit Vesilind/NG Creative; 81 (UP), Joel Sartore/NG Creative; 81 (LO), James L. Amos/NG Creative; 82, O. Louis Mazzatenta/NG Creative; 82-83, Dmitry Saparov/Shutterstock; 83 (UP), Maria Stenzel/NG Creative; 83 (LO), Joel Sartore/NG Creative

Europe
88 (UP), Richard Nowitz/NG Creative; 88 (LO), Priit Vesilind/NG Creative; 88-87, Pavel Svoboda/Shutterstock; 89 (LE), Melissa Farlow/NG Creative; 89 (RT), Richard Nowitz/NG Creative; 90 (UP), Taylor S. Kennedy/NG Creative; 90 (LO LE), Steve Mccurry/NG Creative; 90 (LO RT), Sisse Brimberg/NG Creative; 90-91, Richard Nowitz/NG Creative; 91 (LO LE), Richard Nowitz/NG Creative; 91 (CTR), Nicole Duplaix/NG Creative; 91 (LO RT), James P. Blair/NG Creative; 92 (UP), Karen Kasmauski/NG Creative; 92 (LOLE), Priit Vesilind/NG Creative; 92 (LO RT), Gregory Davies/Alamy; 93, The Art Archive/Corbis; 94 (UP), Richard Nowitz/NG Creative; 94 (CTR), Skip Brown/NG Creative; 94 (LO), Jim Richardson/NG Creative; 95, Richard Nowitz/NG Creative; 96 (UP), Catherine Karnow/NG Creative; 96 (LO), Catherine Karnow/NG Creative; 97 (LE), Sissie Brimberg/NG Creative; 97 (RT), Sissie Brimberg/NG Creative; 98 (UP), James P. Blair/NG Creative; 98 (LO LE), Freesurf69/Dreamstime; 98 (LO RT), Richard I'Anson/Lonely Planet Images/Getty Images; 99, James L. Stanfield/NG Creative; 100 (UP), Steve Raymer/NG Creative; 100 (LO), Steve Raymer/NG Creative; 101, Richard Nowitz/NG Creative

Asia
106 (UP), Taylor S. Kennedy/NG Creative; 106 (LO), Steve Mccurry/NG Creative; 107 (UP), Steve Raymer/NG Creative; 107 (LO LE), Justin Guariglia/NG Creative; 107 (LO RT), David Edwards/NG Creative; 108 (UP), Fred de Noyelle/Godong/Corbis; 108 (LO LE), Jodi Cobb/NG Creative; 108 (LO RT), Justin Guariglia/NG Creative; 108-109, Todd Gipstein/NG Creative; 109 (LO LE), Michael Nichols/NG Creative; 109 (LO RT), Justin Guariglia/NG Creative; 110 (UP), Maria Stenzel/NG Creative; 110 (LO), Steve Winter/NG Creative; 111 (UP), Steve Raymer/NG Creative; 111 (LO), Alexander Zemlianichenko Jr./Bloomberg via Getty Images; 112 (UP), Medford Taylor/NG Creative; 112 (LO), Shamil Zhumatov/Reuters; 113 (UP), Wild Wonders of Europe/Shpilenok/Nature Picture Library; 113 (LO), Dean Conger/NG Creative; 114 (UP), H. Kim/NG Creative; 114 (LO), Justin Guariglia/NG Creative; 115 (UP), O. Louis Mazzatenta/NG Creative; 115 (LO), Roy Toft/NG Creative; 116 (UP), James L. Stanfield/NG Creative; 116 (LO), Alex Webb/NG Creative; 117 (UP), Martin Gray/NG Creative; 117 (LO), Priit Vesilind/NG Creative; 118 (UP LE), Morteza Nikoubazl/Reuters/Corbis; 118 (UP RT), Arthur Thèvenart/Corbis; 118 (LO), Robb Kendrick/NG Creative; 119, Bill Lyons/NG Creative; 120 (UP), Ed George/NG Creative; 120 (LO), James P. Blair/NG Creative; 121 (UP), iStockphoto; 121 (LO), Bobby Model/NG Creative; 122 (UP LE), Paul Chesley/NG Creative; 122 (UP RT), Macduff Everton/NG Creative; 122 (LO), deepblue-photographer/Shutterstock; 123 (UP), Jack Fields/Corbis; 123 (LO), Steve Raymer/NG Creative; 124 (UP), Reuters/Corbis; 124 (LO), Richard Nowitz/NG Creative; 125 (UP LE), Paul Chesley/NG Creative; 125 (UP RT), Tim Laman/NG Creative; 125 (LO), Tim Laman/NG Creative

Africa
130 (UP), George F. Mobley/NG Creative; 130 (LO LE), Michael Nichols/NG Creative; 130 (LO RT), Instinia/Shutterstock; 131 (UP), Skip Brown/NG Creative; 131 (LO LE), Bill Curtsinger/NG Creative; 131 (LO RT), Cary Wolinsky/NG Creative; 132 (UP), Georg Gerster/NG Creative; 132 (LO LE), Digital Vision/Getty Images; 132 (LO RT), Kenneth Garrett/NG Creative; 133 (UP), Cary Wolinskyng Creative; 133 (LO LE), Bill Curtsinger/NG Creative; 133 (LO RT), Michael Nichols/NG Creative; 134 (UP), Thomas J. Abercrombie/NG Creative; 134 (LO), Jose Fuste Raga/Corbis; 135 (UP), Kenneth Garrett/NG Creative; 135 (CTR), Richard Nowitz/NG Creative; 135 (LO), Christian Wilkinson/Alamy Stock Photo; 136 (UP), W. Robert Moore/NG Creative; 136 (CTR), Michael Nichols/NG Creative; 136 (LO), Adisa/Shutterstock; 137 (UP), James L. Stanfield/NG Creative; 138 (UP), Randy Olson/NG Creative; 138 (CTR), Michael Lewis/NG Creative; 138 (LO), Deanne Fitzmaurice/NG Creative; 139 (UP), Suzi Eszterhas/Minden Pictures; 139 (LO), Bobby Haas/NG Creative; 140 (UP), robertharding/Alamy Stock Photo; 140 (LO), AGF Srl/Alamy Stock Photo; 141 (UP), Werner Forman/Corbis; 141 (LO), Xinhua/Alamy Stock Photo; 142 (UP), George F. Mobley/NG Creative; 142 (LO), Tim Laman/NG Creative; 143 (UP), Kenneth Garrett/NG Creative; 143 (LO), Bob Krist/Corbis

Australia, New Zealand & Oceania
148 (UP), Nicole Duplaix/NG Creative; 148 (LO), Frans Lanting/NG Creative; 148-149, Tim Laman/NG Creative; 149 (UP), Art Wolfe/NG Creative; 149 (LO), Nicole Duplaix/NG Creative; 150 (UP), Medford Taylor/NG Creative; 150 (CTR), N.Minton/Shutterstock; 150 (LO), Danita Delimont Creative/Alamy; 150-151 (UP), Tim Laman/NG Creative; 150-151 (LO), travellight/Shutterstock; 151 (CTR), Paul Chesley/NG Creative; 151 (LO), Mark Cosslett/NG Creative; 152 (LE), Jim Agronick/Shutterstock; 152 (RT), Sam Abell/NG Creative; 153 (LE), Jason Edwards/NG Creative; 153 (RT), Paul Chesley/NG Creative; 154 (UP), bumihills/Shutterstock; 154 (LO), Carsten Peter/NG Creative; 155 (UP LE), Martin Gray/NG Creative; 155 (UP RT), Randy Olson/NG Creative; 155 (LO), Jodi Cobb/NG Creative

Antarctica
158, Steve Bloom Images/Alamy Stock Photo; 159 (UP), Vicki Beaver/Alamy Stock Photo; 159 (LO), Alex Huizinga/NiS/Minden Pictures; 160 (UP), Science Source/Getty Images; 160 (LO), Michael Nolan/Robert Harding World Imagery/Getty Images; 161 (UP), Paul Nicklen/NG Creative; 161 (LO), Norbert Wu/Minden Pictures

The Oceans
165 (UP), NOAA; 165 (LO LE), Scripps Institute of Oceanography; 165 (LO RT), NASA; 166 (UP), Wolcott Henry/NG Creative; 166 (LO), Karen Kasmauski/NG Creative; 168 (UP), Tom Murphy/NG Creative; 168 (LO LE), Emory Kristof/NG Creative; 168 (LO RT), John Eastcott and Yva Momatiuk/NG Creative; 170, Hans Fricke/NG Creative; 172 (UP), Nicole Duplaix/NG Creative; 172 (LO), Norbert Rosing/NG Creative

Since 1888, the National Geographic Society has funded more than 12,000 research, exploration, and preservation projects around the world. The Society receives funds from National Geographic Partners, LLC, funded in part by your purchase. A portion of the proceeds from this book supports this vital work. To learn more, visit natgeo.com/info.

For more information, visit nationalgeographic.com, call 1-800-647-5463, or write to the following address:

National Geographic Partners
1145 17th Street N.W.
Washington, D.C. 20036-4688 U.S.A.

Visit us online at nationalgeographic.com/books

For librarians and teachers: ngchildrensbooks.org

More for kids from National Geographic: natgeokids.com

For information about special discounts for bulk purchases, please contact National Geographic Books Special Sales: specialsales@natgeo.com

For rights or permissions inquiries, please contact National Geographic Books Subsidiary Rights: bookrights@natgeo.com

Designed by Rachel Kenny

The publisher would like to thank everyone who worked to make this book come together: Martha Sharma, writer/researcher; Suzanne Patrick Fonda, project manager; Angela Modany, associate editor; Kathryn Robbins, art director; Lori Epstein, photo director; Debbie Gibbons, Mike McNey, and Jon Bowen, map production; Irene Berman-Vaporis, Theodore A. Sickley, Rosemary P. Wardley, Ryan T. Williams, and Scott A. Zillmer, map research and edit; Stuart Armstrong, illustrator; Sean Philpotts, production director; Sally Abbey, managing editor; Joan Gossett, production editor; and Gus Tello and Anne LeongSon, design production assistants.

National Geographic supports K–12 educators with ELA Common Core Resources. Visit natgeoed.org/commoncore for more information.

Trade paperback ISBN: 978-1-4263-3199-2
Hardcover ISBN: 978-1-4263-3247-0
Reinforced library binding ISBN: 978-1-4263-3200-5

Printed in Hong Kong
18/PPHK/1

Metric Conversion Tables

CONVERSION TO METRIC MEASURES

SYMBOL	WHEN YOU KNOW	MULTIPLY BY	TO FIND	SYMBOL
LENGTH				
in	inches	2.54	centimeters	cm
ft	feet	0.30	meters	m
yd	yards	0.91	meters	m
mi	miles	1.61	kilometers	km
AREA				
in^2	square inches	6.45	square centimeters	cm^2
ft^2	square feet	0.09	square meters	m^2
yd^2	square yards	0.84	square meters	m^2
mi^2	square miles	2.59	square kilometers	km^2
—	acres	0.40	hectares	ha
MASS				
oz	ounces	28.35	grams	g
lb	pounds	0.45	kilograms	kg
—	short tons	0.91	metric tons	t
VOLUME				
in^3	cubic inches	16.39	milliliters	mL
liq oz	liquid ounces	29.57	milliliters	mL
pt	pints	0.47	liters	L
qt	quarts	0.95	liters	L
gal	gallons	3.79	liters	L
ft^3	cubic feet	0.03	cubic meters	m^3
yd^3	cubic yards	0.76	cubic meters	m^3
TEMPERATURE				
°F	degrees Fahrenheit	5/9 after subtracting 32	degrees Celsius (centigrade)	°C

CONVERSION FROM METRIC MEASURES

SYMBOL	WHEN YOU KNOW	MULTIPLY BY	TO FIND	SYMBOL
LENGTH				
cm	centimeters	0.39	inches	in
m	meters	3.28	feet	ft
m	meters	1.09	yards	yd
km	kilometers	0.62	miles	mi
AREA				
cm^2	square centimeters	0.16	square inches	in^2
m^2	square meters	10.76	square feet	ft^2
m^2	square meters	1.20	square yards	yd^2
km^2	square kilometers	0.39	square miles	mi^2
ha	hectares	2.47	acres	—
MASS				
g	grams	0.04	ounces	oz
kg	kilograms	2.20	pounds	lb
t	metric tons	1.10	short tons	—
VOLUME				
mL	milliliters	0.06	cubic inches	in^3
mL	milliliters	0.03	liquid ounces	liq oz
L	liters	2.11	pints	pt
L	liters	1.06	quarts	qt
L	liters	0.26	gallons	gal
m^3	cubic meters	35.31	cubic feet	ft^3
m^3	cubic meters	1.31	cubic yards	yd^3
TEMPERATURE				
°C	degrees Celsius (centigrade)	9/5 then add 32	degrees Fahrenheit	°F